1980

W9-ADC-348

3 0301 00090784 6

SPANISH-
AMERICAN
LITERATURE
in Translation

A SELECTION OF POETRY, FICTION, AND DRAMA SINCE 1888

Edited by WILLIS KNAPP JONES

FREDERICK UNGAR PUBLISHING CO.
New York

LIBRARY
College of St. Francis
JOLIET, ILL.

Copyright © 1963 by Frederick Ungar Publishing Co., Inc.
Printed in the United States of America
Library of Congress Catalog Card No. 63-181511

ISBN 0-8044-2436-5

Second Printing, 1977

860.8
Q815
r
2

1-17-80 Main Line Book Co. $15.07

COPYRIGHT ACKNOWLEDGMENTS

The editor and the publishers are grateful for the cooperation of those individuals and publishers who granted permission for the use of their copyrighted material. Every effort has been made to trace and to acknowledge properly all copyright owners. If any acknowledgment has been inadvertently omitted, the publishers will be pleased to make the necessary correction in the next printing.

C. Jonathan Cape. *Doña Barbara*, tr. by Robert Malloy. C. Jonathan Cape and Harrison Smith, Copyright 1931.

Carnegie Endowment for International Peace. Anonymous translations from the lamentably defunct *Inter-America*: Darío, "The Pearl"; Gutié-rrez Nájera, "Lenten Sermon of Duque Job"; Ibarbourou, "Like the Springtime"; Lugones, "Cult of the Flowers"; Angel Pino, "The Christening."

Coward-McCann, Inc. *The Underdogs*, tr. by E. Munguía, Jr., Copyright, 1929, Brentano.

Fantasy (Stanley D. Mayer, Editor). No. 26 (1942): Gabriela Mistral, "Intimate," tr. by Dorothy Conzelman; Guillén, "Execution," tr. by Joseph L. Grucci; Mallea, "Conversation," tr. by Hugo Manning; Silva, "Nocturnal Siesta," tr. by Mary and C. V. Wicker. No. 27 (1943): Carrera Andrade, "Elegy by Abraham Valdelomar," tr. by Lloyd Mallan; Fombona, "I Announce the Kingdom of the Stars," tr. by H. R. Hays; Guillén, "Cane" and "Blade," tr. by Langston Hughes; Huidobro, "Nature Vive," tr. by H. R. Hays; López, "Rubbish," tr. by H. R. Hays; López Velarde, "Ants," tr. by H. R. Hays; Méndez Calzada, "Christ in Buenos Aires," tr. by Edmund C. García; Pedroso, "Five O'clock Tea," tr. by Ben F. Carruthers.

La Gaceta (Mexico). Permission to translate Eclogue of the Blind," from vol. VI, 13 (Sept. 1960).

Hispanic Society of America. From *Hispanic Anthology* (1920): Casal, "Confidence," tr. by Thomas Walsh; Darío, "Portico," tr. by Thomas Walsh; Darío, "Sonatina," tr. by J. P. Rice; Fialio, "Nostalgia," tr.

88549

by Muna Lee; Gabriela Mistral, "Sonnet of Death," tr. by Roderick Gill; González Martínez, "Prayer of the Barren Rock," tr. by J. P. Rice; Herrera, "The Cart, The Priest, The Parish Church," tr. by Thomas Walsh; López, "Village Barber," tr. by Thomas Walsh; López, "Verses to the Moon," tr. by William G. Williams; Lugones, "The Gift of Day," tr. by Garret Strange; Valencia, "Sursum," tr. by Thomas Walsh. From *Translations from Hispanic American Poets* (1938): Banchs, "The Tiger," tr. by Elizabeth du Gué Trapier; Chocano, "Horses of the Conquerors," tr. by Jessie Read Wendell; Darío, "Symphony in Gray Major," tr. by Alice J. McVan; Gutiérrez Nájera, "When I Die," tr. by Alice J. McVan; Ibarbourou, "Fleeting Restlessness," tr. by Elizabeth du Gué Trapier; Lugones, "Drops of Gold," tr. by Alice J. McVan; Nervo, "Not All Who Die," tr. by Helen E. Fish; Nervo, "Purity," tr. by Beatrice Gilman Proske; Storni, "Inheritance," tr. by Jessie Read Wendell.

Holt, Rinehart and Winston. *Don Segundo Sombra*, tr. by Harriet de Onís. Copyright, 1935, by Farrar and Rinehart.

Muna Lee: Carrera Andrade, "Sierra" and "Sunday"; Darío, "Litany for Our Lord Don Quijote"; Herrera, "The Quarrel"; Lugones, "A Journey"; Llorens Torres, "Bolívar"; Torres Bodet, "A Pit"; Vallejo, "Dregs."

Pan American Bulletin. Gabriela Mistral, "The Rural Teacher," tr. by Isabel K. MacDermotte (1924).

G. P. Putnam's Sons. Rivera, *The Vortex*, tr. by Earle K. James. Copyright 1935, by G.P. Putnam's Sons.

Edna W. Underwood. *Anthology of Mexican Poets* (Portland, Maine: The Mosher Press, 1932): Chocano, "Indian Flute" and "A Queen's Breast"; Figueira, "The Southern Cross"; Jaimes Freyre, "Ancestor"; López Velarde, "Spell of Return"; Osorio, "Lament of October"; Reyes, "Quasi-Sonnet A."

Frederick Ungar Publishing Co. Manchester, *Joyas poéticas* (1951): Ibarbourou, "Lullabies"; Silva, "Nocturne III."

University of Pennsylvania Press. Alice Stone Blackwell, *Some Spanish American Poets* (1937): Argüello, "The Eagle and the Leaf"; Díaz Mirón, "To Pity"; Gutiérrez Najera, "To the Wife of the Corregidor"; Hernández Miyares, "The Most Beautiful"; Silva, "Day of the Dead"; Storni, "She Who Understands."

University of Texas Press, T. M. Cranfill, *The Muse in Mexico*, copyright, 1959: Paz, "Hymn Among the Ruins," tr. by Denise Levertov.

Donald D. Walsh. Claudia Lars, "Sketch of a Frontier Woman"; López, "Tropic Siesta"; Tiempo, "Harangue on the Death of Chayim Nachman Bialik"; Vallejo, "Spain, Take from Me this Cup!"

Donald A. Yates. Borges, "Garden of the Forking Path," from *Michigan Alumnus Quarterly Review* (May, 1958) and *Labyrinths* (New Directions, 1962).

TO POLLY
critic, consultant, and typist
whose life it disrupted

ACKNOWLEDGMENTS

An anthology of original translations covering seventy-five years and all of the Spanish-American nations would be a gigantic task for one person. Though more than half the material in this volume appears in English for the first time, it was also necessary to borrow from earlier translators, whose contributions I gladly acknowledge.

Latin American authors collaborated generously. In several conversations in Asunción, Josefina Pla helped select outstanding Paraguayan poets and their representative works, and made suggestions about delicate shades of translation. Novelists Icaza, Alegría, Aguilera Malta, and Arévalo Martínez selected works to represent them and checked the English versions. Dramatists Usigli, Eichelbaum, Rivarola Matto, Aguirre, and Marqués graciously allowed the use of their plays. Claudia Madero made available a scene from her translations of Darthés and Damel.

Many personal friends in this country gave me access to their translations, and their names are attached to their material used. They include the late Edna W. Underwood, Chesley M. Hutchings, Muna Lee, Paul T. Manchester, Donald D. Walsh, and Donald A. Yates. Colleagues at Miami University, Ray L. Moloney and Robert Scott, made translations especially for these pages.

Advanced students of Spanish at Miami, who put to practical use their classroom work in the language, include Marilyn Bauman, Katherine Booher, Malcolm Carmen, Darol Davis, David A. Flory, Robert A. Goldberg, Astrid Hasbrouck, Jane Johnson, Robert McDowell, Robert Monnin, W. P. Negron, Elaine Schaefer, Susan L. Shelby, Sheila Toye, Elizabeth Turner, and Linda Wilson.

For specific references to selections and publishers, see the copyright page.

W.K.J.

PREFACE

An anthology may serve several purposes. Conforming to its Greek root, it may be a bouquet of the compiler's favorite flowers without regard for the bushes from which they were culled. It may single out a few writers, heedless of their relation to the literary currents around them. Or, like the present anthology, it may provide a means of studying literary movements by selections from the writings of representative authors.

The compiler does not claim that translations, especially of poetry, are the ideal way of entering into the literature of another language. Obviously there are two kinds of translations. In one, the translator of verse aims to produce an English poem, taking only the lines and ideas he wants from the original. Thus was *The Rubaiyat* composed and thus did Ben Jonson combine two Greek poems into "Drink to Me Only With Thine Eyes." The other method aims to reproduce the qualities of the original, including the one word that in Spanish may involve a complicated metaphor. To get the full flavor, a reader must, of course, go to the original, but if limitations of language makes this impossible, a good translation will convey some idea of the poem's essence. The contents of this volume try to provide something that neither betrays the original nor discredits the English language.

From the longer forms of literature, selections were made that will give the reader a glimpse of the entire work, enough, it is hoped, to make him want to know more. Because seventy-five years of poetry, prose, and drama from nineteen nations offered an outpouring of riches, careful selection and sometimes abridgment were required.

Militating against the purpose of this anthology to provide a survey of all of Spanish-American literature stands the harsh and saddening fact that by far not nearly enough of the great works from south of the Rio Grande have received adequate translation. If the reader looks in vain for some particular author or work, three explanations are possible: no good English translation is available; the editor considered other writings more important; or, in a few cases, the copyright owner put an exhorbitant value on his property. In general, however, translators and publishers were both generous and gracious. The acknowledgments will serve to guide those who want to explore further into this fascinating field.

Those who are tempted to compare these translations with the very best of the world's literature might bear in mind the comment, some years ago, of the editor of *Poet Lore* regarding publication in English of some Latin-American dramas. "It is quite true that, had some of the translations reached us as contemporary original plays in English, they would have been rejected. However, they are published to give readers the opportunity of examining the outstanding examples of the best products of other countries at the time, or what was significant when produced, irrespective of how they compare with the equivalent best in English. . . . As countries reach their literary maturity, it is interesting to note their progress."

The dating of some authors has presented a problem. Biography, like bibliography, is sometimes treated casually in Latin America. Lack of records or carelessness in keeping them is further complicated by whimsy. With two birth dates to choose from, I consulted the family of one writer. Her husband and her son each sent me another. About these and other details, the editor would be happy to receive corrections or suggestions. The chief aim of this volume is to provide for those not familiar with the field a taste of the literary treasures of our southern neighbors since the beginning of Modernism, and an indication of the reward awaiting those who would search further.

W.K.J.

Miami University
Oxford, Ohio

CONTENTS

Cuba:

Puerto Rico:

Colombia:

Peru:

Bolivia:

Chile:

II. FICTION

III. DRAMA

INTRODUCTION

By 1880 Romanticism, which had reached Spanish America earlier than the 1833 date of its beginnings in Spain, had lost its drive. The masterpieces of the Romantic novels—Marmol's *Amalia* (1855), Blest Gana's *Martín Rivas* (1865), Isaac's *María* (1867), Mera's *Cumandá* (1876), and Silvestre's *Tránsito* (1886)—had palled, and writers were looking for something new.

At this moment, too, the theater of romantic and mysterious heroes struggling amid violent surroundings, was being challenged by a realistic play, full of local color and problems, about a mistreated cowboy, which was being performed in a traveling circus in Argentina. In addition, a postal employe in Valparaiso, Chile, a Nicaraguan with the pen name of "Rubén Darío," was completing an important book of prose and poetry, *Azul* ("Blue"). If anything can mark the beginning of Modernism, it is this volume of 1888. Among its antecedents was an anthology, *Le Parnasse-contemporain* (1866), named by the French poets after the Greek home of the Muses. Poets were in revolt against the subjectivity of the Romanticists and their slipshod writing. They sought to express the feel of things, external and exotic beauty, but with an impersonal attitude and sculpturesque perfection.

Other poets of France, in revolt, were employing such freedom in choice of material that their abnormal, neurotic, morbid products won for the writers the name of Decadents. The return swing of the pendulum touched the color-conscious Symbolists, who objected to the realism of the Decadents.

Darío, working at the Managua Library in his native Nicaragua, and later reading French literature in the library of his Chilean friend Pedro Balmaceda, had concluded that many French "innovations" had really appeared centuries earlier, in Spain, but he did find something new, in literature, in the revolt against the worship of material success. In this lay one of the seeds of Modernism.

Darío did not use the term "modernist" until 1890, when, in reply to critics who found the new technique too much of a departure from the traditional, too modern, he wrote: "Then we are modernists." He defined the movement as "an attempt to give color and life and flexibility to ancient verse that has suffered stiffness of the joints, cramped within stereotyped iron molds."

Its advocates rebelled against the world's lack of sympathy and revealed a consciousness of the sensuous beauty in nature, a longing for escape, for death, melancholic dreams, along with a refinement of expression in musical lines, sometimes carried to incomprehensible extremes. Flexibility in form and musical quality in rhythm are the greatest gifts of Modernism to Spanish poetry.

By his travels Darío carried Modernism to Argentina and Spain, where it renewed and freshened poetry. Then, to complete the circle, it reached France, whose poets had first inspired Rubén Darío.

To voice the universal crisis in letters and spirit in a modern world, a new technique and vocabulary had to be created for literature, as Wagner was then doing for opera, and others for the world of art. Nervo in Mexico was seeking in letters to express the beating heart of earth and the pulsation of modern nerves. Having denied Romanticism and abandoned its norms and forms, its old ideas and themes, the writers could turn in any direction they chose. Some of them went back to folk poetry and to the old Spaniards, Gómez Manrique and Gonzalo de Berceo. In all Modernists, independence and a search for novelty and change were characteristic. So the movement, with its aristocratic and aesthetic tendencies, became a synthesis of all styles of literature before it came to an end about 1910.

The birth of Modernism provides a logical division between the old literature of Spanish America and the new, and a starting point for this volume. To frame the picture, the chief forerunners of Modernism are also included: Manuel Gutiérrez Nájera (1859-1895), of Mexico, with his "Duke Job" poetry and verse; José Martí (1853-1895), with the simplicity of his verse and the modernism of his prose; his fellow Cuban, Julián del Casal (1863–1893), a colorist with a vivid tropical imagination; and José Asunción Silva (1865–1896), of Colombia, author of the charming *Nocturnes*. They had already shown themselves in revolt against the clichés of Romanticism. Tired of such worn phrases as "Ruddy Phoebus sank in the West," Nájera, for instance, was writing: "The melancholy light pulls out its golden net from the green waves."

Modernism developed various offshoots, even one called Neo-Modernism. Their practitioners will be found in this volume. As some poets rebelled against rigidity, they invented an artificial "poetic" language. Others disregarded punctuation or printed their verses in the shape of trees or diamonds. Later, with advocates in all countries of the New World, came Surrealism, based on the subconscious and attempting by shock to strip away the outer layers. Combining symbolistic poetry, the philosophy of Hegel and the revelation of Freud, its followers wanted to revitalize reality, fundamentally reawaken human understanding, and transform the world. In its advanced stages it merged with Existentialism.

Other movements developed. Encouraged by García Lorca, by the Ultraists, by the poets, and by the artists and dancers who in France were using Negro themes, the Afro-Antillian poets began employing authentic dialect and treating realistically the spirit of the black race. The movement was national, however, rather than exotic, as practiced by the Cuban mulatto Nicolás Guillén (1902–   ), and his countrymen, Ramón Guirao (1908–1949), and Emilio Ballagas (1908–   ). The Puerto Rican, Palés Matos (1898–1952), is the chief spokesman, even though he interpreted the Negro through the skeptical eyes of a civilized white man.

Among the nativist poets of the Indians is Fernán Silva Valdés (1887–   ). The tropics and the Andes were glorified by other nationalists like Peru's Chocano (1873–1934). In this anthology, these writers are grouped chronologically by nationality, however, rather than by movements, because most of them were experimenters in many camps.

Each of the nineteen Latin-American nations has had its important poets. Unfortunately, not all who have found translators could be included here. Peru, for instance, boasts Manuel González Prada (1848–1918), who brought conciseness and music; Chocano, who taught his followers sonority; and the bizarre José María Eguren (1874–1942) of the delicate tints, who has been the inspiration for so many modern poets.

Each Central-American nation produced at least one outstanding writer, even though they were frequently unknown outside, even to the rest of the Spanish-speaking world. Of the first period of Honduras' poetry was Padre José Trinidad Reyes (1795–1855), both Classic and Romantic. In the second period came Froylán Turcios (1877–1943) and Darío's friend, Juan Ramón Molina (1875–1908), introspective, melancholy, and a suicide; and from the present epoch are numbered Alfonso Guillén Zelaya (1888–1947); Rafael Heliodoro Valle (1891–1959), and of living poets, "Claudio Barrera," as Vicente Alemán signs his poetry.

Costa Rica has produced Aquileo Echeverría (1866–1909), poet of the countryside; Roberto Brenes Mesén (1874–1947); Alfredo Cardoña Peña (1917–); and the costumbrista "Magón," Manuel González Zeladón (1864–1936), who spent most of his life outside his country. Salvador was the birthplace of Francisco Gavidia (1863–1955) and Manuel Aguilar Chávez (1913–1957). Nicaragua produced, besides the Argüellos, father and son, Ramón Sáenz Morales (1885–1926), Salvador Ruiz Morales (1889–1926) and Juan Felipe Toruño (1898–). Guatemala was the home of José Batres y Montúfar (1809–1844) and its greatest poet, Enrique Goméz Carrillo (1873–1927), whose prose and travel books brought his output to fifty volumes. One representative of Panama was Ricardo Miró (1883–1940).

Paraguay, hidden in the heart of the continent, produced a number of important poets, the chief of whom are represented in this volume, but all this is only a sampling of the many writers of verse in this hemisphere, where even a president of

Colombia was prouder of the poetry he produced than of his political achievements.

Mention should also be made of the many excellent women writers of poetry. "Gabriela Mistral" (1889–1957), of Chile, wrote in *Desolación* about her sweetheart who committed suicide to save his honor. Then she turned to other loves: God, nature, and her fellow creatures. Alfonsina Storni (1892–1938), with a moral nausea about love and a humiliation about the position of women in Argentina, wrote tortured symbolic verse till she felt she had no more to say, then leaped into the sea. Juana de Ibarbourou (1895–   ), hating the idea of growing old, began with charming musical verse, then turned to irregular rhythm and obscure images. Among the many other poetesses, Delmira Agustini (1886–1914) and María Eugenia Vaz Ferreira (1875–1913), of the River Plate, Claudia Lars and María Enriqueta of Central America, Stella Corvalán of Chile, Amparo Rodríguez Vidal of Chile, and Carmen Demar of Puerto Rico, may be remembered only because they achieved a high point of excellence more frequently than hundreds of their sister poets who also wrote, and sometimes published verse. Perhaps such activity by both sexes explains why Latin-American poetry was recognized and esteemed in Europe long before the prose or drama of the continent. Certainly its quantity exceeds that of any other form of Latin-American literature.

FICTION

The advent of Modernism found two literary currents in Latin-American fiction: Costumbrism and Traditionalism. Costumbrism, in its search for American reality, was exemplified in the first regionalist of the continent, Tomás Carrasquilla (1858–1940), of Colombia, now only just beginning to be appreciated. Javier de Viana (1868–1926), of Uruguay, was writing realistic pictures of the pampas. His only novel, *La Gaucha* ("The Cowgirl") (1899), displays Zola-esque naturalism.

Roberto J. Payró (1867–1928) also began as a novelist, presenting the picaresque gaucho in *Casamiento de Laucho* ("Laucho's Marriage") (1906), followed by short stories of the pampas dwellers. Horacio Quiroga (1878–1937), while no novelist, was one of the continent's greatest short story writers, especially with his jungle and animal stories for children.

Chile's first realistic short story writer, Baldomero Lillo (1867–1923), "descended into the coal mines of Lota and came up with the face of Dante and his words cloaked in horror," according to one critic. Vigorous and gloomy souls subjected to terrible woes fill his *Sub-terra* (1904) about the miners, and *Sub-sole* (1905), with more general themes. In his symbolic stories of character, he was equaled only by his countrymen Pedro Prada (1886–1952) and Augusto d'Halmar (1880–1950).

Becoming conscious of social problems, after Zola's novels reached Lima, two Peruvian women were moved to produce novels attacking national evils. Mercedes Cabello de Carbona (1847–1909) wrote romantically about inherited traits and a craving for importance in *Blanca-Sol* (1889), her country's first novel, although preceding by only a few months the more literary *Aves sin nido* ("Birds without Nests"), with its exposure of unjust treatment of Indians by politicians and priests, the work of Clorinda Matto de Turner (1854–1909).

Traditionalism, the other literary movement, also had its practitioners who made some impression on the Modernists. By the end of the nineteenth century, money was becoming abundant, and young people could afford to travel in search of the foreign and erotic. Darío felt its allure and wrote a Russian story, *La matushka* (1889), as well as *Queen Mab* and *The Death of the Empress of China*.

Carlos Reyles (1868–1938), after writing *Beba* (1894) which dealt with family breeding as if it were cattle breeding, and the violent *Raza de Caín* ("The Race of Cain") (1910), turned his face toward Spain in *El embrujo de Sevilla* ("Castanets") (1912), so full of the spirit of that Andalusian city that the author was made an honorary citizen. Reyles later returned to his own soil in the authentic *El terruño* ("Native Soil") (1916), which some consider the continent's first psychological novel, and in *El gaucho Florido* (1938).

Enrique Rodríguez Larreta (1873–1961) began his career by writing about Sophist Greece in *Artemisa* (1896), followed by that great historical novel of Philip II, *La gloria de don Ramiro* ("The Glory of Don Ramiro") (1909). Then he wrote *Zogoibi* (1926) about gaucho life, in which he provided one of the finest expressions in Latin-American literature of the spiritual value of the soil.

When the super-refinement of the Modernists and exaggerated realism tending toward Naturalism converged, both schools gained. As Angel Flores put it: "If Realism exposed American layers never before seen, Modernism opened the windows to let the light from outside into the fertile and robust literary expression of Hispanoamerica."

First to demand attention from the outside world were the authors of "Green Hell" novels, full of the terror of wild nature. José Eustasio Rivera (1888–1928) began it with *La vorágine* ("The Vortex") (1924), about the rubber-latex collectors in Colombia. Though weak in its stringing out of events, it is a powerful protest against exploitation of the natives. Rivera was followed by Rómulo Gallegos (1884–), later elected president of Venezuela. His *Doña Bárbara* (1929) follows the descent into barbarity of a woman in the selvas, embittered by the assassination of the only man she ever loved and taking revenge on all men for his death. Gallegos completed his panorama of the jungles with *Canaima* (1935), the tragic defeat of Marcos Vargas by the selvas. It is also a tribute to the singer Florentino of the race of Martín Fierro and Santos Vega. *Toá* ("The Flame Girl") (1936) by Dr. César Uribe Piedrahita (1906–) is another violent jungle novel, based on the doctor's own experiences.

Across the Andes, Raúl Botelho Gosálvez (1917–) wrote of the Bolivian jungles in *Borrachera verde* ("Green Intoxication") and *Coca* ("The Coca Drug"). Among the novels by Ciro Alegría (1909–) is *Serpiente de Oro* ("Golden Serpent") (1935), the first great novel of Peru's selvas. The war in the jungles between Bolivia and Paraguay from 1932 to 1935 is covered in Roberto Leiton's *La punta de los cuatro degollados* ("Slit-Throat Point") (1933, published in 1946). Paraguay's side was upheld by the Costa Rican José Marín Cañas (1904–) in *Infierno verde* ("Green Hell") (1935) and in short stories by José Villarejo (1907–). Bolivia had other spokesmen: the diplomat Augusto Céspedes (1904–) in *Sangre de mestizos* ("Mixed Blood") (1936) containing the excellent short story "The Well"; Oscar Cerruto (1907–) in *Aluvión de fuego* ("Rain of Fire") (1935); Augusto Guzmán (1903–) in *Prisioneros de guerra* ("Prisoners of War") (1937); and the two-volume novel *Cuando el viento agita las banderas* ("When the Wind Flutters the Flags") (1950) by Rafael Ulises Peláez (1902–). Short fiction by Aquiles Vergara Vicuña, *Del caldero del Chaco* ("From the Chaco Cauldron"), and poetry especially were even more strident in recording the terrors of the Chaco conflict that made it seem so much grimmer than the earlier Paraguayan war, as recalled in the historical trilogy by Manuel Gálvez (1882–1951), of Argentina.

Besides the jungle tales, novels about the Indians attracted the attention of European and North American readers. Since most of the Spanish-American countries had their Indian problem, some of the continent's greatest novels deal with it. The earliest novels, like the plays about the Indians, were romantic in tone, following the Chateaubriand and Fenimore Cooper tradition, till three novels put an end to that phase: the Matto de Turner novel of 1889, *Aves sin nido*, previously cited; *Raza de bronce* ("Race of Bronze") (1919) by Alcides Arguedas (1879–1946) of Bolivia; and *Plata y bronce* ("Silver and Bronze") (1927), the work of Ecuador's Fernando Chaves, who also wrote *La embrujada* ("Bewitched").

Other nations also produced their novels of protest against the treatment of the Indians. As far back as 1905, Mexicans were shuddering over the massacre of the Indians in battle as described in *Tomochic* by Lieutenant Heriberto Frías. And when restoring the land to the Indians became one of the four-

and other novels. Still later, Pedro Jorge Vera (1915–) showed the results of his long visit to Russia in *Animales puros* ("Complete Beasts") (1946), a powerful but pessimistic story of Communists trying to live up to their convictions.

Loja produced several novelists; in Cuenca, G. Humberto Matta began putting real Indians into his poetry and then wrote the novels *Sumag-Allpa* ("Beautiful Land") (1940), and *Sanaguin* (1942).

Mexican novelists have been inspired by their country's history. Francisco Monterde (1894–) in *La madrigal de Cetina* ("Cetina's Madrigal") and *El secreto de la escalera* ("The Secret of the Ladder") (1918), was followed by Artemio de Valle-Arizpe (1888–) with *Ejemplo* ("Example") (1919), *Vidas milagrosas* ("Miraculous Lives") (1921), *Doña Leonor de Cáceres* (1922) and especially *El Canillitas* (1942). Julio Jiménez Rueda (1896–1959) wrote *Sor Adoración del Verbo Divino* ("Sister Adoration of the Divine Word") (1923) and *Moisén* (1924).

It was the Revolution, however, centering in the overthrow of Díaz in 1910, that provided the greatest stimulus to Mexican letters. Mariano Azuela (1873–1952) was its first and most complete historian in fiction, covering the twenty-five year period from Díaz through Cárdenas. Martín Luis Guzmán (1887–), newspaperman and government employee, followed him. Gregorio López y Fuentes (1897–) fictionalized the aims of the Revolution, and Mauricio Magdaleno (1906–) also described its Indian aspects in *El Resplendor* (1937). From his experiences as a young soldier, José Rubén Romero (1890–1952) wrote *Desbandada* ("Disbanded") and *El pueblo inocente* ("The Innocent People") (1934), but he will be longest remembered for his humorous *La vida inútil de Pito Pérez* ("The Futile Life of Pito Pérez") (1938).

Other practitioners of humor on the continent include Arturo Cancela (1892–) of Argentina with his *Los tres relatos porteños* ("Three Buenos Aires Stories") (1922); the Chilean, Jenaro Prieto (1889–1946), author of *El socio* ("The Partner")

(1928); and purveyors of brief humor and satire like "Ángel Pino" of Chile and the Ecuadorian "Jack the Ripper" included in this volume.

The gaucho inhabitants of the Argentine pampas, that cover an area 600 by 1,000 miles, have inspired many works of fiction. Sometimes believed to have taken their name from the Indian word *guacho* "orphan," these cowboys have been adopted by many writers since they first appeared in literature about 1775. During the period covered by this volume, Eduardo Gutiérrez (1852–1890) wrote dime novels about them, serialized in the newspapers: *Juan sin tierra* ("John Lackland"), *Juan Moreira* (1880) and *Hormiga negra* ("Black Ant") (1883). The second was dramatized to provide an important step in Argentine drama. Eduardo Acevedo Díaz (1851–1921) first put the cowboys into formal novels in his Hymn of Hate trilogy about the Uruguayan struggle for independence: *Ismael* (1888), *Nativa* (1890), and *Grito de gloria* ("Shout of Glory") (1894), but it was his realistic *Soledad* (1894) that provided the model and even some episodes for later gaucho prose.

Benito Lynch (1885–1952) put a pair of murdering Gauchos into his *Los Caranchos de la Florida* ("The Florida Hawks") (1916–6). He also wrote *Romance de un gaucho* (1934), and *El inglés de los güesos* ("The Englishman of the Bones") (1924), the love story of the English archaeologist James Gray and the gaucho girl Balbina, whom he abandoned. The greatest example of the gaucho fiction, however, was *Don Segundo Sombra* (1926) by Ricardo Güiraldes (1886–1927). The ideal but phantom "good gaucho" of this tragedy about the disintegrating cowboys of the pampas has been compared to Don Quixote. The story follows the education of young Fabio Cáceres, Jr., in the customs of the cowboys. Though it does contain episodes, it is really a character study. As the figure of the old gaucho passes out of sight at the end, the author, repeating the concept expressed by Florencio Sánchez in *La gringa*, twenty-two years before, declares: "What was disappearing was more an idea than a man."

The transformation of the gaucho tragedy into the rural

tragedy is seen in *El caballo y su sombra* ("The Horse and His Shadow") (1926) by the Uruguayan Enrique Amorím (1900–1960). He also wrote *La carreta* ("The Cart") (1929) and *El paisano Aguilar* ("Rural Aguilar") (1934), besides social and psychological works and even a few detective novels, a field not very deeply cultivated in Latin America except by the Chilean, Camilo Pérez de Arce under the pen name of "James Ernhard," and by the Mexicans, Rafael Bernal (1915–), Maria Bermúdez, and Antonio Elú.

Of all Latin-American novelists, almost the only ones able to make a living from their pen have been two Argentines: Gálvez, and Hugo Wast. Manuel Gálvez (1882–1951) made his reputation with the naturalistic *La maestra normal* ("The Normal School Teacher") (1914) and *Nacha Regules* (1919) set in Buenos Aires, and with the historical novels of the Paraguayan War already mentioned. Gustavo Martínez Zuvirría (1883–) transposed the letters of his first name into his pen name "Hugo Wast," and wrote a series of historical and costumbristic novels like *Casa de los cuervos* ("House of the Ravens") (1915) and *Desierto de piedra* ("Stone Desert") (1925), that were so popular that he followed the example of the creator of Tarzan in incorporating and industrializing himself.

Among recent Argentine novelists, the chief ones are the philosophic Jorge Luis Borges (1899–) and Eduardo Mallea (1903–), whose worries about human existence produced *La bahía de silencio* ("The Bay of Silence") (1941), *La torre* ("The Tower") (1951), and other Existentialist writing.

In the last seventy-five years there have been many other types of novels, covering many subjects. Bernardo Arias Trujillo (1905–1939) bared the souls of Colombia's downtrodden Negroes in *Risaralda*, as did Adalberto Ortiz (1914–) of Ecuador in *Juyungo* ("Negro") (1943). Like them was Gallego's *Pobre negro* ("Poor Negro") (1937).

Politics have been exposed by Rufino Blanco Fombona (1874–1944) who wrote his ironic *Hombre de oro* ("Man of Gold") (1907) while imprisoned in Ciudad Bolívar, a political victim of dictator Gómez. Finally escaping, he went to Paris, then returned to his homeland after the overthrow of Gómez. Azuela probed the social and political injustices of Mexico in *Mala yerba* ("Weeds") (1909) and *Los de abajo* ("The Underdogs") (1915).

The earthy themes of Criollism, beginning with *Peonía* ("Bondage of Labor") (1895) by the Venezuelan Manuel Vicente Romero García (1865–1917), were used by others with techniques developed through Modernism. Two of the greatest practitioners were the Chileans Mariano Latorre (1886–1955) and Marta Brunet (1901–   ). Latorre analyzed the souls of the hunters and the fishermen in *Cuentos del Maule* (1912), *Cuna de cóndores* ("The Condors' Cradle") (1918), and *Chilenos del mar* ("Seagoing Chileans") (1929). Miss Brunet, brought up in Europe, started with a regional novelette, *Montaña adentro* ("Deep in the Mountain") (1923), and by its success was encouraged to continue writing. Oscar Castro Z. (1910–1947) was one of their worthy disciples, in addition to writing Whitmanesque blank verse.

Historical fiction can be found in all parts of the continent. One of its most fertile producers, the Peruvian Ricardo Palma (1833–1919), whose stories cover all periods of his country's history, wrote most of his "Tradiciones" before the beginning of this volume. However the Chileans Manuel Rojas (1896–   ) with *Ciudad de los Césares* ("The City of the Caesars") (1928), and Hugo Silva, in *Pacha Pulai* (1937), dealt with a legendary period. The Inca empire figures in *Wuata Wuaru* (1904) by Alcides Arguedas (1879–1946). Fernando Alegría (1918–   ) told of Valdivia's servant and executioner in *Lautaro* (1943).

Seventeenth-century Potosí is the scene of *Era una vez* ("Once Upon a Time") (1935) by Abel Alarcón (1881–1954). *La Sombra del Corregidor* ("The Mayor's Shadow") (1927) by Chile's Sady Zañartu (1893–   ) tells about his eighteenth-century ancestor. Colombia's revolutionary period provides the background for *Lanzas coloradas* ("Colored Lances") (1931) by Arturo Uslar Pietri (1906–   ) and *El alférez real* ("The Royal Ensign") (1886) by Eustaquio Palacios (1830–1898), set in Cali. Chile's fight for independence in 1810 brought a stream of historical stories and novels, including two big volumes by Liborio Brieba (1841–1897) in 1871 and 1875, reprinted as the ten-book *Episodios nacionales* for Chile's sesquicentennial in 1960. Blest Gana's story of this period, *Durante la reconquista* ("During the Reconquest") (1897) is the best-known Chilean historical novel, but Fernando Santiván's (1886–   ) *El mulato Riquelme* ("Riquelme the Mulatto") (1951) also gives a fine picture of the times of O'Higgins.

Sugar-coated history of almost any period can be found within the covers of one novel or another, but of all the Spanish American countries, only Ecuador has produced the number and quality of novels to compare with the literary output of Brazil.

DRAMA

The dramatization of Eduardo Gutiérrez's (1853–1890) *Juan Moreira* in the Carlo Brothers' Circus, first as a pantomime and then in 1886 with dialogue, did not begin the national drama in Argentina or elsewhere. Other dramatists had been writing plays before it and went on writing afterward without knowing this landmark of the Argentine stage. But *Juan Moreira* did serve to focus attention on the gaucho as a subject for dramas. He quickly appeared in other plays: *Calandria* (1896) by Martiniano Leguizamón (1858–1935), and *Jesús nazareno* (1901) by Enrique García Velloso (1881–1939), among others.

With the end of the gaucho epoch, following the arrival of railroads and barbed wire fences, came the hard-working immigrant to provide economic competition for the easy-going Creole. The foreigners provided a new series of themes for the new technique developed from Ibsen, Strindberg, and others.

Roberto Payró (1867–1928) dramatized this conflict of old customs and new science in *Sobre las ruinas* ("On Top of the Ruins") (1902), then went on to bring the immigrant onto the stage in every phase from his arrival aboard ship to his eventual settlement, a task in which he was imitated by Pedro E. Pico (1882–1945). Their handling of social protest opened the way for Florencio Sánchez (1875–1910), greatest of the continent's dramatists, who evolved from rural plays involving gauchos like the economic clash in *La gringa* ("The Foreign Girl") (1904) and *Barranca abajo* ("Down the Gulley") (1905), to naturalistic dramas of the city that attacked hypocrisy, alcoholism, and the callous treatment of illegitimate children.

Sánchez did not succeed in establishing a following, except, perhaps for Ernesto Herrera (1886–1917). *El león ciego* ("The Blind Lion") (1911) by this Uruguayan bohemian, giving poignancy to a gaucho who outlived his generation, is credited with lessening the number of civil wars in Uruguay. His *La moral de Misia Paca* ("Miss Paca's Morality") (1911) represents an advance in psychology over his master, Sánchez.

Gregorio Laferrère (1867–1913) brought the modern comedy into being with plays like *Jettatore* ("Jinxed") (1904), *Locos de verano* ("Midsummer Madness") (1905), and especially *Las de Barranco* ("The Barranco Family") (1908). He was followed by many dramatists, writing alone or in partnership, like Darthés and Damel. Francisco Defilippis Novoa (1890–1930) and Armando Discépolo (1887–) deserve to be known by students of the theater, as should Conrado Nalé Roxlo (1895–), author of varied and successful comedies like *La cola de sirena* ("The Siren's Tail") (1941) and *Una viuda difícil* ("A Difficult Widow") (1944).

Samuel Eichelbaum (1894–) among the outstanding successors of Sánchez, and the popular and fertile Alberto Vacarezza (1896–) are other important Argentine dramatists of the passing generation. New River Plate dramatists are constantly appearing, to be noted by future historians of the theater, like Fernán Silva Valdés (1887–), Juan Bautista Devoto and his collaborator Alberto Sabato, and Carlos Gorostiza (1920–), Juan Carlos Ferrari, Agustín Cuzzani, and Carlos Carlino.

Chile produced few important plays until the twentieth century. Antonio Acevedo Hernández (1886–1962) wrote his first tragedy, *En el rancho* ("On the Farm"), in 1912, followed by gloomy plays like *Almas perdidas* ("Lost Souls") (1917), and folklore like *Camino de flores* ("The Flower Path") (1917) and *Chañarcillo* (1933), set in the mining region of Chile, near Copiapó. Armando Moock (1894–1942), whose dramatic career began in 1914 with *Crisis económica* ("Economic Crisis"), was author of about four hundred plays of all sorts, charming local color plays like *Pueblecita* ("Small Town") (1918) and *Mocosita* ("The Youngster") (1929), plays of ideas like the Ibsenesque *La serpiente* ("The Serpent") (1920), and a number of experiments like *Del brazo y por la calle* ("Arm in Arm Through the Street") (1939), also successfully performed in Brazil. Indeed probably more of Moock's plays have been performed in more Spanish-speaking countries than those of any other Latin-American dramatist. Germán Luco Cruchaga (1894–1936) is the third of the trio of Chile's early dramatists, and he is remembered especially for his *Viuda de Apablaza* ("The Widow of Apablaza") (1928), recently successfully revived.

It was a long time before other dramatists in Chile attained to their levels. A few wrote entertaining plays, but the usual Latin-American difficulty in finding available actors and audiences who were willing to attend performances by local writers when they might enjoy imported plays from the United States or Europe, delayed any great activity and consequent development of ability. The chief exceptions were a few labor unions that organized performances for propaganda purposes.

In the forties, the National University in Santiago developed an interest in drama and organized a professional company, followed by similar activity in the Catholic University of Chile. That encouraged a group of young writers: Gabriela Roepke (1920–   ), author of psychological plays; Isidora Aguirre (1919–   ), writer of plays about Chile culture; and María Asunción Requena (1918–   ), author of historical tragedies, among the women; and Egon Wolff (1926–   ), Sergio Vodánovich (1928–   ), Dr. Roberto Sarah (1918–   ), and Alejandro Sieveking (1936–   ).

The only other country to show great activity in the theater is Mexico. There, several dramas were based on the Revolution of 1910. Others were on proletariat themes. Julio Jiménez Rueda (1895–1959) labored before 1920 to create a national theater. Later El Teatro Ulises came into being, the first of a number of small theaters that introduced modern movements from abroad, besides providing local dramatists with their opportunities. Xavier Villaurrutia (1903–1950), Celestino Gorostiza (1904–   ), Salvador Novo (1904–   ), and especially Rodolfo Usigli (1905–   ) contributed to the developing stage. More recently have appeared Luis G. Basurto (1920–   ), Wilberto Cantón (1923–   ), Hector Mendoza (1932–   ), and Sergio Magaño (1924–   ), whose *Signos de zodíaco* ("Signs of the Zodiac") (1951) has been called one of the greatest plays of the Mexican stage.

The theater is also showing activity in other nations. The products of some of them are included in this volume. Puerto Rico, the home of Francisco Arriví (1915–   ) and René Marqués (1919–   ), supports an annual theater festival where local works are produced. And even Paraguay has shown surprising activity, not only with a short-lived theater in the Guaraní Indian language, of which Julio Correa (1890–1953) was the chief figure, but one in Spanish under the urging of Josefina Pla (1907–   ), Arturo Alsina (1897–   ), Jaime Bestard (1892–   ), and José María Rivarola Matto (1917–   ).

To a greater or lesser degree, all the Latin-American countries have produced works for the stage, but that form of literature has attracted fewer writers than either poetry or prose. However in all fields, the tempo is increasing. Spanish-American works do have importance in world literature, and the translated samples in this anthology will give some idea of the themes, currents, and techniques.

I

POETRY

RUBÉN DARÍO

1867–1916   Nicaragua

Félix Rubén García Sarmiento, who adopted the name
of a relative for his pen name, was the greatest figure
in modern Latin-American poetry. Influenced by old
Spanish poets and by modern French Parnassians, he
became the leader of Modernism, with its emphasis on
beauty of diction and variety of metrical forms. His
travels in South America and Europe, as diplomatic
representative of various countries, increased his influence among poets seeking new freedom.

Darío's first volume, *Azul* ("Blue") (1888) revealed
color and music unknown through previous technical
resources but created by his genius. His *Prosas profanas*
("Worldly Prose") (1896) further revealed his ex-
oticism. *Cantos de vida y esperanza* ("Songs of Life
and Hope") (1905) introduced a more human side
that tended toward universality by the time of *Canto
a la Argentina* (1910).

Among the poems here translated, "Sonatina,"
popular among elocutionists, is an example of Darío's
musical touch, and presents many of the exotic qualities
of Modernism: swans and marble palaces, later fore-
sworn by him in "Pórtico." An example of his prose is
also included.

SONATINA

The Princess mourns—Why is the Princess sighing?
Why from her lips are song and laughter dying?
    Why does she droop upon her chair of gold?
Hushed is the music of her royal bower;
Beside her, in a vase, a single flower
    Swoons and forgets its petals to unfold.

The fool in scarlet pirouettes and flatters;
Within the hall the silly dueña chatters;
   Without, the peacock's regal plumage gleams.
The Princess heeds them not; her thoughts are veering
Out through the gates of Dawn, past sight and hearing,
   Where she pursues the phantoms of her dreams.

Is it a dream of China that allures her,
Or far Golconda's ruler who conjures her
   But to unveil the laughter of her eyes?—
He of the island realms of fragrant roses,
Whose treasure flashing diamond hoards discloses,
   And pearls of Ormuz, rich beyond surmise?

Alas! The Princess longs to be a swallow,
To be a butterfly, to soar, to follow
   The ray of light that climbs into the sun;
To greet the lilies, lost in Springtime wonder,
To ride upon the wind, to hear the thunder
   Of ocean waves where monstrous billows run.

Her silver distaff fallen in disfavor,
Her magic globe shorn of its magic savor,
   The swans that drift like snow across the lake,
The lotus in the garden pool—are mourning;
The dahlias and the jasmine flowers adorning
   The palace gardens, sorrow for her sake.

Poor little captive of the blue-eyed glances!
A hundred Negroes with a hundred lances,
   A hound, a sleepless dragon, guard her gates.
There in the marble of her palace prison
The little Princess of the roving vision,
   Caught in her gold and gauzes, dreams and waits.

"Oh" (sighs the Princess), "Oh, to leave behind me
My marble cage, the golden chains that bind me—

—The empty chrysalis the moth forsakes—
To fly to where a fairy Prince is dwelling,
Oh, radiant vision past all mortal telling,
    Brighter than April or the day that breaks!"

"Hush, little Princess," whispers the good fairy.
"With sword and goshawk, on his charger airy,
    The Prince draws near—the lover without blame.
Upon his wingéd steed the Prince is fleeting,
The conqueror of Death, to bring you greeting,
    And with his kiss to touch your lips to flame!"

                                        John Pierrepont Rice

PORTICO

I am the singer who of late put by
    The verse azulean and the chant profane,
Across whose nights a rossignol would cry
    And prove himself a lark at morn again.

Lord was I of my garden-place of dreams,
    The heaping roses and swan-haunted brakes;
Lord of the doves; lord of the silver streams,
    Of gondolas and lyres upon the lakes.

And very eighteenth century; both old
    And very modern; bold, cosmopolite;
Like Hugo daring, like Verlaine half-told,
    And thirsting for illusions infinite.

    .   .   .   .   .   .

All longing and all ardor, the mere sense
    And natural vigor; and without a sign
Of stage effects or literature's pretence—
    If there was ever soul sincere, 't was mine.

The ivory tower awakened my desire;
   I longed to enclose myself in selfish bliss,
Yet hungered after space, my thirst on fire
   For heaven, from out the shades of my abyss.

.   .   .   .   .   .

But through the grace of God, my conscience
   Elected unto good the better part;
If there were hardness left in any sense,
   It melted soft beneath the touch of Art.

My intellect was freed from baser thought,
   My soul was bathed in the Castalian flood,
My heart a pilgrim went, and so I caught
   The harmony from out the sacred wood.

.   .   .   .   .   .

Life, Light and Truth, as in a triple flame
   Produce the inner radiance, infinite;
Art, pure as Christ, is heartened to exclaim:
"I am indeed the Life, the Truth, the Light!"

The Life is mystery; the Light is blind;
   The Truth beyond our reach both daunts and fades;
The sheer perfection nowhere do we find;
   The ideal sleeps a secret in the shades.

Therefore to be sincere is to be strong.
   Bare as it is, what glitter hath the star?
The water tells the fountain's soul in song
   And voice of crystal flowing out afar.

Such my intent was,—of my spirit pure
   To make a star, a fountain music-drawn,
With horror of the thing called literature—
   And mad with madness of the gloam and dawn.

From the blue twilight such as gives the word
   Which the celestial ecstacies inspire,
The haze and minor chord,—let flutes be heard!
   Aurora, daughter of the sun,—sound lyre!

Let pass the stone if any use the sling;
   Let pass, should hands of violence point the dart.
The stone from out the sling is for the waves a thing,
   Hate's arrow of the idle wind is part.

Virtue is with the tranquil and the brave;
   The interior fire burneth well and high;
The triumph is o'er rancor and the grave;
   Toward Bethlehem, the caravan goes by!

Thomas Walsh

SYMPHONY IN GRAY MAJOR

The sea like a vast quicksilvered glass
Reflects the zinc of the graven sky;
The burnished background of pallid gray
Is flecked with distant birds flying by.

Round, opaque glass, the sun is climbing,
Slow as an invalid, weak and worn;
The Triton sea wind rests in shade
Pillowed upon his curved black horn.

Leaden waves moan beneath the pier,
Shifting their swollen expanse of gray.
Upon a cable, smoking his pipe,
A sailor dreams of the misty shores
Of a hazy country far away.

An old sea dog. The fiery rays
Of Brazilian suns have tanned his skin,

88549

College of St. Francis Library
Joliet, Illinois

The fierce typhoons of the China Sea
Have seen him swig his flask of gin.

Pungent with nitre and iodine
The sea foam knows the sailor well
From his curls and biceps and ruddy nose
To his canvas cap and blouse of drill.

In the cloud of gray tobacco smoke
He visions a country far away
And a brigantine that spreads its sails
For that warm shore on a golden day.

Tropic siesta. The mariner sleeps.
All is wrapped in the gamut of gray.
Dim and more dim grows the curved horizon
As if it were softening and faded away.

Tropic siesta. A harvest fly
Plucks his guitar in a senile drone;
On the single cord of his violin
A cricket preludes his monotone.

Alice Jane McVan

LITANY FOR OUR LORD
DON QUIJOTE

King of all cavaliers, lord of the sorrowing,
From warfare your sustenance, from dreams your cloak borrow-
　　　ing,
　　Crowned with illusion's golden crest;
Of whom none has ever beat down the daring,
As the shield on your arm all vision bearing;
　　And all hearts as your lance in rest;

Noble pilgrim, all pilgrims surpassing,
Who sanctify all roads by your passing,
    With tread heroic, august, uncouth;
Against certainties and against consciences
Against laws and against sciences,
    Against falsehood, against truth;

Errant knight of all knights-errant,
Baron of strong hearts, prince of the valiant,
    Peer among peers, I hail you aloud!
    Hail! for today obscure is your station
And the disdain and adulation,
Amid the crowning and ovation,
    And all the idiocies of the crown.

                ·   ·   ·   ·   ·   ·

Pray for us, too avid of living,
Tempted souls, faith lost past forgiving,
    Filled with disease, orphaned of sun;
And for those upstarts, with wide sleeves trailing,
At the noble figure of La Mancha railing,
    At that generous and most Spanish one.

                ·   ·   ·   ·   ·   ·

Pray for us, generous, pious, and most proud one;
Pray for us, chaste, pure, heavenly, unbowed one;
    Pray for the worthless, intercede for our sod!
Since we are now without vigor or glory,
Without soul, without life, without your grand story,
    Without foot or wing, without Sancho or God!

From so many sorrows, from griefs heart-wringing,
From supermen of Nietzsche, from Aphonic singing,
    From the prescriptions that doctors give to us
From the epidemics of horrible blasphemies

Of the Academies,
  Good Lord, deliver us!

      .   .   .   .   .   .

Pray for us, Lord of the sorrowing,
From warfare your sustenance, from dreams your shield borrow-
    ing,
  Crowned with illusion's golden crest;
Of whom none has ever beat down the daring,
As the shield on your arm all vision bearing,
  And all hearts as your lance in rest!

Muna Lee

THE RUBY

When the gnomes were gathered, some with their hammers
and short axes in their hands, others in gala attire—with
pointed caps, red and flaming, covered with precious stones, all
curious, Puck spoke thus:

"You have asked me to bring you a specimen of the new
human falsification, and I am satisfying your desires. In the
great city of Paris, flying invisible, I saw rubies everywhere.
They shone in the necklaces of the courtesans, in the rings of
the Italian princes, in the bracelets of the prima donnas."

With a knavish smile, he continued:

"I entered a certain rose-colored boudoir where a beautiful
woman was asleep. From her neck I snatched a medalion containing a ruby. Here you have it."

They all burst into laughter. What a tinkling! Afterward
they gave their opinion of the false stone, the work of a man, of
a savant, which was worse:

"Glass! Black art! Poison and cabala! Chemistry! The idea
of pretending to imitate a fragment of the rainbow!"

The oldest gnome, walking about on his twisted legs, with

his great snowy beard, his aspect of a patriarch, his face filled with wrinkles, said:

"Señores, you know not what you are saying. I, that am the oldest among you, shall tell you how the ruby was made. Harken:

"One day, we, the bands that have under our charge the mines of diamonds, had a strike that stirred the whole earth, and we went forth in flight through the craters of the volcanoes.

"The world was full of glee; all was vigor and youth; and the roses and the fresh green leaves and the birds, into whose crops enters the grain and whence emerges the twitter, and all the countryside, saluted the sun and the fragrant springtime.

"The mountain was flushed with flowers and glad with song, filled with the trills of birds and with bees; it was a great and holy nuptial celebrated by the light, and in the tree the sap was boiling ardently, and in the animal all was quivering or bleating or song; and in the gnomes were merriment and laughter.

"I had come forth through an extinct crater. Before my eyes was an extensive country. With a bound I set myself upon a great tree, a hoary oak. Then I slid down the trunk and found myself near a brook, a river small and clear, where the waters babbled, telling crystaline jokes to themselves. I was thirsty. I wished to drink there. . . . Now, listen better.

"Arms, backs, naked bosoms; lilies, roses, loaves of ivory crowned with cherries; echoes of golden, festive laughter; and there, amid the foam, amid the shattered lymph, beneath the green boughs . . ."

"Nymphs?"

"No; a woman!

"I knew which was my grotto. With a blow on the ground, I opened the black sand and I reached my dominion. You— poor, little, young gnomes—have much to learn.

"Under the shoots of some new ferns, I scrambled over the rocks worn by the foamy, babbling current, and her, the beauty, the woman, I seized by the waist with this arm, formerly so muscular. She cried; I beat the earth; we descended. Above was left astonishment; below was the proud, triumphant gnome.

"But, in the depths of my dominion, my queen, my beloved, my beauty, deceived me. When man loves truly, his passion penetrates everything and is capable of passing through the earth.

"She loved a man, and from her prison she wafted him her sighs. They passed through the pores of the terrestrial crust and came to him; and he, loving her also, kissed the roses of a certain garden; and she, the beautiful one, had—I noted it—sudden convulsions in which she stretched her lips, fresh and rosy as the petals of the centifolia. How was it that the two felt thus? Being who I am, I know not.

"I had finished my work one day: a great pile of diamonds. The earth opened its cracks of granite like thirsty lips, awaiting the brilliant shivering of the rich crystal. Finally, tired, I struck a hammer blow that burst a rock; and I went to sleep.

"I awakened after a little, at hearing something like a moan.

"From her couch, from her mansion, richer and more luminous than those of all the queens of the Orient, had flown, fugitive, desperate, my beloved, the stolen woman. Ah! She, minded to flee through the hole opened by my club of granite, and naked and beautiful, tore her body—white and soft as if of orange-blossom and marble and rose—upon the edges of the broken diamonds. Her sides, wounded, jutted blood; her plaints moved even me to tears. Oh, agony!

"I awakened, took her in my arms, gave her my most ardent kisses; but the blood flowed, flooding the spot, and the great diamantine mass was dyed red. It seemed to me that I felt, as I gave her a kiss, a perfume issue from that burning mouth: the soul; the body became inert.

"When our great patriarch, the centenarian demigod of the bowels of the earth, passed thereby, he found that multitude of ruddy diamonds."

The gnomes, very grave, arose.

They examined more nearly the false stone, the workmanship of the savant.

"Look; it has no facets!"

"It shines palely!"

"It is round like a beetle's breastplate!"

In a flurry, one here, another there, they darted to tear from the walls pieces of arabesque, rubies large as oranges, red and sparkling like diamonds turned to blood; and they said:

"Behold, ours, O Mother Earth!"

And they tossed into the air the gigantic, shining stones, and they laughed.

Afterward they took the false ruby, crushed it to pieces and tossed the fragments with terrible disdain into a hole that opened below on a very old charred forest.

Puck was already flying abroad, in the glimmering of the new-born dawn, toward a meadow in flower; and he murmured —always with his roseate smile: "Earth! . . . Woman! . . ."

For thou, O Mother Earth! art great, fecund, of an inextinguishable and sacred bosom; and from thy brown womb spring the sap of the stout trunks and gold and diamantine water and the chaste fleur-de-lis. The pure, the strong, the unfalsifiable! And thou, woman, art spirit and flesh, all love!

Anon. (Inter-America, Vol. 4)

SALVADOR DÍAZ MIRÓN
1853–1928   Mexico

One of the most original of Mexican poets is Díaz Mirón, put by Anderson Imbert "between Justo Sierra who announced Modernism and Gutiérrez Nájera who opened the door." Perhaps Mirón came in through the window. His romantic exuberance, in the spirit of Byron and Victor Hugo, made him immensely popular. He lived Romanticism, even to fighting duels and getting imprisoned. Later, when he became conscious of form, he controlled his language and disciplined his thoughts in *Lascas* ("Stone Chips") (1906), which he declared the beginning of his career. While it shows originality of thought and force and clearness of expression, it lacks the spontaneity of his discarded earlier poetry.

Darío praises his work in *Azul*, and Chocano, along with many Mexican poets, acknowledged his influence. In describing daily life, Díaz Mirón adapted an eleven-syllable stanza, previously used chiefly in religious poetry. Each quatrain is independent and made up of an initial general statement, followed by an application or a metaphor. "A piedad" ("To Pity") here translated is an example, as is "A Gloria" ("To Gloria"), written to his wife who was trying to prevent his duel with a fellow congressman.

TO PITY

You came to me in pride of gentle beauty.
What various forms hath pride! It shows to view
In the strong lion, rough mane and mighty roaring,
And in the dove, soft note and changeful hue.

A heavenly power comes with you to my sorrow;
It dawns upon the cavern's darksome night,
And enters in and spreads there like a music,
Like a sweet fragrance, like a shining light.

You give to sadness, like a good magician,
A happy truce; moved sweetly by your graces
I bless the wound because of its pure balsam;
I love the desert for its green oasis!

Alice Stone Blackwell

TO GLORIA (fragments)

Use for my doings no abusive term.
No madness of your mind my actions thwarts.
My reason is at once both clear and firm,
As firm and lucid as the crystal quartz.

Like no nocturnal pilgrim with bent head
Do I go forth, my gaze upon the ground,
For there one sees but shadows dark. Instead
I contemplate the skies where hopes abound.

All that illuminates is bound to perish.
My inspirations all my powers consume;
From wounded mollusk comes the pearl we cherish;
And Venus sprang from bitter, salty spume.

. . . . . .

Conform, then, woman! That is always best,
For in this Vale of Tears we find our fate:
You like the dove so tranquil in its nest,
I like the lion, for combat and for hate.

W.K.J.

IN HOC SIGNO

(For my daughter Rosa)

A small, captive sparrow
To a star raised his eyes:
"I hope I can send my
Sweet song to the skies."

By luck or hard striving,
From his prison he flies,
And free, to the heavens
You could then watch him rise.

If a star and a sparrow
Could knot their love ties,
Neither bars nor great distance
Love's triumph denies.

W.K.J.

MANUEL GUTIÉRREZ NÁJERA
1859–1895   Mexico

As exquisite in his verse as he was ugly in body, Gutiérrez Nájera is considered Mexico's greatest poet since Sor Juana de la Cruz. In his ambition to "fuse French thought and Spanish verse," he was a forerunner of Modernism, and his *Revista Azul* (1892) encouraged the movement by printing the work of experimenters like Silva, Casal, and even Darío. Some of his own published poetry, characterized by elegance and melancholy, appeared there, but his light verses signed "El duque Job," that rank him as Mexico's most intimate poet, were not collected till 1896, after his death.

A pianist himself, he put music into his poetry and even wrote a long romantic poem to be recited as Schubert's "Serenade" was being played. His earliest work was religious poetry, and he continued to write religious prose, like the *Sermons of Duke Job*. His final poem, "A la corregidora" ("To the Wife of the Corregidor"), was written to be recited at the erection of a monument to the wife of Mayor Domínguez, who, though locked in her room, managed to send warning to Manuel Hidalgo, enabling him to escape arrest and to utter the *Grito de Dolores* (1810) that began Mexico's struggle for independence. Using an ancient Spanish verse form, the poem attempted to make the sounds of the words help paint the picture, as Darío did in his "Era un aire suave" ("It was a Gentle Air").

WHEN I DIE

Let me die with the sun's last gleam
Upon the sea, my face to the sky,
The pangs of my death but a distant dream,
The soul a bird to mount and fly;

Hearing naught those moments save—
Alone there with the sky and the sea—
The voices of the tossing wave,
No other sobbing prayer for me.

Death to come as the light redeems
From green-hued wave its nets of gold,
Death like that of the sun whose beams
Are lost in flaming color bold.

To die while young, ere treacherous time
Destroys my fragile crown of youth,
With Life still saying: "I am thine!"
Though well we know 't is not the truth.

Alice J. McVan

THE DUCHESS JOB

Around the table when the dinner's through
We'll eat strawberries, sup coffee, too.
Under the table sleeps our dog Bob.
And while we're chatting, I'll draw for you
A sketch of the Duchess, wife of Duke Job.

She's not the Duchess in caricature
Of Villasana, nor—to be sure—
That country maiden, red skirt aflair,
Loved by Prieto, nor servant maid
Dreaming of dandies thick with pomade,
Products of Nicolo's barbershop chair.

My little Duchess—she who loves me—
Has no pretensions a model to be.
To her the Boston's complete mystery.
Nor does she figure in novels by Kock,

Never drinks tea when it comes five o'clock.
She is no leader in society.

Thick and soft rugs are not for her feet.
Though she may wander in Plateros Street
Where perhaps Madame Marnet will bow,
Not as a client is she there, at least.
That's just her route to a cheaper modiste
Who, early rising, waits for her now.

My little Duchess, no jewels has she,
But she's so chic, with such gaiety
And such a figure that draws every glance!
She's far more charming, likewise more cute
Than all the clients of Helène Kossut,
And not behind them in sheer elegance.

.   .   .   .   .   .

On Sunday mornings in bed she'll stay
Till through the windows come sounds of day,
And in the tower the clock strikes nine.
If you could see her, you'd not forget
My Duchess under her pink coverlet,
But we're alone in this house of mine.

.   .   .   .   .   .

Finally she rises, a smile on her face,
And on the table the food we place:
A couple of eggs and a thick beefsteak.
Then a half bottle of delicious wine,
And afterward, when the weather is fine
Gaily we drive out to Chapultepec.

In all the city, from Surprise Store
Down to the corner of Jockey Club's door,
There's nobody Spanish, or Yankee, or French,

Prettier or sweeter than my sly wench,
My Duchess her Duke Job sure does adore!

                                              W.K.J.

TO THE WIFE OF THE
CORREGIDOR

For primates old, pale incense eddying round;
For heroes, hymns; For God, the solemn sound
Raised by the forests and the seas, with power;
For the prize-wrestler, murrine wine-cup be;
Palm for the martyr; heroine, for thee,
Leaves of acanthus and the clover flower!

Poems of gold there are, and silver notes;
Stanzas I seek where crimson color floats.
Stanzas of blood, such as the Orient knows;
And moist and living, red and warm to see,
The trembling leaves outstretch themselves to me
That sway in graceful nets upon the rose.

Bloom out, fresh flowers! Arise from out the mould!
Unfold thy wings, gardenia, chilled with cold!
Buds, open! Myrtles, light your flame so fair!
Ye poppies, let your rich skirts gleam and glow!
Your Persian shawls, luxurious roses, show,
Spreading their glossy silk to greet the air!

Hear'st thou a murmur, faint and cool and low,
Like silken trains that softly sweeping go
O'er marble smooth or polished ivory white?
It is the fruitful sap that upward flows
And swells the shoots, and breathes and burns and glows
In all Prince April's buds, now ruddy bright.

O noble lady, Earth sings unto thee
The psalm of life; the plants awake and free,
The bursting bud, arise toward thee aloft,—
The iris bold, with flower erect and bright,
The insect, shining, quivering and light,
That breaks, impatient, from its prison soft.

The lily chaste, a timid nun, perfumes
Thine altar; filled with pride the dahlia blooms,
Seeming a bird for eager flight soon bound.
Daringly fixing to the stone its lace
The ivy with festoons of curving grace,
Jealous and faithful, wreathes thine altar round.

Come to the shade that offers welcome here,
Swift birds of gorgeous plumage, without fear!
Nests wait for thee. Come sing here, everyone!
Sing to the lark that to the warrior cried,
Announcing daybreak: "Draw thy sword with pride.
Awake thy comrades! 'T is the hour. March on!"

Alice Stone Blackwell

LENTEN SERMONS OF
"EL DUQUE JOB"

First series: The Sunday of Temptation

Do you recall having seen in our Academia de Bellas Artes a picture that represents the temptation of Jesus? The devil shows to the Son of God several trays filled with fruits and flowers and borne on the hands of some angels, about whom I am in doubt, as to whether they are men or women; for angels have no sex.

The devil seems to be saying to him: "If thou wilt obey me, if thou wilt deliver thyself to me, thou shalt eat of all these grapes, all these peaches, all these pears!"

Do you remember seeing that picture? Well, the temptation of Jesus was otherwise. There is another canvas—another, indeed!—that has the same subject as a motive. It is by Ary Scheffer and I recall having contemplated it in a marvelous article by Renan (suppress the adjective "marvelous" as useless and the phrase will lose nothing of its force); in an article by Renan. In it, the devil is beautiful. Why must we make him ugly, when God made him beautiful? Why must we give him horns if we are not women? Why must we imagine him repulsive if to all of us he is, unfortunately, so attractive? And in a gallant attitude and haughty, he offers to Jesus mastery and dominion over all the earth.

The temptation in this picture is seductive, as true temptation must be! That of the serpent in paradise was very silly. What did the serpent offer? What any Indian woman offers on any corner: an apple! For the honor of Adam and for the honor of Eve, for we are, after all, of one family, I should like to believe that all this about the apple was a mere symbol and that the serpent in reality offered Eve something else. Moreover I should like to believe that there was no such serpent, for serpents could not have been made by God, not could they have been in paradise; besides, women from the first to the last of them, are and always will be, incapable of holding conversation with such a creature.

Temptation is beautiful in itself, señoritas, and it not only displays its charms to seduce the creatures that can lead all humanity to perdition, as Eve did; it not only speaks on the top of the mountain, at every step, in every showcase, now offering a hat, now a gown, now a jewel, it speaks to us . . .

Temptation, from the most remote times, has enamoured women with the glance of golden coins and with the rays of precious stones. Jupiter to possess himself of Danaë, changed himself into a shower of gold. The enemies of the soul are three: I do not know how many are the enemies of women, but one of them, señoritas, is the diamond.

I have no reason to dislike this stone, perhaps because I am not intimately acquainted with it, except by sight only; but

when I think of the evils it has caused, I can do no less than
condemn it. To possess this piece of carbon ennobled by light,
a woman will tie herself to a rich husband. The evils that
spring from yielding to this temptation will be, señoras and
señoritas, the theme of my discourse . . .

What I would charge you is not to seek the diamond;
await it. When it comes naturally, as dew on the petal, it is
beautiful and good. I speak in the presence of a distinguished
audience, of whose religiosity and good conscience I have evident signs, and therefore I consider it useless to say to you that
you should not seek the diamond by other means; but always,
señoritas . . . do not seek it!

Anon. (*Inter-America*, Vol. 5)

ENRIQUE GONZÁLEZ MARTÍNEZ
1871–1952   Mexico

González Martínez, last great poet of the Modernist
movement, wrote his first volumes, *Preludios* (1907)
and *Lirismos* (1908) while practicing medicine in
Mazatlán. Before coming to the capital in 1909, he
broke with Modernism in a sonnet, "Tuércele el cuello
al cisne" ("Twist the Neck of the Swan"), proposing
the owl of wisdom for its symbol. It has been compared to Hugo's *Manifesto* for Romanticism. Its author did not intend to attack Darío, for he had already
abandoned swans and ivory towers in his *Songs of Life
and Hope* (1905). González Martínez was speaking to
imitators of the old Darío.

Nearly a score of his early volumes are combined in
his three-volume *Poesías* (1944), that shows his concern with death, yet expressed with a serenity and an
idealism that were imitated by his followers. The poet
was a pantheist who deified nature and contemplated
it with love and devotion. As a diplomat, he represented Mexico in Argentina and Spain.

TWIST THE NECK OF THE SWAN

Twist the neck of the swan with its deceptive plumage
Giving his white to the azure pond's appeal.
He only parades his beauty and cannot feel
The soul of things, nor hear the voice of the herbage.
So shun all visible forms and audible language
Through which Life's deep and latent rhythms steal
Not, nor beat; adore Life till your senses reel,
And let all Life receive your reverent homage.

Behold the wise owl—how he spreads his wings
Leaving the lap of Pallas, and from Olympus swings
Down to the distant tree to end his flight . . .
The owl lacks swan-like beauty, but his restless eye
Is fixed on Life's dark shadow and can descry
And read the mysterious book of silent night.

Read Bain

THE PRAYER OF THE
BARREN ROCK

Lord, round my brow the winds of heaven are hurled;
Under the burning sun I bend my head;
The cloud that passes like a bird is sped
Forth to another world.

I know the winter blasts that freeze and sting,
The long monotony of summer rain;
My eyes upturned to heaven implore in vain
The miracle of spring.

No forests crowd upon my barren crest,
No singing streams of water, running bright

Through beds of moss and drowsy flowers, invite
The traveler to rest.

But even as spectres in their tombs awake,
Haunted by dreams of Paradise denied,
My dull heart stirs, and in my soul I hide
A thirst I cannot slake.

My feet are buried in the mountain height,
My feet are chained; my hope soars to the sky.
Men know me not; like strangers they pass by
My prison bars of light.

And since I am denied the friendly flowers,
The fragrant bed of moss, the singing stream,
Lord, let the nesting eagles mate and scream
Above my mountain towers.

Yet by my loneliness would I express
As in a symbol, that exalted mood
Which in impassioned solitude
Finds everlastingness.

John Pierrepont Rice

TOMORROW

Tomorrow poets shall hold the world in thrall,
And war shall be no more, when greed and pride,
Writhing like horrid serpents, shall have died;
And man shall then look up and cease to crawl,
And face the stars; the trite, the smug, the small,
Like cruel, childish toys, be laid aside:
Lust, traffic, hate, and fear. Then dreams denied
(Since factory smoke first spread its murky pall)
Shall blossom into beauty. Yes, tomorrow

Poets shall rule in awful humbleness,
And all our paltry cares submerge in sorrow
Tall and divine, that only poets guess;
And none shall hunger save for cosmic loss,
The shadow of a god upon a cross.

Chesley M. Hutchings

AMADO NERVO
1870–1919   Mexico

Of Nervo's large amount of writing, filling thirty volumes, only a small quantity is likely to endure. Beginning as a Modernist, he turned to Mysticism in 1912, following the death of a woman he loved. It is the product of this period that will keep his name remembered among Mexico's poets. See the prose section for other details and an example of his prose.

PURITY

Let nothing stir the quiet lake
Of Life. If there is mud down deep,
What matter? Clear the waters keep;
They never cloud the shining glass.
There tranquil waters make
A mirror and an image take
Of summer branches where they greenly mass.

Mud will not roil
The pure, transparent surface of the spring
If deep it lies where none can spoil
Its slumbering.
It only shows its presence there
By water lilies pale and fair;

Fainting with love upon the crystal clear,
They float on slender stems that grow
So long they reach to bring us near
The flowers, but leave the mud below.

Beatrice Gilman Proske

OLD BURTHEN

Who is yon siren whose voice is so dolent,
Whose body gleams white under the dark tresses?
Only a ray of moonlight, bathing in the fountain,
   only a ray of the moon.

Who is it goes seeking me through all my dwelling,
Calling my name all night with tremulous accent?
Only a breath of wind, sobbing in the tower,
   only a breath of wind.

Who are you, Archangel, whose bright wings kindle
In divine fire of sunset, swiftly descending
Through the glory of the ether? Only a cloud passing,
   see, it is only a cloud!

Who spilled in the water the gems of her necklace,
A shower of diamonds, fallen on blue velvet?
Only the face of the sky, quivering on the river,
   the face of the sky.

So then, Lord, beauty is just a mirage!
Only Thou art real. Be Thou my ultimate master.
But where shall I find Thee: in sky, on earth, within me?
A bit of a dream shall guide me through all dark places,
   a bit of a dream.

Chesley M. Hutchings

NOT ALL

Not all who die see God, and thinkest thou
That merely dying will suffice to gain
For thee the vision that thou seekest now?
The veil of Isis it will rend in twain?
Illusion vain!
Not all who die see God!

But souls heroic, scorning self—if they
Have learned to soar—shall, living, see His light,
As Andean summits see the flame of day
While lowlands still lie buried in the night.

Helen Eldredge Fish

RAMÓN LÓPEZ VELARDE
1888–1921   Mexico

Mexico's greatest Symbolist was López Velarde, reminiscent of Rimbaud. His abandonment of the seminary
to study for the bar may have set up an inner conflict
between Christianity and paganism, that is visible in
his writings. Though he wrote only a small amount of
poetry, he revealed a mastery of technique, color, and
music that gives him high rank. *La sangre devota*
("Devout Blood") (1916) deals with pure love.
Zozobra ("Anguish") (1919), his best volume, voices
his conflict with carnal love. His manuscript for *El son
de corazón* ("The Heart's Rhythm") (1932), found
after his death, is full of his disillusionment because of
surrender. His complete output, edited by Villaurrutia
in 1935, shows López Velarde as a forerunner of many
Mexican poetic movements that developed later: In-
dianism, Nationalism, and the cult of rural regions.

THE SPELL OF RETURN

Never perhaps to go back again to my lonely village
Would be just as well,
To my ruined paradise, silent grown
Under the rain of shot and shell.

Even the ash-trees are maimed and split;
Pompous and dignified, showy of dome,
Still they sway greenly round the grieving resentful tower,
Pitted, wind-stung, in an evil hour.

Shot and shell cut the plaster deep
In all the walls
Of my little old spectral village,
Slashing maps that are sharp and black,
That everywhere the prodigal
When he returns to his ruined home,
On some luckless night of witchcrafterie,
May read by the flickering light of a ghostly match
The ruin of all his hopes.

Edna Worthley Underwood

MY COUSIN AGUEDA

My godmother often invited my cousin Agueda
To come and spend the day.
My cousin used to arrive
Appearing in a mixed-up way,
Suggesting starch and fearful
Mourning of a funereal day.

Agueda would appear rustling
With starch, and with her eyes green,

And her rosy cheeks
Protecting me against the mourning
That I'd seen.

I was a kid
And knew nothing at all,
And Agueda, who was moving
Tamely and persistently in the hall,
With her rustling brought excitement
About which I knew nothing at all.

(I even think she is responsible
For my mad habit of talking to myself.)

At the dinner hour in the quiet
Shadows of the dining room,
How delightful the fragile
Intermittent rattle of the dishes
And the affectionate tone
Of the voice of my cousin.
                         Agueda
(in her black mourning, her green eyes, and
Pink cheeks) was a many colored basket
Of apples and green grapes
On the ebony of our ancestral sideboard.

                                              W.K.J.

ANTS

To the warm life that musically passes
In the dress of a woman without domino or letters,
To the unconquered beauty that saves and enamours
In the enchanting hour's intoxication,
In my ravenous veins a fester of ants replies.

In the well of silence and the multitude of noises,
The flour, sliced like a double trophy
In fertile bosoms; the Hell I believe in,
The last death rattle and the prelude of the nest
Lash the excess of the perpetual anthill.

But then my ants deny me their embrace
And must fly from my poor and laboring fingers
Like a bit of cold refuse forgotten in the sand;
And your mouth which is emblem of erotic braveries,
Your mouth, my rubric, my food, my adornment
(Your mouth whose tongue quivers, thrust at the world
Like flames of perdition shooting out from an oven
In the murky time when the north wind is moaning,
When the moon sulks as it seeks to rob you),
Has to smell its shroud and crushed glasses,
Like drug and responsory, like wax and candlewick.

Before my ants desert me, Beloved,
Let them travel the way of your mouth
To drink the viaticums of the bloody fruit
Which provoke me from Saracenic oases.

Before your lips die, give them to me
For my mourning, in the critical shade of the cemetery,
As perfume, and bread, and poison, and cautery.

H. R. Hays

JAIME TORRES BODET

1902–   Mexico

González Martínez provided the foreword to Torres
Bodet's first volume, *Fervor* (1918). As a member of
the Ulises group, the sixteen-year-old poet was interested in French literary trends and experimented with
meters and movements. Surrealistic tendencies as well

as neo-Symbolism can be found in his *Poesía* (1926), culled from his earlier volumes, and in his later collections. He has also written essays, excellent short stories, a couple of novels, and some amusing light verse.

A PIT

"Shall I compare thee to a Summer's day?" Shakespeare.

I touched—amid the blond
and delicate flesh—of what fruit?—
the black, harsh pit of the Summer.

And suddenly I felt, before
the seed's mute, cruel sincerity,
like one finding on a tomb the name
of the woman never imagined,
living, as sustained
by the hidden skeleton
—of misery, of anger, of boredom—
which even after death espouses her.

Muna Lee

MIDDAY

To open the dining room window at midday.
To feel the sun's rays pour in from above.
To smell the warm fragrance of sun and apples.
To say simple things, inspirations of love . . .

To drink of pure water and see in the goblet
Reflected, the cherished sites of my farm range.
To sense the earth's globe in the roundness of peaches.
To know that in spite of all there is no change.

To feel at last ripe, to see in all things
Nothing more than those things: sun, honey, bread . . .
To be only a man pulling petals off roses,
To trace at the table a name on the spread . . .

Donald Malcolm

OCTAVIO PAZ
1914–   Mexico

One of the authentic voices of Mexican literature today, both as a poet and as a critic, is Paz, who began
in 1933 with an adolescent volume of poems, *Luna
silvestre* ("Sylvan Moon"). Then, matured by the
Spanish civil war, he published *No pasarán* ("They
Shall Not Pass") (1936). He struck his stride in *Raíz
del hombre* ("Man's Root"), praised for its humanity,
no less than for its virile style and profound lyricism.
Till 1941, he was associated with the Taller group that
followed current European poetic techniques in describing the Mexican scene. While his work is intensely personal, it is also extremely national. In 1950, Paz published a series of essays on the Mexican scene, *Laberinto
de la soledad* ("Labyrinth of Solitude"). His recent
volume of poetry, *La estación violenta* ("The Violent
Season") (1958) shows evidence of his attraction toward Surrealism, but at the same time expresses his belief that man must re-establish himself.

HYMN AMONG THE RUINS

Self-crowned, the day extends its plumes.
A high yellow cry,
a hot geyser in the center of
an impartial, beneficent sky!
Appearances are beautiful in this momentary truth,
The sea climbs the coast,

gasps among the cliffs, a dazzling spider;
the purple wound of the mountain shines;
a handful of goats is a herd of stones;
the sun lays its golden egg which melts over the sea.
All is god.
Broken statue,
columns eaten by light,
living ruins in a world of living dead!

Night falls in Teotihuacán.
Atop the pyramid, boys smoke marijuana,
harsh guitars sound.
What life-giving herb or water will give us life,
where unearth the word,
the proportion that rules the hymn and the speech,
the dance, the city, and the scale?
The Mexican song explodes in an oath,
in a colored star that dims,
in a stone that seeks the door of contact to us.
The earth has an aged taste.

Eyes see, hands touch.
Here a few things are enough:
prickly pears, thorny coral planet,
hooded figs,
grapes tasting of resurrection,
clams, intractable virginities,
salt, cheese, wine, ancestral bread.
From the summit of her dark beauty
an islander looks at me,
slim cathedral clad in light.
Towers of salt, the boat's white sails
Surge against the green pines of the shore.
The light engenders temples on the sea.

New York, London, Moscow.
The shadow covers the plain with its phantom ivy,

its wavering, spine-chilling vegetation,
its sparse down, its scurrying rats.
At intervals, an anemic sun shivers.
With elbows propped on mountains
that yesterday were cities
Polyphemus yawns.
Beneath, among the pits, crawls a herd of men.
(Domesticated bipeds, their flesh
—in spite of recent pious bans—
the wealthy much enjoy.
They were impure beasts to the vulgar till lately.)

To see, to touch beautiful forms of day.
The golden light hums; darts and wings.
The wine stains on the napery smell of blood.
Like the coral's branches in the water,
I stretch my senses in the living hour;
the instant is fulfilled in a yellow concordance.
O noon, ear of grain swollen with minutes,
cup of eternity!

My thoughts divide in two, meander, mingle,
and then begin again,
are motionless at last, rivers without mouths,
blood delta under a sun devoid of twilight.
Is it all to end in this splashing of dead waters?

Day, round day,
a luminous orange of twenty-four sections,
each crossed by a same and yellow sweetness!
The mind at last is incarnate in form,
its enemy halves are reconciled
and liquefy the conscience-mirror,
again become fountain, fabled spring:
Man, tree of images,
words that are flowers that are fruits that are acts.

Denise Levertov

THE STREET

The street is very long and filled with silence.
I walk in shadow and I trip and fall,
And then get up and walk with unseeing feet
Over the silent stones and the dry leaves,
And someone close behind, tramples them, too.
If I slow down and stop, he also stops.
If I run, so does he. I look. No one!
The whole street seems so dark, with no way out,
And though I turn and turn, I can't escape.
I always find myself on the same street
Where no one waits for me and none pursues.
Where I pursue, a man who trips and falls
Gets up and seeing me, keeps saying: "No one!"

W.K.J.

ALFONSO REYES
1889–1959   Mexico

Dead just as he was being considered for a Nobel Prize
for Literature, Reyes has been regarded as the grand
old man of Mexican letters. He contributed to every
phase of it. Poetry, essays, criticism, and fiction have
served to express his idea, first formulated in *Ultima
thule* (1942) that America is a Utopia. Because of his
versatility, he has been called a "Man of the Renais-
sance." One of his *5 casi sonetos* (1931) is translated
here, as well as a symbolic closet drama written in Paris
in 1925 and lost for many years. Readers may think it
an Existentionalist picture of man's search for knowledge.

QUASI-SONNET

When did I breathe down such rare dusk as this?
Hair dripping, unbound, and a bath-thick air,
Strong stable-scent, throat-gripping freshness there,
Wide spring bloom, and moisture dissolved like this.
The grating is opened and to horse we leap,
The sky is but song and the fields are delight,
And the promise of rain there's not to keep,
That joy that slips from the mountain crest's height.

Every leaf it trembled and it was mine,
And you likewise who were shaken with fear,
'Twixt your own forebodings, the lightning near,
'Twixt clouds went pulsing the little star shine
And the pulse of the earth came to us, too,
In the long light stride that our horses knew.

Edna Worthley Underwood

ECLOGUE OF THE BLIND

Characters

Máximo, blind from birth, venerable.
Primitivo, blind by accident, pathetic.
Segundo, wrathful, blind with occasional glimmerings, horrible.
Cándida, supplicant, beautiful.
Blas, feigned blind man, talented no-good.
Young almsgiving gentlemen.
Stray dogs which pay no attention to the blind.

A place somewhat like a small Plaza del Conde Barajas in Madrid. It smells of boredom and hidden crime. A sunny

*day. Public garden amidst houses with drawn Venetian
blinds. The time, a static hour of the day. As the fable unfolds, the trees stop the habitual sweep of their shade, still-
ing themselves like clocks in a state of ecstasy. Midsummer
trees, ashen colored, with thorny twigs. An occasional bird
traces a line on sky of tin, chirping like a flying noisemaker;
it is thirsty.*

*The ground, pinched together, reveals footprints coming
and going. The close vulgarity of things gives them a monu-
mental air. The hollow statue, consecrated to tedium, jumps
forever on one foot on the fountain's heap of sculptured
mud. The last vomit of water spewed left the buccal corners
with salty residue.*

*Above, eaves appear. Human sweat evaporates in air-
quakes. Below, among the street lights, a bench imprisoned,
where knives of the uncouth have whittled cuneiform stories
and rupestrian obscenities. The bench, tottering, its legs
askew, a lame trapezoid, appears to slope downward like
camels beginning to strain against the load; and it seems
ready to trot off on its uneven stick legs across the deserted
city district, bearing its bundle of three bodies.*

*There are the three blind men, three bearded faces, eyes
obfuscated by spider webs and clouds of bronze. Máximo in
the center, Segundo and Primitivo on either side of him.*

*Riders on the bench. They do not see the Plaza which, in
contrast, seems to contemplate them in a certain unreal,
mystical way. And we can imagine that they feel suspended
in Nothingness: Don Quixote and two Sanchos, blindfolded,
mounted on their interplanetary Clavileño.*

MÁXIMO: This even slope, without temptations:
               solid stagnation, lazy time. . . .
               You are a rocking lullaby,
               a cage of solitude which I bear everywhere.
               No one penetrates in me.
               But words, produced by eye,
               never will reveal the forms I dream;

science without space,
savory mass impervious to touch,
avenues of comforting voices,
along which I go with rudder of cane
through waves of force whose color I render null,
plowing my boat's course through capsize after capsize.

PRIMITIVO: Yes, but I, drugged, another Segismundo,
from the open windowed palace
down to Plato's shadowy cave,
where today I ravel, thread by thread,
the whole tapestry of Nature,
whose reverse I traverse
in guise of mythological chastening,
and the rope of Ocnus once woven by my eyes
today untwisted by my hands benumbed.
Oh, throbbing blackness phantomed!
New asphyxia, I breathe no light.
Castaway thrown overboard,
worse than Palinarus, without joy nor ecstasy;
in the street, a castaway who opens out his bundle
of limbs
to see if he can bounce against the other bank,
afraid of those invisible beasts
whose natatorial gasps are born
in lightless place.
Oh, other wheel of Time,
Oh, other corridors of Being,
do not believe that we crash against bodies of yore,
but rather against other animal embryos
which begin to breathe when you close your eyes.
And this fright, stronger than memory,
child of freedom, holds me enslaved.

MAXIMO: Oh, compassionate Philosophical Father,
who witnessed my birth in your system,
in your truth!
This one, astride of two horses,

daily rolls, split in two;
he cries for unknown human faces
whose grimaces suddenly did curdle into shadow.
He cries for unknown white roads
trod upon yesterday, if it is as I understand it.
I, wrapped up in you whose power invades me,
am a creature in your robe,
a domestic gift upon your knees,
withal tangled up at your feet.
And tell me, Primitivo, if you listen not
to the whirling of the organs,
the persuasive clamor
with which life invites you to repose?
I forget myself in her arms
so much more lulling because unknown;
order, peace, pillow,
breathing of tender breasts.
All enter, walking on tiptoe—
Oh, gratitude—; everything becomes slow and sweet
so as not to startle the blind man.
Every hand I proffer finds a hand
provident, solicitous.
A steady, even pity subdues Time,
and each instant gives forth
its full charge of human warmth.

SEGUNDO: What, Sir Primitivo, Sir Máximo,
you who label me insensate?
I perceive glints of wisdom,
and at times, amidst spinning sparks,
some errant crosses appear
which men are said to be;
and my burning nails, my phantoms, do me engulf,
but I am going to tell you my secret:
I alone live in perpetual life,
and the rest persists in flashes.
It flares; it is snuffed out;
it lives and dies without surcease.

The weft has holes
and the world is a tenuous web.
Take care! Tread not! It will disintegrate!
Here I remain on my steed of sticks
seeing temptations rise and fall
as if astride of currents of alternate sensation
which now seem noise, again wind;
for I alone live in perpetual life,
and the rest moves along in flashes.

PRIMITIVO: If you would permit me, Segundo, I would tell you
that that palpitation which to you brings torture
was called in my time and when I could see
night and day, that seesaw of nature;
but you, since you are a Time in miniature,
make sum and flash of hours twenty-four,
reduce to seconds the acts of theater,
and your scenario scarcely does endure
as far as your hand can reach in folly.
Do not forget that I was schooled by my eyes.
If today I inhabit the deep bleak,
yesterday I trod on mountain peak.
I give to you in souvenir what you do see
as scraps of bursts and fires.

SEGUNDO: If the slender instrument, Primitivo,
thins the essence of the hours which I live;
if because of having a weakly hand,
the world becomes weakened as it I heft;
this then is no world; this is an underdraw
which elsewhere rocks, another reality bereft,
its sea of wind and its hammock seesaw.

MÁXIMO: Heresy, Segundo! You with science sleep
and lie awake amidst deliria
and in your conscience do invert
the course of these fountains which men call senses.
Why to encompass all do you seek
from your clod of mud, your nothingness?

SEGUNDO: And why was I given a key which opens not?
            And why was I told:
            "Thou shalt not taste this fruit which I have placed
                    before thee,
            nor that water thy lips will never reach?"
            And why, Primitivo, Máximo,
            and why, Máximo, Primitivo,
            with a host of questions do me endow
            when they ever fall into the abyss condemned
            to bits, smashed, and answerless?

PRIMITIVO: Worse than my fear is your distrust.
            I at least know for what I suffer and endure:
            I am the one despoiled.
            You are the one who caresses with hopeful trust
            of turning venom into cure;
            you are deceit and I the undeceived.

SEGUNDO: Worse than your spoils is my agony
            And worse than the perfect night, Máximo's gift.
            He had no yesterday; you of yours have made a
                    memory.
            I am a prisoner spying on light through cleft.
            (*Cándida appears, followed by dogs.*)

CÁNDIDA: My grief, what good is it,
            what good is my pain,
            if there is no one to relieve me
            of my weighty chain?
            May Saint Lucia deliver you
            from evil gout serene!
            My grief, what good is it,
            if there is no helping hand
            to support those who beg
            for the mercy of another?
            May Saint Lucia deliver you
            from evil gout serene!
            What good is my pain?
            Pity achieves naught?

Alms for the blind!
Alms for the blind!
May Saint Lucia deliver you
from evil gout serene!

(A *young almsgiving gentleman passes, leaving alms in the blind maid's hand. He contemplates her an instant, awed by her beauty.*)

YOUNG GENTLEMAN: What is your name?
CÁNDIDA: Cándida, sir,
YOUNG GENTLEMAN: And are you blind?
CÁNDIDA: More blind than Love.
YOUNG GENTLEMAN: You never, then, have seen yourself in a
                     mirror.
CÁNDIDA: I am an image, but I reflect not.
YOUNG GENTLEMAN: Image enough
                     which ignores its appearance yet!
CÁNDIDA: May Heaven repay you and prosper you
         :   and may Saint Lucia deliver you, sir!
MÁXIMO: Come! Cándida, followed by your dogs.
          Room there is left on the bench for the blind maid.
          We three are here as on every day,
          attentive to your prayers and your Saint Lucias.
CÁNDIDA: You, Máximo, perfect,
          are cause which disdains effect.
          You, Primitivo, are the one who a world has lost,
          and you, Segundo, who divine it toss by toss.
(*Blas appears with his cane, feigning to be stumbling.*)
BLAS: And you, diplomaed and doctored and all the rest,
          you, who ignore Blas but know every all else.
          Because I, Blas, escape from your center;
          when you think that I flee, I am about to enter.
          Come to my arms, Cándida, for I believe I hear
              you,
          I absorb your enchantment, though I do not see
              you.

(*He opens her vestments, without her being able to prevent it, to uncover her secrets.*)

MÁXIMO: Rascal.

PRIMITIVO: Schemer.

SEGUNDO: Scoundrel.

CÁNDIDA: May the restless have peace and the evil forgiveness!

MÁXIMO: For blind faker may there be forgiveness no more.

CÁNDIDA: Forgiveness, forgiveness! Close not your ears to my prayer!

PRIMITIVO: Take club to him!

SEGUNDO: Sick! Sick! Hounds!

(*Harum-scarum of arms, clubs, jumps, dogs biting. Blas, rent and in agony, murmurs.*)

BLAS: Pity! Pity! Suffering Acteon
dies amidst canine humans and human dogs,
with no other guilt than. . . . .

(*He dies. The blind men disappear taking Cándida with them. The dogs remain licking the blood flowing from the cadaver of Blas, the blind faker.*)

R. L. *Moloney*

FROYLÁN TURCIOS
1877–1943   Honduras

Nearest in spirit to Juan Ramón Molina (1875–1908), greatest poet of Honduras' second period, was Turcios, originally a writer of local-color short stories, and later a poet of sentiment and sorrow. His brother married Rubén Darío's sister. Turcios saw in nature a reflection of his own woes, and passed on to his followers a tradition of nostalgia. However after his period of immense sadness, exemplified in *Ojos azules* ("Blue Eyes") came a period in which Turcios mocked the melancholy night, challenged the dark waves of the sea, and instead of committing suicide, like Molina, recovered his faith.

BLUE EYES

Blue eyes that cast a spell upon my soul
In autumn afternoons when twilight comes,
When the gray silken veil of the last light
Over the mountain peaks in silence falls,
Blue eyes that in the peacefulness
Of countryside, upon my life have shed
A comfort sent from heaven, ineffable
Balm after strife for glory, and my tears.

No more shall I the mirrored image see
In your clear crystal gaze, of all my woes,
Or the bright gleam of fleeting happiness,
Or all my gloomy, pain-filled nights that left
Funereal seal upon my brow till you
Transferred them as the moonlight changes night.
You sleep beneath the earth, beneath the sad
And faded blossoms of forgetfulness.

My tremulous lips, alas, never had chance
To close in sleep your eyelids, chilled in death.
The warmth of one last glance I never had,
But in my feverish nights of wakefulness
You'll burn forever like a far-off light;
Like lilies blue, your eyes—like violets
Of heavenly brightness, like two gleaming stars
To shine within my soul eternally.

W.K.J.

CLAUDIA LARS
1899–   Salvador

Under a pen name, the Irish-Salvadorean Carmen Bran-
non de Samoya Chinchilla became the greatest lyric

poet of her country. *Estrellas en el pozo* ("Stars in the Well") (1934) was her first volume, with *Canción redonda* ("Round Song") (1937) following. Her sonnet sequence, *Sonetos del arcangel* ("The Archangel's Sonnets"), won the Central American literary contest of 1941. She came under the influence of García Lorca, especially in her *Romances del norte y del sur* ("Ballads of the North and South") (1946), but later she provided her own inspiration in *Donde llegan los pasos* ("Where the Steps Lead") (1953), full of powerful lines and metaphors.

SKETCH OF THE FRONTIER WOMAN

Walking erect in the mire.
Unlike the flower's stalk
and the butterfly's eagerness . . .
Without roots or fluttering
more upright, more sure,
and more free.

Familiar with the shadow and the thorn.
With the miracle uplifted
in her triumphant arms.
With the barrier and the abyss
beneath her leap.

Absolute mistress of her flesh
To make it the core of her spirit:
vessel of the heavenly
domus aurea,
a lump of earth from which, budding,
the corn and the tuberose.

Forgotten the Giaconda smile.
Broken the spell of centuries.

Vanquisher of fears.
Clear and naked in the limpid day.

Lover without equal
in a love so lofty
that today no one divines it.
Sweet, with a filtered sweetness
that neither harms nor intoxicates him who tastes it.

Maternal always,
without the cares that hinder flight,
or the tenderness that confines,
or the petty yieldings that must be redeemed.

Pioneer of the clouds.
Guide to the labyrinth.
Weaver of tissues and songs.
Her only adornment, simplicity.

She rises from the dust . . . ;
Unlike the flower's stalk
which is less than beauty.

Donald D. Walsh

SANTIAGO ARGÜELLO BARRETO
1872–1942   Nicaragua

Ranking second only to Darío among Nicaragua's poets
was Argüello, a personal friend of the great Modernist.
Argüello's melancholy concern with life took form in
many profound and reflective poems like "El águila y la
hoja," here translated. He spent much of his life outside his country. His *Ojo y alma* ("Eye and Soul")
(1908) was published in Paris. His concern with rural
themes is evident in *De tierra cálida* ("From Tropic
Lands") (1909) that marked him as one of the great
Central American literary figures.

THE EAGLE AND THE DRY LEAF

One day an eagle said with pride: "None can soar up like me!
Sick shivering and giddiness reign where I dare to go.
My Adriatic is the air, my gondola the cloud,
My canopy a background like purple satin's glow.

"No other can rise up like me! Alone I have the power,
When creeping worms are trembling with the icy chill of night,
To pierce to skies inviolate, and in a garden fair
Of morning stars, to drink long draughts from chalices of light.

"Oh, with my mighty pinions, on days of snow and storm,
To cleave the mist in quest of clouds that glow with evening's
         red,
And drink the hot, consuming beams of sunshine fierce and
         bright,
My talons on the sun's keen disc, from which his rays are shed!"

She spoke and looked again upon her ornaments of power,
And shook her wings as shakes a queen her mantle, royally.
"No other can soar up like me!" Into the clouds she flew,
Repeating ever while she rose: "None can soar up like me!"

"Who art thou?"
                    "A dry leaf."
                              "And whence?"
                                        "I come from far
                                              above."
"And hast thou wings?"
                    "Nay!"
                              "Wingless leaf that in my path I
                              find,
Who has breathed into thee this breath which gives thee power
      to rise

Yet higher in the ether than my sovereignty?"

"The wind!"

You hear it, O ye ragged men in yonder neighboring street!
Take courage, all ye foolish ones! Be faint of heart no more,
Ye ignorant! When o'er the world a strong, mad whirlwind
    sweeps,
Then higher than the eagles, the dry leaves rise and soar!

Alice Stone Blackwell

LINO ARGÜELLO
1890–1935   Nicaragua

Another Argüello, son of Santiago, was a traditionalist,
who wrote extensively in the sonnet form. At other
times he was a disciple of Baudelaire. But occasionally
he became bucolic, as in this "Día del campo," with its
unrhymed lines of irregular length.

A DAY IN THE COUNTRY

The paths were displaying their verdure
    Full of the love of God.
The birds in the early morning
    Were asking the Lord for a drink.
The dawn was like blue silk . . .
The sun was a sweet caress
When we finally glimpsed the hut
    Where the fortunate farmer
Lived without dreams or shirt,
    As Tolstoy described him!
We entered by the portal that seems
    A note on the musical staff.
In the barnyard our daylight pleasures grow;

They are preparing to milk!
How white is that delicious nectar
    That intoxicates without after-effects!
There is a bull, black and beautiful
Who shakes the earth with his bellow;
The thundering waters make echo.
How delightful the voices of water
    In sky and sea!

W.K.J.

FABIO FIALLO
1879–1926   Dominican Republic

Fiallo, who as a politician opposed the entrance of the
United States into his island, was known beyond
Santo Domingo for both prose and poetry. Though a
friend of Darío's and often called Leader of Dominican
Modernism, he was basically a Romanticist, a poet of
the tropics and nightingales. Much of his fiction, especially in his *Cuentos frágiles* ("Fragile Stories")
(1908) was a prosification of his poetry. *Canción de
una vida* ("A Song of Life") (1928) was his only published volume of verse, though his writings were widely
printed, separately.

NOSTALGIA

There we were and the good St. Peter
    Who came to God on high:—
A dauntless fellow of a crusader,
    A pretty maid, and I.
The soldier prayed that he might ever
    Fight as on earth he fought;
And St. Michael gave him his own picked legion
    As the boon he sought.

The maid sobbed out a stammering prayer
    To return to her lover's sight,
And she became the kiss of dawn by day,
    A ray of the moon by night.
My turn next; and God said blandly:
    "Already I know your will.
You desire the harp of My singer David!"
    My pride leaped up, but still—
"Oh, no, Lord; another thing!
    To be a tree on the tropic shore
Watered by my own Ozama,
    And there, deep-rooted, to live once more!"

Muna Lee

ENRIQUE HERNÁNDEZ MIYARES
1854–1914   Cuba

Hernández Miyares represents the transition between
Cuba's colonial status and the period when it achieved
independence. Of all he wrote, he is remembered
chiefly for this one sonnet, "La más fermosa," often
called the best sonnet of the epoch. In praising Don
Quijote, it pays tribute to all who fight, undiscouraged,
for their beliefs.

THE MOST BEAUTIFUL

O Knight, pursue thy way with courage free,
Redressing wrongs and woes with mighty spear!
Such noble obstinacy will bring near
The founding of just laws in equity.
Mambrino's broken helmet take to thee;
Ride forward proud, victorious, without fear;
To Sancho Panza's proverbs lend no ear;
Trust in thine arm and in thy destiny.

For the disdain of Fortune have no care;
And if the Knight of the White Moon should dare
Measure his arms with thine, and thou shouldst fall
By evil fate, say with thy final breath,
Of Dulcinea, 'mid the pangs of death,
That she will ever be most fair of all.

Alice Stone Blackwell

JOSÉ MARTÍ
1853–1895   Cuba

As Martí was the apostle of Cuban liberation, losing
his life in battle before freedom was achieved, so he
started a trend in poetry that only after his death became an organized movement under Darío and
Gutiérrez Nájera. Said Darío in 1913: "Should you not
call Martí a forerunner of the Modernist movement
that I initiated years later?" Unamuno, the other pole
of Modernism, called Martí the foundation of his
literary position. His *Ismaelito* (1882) containing many
of the elements of Modernism, is a "How to be a
father" textbook. His *Versos sencillos* ("Simple
Verses") (1891) was a point of departure for the great
literary revolution. Like Darío, Martí experimented
with old Spanish verse forms, but he was contemporary
as well, introducing Emerson and Whitman to Latin
America. In his poetry, prose, and oratory he inspired
many followers who wanted to be simple without being
commonplace.

MY LITTLE HORSEMAN

Early each morning
My little horseman
Used to awaken

Me with fond kisses.
Then he would clamber
Astride my body
Seizing my forelock
To serve as bridle.
Gaily he'd ride me
And I as gaily;
The heels of my horseman
Would kick as they spurred me.
What gentle spurs were
The feet of my baby!
How he would chuckle,
Ismaelito!
And with my kisses
I'd cover each white foot.
Two feet I covered
With one of my kisses.

W.K.J.

YOKE AND STAR

When I was born, my mother said to me:
"My son, Homagno, Flower of my breast,
Reflected sum of me and of the world,
Fish that to bird and horse and man has turned,
See these two signs of life I offer you
With hope and sorrow. Look and make your choice.
This is a yoke. He who accepts it lives.
By it the ox is tamed, and since he gives
Full service to his master, in warm straw
He sleeps and eats good and abundant oats.
But this, O Mystery sprung from my womb
As peaks from lofty mountain range take shape,
This thing that gleams and slays, this is a star!
All sinners flee from one who bears its mark,

And from its spreading light; and so in life,
As though the one who wears it were a beast
Burdened with crimes, he will be shunned by all.
The man who imitates the care-free ox
Becomes himself a dumb, submissive brute
And has to start again the eternal climb.
But he who, confident, shall choose a star
To be his symbol, grows.
                              When for Mankind
The living person freely pours his cup;
When for the bloody human festival
The good man sacrificed his beating heart
Quickly and gravely; when to wandering winds
Of North and South, he gave his sacred words;
The Star, a mantle now, envelops him
And the clear air is bright, as in festive days,
And the living man, who did not fear to live,
Knows he is not alone in dark and death."

"Give me the yoke, O Mother, so that I
Can stamp it under foot, then let the Star
That lights and kills glow brightly on my brow!"

                                        W.K.J.

POETRY IS SACRED

A poem is something sacred. Let no one
Take it for anything except itself.
Let no one force it to his will, as slaves
Are forced with tear-filled eyes by mistress cruel,
And then, pale and unloving it will come,
Like that unhappy slave who, while she may
Obey behests, with weak, unwilling hands
Will comb her mistress' tresses; in some tower
That rises like a cake against the sky,

She'll press the hair in form, or with false curls
Destroy the flowing line of noble brow
That shows the soul's essential honesty.
But while the slave obeys her mistress' whims,
Her melancholy heart, like a red bird
With wounded wings, dreams she is soaring far
From there to where her absent sweetheart is.
God's curse on masters and on tyrants, too,
Who force the luckless bodies to abide
In places where their hearts unwilling dwell!

                                                                    W.K.J.

JULIÁN DEL CASAL
1863–1893   Cuba

Though Casal was later to die of tuberculosis, when he
was writing his early poetry he was not experiencing
any of the ills he described. Similarly, he wrote one of
his most representative poems "En el campo" ("In the
Country") while living in Havana. During his short
lifetime, Casal published two volumes of poetry: *Hojas
del viento* ("Leaves in the Wind") (1890), revealing
the influence of Romanticism, and *Nieve* ("Snow")
(1893) with Baudelaire, Darío and Gutiérrez Nájera
as his models. After his death appeared *Bustos y rimas*
("Busts and Rhymes") (1893) to reveal his own originality. He was especially skilled with the sonnet, and
he showed his Modernist tendencies in a series of them:
"Elena," "Prometeo," and "Salomé" that colorfully
describe French paintings in a Cuban exhibit.

Though his only European experience was a brief
trip to Spain, Casal dreamed of ancient Greece and
modern France. As an ultra-refined soul who sought
beauty as an escape from life, he took up Japanese art
and kept incense burning before an image of Buddha
in his home. But at the same time, Casal could produce
such decadent lines as "The sunset, like a knife-gashed
belly, bleeds," that begins his sonnet "Crepuscular."

FLOWERS

My heart was a crystal vase,
And in solitude fragrant grew there
Under the starlight, a lily white,—
    It was a prayer.

Like a virgin anaemic and pale,
All withered this flower I see.
Now in my heart grows a purple bay rose,—
    It's blasphemy.

W.K.J.

CONFIDENCES

Why weepest thou, my sweetheart pale,
    Why bendest down thy lovely head?—
A dread idea doth assail
    My mind and turn my heart to lead.—

Tell me, have they not loved thee well?—
    Never!—Come, tell the truth to me.—
Ah, then, one lover only can I tell
    Was faithful.—Who?—My misery.

Thomas Walsh

THE FRIAR

Barefooted in his cloak of brown,
Mounted upon his burro's chubby back
To beg the pious alms that fill his sack,
The old Franciscan starts at dawn for town.
Behind him sounds the early belfry down
The call to Mass the faithful in his track;

The summons floats afar into the wrack
Of pink and golden clouds, the dawning's crown.

His breviary at his elbow tucked away,
His rosary rattling heavily with his sway,
He reckons that his givers will not lag;
And hearkens as he paces down the road,
Between the burro's braying for the load,
The wind that whistles through his empty bag.

Thomas Walsh

NICOLÁS GUILLÉN
1902–   Cuba

Negro poetry developed in the Caribbean chiefly
through imitation of similar folklore trends in France
among the Ultraists, in the United States with its
Negro music, ballet, and plays, and in the example of
García Lorca. Its earliest practitioner in Cuba was
Guillén, himself a mulatto, whom some critics class
with the Dadist school. From his first book, *Motivos
de son* ("Son Themes") (1930), he was the authentic
voice of his race, frequently using dialect. "*Sensemaya*"
is an African word and "*mayombe*" is the distortion of
a geographic name.

Humor as well as tragedy, and daily tasks as well as
social and political injustice, provided him with themes.
His visits to France and Spain during its civil war inspired anti-Fascist verse. But it is his popular *sones* that
are best known, and a number have been set to music.

CANE

Negro
In the cane fields.

White man
Above the cane fields.
Earth
Beneath the cane fields.
Blood
That flows from us.

Langston Hughes

BLADE

Knife-toting pimp
becomes a knife himself:
whittling chips of the moon
until the moon runs out,
whittling chips of shadow
until the shadows run out,
whittling chips of song
until the song runs out—
and then,
sliver by sliver,
the dark body
of the one he loves.

Langston Hughes

SENSEMAYA

(*Chant to kill a snake*)

¡Mayombe - bombe - mayombé!
¡Mayombe - bombe - mayombé!
¡Mayombe - bombe - mayombé!

The snake has eyes of glass;
The snake coils on a stick;

With his eyes of glass on a stick,
With his eyes of glass.

The snake can move without feet;
The snake can hide in the grass;
Crawling he hides in the grass,
Moving without feet.

¡Mayombe - bombe - mayombé!
Hit him with an ax and he dies;
Hit him! Go on, hit him!
Don't hit him with your foot or he'll bite;
Don't hit him with your foot, or he'll get away.

Sensemayá, the snake,
sensemayá.
Sensemayá with his eyes,
sensemayá.
Sensemayá, with his tongue,
sensemayá.
Sensemayá, with his mouth,
sensemayá.

The dead snake cannot eat;
the dead snake cannot hiss;
he cannot move,
he cannot run!

The dead snake cannot look;
the dead snake cannot drink;
he cannot breathe,
he cannot bite.

¡Mayombe - bombe - mayombé!
Sensemayá, the snake . . .
¡Mayombe - bombe - mayombé!
Sensemayá, does not move . . .

¡Mayombe - bombe - mayombé!
Sensemayá, the snake . . .
¡Mayombe - bombe - mayombé!
Sensemayá, he died!

W.K.J.

EXECUTION

They are going to execute
a man with his arms tied;
four soldiers are there
to do the firing.
They are four soldiers,
silenced,
four soldiers tied,
like the man they are about to kill.

"Could you escape?"
"I cannot run!"
"They are ready to fire!"
"What can we do!"
"Maybe the rifles aren't loaded . . ."
"They have six bullets of cruel lead!"
"Maybe those soldiers won't fire!"
"You're such a fool!"

They will shoot.
(How could they shoot?)
They will kill.
(How could they kill?)
They were four soldiers,
silenced,
and an officer signaled with his saber;
they were four soldiers,

tied,
like the man the four just killed.

Joseph Leonard Grucci

REGINO PEDROSO

1898–   Cuba

Pedroso, awarded a prize in 1938 as that year's best
Cuban poet, claims to be a citizen of the world. Of
Negro and Chinese blood, he had the varied experi-
ences of a factory worker and a sugar cane harvester,
and more recently as an employee of the Ministry of
Education.

Pedroso's poetic career began with *Nosotros* ("We")
(1933), followed by *Antología poética* ("Poetic Anthology"): 1918–1938 in 1939, the same year as his
Más allá canta el mar ("The Sea Chants Over Yonder"). Declaring that art is the supreme manifestation
of beauty when it interprets anguish and dreams,
Pedroso's ambition has been to "contribute to Cuba
the affirmation of the existence of a social lyricism." He
is one of the hemisphere's most powerful proletariat
poets.

FIVE O'CLOCK TEA

I walk along, my hands all thick with grease . . .
the shiny taxis do not stop when I call;
I walk along all filled with greetings;
but men ignore me, passing by;
for in the splendid festival of this rich town,
my hands are thick with grease.

Only the landscape and the sunset do embrace me
and the old sidewalk
which recounts the rosary of my steps.

But the shop-windows of elegance
have closed their doors to me;
the elevator of opulence will not lift me to the terraces
where life is sung and laughed;
for in the ebriate hour of the fragrant golden tea
which does enrich the world,
I walk along with hands all thick with grease.

Ben F. Carruthers

LUIS LLORENS TORRES

1878–1944   Puerto Rico

Llorens Torres is only distantly connected with the Modernists. As a poet, he was conservative. His language was simple, yet he has few equals in expressing the Puerto Rican soul with its combination of Spanish and New World elements. Llorens showed his pride in Spanish traditions in his volume *Al pie de la Alhambra* ("At the Foot of the Alhambra"). He also voiced his American pride by collecting into *Alturas de América* ("Heights of America") (1940), works from all his periods that hymn the New World. Best known is his "Bolívar," which is an outstanding example of Llorens' experiments in *vers libre*. But he was also a conscious artist, as proved by the preface to his second book of verse, *Sonetos sinfónicos* ("Symphonic Sonnets") (1914), which stated his theories of metrics and aesthetics.

BOLÍVAR

Poet, soldier, statesman, hero, he stands—
Great, like the nations whose freedom he won;
He whom no country can claim as her son,
Though as his daughters were born many lands.

His was the valor of who bears a sword;
His was the courtesy of who wears a flower;
Entering salons, he laid by the sword;
Plunging in battle, he tossed away the flower.

The peaks of the Andes to him seemed to be
But exclamation points after his stride;
Soldier-poet he was; poet-soldier was he!
Each land that he freed
Was a soldier's poem and a poet's deed:
And he was crucified.

Muna Lee

LUIS PALÉS MATOS
1898–1959   Puerto Rico

One of the great contemporary post-Modernist poets,
Palés Matos published his first book at the age of fourteen. In 1926, preceding by four years the appearance
of *Motivos de son* by the Cuban Nicolás Guillén,
Palés was writing poems in Negro dialect, and most of
his *Tuntún de pasa y grifería: poemas afroantillanos*
(1937) had already been completed. Both poets wrote
realistically about the spirit of the black race, but
Palés was ever the skeptical and civilized white man.

He had other themes. Disenchanted with civilization, he went back to the primitive life of Guayama,
and as a descriptive poet wrote of his delight in the sea.
However he was very critical, destroying more than he
preserved. In 1957, he collected 104 poems of those
written during forty-one years, for his definitive volume.
Two of the best are "El pozo" and "Lagarto verde,"
here translated. "The Green Lizard" is a satire on the
courtiers of Emperor Christophe of Haiti, who were
so close to their monkey ancestors that mention of a
reptile was enough to throw them into a panic.

THE WELL

My soul is like a well of water, quiet, deep,
Within whose solemn and imperturbable peace
The days roll by, with all their worldly murmur stilled,
Like something drowned within the silent cavity.

Down deep, the water cries its bright-hued agony,
A morbid iridescence that in gloom ferments
As it coagulates in blackened trails of slime
And then exhales in phosphorescence, bloodless, blue.

My soul, I say, is like a well. The sleeping world
Takes blurred and obscure form in it, then fades away.
Down low, within the depths perhaps of centuries,
A crouching misanthropic frog hides, lost in dreams.

Sometimes, under the influence of the far-off moon,
The well seems to take on a legendary spell.
One hears the deep croak-croak of the frog within the well
Which then assumes a feeling of eternity.

W.K.J.

GREEN LIZARD

The little Count of Lemonade,
So tiny and so playful, strayed
Among the halls and rooms of state
Where lives Christophe the Great.
His monkey face alive with glee,
With Monsieur Haiti, he'll agree.
To Madame Coffee 'n' Cream, he'll say:
"This way, this way!"

And while the squat aristocrats
Pass, armed with coconut brickbats,

Solemnly black,
This tiny, playful count is all
A flowing stream of charm and tact,
Who fills with niceties the hall:
"Yes, Monsieur Haiti! Madame, dear,
Right over here!"

Just watch him dance. He struts his gait
In rigadoon or minuet.
None of those near Christophe the Great
Wears half so well the robes of state,
Moves with more genteel etiquette.
His social formula: *"S'il vous plaît."*
His word of elegance: *"Volupté."*

Ah, but before His Highness, never,
Never say "lizard," or you'll see
That in one instant gone forever
Is every trace of aristocracy.

Then flees your Count of Lemonade,
His red coat trailing. He's afraid.
His proud jaw, once so undismayed,
Is stiff in epileptic state.
Yes, there he goes, with terror pangs!
The mirrors of Christophe the Great
That usually reflect the lords,
Now multiply him into hordes
Of squat orangutans.

                                              W.K.J.

CESÁREO ROSA-NIEVES
1901–   Puerto Rico

Important in Puerto Rican literary life, Dr. Rosa-Nieves has not only written prize-winning poetry; he has been critic and historian of his fellow poets in *Poesía en Puerto Rico* which, after earning him a doctorate at the University of Mexico, has gone into several editions, the latest in 1958. A three-volume anthology of his country's poetry, a collection of his own short stories, and several plays have also come from his study.

Beginning with *Las veredas olvidadas* ("Forgotten Paths") (1922) under the influence of Herrera y Reissig, he passed through stages of Noism, an offshoot of Vanguardism, when his *Estampas sinfónicas* ("Symphonic Pictures") received the 1930 Ateneo Roosevelt Prize. Later he experimented with classical forms and published a study of Spanish meters. Since 1954, however, he has been the spokesman for the Ensueñista movement, seeking universality through nativist themes. His recent *Los nísperos del alba maduraron* ("Dawn's Medlars Ripened") (1958) from which these samples are taken, won Barcelona's Rumbos Poetry Prize. Along with elaborate figures in poetic language, lyrical quality with a stressing of light and color characterize Dr. Rosa-Nieves' writing.

THE ENSUEÑISTAS'
"ARS POETICA"

Our Country, who art in our souls,
Enter Boriquen completely and penetrate into its Saturnalian
    protons, a golden shower down to the very roots;
In the incarnate island of the firmament, our landscape at dawn,
    twilight, and night in a sea of watery moons;
Intimate reflection of soothing balm in the mirror of the earthly
    heart, fruity essence of the tropics in infinite Spring-
    time . . .
Each day the sun must dawn for us, a golden Polyphemus,
    and from early mass to matins, from our sea-swept balconies
    we shall greet the whole Universe: "Hail, comrade, hail!"

Then thou, O Knight of the Continents, shalt be our guest;
    We shall embroider stars on the crystal distaff of our rivers;
And later must we journey everywhere, to return weary
    of foreign scenes, casting off foreign garments of ports,
    planes and ships, and turn to the native *batey*,
To the native sugar plantations, bound by green horizons
    And symphonic and diaphanous silences,
But more intimate:
Mine, yours, and possessed by the four poles of winters and
    summers.
Always generously loving shall we be.
You will voice it in the songs of your sad fraternal poets,
Savoring our white affection, good brother . . .

                                    W.K.J.

I AM THE TROPICS

I adore bitter bread, loaves of woe, woe of woes;
Out of the sea come green and red fish of the sun
    with wings of white foam.
To me from the stars comes the gold of dawn amid alabaster
      mists,
Chaste,
And from the sky, seraphic covering of soft blue velvet;
Mallow moon of the centuries,
From beyond the stars.
I bear woe in my soul,
Woe that kisses me and wounds me,
That hates me and loves me:
Anguish that conquers me and anguish that delights me.
I prefer it to remain, and never go away:
Malignant kindness that loves me.
A comradely, Edenly pang!
O woe, I have existed for you in the flower,
    the star, the nest, and the leaf;
In everything that aches and in everything that suffers in silence.

Celestial leavening, Eucharistic light of dreams and wounds.
My complaining bread of blood, happiness and torment,
Sea without shores, Night without dawn; flower of sadness, joy-
      giving thorns;
Moonlight woe of my most painful dreams,
May I never lose you,
May you never leave me,
And never, no never take away my sweet and mortal martyrdom!

Flowering daisy along my route,
Tip of the dagger that opens my uncomplaining suffering
Of my yesterdays that never came.

My beloved enemy,
Bitter medlar nectar of my euphoric sleeplessness,
Of my most dolorous delights
Sensitive,
Infinite!
Pain deep within my heart: Hail, my fragrant Bread and Master,
Master of all my hopes and all my forgettings!
I am the tropics
Singer of sadness, I am brother to the sun
    the sky, the flower, and the sea.

                                  W.K.J.

JOSÉ ASUNCIÓN SILVA
1860–1896   Colombia

Silva cared nothing for what the public thought of his
writing. He had nothing in common with the rigid
atmosphere of Bogotá. He was a rebel, a nonconform-
ist. He published little of what he wrote, so preventing
any study of his development until the appearance of
his *Obras* ("Works") in 1956. Yet this pessimistic and
most sensitive of poets who wrote at the beginning
of Modernism had a greater influence on those who followed him than did Martí, Casal, or Gutiérrez Nájera.

Poe was his early idol, and if the death of his sister Elvira inspired his "Nocturnos," he also had Poe's "Annabel Lee" and "The Bells" in mind. Traces of Mallarmé, Verlaine, Baudelaire, and even Bécquer can also be found in his writing.

He was a poet of mystery, moved by the sense of death. With a feeling that sorrow always ends in oblivion, he could laugh ironically at martyrdom and death in his "Día de los difuntos" ("Day of the Dead"). Unamuno declared his poetry the "music of wings." Like other Modernists, his motto was: *Sufrir, soñar, cantar* ("Suffer, Dream, and Sing"). Finally persuaded to publish his works, he shipped them to France, only to have them all lost with the wreck of *L'Amérique*. Critics declared his lost *Cuentos negros* ("Black Tales") the equal of his master Poe's.

Committing suicide, more probably because of his inability to repay his father's debts than because of the loss of his manuscript, he was buried in unhallowed ground by the very religious people of Bogotá.

THE THIRD NOCTURNE

One lone night,
One lone night intoxicated by the murmurs, by the perfumes
     and sweet music of soft pinions;
One lone night,
While there glimmered in the humid nuptial shadows the
     fantastic light of fireflies,
To my side so tightly pressing, yet so closely, gently clinging,
     mute and pallid,
As if sordid apprehensions of afflicting woes transcendent
Made you tremble to the inmost, deep recesses of your being,
Down the flower-embellished pathway leading to the open
     prairie
   You came strolling
   And the moon in fullness

Through the deep, enfolding curtains of the infinite velvet of
        the skies displayed her brilliance;
    And your shadow,
    Fine and languid,
    And my shadow
    By the moon's bespangled rays delineated
    On the canvas of the sands
    Of our pathway were united;
       And were one,
         And were one,
       And were one distinct, long, single shadow,
         And were one distinct, long, single shadow.

    This lone night,
    Alone my spirit,
Filled with infinite obsessions, bitter agonies and sorrow for
        your passing,
Separated from your spirit by the tomb, by time and distance,
    By the infinite deep blackness
    Where our voices find no answer,
    Mute and lonely,
    Down that path I slowly wandered . . .
And the barking of the watchdogs at the moon, so white and
        pallid,
    Broke the all-invading stillness,
    And the croaking of the frogs . . .
I felt cold. It was the coldness and the numbness of your cham-
        ber,
Of your cheeks, and of your temples which I worshipped
    Lying 'neath the snowy whiteness
    Of the winding sheet that hid you.
'Twas the coldness of the sepulchre, the iciness of death,
    'Twas the chill of annihilation.
    And my shadow
By the moon's full rays projected,
    Walked alone,
       Walked alone.

Walked alone across the solitary prairie;
And your shadow, tall and agile,
Thin and languid,
As on that warm night of Springtime, of the agonizing Spring-
time,
As upon that midnight filled with murmurings, with sweet
perfumes and the stress of wingéd music,
Wandered close and joined my shadow,
Wandered close and joined my shadow,
Wandered close and joined my shadow . . . Oh, the shadows
interwoven!
Oh, the shadows of the bodies that were melted in the shadows
of the spirits!
Oh, the shadows that seek shadows in the lonely nights of tears
and haunting sadness!

Mary Newman and *Paul T. Manchester*

THE DAY OF THE DEAD

The light is dim, the day opaque. The drizzle falls and wets
with its penetrating threads the cold, deserted city. Through
the shadowy air, an unknown hand throws a thick, dark veil of
deathly sadness; and there is no one who does not in his inmost
heart feel quiet and gather himself together as he sees the gray
mists of the gloomy atmosphere, and hears in the dark, sad
heights the resigned, sorrowful, wavering notes that speak to the
living of the dead.

And there is something painful and dubious which mingles
its sound with that sound, and vibrates as a discord in the concert raised by the bells of bronze as they toll for the dead, for all
who have been. It is the voice of the bell that keeps on marking the hours, today the same as tomorrow, rhythmical, even,
and sonorous. One bell complains and another weeps; this one
has the voice of an old woman, and that one of a girl who is
praying. The largest bells, which have powerful voices, sound

with an accent of mysterious disdain; but the bell that tells the time laughs; it does not mourn. It has subtle harmonies in its dry timbre; its voice seems to speak of festivities, of gaities, and rendezvous, of pleasures, of songs and dances; of the pre-occupations that fill our days. It is the voice of the century, amid a chorus of monks, and with its notes it laughs sceptically and mocks the bell that laments, the bell that entreats, and everything which that chorus commemorates; and it is because with its tinkle it has measured human sorrow and marked the sorrow's end.

Therefore it laughs at the solemn bell that rings up there with funereal notes; therefore it interrupts the sad concert in which the bells of sacred bronze mourn for the dead. Do not listen to it, O bells of bronze; do not give ear to it, ye bells that with the solemn voice of your knell are praying for the beings who sleep today far from life, free from desire, far from the rough struggles of humanity; do not listen to it, O bells! Against the impossible, what power has desire?

Up there it rings, rhythmical and sonorous, that golden voice, undeterred by its grave sisters that are praying in chorus, the bell of the clock rings, rings, rings today, and says that it marks, with its sonorous vibrations, the hours of forgetting; that after the night-long watch held over each dead person in a room draped in mourning, with the family gathered near in atti-tudes of grief, while the light of the candles illuminated the coffin and the wreaths of lilies; after the sadness, the cries of grief, the words of sorrow, the touching tears, it marks in just the same way the moment when, with the heaviness of the mourning, the thought of the dead person and the feeling about him has vanished, six months later—or ten.

 And today, the day of the dead—today when sadness hovers in the gray mists, while the drizzle falls drop by drop and stupifies the nerves with its melancholy, and wraps the gloomy city in a mantle, this bell, that has marked the day and the hour when to each dismal and empty house, after a short period of mourning, gladness returned; this bell that has marked the hour of the dance when, after just a year, the girl whose mother

sleeps forgotten and alone in the cemetery, tried on for the
first time a light dress—rings indifferent to the monk's voice
of the solemn bell and its grave song . . . it sees everything in
life under a merry aspect, and keeps on marking in the same
way, with the same enthusiasm and the same disdain, the flight
of time that blots out everything.

And this is the something of pain and doubt that hovers in
the sound; this is the note of irony that vibrates in the concert
raised by the bells of bronze when they toll for the dead—for all
those who have been. It is the keen and subtle voice of crystal
vibrations, which with child-like accents, indifferent to good
and evil, measures the base hours equally with the sublime
and fatal hours, and resounds in the sad, dark heights without
having in its clear, rhythmic and sonorous playing the intensely
sad, dejected and wavering accents of that mysterious chorus
rung by the bells—the mournful bells that speak to the living
of the dead!

                                              Alice Stone Blackwell

MIGUEL ÁNGEL OSORIO
1880–1942   Colombia

This Colombian lived and wrote under many names:
as Ricardo Arenales he became a Mexican citizen, and
as Porfirio Barba Jacob, he inspired one of Latin America's most famous stories, "The Man Who Resembled
a Horse," by Dr. Arévalo Martínez.

In his poetry, Osorio bridged the gap between Silva
and Valencia, though lacking the delicacy of Silva in
his romantic verse and failing to achieve the modern-
istic artistry of Valencia. Some point to "Barba Jacob"
as closing the cycle of Latin-American Modernism.

He was a tangle of doubts, temptations, and im-
morality, whose poetry reveals his attempts to seek refuge within himself. Solitude and a sense of being lost

in an Oriental fatalism are expressed in a lyricism that is often so dense as to be obscure. But he was capable of powerful poetry, though he cared so little about it that he never tried to collect it into a book.

THE LAMENT OF OCTOBER

I did not know that the azure of morning
Is merely the ghost of some sad yesterday,
That whipped with the winds of the centuries blowing.
The heart is consumed with desire, with desire;
I can feel its sorrow and its sad beating,
And light if I wish all the fires that burn,
> *But the voice of life already is calling,*
> *And the hour has not come yet for me to learn.*

I did not know that your sun, that loving,
Alone makes rosy the sky of childhood,
That even 'neath laurels the rugged hero
Must remain something of the child that he was.
Oh! who, could he once with all old love teeming,
Would not unto innocent joy return!
> *But the voice of life already is calling,*
> *And the hour has not come yet for me to learn.*

I did not know that the peace so profound once
Of love, the lilies of joy purest,
The magnolia of light of all our emotions,
The mother must bear in her gentle breast,
My heaven of rest and such love long lies shattered,
A man to be once now in truth I yearn,
> *But now life draws too near to its ending,*
> *And the hour has not come yet for me to learn.*

Edna Worthley Underwood

STANZAS

The air it is tender and milky with sweetness;
In Spring's fire I watch roses flame to their doom;
I drink down their pleasure which keeps too much fleetness,
But how many more lovely will never bloom!

The wind from the sea here while the twilight is sighing
Breathes softly and then spreads its soft tulle sails divine
Fringed with the amber of a sun that is dying,
But how many more splendid will never shine!

Edna Worthley Underwood

GUILLERMO VALENCIA

1873–1943   Colombia

Valencia was wealthy, aristocratic, and even once a
candidate for the presidency of Colombia. To him,
poetry was an escape. After his experiences in politics,
his travel in Europe where he met Rubén Darío, and
published *Ritmos* (1914) in London, he retired to
Popayán in the Cauca Valley and wrote for the rest of
his life.

He translated French, Italian, and Portuguese poetry,
and experimented with many techniques. Anderson
Imbert called him "a romantic soul with Parnassian
eyes and Symbolist ears." He was also briefly a Van-
guardist, setting himself problems to solve with an
emotional approach, but with the technical skill to get
the images into words. In his regard for form and perfection in rhythm, Valencia was leader of the Parnassian branch of Modernism. His first volume, *Poesías*,
(1898) contained the symbolic "Los camellos" for
which each reader can supply his own interpretation.

The poet, suggested by the camel, is alone in the desert. The other camel (perhaps José Asunción Silva, who died in 1896) has left him, and only in his sweetheart can he find consolation. Some think the Byzantine reference is to Darío. The other details, the hump that makes him unlike others, but suggestive of the Pyramid, a symbol of wisdom, the Sphinx, and the palms, can have many possible interpretations. Another poem, showing Valencia's feeling for sensuous beauty, is his lengthy and famous "Leyendo a Silva" ("On Reading Silva") discussing the poetry of his friend.

SURSUM

A pallid taper its long prayer recites
Before the altar, where the censers spread
Their lifted clouds, and bells toll out their dread,
In grief's delirious sanctuary rites.
There—like the poor Assisian—invites
A cloistered form the peace All-Hallowéd;
Against the dismal portals of the dead
Resting his wearied brows for heavenly flights.

Grant me the honey-taste of the Divine;
Grant me the ancient parchments' ruddy sign
Of holy psalmody to read and prize!
For I would mount the heights immortal crowned,
Where the dark night is 'midst the glories drowned,
And gaze on God, into His azure eyes!

Thomas Walsh

THE CAMELS

Two tired camels with their clear green eyes,
   Extended nostrils, supple necks, wind-fanned,

And silken, tawny skin that sun defies,
    Measured with lengthened tread the Nubian sand.

Raising their heads to scan the wilderness,
    They saw afar, beneath that ruddy dome
Whose zenith was of fire, a spot to bless,
    A green oasis in their desert home.

Their eyes were glazed and tortured by the sun.
    A fever coursed within them. Years they'd spent
Perhaps deciphering slowly, one by one,
    The hieroglyphics of some monument.

Over the sleepy carpet of the vast
    And dismal desert by the last faint ray
Of light, their sombre silhouette was cast.
    Like weary marchers on dark sand it lay.

In the sad faces of these desert kings
    Chimera etched deep lines of weariness.
"We love fatigue that search for wisdom brings,"
    They heard the sun-scorched Pyramids confess.

Upon their faces streamed the Sphinx's hot breath.
    Their humps with powdery sand were gold, when blew
Wild whirlwinds in that fevered land of death,
    Which, womanless, but thirst and hunger knew.

Debris of caravans and scattered pile
    Of bleaching bones they saw. No friendly shade
Of whispering palm or tinkling bells beguile
    This realm of loneliness; no joys pervade.

Learn grief of them, ye of the Byzantine!
    Play their sad song, slave flutists, when you blow!
Ah, eyes of weariness! What anguish thine!
    What tales you tell of lassitude and woe!

You hump-backed camels of the sand-swept plain,
  You whose chaste lover is the virgin palm,
Sad as the Sphynx, what surcease has your pain?
  Thirst for the infinite alone brings calm.

The caravan has gone. I'm left behind,
  A camel ridden by grief. Shall I pursue?
Nay! I shall rather seek two eyes and find
  A fountain, source of inspiration new.

There grieving, I shall drink till verse subdued
  Finds new and mystic threads. Should crowds of fools
Pass by, a camel they would say they viewed,
  Gazing in silence in two sapphire pools.

W.K.J.

LUIS CARLOS LÓPEZ
1880–1950   Colombia

Satirical poets are hard to find in Latin America, but
the Colombian López makes up for the lack. From his
first *De mi villorio* ("From My Small Town") (Madrid: 1908) and *Posturas difíciles* ("Difficult Pos-
tures") (1909) to *Por el atajo* ("Short Cut") (Carta-
gena: 1928), he railed at provincial life and poured out
his contempt on politicians, priests, and bureaucrats.
Bitter humor, that is at times brutal, characterizes his
verse. Parody of the sonnet, with uneven lines, faulty
rhymes, and foreign words, was another form of his
humor. Occasionally he slipped into sentimentality
with his longing for the "good old days," and his yearning for his farm or his *"ciudad nativa."* López has influenced, and been influenced by, few poets of the
hemisphere.

RUBBISH

The shadow which my bedroom throws
Sketches on a roof
And on a wall an ass's ear
And a frying pan. The ear
Grows longer in the purple twilight,
Giving the impression
Of an old slipper walking,
And the frying pan intrudes upon a balcony.

Is not this a matrimonial
Presentiment? . . . And like a demonstration,
An audible disturbance
Invades my bedroom's quietude:
It's a hen being run down by a rooster.

H. R. Hays

THE VILLAGE BARBER

The village barber in his old straw hat
And dancing pumps and waistcoat of piqué
Plays sharp at cards, and on his knee-bones squat
Hears mass, and rails at old Voltaire all day.
An old subscriber to *El Liberal*,
He works and sparkles like a merry glass
Of muscatel, his razor's rise and fall
Timing his gossip of what comes to pass.

With mayor and veterinary, pious folk,
Who say the rosary, he speaks no joke
Of miracles by Peter Claver wrought;
A tavern champion and a cock-pit sage,

Amid the scissors' clip his war he'll wage,
Sparkling like the muscatel the light has caught.

Thomas Walsh

VERSES TO THE MOON

O Moon who now looks over the roof
Of the church in the tropical calm
To be saluted by him who has been out all night,
To be barked at by the dogs of the suburbs;
O Moon, who in your silence has laughed at
All things! In your sidereal silence
When, keeping carefully in the shadow, the
Municipal Judge steals from some den—

But you offer, saturnine traveler,
With what eloquence in mute space
Consolation to him whose life is broken,
While there sing to you from a drunken brawl
Long-haired, neurasthenic bards,
And lousy creatures who play dominoes.

William G. Williams

TROPIC SIESTA

Sultry Sunday, noon
of shimmering
Sun, a policeman
as if embedded in the curb,
profoundly asleep. A dog's
filth smeared on a fence. An abbot's
indigestion, the muffled
cacophony of a locust . . .

Solitude of the grave, complete
and sullen silence. But
suddenly in the ugly town,
the dominical hush is broken,
for a raving drunkard screams:
Hurray for the Liberal Party!

Donald D. Walsh

JORGE ESCOBAR URIBE
1886–1918   Colombia

Son of an influential Colombian family, Escobar was
exiled for life at the age of fourteen for his part in the
revolt of 1900 by General Avelina Rosas. He visited
many lands before finally settling in Argentina. Gloom
fascinated him. He collected postcards of cemeteries,
and had a skull on his desk to which he wrote "Ante
un cráneo" ("In the Presence of a Skull"), much
quoted by university students. In Chile he adopted the
pen name "Claudio de Alas" to describe his feelings
about the sad, monotonous waltz by Octavio Barbero,
"Cuando escucho el vals Francia." Finally he gathered
all his poetry into one volume, wrote a foreword: "Fiat
Lux" ("Let There Be Light"), then after shooting his
dog to provide himself with a companion in the Hereafter, this Romanticist committed suicide. A Chilean
critic summed him up: "He felt deeply and expressed
himself beautifully."

IN THE PRESENCE OF A SKULL

I know you not, offscouring of grim life,
    You hoary, voiceless proof of nothingness;
How many years ago your fire and strife
    Was dulled by Death in just one brief caress!

Naught do those holes that once were eyes aver;
  There, mysteries of existence left no trace.
I only know that in some sepulchre
  The slowly toiling worms destroyed your face,
And that in murkiest depths of sealed Hereafter,
  Death, coveting all things you now despise,
Left on your countenance its fearful laughter,
  And buried shadows deep within your eyes.

                                        W.K.J.

WHEN I HEAR THE
FRANCIA WALTZ

Once upon a night of love, of silence, yet of flame,
A melancholy singer,
A gentle troubadour,
All close muffled from the world in cape of black I came
Thinking upon a sweet amour,
Thinking on a sweet amour.

And as I looked upon you with devotion,
Seeing the demon, I beheld the woman, too,
And my emotion,
And your emotion,
Were burning flames to light me unto you.

(*These two stanzas are repeated in reversed order.*)

Oh, sad love that could not last,
But fled with you,
And with your song—
Lovely song of the past!—
A traveler without love and without home, I hie
Like other troubadours,
Hymning amours,
But I shall dream your beauty till I die.

And if 't is you who are the first in dying,
Along the path your footsteps tread
I'll follow close that soul so sped;
A singer sad beyond belief
I'll weep my grief,
I'll weep my grief.

W.K.J.

FIAT LUX

With the pure boldness of a statued nude
  This sonorous book I give mankind.
Within it, Death and Sin and Doubt are viewed
  In words my Soul's blood wrote for all to find.
Its harmony is boisterously crude
  Bearing a threat for carping critic's mind;
But—Volume of my Life—with life endued
  Because by soul and hand together 't was designed.

Read not this book, satanical and sad—
  Read not this book, for Hell in it finds room—
Read not this book, which weeps for all man had.
  Hope in its pages, pitiless in gloom
Ironic is, depraved and always sad.
  Grant that its final page shall be my tomb.

W.K.J.

JACINTO FOMBONA PACHANO
1901–1951   Venezuela

Originally a student of political science, Fombona
Pachano went into diplomacy after the romantic prose
and poetry of his local color *Virajes* ("Here and
There") (1932) had won him election to the Vene-

zuelan Academy. While serving in Washington,
he wrote *Las torres desprevenidas* ("Improvident
Towers") (1940), with a cosmopolitan point of view.
After that, he experimented with Surrealism. His recent writings express the horrors of war and man's longing for a better world.

I ANNOUNCE THE KINGDOM
OF THE STAR

And now I have spoken my word to the men of peace,
To the men who suffer in silence.
To those who still utter the feelings of the tree,
Of the sheepskin and the child, of the roof and the bell.

There is a place in the world, my brothers,
There is a place in the world beyond the burnings,
Farther than the useless nosegays of the grenades,
Farther than the hooks, the blades, the armorplate, and the
    nets,
Behind carbon and ashes,
Behind paper cheeks and crushed bones,
For the flower, the wheat ear, the fleece and the milk,
For all the rancorless mothers of the world,
For the honeycomb, there has to be a place.

Over the smoke, over the hospital and the ravens,
If you pass the ramparts of stenches and screams,
If you pierce the gangrene that seizes you in the air,
On the other side, brothers, under the unarmed skies,
Amid fields of sweet shadows along the high clouds of joyful
    water,
Seas of sheep kiss a certain place in the world.

Do not ask, Oh, do not ask: Where is it?
Look first at your nails, your jaws, to see

Whether scythes and saws do not grow out of them,
Whether mouth and hands have the savor of wool and lily,
Whether on your fingers there are signs of extinguished butter-
    flies,
Dead bells and mute cicadas.

Go for the first honey, the most profound.
The gayest, which joins your heart to the bees.
Look to see if in each breast the stars are duplicating themselves
And if from their margins a child may peep in without fear,
Or a flute, a roof, an entire dovecote, without being effaced.

Tell me what have you done with fire,
What have you done with the garden air and the birds,
With so much olive of sea as your ships have been sunk,
With so much earth, pregnant with unhappy springtimes?

Tell me what coin of sweat or of tears
Dies in your pocket or is blood on your teeth.

And if you are truly the men of peace
And if you are truly nard and linen and go naked,
Then, Oh, then, you will know that there is a place in the world.
A place, indeed, that is being born of your cleanest light,
A place where the bonfires forge skies of purity,
Where the air links rings of contented perfume,
Where the water between two shores spreads warm bowknots,
Where the earth is mother of cheeks and kisses.

If you, yourselves, want it, there is a place in the world,
There is a place beyond the burnings,
Farther than the pregnant wombs that plead with you
Through their cracks of mutilated cemeteries,
The white, sweet kingdom of the star.

                                        H. R. Hays

MEDARDO ÁNGEL SILVA
1900–1929   Ecuador

Best of the Negro poets of Guayaquil, Ecuador, was
youthful Silva, who shot himself, leaving—besides a
novel—only a few poems published in newspapers and
magazines, that deal with scenes in Ecuador's chief
port. They are witness to what he might have done had
he lived longer.

THE SLEEPING MALECÓN

The sleeping Malecón, these nights foggy and dark,
Recall the frightening legends of colonial days.
The river seems alive with many a phantom bark;
In silhouette through mist each like a cradle sways.
Street lights beneath whose globes are eerie shadows made
By feeble glow that spills through grime-incrusted glass,
Stand like malignant Cyclops in a long parade
And through their bloodshot eyes they glare at us who pass.

The whole world sleeps. Scarcely can listening ears at times
Hear from some far-off clock the even-stroking chimes,
And echoing steps of guards through lonely streets and park.
But suddenly like wasps swarming by millions, rise
Bright bursts of dazzling sparks into the midnight skies,
As scarce-seen steamer slips through waves deathlike and dark.

                                                      W.K.J.

NOCTURNAL DETAIL

On a near-by gable, a cat, solemn and cold,
Is sunk in deep contemplative vagary,

His green eye like a living emerald
Fixed on the ruddy moon of January.

Plato himself, he sits with head bent low,
Immobile, abstract in grand hypotheses;
Nothing disturbs his monologue's silent flow
But the fragrant singing of a passing breeze.

Mary and *C. V. Wicker*

JORGE CARRERA ANDRADE
1903–   Ecuador

Dr. Carrera Andrade, diplomat and aristocrat, was
editor of his own magazine, *Idea*, before he was twenty.
In 1928 he went abroad to study. Since then he has
lived mostly in foreign countries, in his nation's service. His tour of duty in San Francisco resulted in one
volume of poetry.

Early influenced by Góngora, as well as by Francis
Jammes and other French Romanticists and Symbolists, Dr. Carrera has employed many styles of verse,
even Surrealism, following Bretón and Eluard. Indian
themes prevailed in his *Tiempo manual* (Madrid,
1935), while the delicacy of a miniaturist can be observed in *Microgramas* (Tokyo, 1940). His poetic career can be followed in *Edades poéticas* ("Poetic
Ages") (1956), which includes the best of his work
since 1922. It shows his use of description and metaphor, his pride in his country, and his universality and
sense of the comradeship of mankind. Symbolism is
apparent in some of his most recent verse.

SIERRA

Corn hangs from the rafters
by its canary wings.

Little guinea-pigs
bewilder the illiterate silence
with sparrow twitter and dove coo.

There is a mute race through the hut
when the wind pushes against the door.

The angry mountain
raises its dark umbrella of cloud,
lightning-ribbed.

Francisco, Martín, Juan,
working in the farm on the hill,
must have been caught by the storm.

A downpour of birds
falls chirping on the sown fields.

Muna Lee

SUNDAY

Fruit-vender church,
seated at a corner of life:
crystal oranges of windows.
Organ of sugarcane stalks.

Angels: chicks
of Mother Mary.

The little blue-eyed bell
runs out barefoot
to scamper over the countryside.

Clock of the Sun;
angelical donkey with its innocent sex;

handsome Sunday wind
bringing news from the hill;
Indian women with their vegetable loads
bound to their foreheads.

The sky rolls up its eyes
when the little barefoot bell
comes scampering out of the church.

Muna Lee

ELEGY FOR
ABRAHAM VALDELOMAR

Parasites storm this poet's mansion.
Large fungi grow within its quiet shadow
while a trickle of soundless dreaming water shudders.
Everything waiting his return. Except the faintest chatter
upon the roof: the village pigeons
or perhaps the spread wing of the wind
scattering carefree leaves
while grasses between the roof-tiles dance so sadly.
But the old pastorals with their foolish little bells
and their loving flutes
no longer move through the willows
and the young girls now no longer
follow their burros into town.

Enchanted furniture in these rooms
still holds the fragrance of days gone by,
but all of this, all these things,
exude a dream without horizons.

Valdelomar, my friend: everything is waiting for you!
Your house yet fresh with soft sea winds,
that little path of wooded shadow—
they're listening to hear your warm familiar steps . . .

And there on the foam-fringed beach—
foam like lemon blossoms—
crawls the deliberate turtle like a decoration done in lacquer,
and that small old boat of yours lashed to the pile
seems, from time to time, to be a pattern on Biscay linen,
while all your poems still remember me
from long ago, my friend.

Lloyd Mallan

MANUEL GONZÁLEZ PRADA
1844–1918   Peru

González Prada, author of a number of volumes of
post-Romantic poetry noted for its perfection and
polish, like *Minúsculas*, and of magnificent prose,
Páginas libres ("Free Pages") and *Horas de lucha*
("Hours of Strife"), with a style "as clear as distilled
alcohol," was also a rebel and fighter for justice, who
influenced Peruvian young people along political lines.
While he did introduce German literary currents into
his country, many of his poems followed French forms
like his famous "Aves de paso," ("Birds of Passage"),
and these triolets.

TRIOLETS

Treasures of life and glories men desire
Never arrive, or reach us far too late.
Gleaming, they pass before one can acquire
Treasures of life and glories men desire.
Woe to the man who, full of youth and fire,
Delays too long to seize the gifts of fate.
Treasures of life and glories men desire
Never arrive, or reach us far too late.

If you must sigh, my heart, sigh quietly
That no one hears the echo of that sigh.
Lest you disturb a happy revery
If you must sigh, my heart, sigh quietly.
Pretending you are full of gaiety,
As in some quiet nook, lonesome you lie,
If you must sigh, my heart, sigh quietly
That no one hears the echo of that sigh.

W.K.J.

JOSÉ SANTOS CHOCANO
1875–1934   Peru

Most thoroughly American of the Modernist poets
was the self-complacent Chocano of Peru, for whose
first published volume, Alma americana ("American
Soul") (1906), Rubén Darío wrote the Preface. However Chocano departed from Darío's practices in pre-
ferring Whitman to the French poets and in substitut-
ing the condor and the snake for Darío's swan. While
championing the Indians, he did not forget racial
bonds with Spain. His lyrical ability is exhibited in
poetry ranging from Whitman-esque free verse to formal sonnets of twelve syllables, like "Blasón" ("Coat
of Arms") here translated.

Chocano's exuberant life paralleled his writing. A
political revolutionist, he was imprisoned and barely
escaped a firing squad, only to be murdered on a street
car in Chile. Toward the end of his life, he and his
poetry lost their arrogance, and he could write such a
humble poem as "¡Quién sabe!" ("Who Knows?")
(1922).

COAT OF ARMS

My savage native soil inspires this singer's lay;
America's ideals I chant; my lyre has soul.

Not from some palm tree hanging do my verses sway
Like lazy hammock at the tropic wind's control.
When I feel purely Inca, then I give my king,
The Sun, a vassal's homage and his scepter own.
When Spain's blood courses and colonial days I sing,
Then do my verses seem from crystal trumpets blown.

My flights of fancy spring from Moorish mold,
The Andes give me silver; Leon gives me gold,
And these two substances I fuse with epic roar.
Its blood is Spanish, but from Inca heart it throbs,
And were I not a poet, perhaps I'd seek new jobs,
As white adventurer or Inca emperor.

                                                    W.K.J.

HORSES OF THE CONQUERORS

The horses were agile.
The horses were strong.
Their necks were arched and their haunches gleaming,
Their flying hoofs a rhythmical song . . .
    The horses were agile.
    The horses were strong.

No, it was not the warriors alone
Who in armor and plumage and banners, at last
Through the forest and the Andes
Conquering passed.
The horses of Andalusia, whose sinews
Are sparks from the breed of swift-running Arabs were they
Who stamped their glittering shoes
On the rocks of the way,
On the loud river's strand,
On the muffled snow,
On the wet marsh-land,

On mountain and valleys and plain, as they thundered along.
  The horses were agile.
  The horses were strong.

A horse was first in the torrid glen
When Balboa the drowsy silence broke
With shouts of marching men,
And was even the first
To discover the unknown Pacific and suddenly halt
At a breath in its nostrils,
The odor of salt.

And what of that other,
Mighty of girth and rearing his proud magnificent height,
In whose sparkling stirrups rode
Hernán Cortés one night,
From Mexico on to Honduras,
Over boulders and bushes, fortnights and leagues, in its flight?

An epic of horses is seemly,
A poem that is sung;
As fabulous wing-clipped hippogriffs hover,
As down from the Andes a river is flung,
All panting, dusty and hot,
They come over
From worlds still unborn,
Other worlds to conquer,
And suddenly start at the sound of horn
That swells with a mighty hurricane blast,
And nervously neighing, a call so profound
It seems it forever would last . . .
And out on the wide, unlimited plain
They gaze where the sorrowful distances lie
With alluring horizons, and off to the ages
Jostling and pawing and snorting . . . they fly
Ascending the air

In a cloud-bank of glory . . . they clamber . . . they throng
  . . .
The horses were agile.
The horses were strong.

Jessie Read Wendell

THE INDIAN FLUTE

Not the gay reed the god was wont to play
Among the groves of Greece in days of old;
Its voice is like a dying dove's, this flute
That sounds by night among the Andes cold.
The *quena's* low lament, how deep it is!
In the chill desert of the mountains high
It lingers out its long-drawn melody,
The calmer, the more piercing, 'neath the sky.

Pearls of its tears it streams along the height;
It sometimes, moaning 'midst those wastes that freeze,
Sinks in an echoing jar its plaintive dole;
And then it seems, amid the tranquil night,
Breath of a soul that has become a breeze,
Breath of a breeze that has become a soul.

Alice Stone Blackwell

A QUEEN'S BREAST

She was a Queen of Spain. Her name beside
We know not, nor her lineage—just the grace
With which she stopped her carriage, left her place,
Hearing a child that in a corner cried.
"Why is he crying?" Cold the eventide,
Hungry the child. She op'ed her robe a space,

And gave him the white breast from its white lace,
Like Hungary's queen, of old a saint who died.

Our pride is that she fed that hungry child—
Who later, haply, felt his blood inflame
With some strange royal right, unknown, unguessed.
Our pride it is, that fostering love and mild
With which her breast she gave him, is the same
With which Spain to a whole world gave its breast.

Alice Stone Blackwell

CÉSAR ABRAHAM VALLEJO

1892–1938   Peru

Vallejo, mestizo son of a small-town mayor, started
with pessimistic poems about dull rural life, collected
in *Los heraldos negros* ("Black Heralds") (Trujillo,
1918). After an absence while teaching in Lima, he returned home, only to be jailed unjustly. While in
prison he completed *Trilce* (1922). When finally released, he turned his back on Peru for Russia and Paris,
where he died in poverty. His disillusionment and despair, along with his yearning for social progress and
horror over Spain's civil war, expressed in powerful
verse that rejuvenated Peru's poetry, established him as
one of Latin America's great poets. He exerted tremendous influence all over the continent. At the close of
his life, when his keen imagination was expressing itself in almost incomprehensible poetry, some see him
as a follower of Huidobro and Creationism.

DREGS

This afternoon it is raining as never before, and I,
My heart, have no desire to live.

This afternoon is sweet. Why shouldn't it be?
It is dressed in grace and sorrow; dressed like a woman.

It is raining this afternoon in Lima. And I remember
the cruel caverns of my ingratitude;
my block of ice crushing her poppy,
stronger than her: "Don't be like this!"

My violent black flowers; and the barbarous
and enormous stoning; and the glacial interlude.
And the silence of her dignity will mark
in burning oils the final period.

And so this afternoon, as never before, I go
with this owl, with this heart.

And other women pass; and seeing me so mournful,
they take a little of you
from the grim convulsion of my pain.

This afternoon it is raining, pouring. And I,
My heart, have no desire to live!

Muna Lee

SPAIN, TAKE FROM ME THIS CUP

Children of the world,
if Spain falls—I say, if it should happen—
if they tear
down from the sky her forearm, held
in a halter by two terrestrial rings:
children, what an age of hollowed temples.
How soon the sun will bring what I foretold!
How quick in your breast the ancient shouting!
How lost the B+ in your notebook!

Children of the world,
Mother Spain sweats with weariness;
our teacher with her ferules,
our mother and mistress,
our cross and our wood, for she gave you height,
dizziness and division and addition, children;
she is hard pressed, fathers of tomorrow!

If she falls,—I say, if it should happen—if
Spain falls, from earth downward,
children, then you will grow no more!
Then the year will punish the month!
Then the teeth in your mouth will stop with ten,
the diphthong will end on a downstroke, the medal in tears!
The little primer lamb will be left
in the big inkwell, unread, unwritten!
You will go down the steps of the alphabet
as far as the letter at which pain was born!

Children,
sons of warriors, meanwhile
hush your voices, for Spain even now is parting
her strength among the animal kingdom,
the little flowers, the comets, and man.
Hush your voices, for she is
in agony, great agony, not knowing
what to do, and in her hand
is the talking skull that talks and talks,
the skull with braided hair,
the skull of life!

Hush your voices, I tell you;
hush your voices, the chanting of syllables, the wailing
of lessons and the minor murmur of the Pyramids, and even
that of your temples which throb with two stones!
Hush your breath, and if
her forearm falls,

if the ferules rap, if night comes,
if the sky is contained in two terrestrial limbs,
if there is a creaking in the sound of doors,
if I am late,
if you see no one, if you are frightened
by pencils without points, if Mother
Spain falls—I say, if it should happen—
go forth, children of the world; go and seek her!

Donald D. Walsh

RICARDO JAIMES FREYRE
1870–1933   Bolivia

Jaimes Freyre, son of a famous Bolivian painter and a
Peruvian playwright, looked like an artist with his
fierce mustache, uncombed hair, and long cape.
Though he spent little of his life in Bolivia, he is considered one of its greatest writers. Buenos Aires was his
home. There, with Darío and Lugones, he published
the influential, if short-lived *Revista Americana,* and
there his *Castalia bárbara* ("Barbaric Muses' Fountain") (1897) was published, with its experiments in
rhyme and meter. Later he wrote an important study
of poetic theory, *Leyes de la versificación castellana*
("Laws of Spanish Versification") (1912). *Los sueños
son vida* ("Dreams are Life") (1919) shows Parnassian
influence, but Nordic mythology and Christianity likewise found place in his melancholy poetry. He helped
found the University of Tucumán and served Bolivia
as ambassador in Brazil and the United States.

THE ANCESTORS

Lake of the Sun, that near the clouds dost slumber,
Where snows eternal guard thy silent sleep!

Lake of green waters, to the sky uprising
  When the winds issue from their caverns deep!

The wandering lord of workmen and of warriors
  Was born within thine icy waves of old;
The Inca Manco Capajh, wise, celestial,
  Cast his vast shadow on the glaciers cold.

From Tucumán to Quito, Maule to Guayas,
  Followed the crown whose worship he had won;
By plains and forests, mountain chains and sea-coasts,
  The Emperors went, the children of the Sun.

The Indian, 'neath the sceptre of those rulers,
  Patient and calm, magnanimous and brave,
Was like the bee or the industrious beaver;
  He was not as a servant or a slave.

Noble and quiet nation! Life that pleased thee
  Was crystallized in dreams of misty grace.
How through thy broad wound flowed away in bloodstreams
  The mournful souls of thine ill-fated race!

A heritage thou gavest to the Spaniard
  Of melancholy that no cure may know,
Softening the vivid light of Spain's bright heaven
  With the dim twilight of thy dying woe.

The grandsons of those conquerors rough, whose valor
  Has made the centuries wondering awe confess,
Join to the noble pride of those forefathers
  A world of vague ancestral sadnesses—

Sadnesses that are blended with their pleasures,
  That mingle with their love a secret pain,
That sigh upon the lips of their sweet women,
  And in their poets' mournful songs complain.

Vainly the dread red sword that smote the Incas
  And the proud Aztecs, and in years long fled
Made its imperial flag blaze o'er Granada,
  Civilizations three hath stricken dead.

It was perhaps a deep and secret mystery,
  Full of wild grandeurs mixed with shadows gray,
That fused the Indian, Saracen, and Spaniard
  To make the New World's race that lives today!

Alice Stone Blackwell

JULIO VICUÑA CIFUENTES
1865–1936   Chile

Poet, critic, professor, and student of languages, the many-sided Chilean Vicuña Cifuentes published only one volume of verse, fittingly titled *Cosecha de otoño* ("Autumn Harvest"), since it was completed during his own autumn, in 1920. In his youth, he translated Virgil, Horace, and Italian, Portuguese, and French poetry, and wrote an authoritative *Studies in Spanish Metrics*. His poetry, ranging from love to religion, has a smoothness and a slyness that the post-Modernists have failed to appreciate. "La ocasión," here translated, and his "La mimosita" ("Little Darling") are among his better known poems.

CIRCUMSTANCES

"The rose that you plucked in the garden at eve
Was gone from your breast when you came from the dance.
Tell me, who could have stolen it without your leave?"
  " 'Twas circumstance, Mother, circumstance."

"On your cheek, daughter dear, there are signs you've been kissed.

(Stolen kisses leave trace to be seen at a glance.)
Tell me who could do that if you tried to resist?"
   "It was circumstance, Mother, circumstance."

"Your face looks so pallid. Your skirt's growing tight,
And your belt can't hold in your continued expanse.
Who could blemish your name unless *you* gave that right?"
   "It was circumstance, Mother, circumstance."

                                                        W.K.J.

JUAN GUZMÁN CRUCHAGA
1896–   Chile

Guzmán Cruchaga is a world-girdling Chilean consul,
having lived outside his country more years than in it,
but publishing in Chile a series of volumes of poetry of
increasing power, beginning with *Junto al brasero* ("Beside the Brazier") (1914). His *Aventura* ("Adventure") won a Santiago Municipal prize for verse.
"Canción," his most popular poem, here translated,
became the title of his recently-published anthology.
One of his philosophic phases was a sort of mystic
pantheism, exemplified in "Canción del humo," also
translated here.

SONG

O Soul, say naught to me!
My door I tightly close,
And though you seek repose,
You'll find no vacancy.

Long years had I been yearning
In vain for your returning.

Today when you return,
You'll find that no lights burn.

The cold autumnal blast
Entered my wounded heart
Through shutters blown apart.
No flame against it could last.
I saw its light depart.

Today no lights there burn.
My Soul, say naught to me,
For though you may return
You'll find no vacancy!

W.K.J.

THE SONG OF SMOKE

Like loosened tresses I unfurl myself,
All marveling to all the winds of God.
I am the ladder of light unto the skies,
I am the humble anthem of the earth,
A dream, a cloud, a ruined altar stone—
I sketch in air. My sorrow is profound,
For I am slowly dying as I rise.

My life is nothing but a water drop,
Heaven and light, a dying at a breath—
I have the airy lightness of a thought,
And yet the weakness of a still-born babe
Who sighs in Limbo; and my sadness is
Slender and starlike, as a virgin who,
Afraid of life, flees from her very soul.

The sun absorbs me even as the sands
Of desert drink the brook; and yet I move

Like to the seraphim across the sky;
And all the stars and all the things of earth
Behold me die in space. My loneliness
Crosses the face of life as minutes march
Across the face of God, and leave no trace.

Chesley M. Hutchings

GABRIELA MISTRAL
1889–1957   Chile

Lucila Godoy Alcayaga was born in northern Chile. As
the daughter of a schoolteacher, she entered that profession at the age of fifteen and taught for twenty years
in rural schools. Finally she was made director of an
important school in Santiago. As her poetry shows, she
never lost interest in education, and it was as a school
consultant that she toured America and Europe, an
activity that somewhat influenced the award to her of
the 1945 Nobel Prize for Literature.

The suicide in 1909 of her sweetheart Romelio Ureta
turned her to poetry. First recognition came with the
award to her *Sonetos de la muerte* in the 1914 Juegos
Florales, under the pen name of "Gabriela Mistral,"
derived from the first name of Rosetti and the last
name of a Provençal poet who had just died. She continued to write tragic verse on such themes as the awakening of love, maternity, religion, and nature. She cared
little for form. Her language was that of the rural people, archaisms and all. Her volume *Desolación*, published in New York in 1922, made her widely known
as one of the great poetesses of the hemisphere. Not
till 1938 did she follow it with *Tala* ("Desolation"),
the work of her maturity, that showed greater care
about style. Finally came *Lagar* ("Wine Press")
(1954), with its stylized love of nature and its creatures.

While not a Modernist, Gabriela Mistral learned
from them. Her poetic gifts are evident even in her
excellent literary criticism and her personal letters.

A SONNET OF DEATH

The hands of evil have been on your life
Since when, at signal from the stars, I sowed
It 'mid the lilies. Beauteous was it rife
Till hands of evil wrecked the fair abode.
Unto the Lord I said: "From mortal paths
Oh, let them bear him,—spirit without guide—;
Save him, O Saviour, from the grip of wraths,
And plunge him in the dreams Thine arms provide!"

Lament is vain—in vain I strive to follow;
Black is the tempest that drives on his sail;
My breast for him, or mow away his flower!—
Woe! Woe!—the seas his bark of roses swallow—
Is pity in my heart of no avail?—
Thou that shalt judge me, Lord, speak Thou this hour!

Roderick Gill

INTIMATE

—Do not press my hands.
There will come
The lasting time
Of resting with much dust and shade
Between the interwoven fingers.

You will say:
"I cannot leave her now.
Already her fingers
Are threshed-out grain."

—Do not kiss my mouth.
—Will come the moment
Full of waning light,

When I shall stand
Without lips
On a moistened ground.

And you will say:
"I loved her,
—But how love her now?
She does not breathe
The cedar fragrance of my kiss."

And I will be anguished hearing you,
Speaking wild and blind:
When my fingers are dust,
My hands will touch your brow.
And on your grief-worn face
My breath will fall.

—Do not touch me, therefore.
It were a lie to say
I reach you, my love, in these outstretched arms,
In mouth, and throat . . .
—You, believing that you drank it all,
Would be deceived as an unseeing child.

My love is not alone
The stubborn weary body's sheaf,
Shrinking from the hair shirt's rasp,
Shed in every flight.

My love is what is in the kiss
And is not lip;
What sounds forth voice
And is not breast.
My love is a wind of God that passes,
In its blast
Stripping the clusters
Of the flesh.

Dorothy Conzelman

THE RURAL TEACHER

The teacher was pure. "The kindly gardeners," she said,
"Who till this soil, the garden of our Lord,
Must have pure eyes, unstainéd hands, and ever
Keep clean their oil, a clear light to afford."

The teacher was poor; her kingdom not of men
(Like His who sadly mowed o'er Israel's field.)
Her garments dull in hue, her hands unjeweled;
But her soul one great and loving gem revealed.

The teacher was glad of heart. Poor wounded woman!
Her smile was token of a grief benign.
Over the sandals torn and blood-stained shone
That smile, of saintliness the blossom fine . . .

O peasant woman, you recall how oft
From her name some coarse or brutal jest you drew;
You've seen her a hundred times, yet never known her;
In your son's face there is more of her than you!

Her soul was made as an o'erflowing vase
To scatter pearls before our human sight;
And her life on earth was but the widening breach
That the Father makes to shed His own clear light.

Hence even the dust to which her frame has come
Sustains red roses of a violent flame,
And the sexton tells how the feet of those who, passing
Tread on her bones, are perfumed with the same.

Isabel K. Macdermotte

VICENTE HUIDOBRO
1893–1948   Chile

Vicente García Fernández, under the pen name of "Vicente Huidobro," was one of the first Latin-American poets to reflect the French postwar poetry. In 1912, with Guzmán Cruchaga, Latorre, and other Chileans, he published *Musa joven* ("Young Muse"). In 1916, his wealthy parents sent him to France, where he began publishing with the original Cubists. Though Pierre Réverdy later claimed the distinction, García Fernández originated Creationism, in a Buenos Aires lecture of 1916, in which he declared: "It is a poet's first duty to create; his second, to create; his third, to create."

His first volume of verse, in 1916, bore the title *El espejo de agua* ("The Mirror of Water"). The next three carried titles in French; it was his belief that the image, rather than the language, was what mattered. With the publication of *Ultra* (1921–2), Huidobro became an Ultraist, trying like Apollinaire, to develop a poetic and unpunctuated language. He commenced printing his poems in pictorial shapes, for example "Paisaje" ("Landscape").

For his "Manifestos," like the one of 1917, for his volume of 1925, for his intellect, rather than his emotion, and for the stir he caused, "Vicente Huidobro" gets a place in most anthologies, though he was a second-rate poet. After his death, his friend Eduardo Anguita, himself a poet, collected his work into a single volume.

LANDSCAPE

AFTERNOON PROMENADE TO BE CONDUCTED
IN PARALLEL ROWS
THE TREE
WAS
TALLER
THAN THE MOUNTAIN
BUT THE
MOUNTAIN
WAS SO WIDE   THE
THAT IT CROSSED   RIVER
THE BOUNDARY-LINE   WHICH
                               FLOWS
                               OVER
                               THE
                               FISH

WARNING! DON'T
PLAY ON THE GRASS!
FRESH PAINT
A SONG LEADS THE LAMBS TO THE STABLE

Arturo Torres-Rioseco

NATURE VIVE

He leaves the end of the world to the accordion
Pays for the last song with rain
Yonder where the voices unite an enormous cedar is born
More comfortable than the sky

A swallow says to me papa
An anemone says to me mama

Blue blue over yonder and in the mouth of the wolf
Mr. Blue Sky departing
What do you say   Where are you going

Ah what a beautiful blue blue arm
Give your arm to Mrs. Cloud
If you're afraid of the wolf
The wolf with the blue blue mouth
With long long teeth
to eat up grandmother nature

Mr. Sky scrape off your swallow
Mrs. Cloud put out your anemones

The voices unite over the bird
Larger than the tree of creation
Lovelier than a current of air between two stars

H. R. Hays

PABLO NERUDA
1904–   Chile

Neftalí Ricardo Reyes, who writes under the name of
"Pablo Neruda," was early recognized as one of Latin
America's outstanding poets. An admirer of García
Lorca, he became a poet of the senses, deeply subjec-
tive, and with a dramatic outlook on life, which he saw
as a nightmare, full of romantic qualities. In his early
period, beginning with his first volume, *Crepusculario*
("Twilight"), influenced by the Ultraist school of
Guillermo de Torre and Cansino Assens, he glorified
animal instincts, with poems full of sex and sensual
images. Later, in revolt against the artificiality created
by a search for perfection in form, he studied Whitman
and his style became more realistic. However, his poems
still contain violent symbolism, with grapes, flowers,

bees, fish, etc., along with smells and noises, in a kind
of personal shorthand. Some of his metaphors are most
unpoetic. In his most recent period, he has abandoned
Symbolism, though not going as far as Surrealism. In
most of his verse, one sees the spiritual doubts of a soul
full of grief and despair. As the most widely published
and translated of Latin-American poets, his influence
on post-Modernist poets has been second only to Darío.

SONATA: THERE'S NO FORGETTING

If you should ask me where I've been,
I must reply: "It happens."
I must speak of the soil obscured by the stones,
Of the river destroyed while still existing.
I know only things that birds lose,
The ocean left behind, or my weeping sister.
Why are there so many regions? Why does one day
Join with another day? Why does a black night
Accumulate in the mouth? Why do the dead exist?
If you should ask from where I came, I must speak about broken
    things,
About utensils far too bitter,
About huge beasts often decayed, and about my distressed
    heart.

All that have passed have not been memories,
Nor is what sleeps in forgetfulness a yellow dove,
But rather, faces wet with tears,
Fingers at the throat,
And all that collapses from the leaves;
The obscurity of a day gone by,
A day fed with our sad blood.

I'll show you violets, swallows,
And all that pleases us and appears

On the pretty, large postcards
Sent back from places that time and sweetness visit on their
    trip.

But let's not penetrate beyond the teeth.
Let's not chew on the husks that silence accumulates.
Because I don't know what to answer:
There are so many dead,
And so many seawalls that the red sun has damaged,
And so many heads that the ships strike,
And so many hands that have imprisoned kisses,
And so many things that I want to forget.

W.K.J.

THE SEA GULLS OF ANTOFAGASTA

You know nothing of sterile lands;
You know nothing of parched Cordilleras,
And skies marred by infinite scars,
And dead ochre at mid day
Beside the death-like color of tungsten,
Beside the still, immoveable
Mountains of a dead world
With heights and unrelieved catastrophes
Bathed in cruel light of sandy *paramos*.

Such was my harsh welcome
From the calcified North of my country.

Then at the line
Where blue metalic sky
Meets the insurgent waves
Above the cruel mountains of mineral
Behind my ship,
I saw man and love arise

In a farewell flight of sea gulls.
Triangular and gray
They took form
Above the disappearing Antofagasta,
And in their flight, they cut
Fugitive rectangles.
Light and geometry criss-crossed
Immoveable, they came nearer.
They seemed to rise in their own foam
And suddenly they became lines of salt,
Eyes of the sky or eyebrows above the snow.

Over the sea, long as a month,
Leaving behind the calcareous shell
Of the cliffs of Antofagasta,
Came a cluster of birds,
Bunched like grapes.
The pure cycle of their flight,
The voiceless music of the gulls,
And above the horrendous world,
Above the dry death of a lunar desert,
They rise with the sea
In a broken flight of orange blossoms,
An accompaniment
Of balance and whiteness.
And it was, at the end of the day,
A dance suspended,
The purest repertory of air,
The chapter of sweetness.

Farewell, farewell, gulls!
Turn back, back
Toward the cruel, infernal wealth
Of calcinated nature,
Toward darkening night,
Toward what departs when the circle
Of the sea begins closing around my ship,

While I, in my voyage,
Endless, senseless, luckless,
Sailing night and day,
Stop there and question myself
About the brave light of those rocks,
About the erratic wings that followed
My pilgrim heart into the open sea.

Farewell, farewell,
Lone souls of a dead moon,
Lofty questions of marine light!
Farewell, until I lose
In space
All that accompanied me on my voyage:
The light of the gulls that rose
Behind me in their flight
And bore me up in their wings,
That honor of the sea, that purest of towns.

W.K.J.

POEMAS DE AMOR

> *"And I will make the poems of my body
> and of my mortality,
> For I think I shall then supply myself
> with the poems of my soul and of
> immortality."*
>
> Whitman.

No. I

Hold not my hands,
And leave my heart free!
Let my fingers pass
Over the paths of your body.

Passion—blood, fire, kisses—
Starts trembling flames within me . . .
Ah! You have no idea what this is!

It is the storm of my senses
Bending the sensitive forest of my nerves.
It is flesh, crying with its ardent tongues!
It is fire!
And here you are, woman, like untouched timber
While all my being flies, turned to ashes,
Toward your body that's filled with stars, like night.

Hold not my hands,
And leave my heart free!

Only you do I desire, only you!
It is not love. It is a self-consuming and destroying desire.
It is an onslaught of furies,
The onrush of all that is impossible,
But you are there,
There to give me everything
And to give me what you have, you came to earth,
And I am come to hold you,
and desire you,
and receive you.

W.K.J.

THE SHIP

But if we've paid our passage through this world,
Then why, oh why, will they not let us sit and eat?

We desire to look at the clouds,
We want to take sun baths and smell the salt;
Frankly we have no wish to bother anybody.
It's all so simple: we're just passengers.

We're all passing by, and time along with us.
The sea goes by; a rose is only fleeting,
Earth travels on in shadow and in light.
And you, like us, pass by, as passengers.

So what is troubling you?
Why do you strike so angrily?
And whom go seeking, with revolver armed?

We did not know
That you had occupied it all.
Are yours the cups, the seats,
The beds, the mirrors, too,
And sea and wine and sky?

And now it seems
There is no table left.
But that can't be true, we think.
You can't convince us of it.

It was all dark when first we reached the ship
And we were naked, too.
We all came from the self-same place;
All of us came from women and from men,
All born with hunger, and our teeth came soon.
And all of us developed hands and eyes
That we might work, and yearn for what we saw.

Yet now you tell us that we have no rights;
There's no room on the ship.
You will not speak to us;
You will not play with us.

So many advantages for you! Why?
Who gave you spoons while yet you were unborn?
Here you are discontented.
Things shouldn't be like that.

On the voyage, I don't like
To find in hidden corners
Dull eyes without a love-light, hungry mouths.

There are no clothes for the approaching autumn;
And less, much less, for winter soon to come.
And without shoes, how can we walk about
The world on paths with sharp stones strewn?

Without a table, where are we to eat?
Where shall we sit if we're deprived of chairs?
If this is some sad joke, gentlemen, please decide
To end it soon,
To talk now seriously.
The sea is harsh.
It's raining blood.

                                                    W.K.J.

STELLA CORVALÁN
1919–   Chile

Like her fellow countrywoman Gabriela Mistral, Miss
Corvalán has been a world ambassador of culture and
poetry. Juana de Ibarbourou and César Tiempo were
the first to recognize her poetic talent in her *Sombra en
aire* ("Floating Shadow") (1940). Her first ten volumes were collected into one of 784 pages in 1958. She
also began a series of *Sinfonías* in 1951, long poems
about the elements. In her shorter love poetry, she
shows herself a disciple of Alfonsina Storni, whom in
one of her poems she calls *"hermana"* ("sister")

ANXIETY

In what remote abode,
In what far nation, or wide open space,

Dwells he of whom my body dreams?
That man who with encompassing hands
Shall rediscover me, and with his kiss
Bring into life, to dwell against my heart,
The son for whom I hope?
Within what honeycomb of shadowy woods
Or in what continent, all limitless,
Is he now waiting till I come,
With the audacious kiss of his desire?
Not in these cold walls nor in this anguished heart,
Not in the beat of empty words
That echo loud and sadly in
The attic where my patience waits.
This surfeiting of sweets, unsought,
This wandering soul that goes so eagerly
Seeking some hidden trace, some obvious track,
So avidly along the highways of the world.
My flesh in weariness
Seems like a pulsing rose that every day
Opens its empty petals all in vain.
Never to know illusions on my mouth,
Never to feel the river of my blood
Course with the pulsing, ardent ecstasy,
Body and soul aflame.
I would go calling his name from street to street;
"Hello, you! Man! Man, who will crush
All the chill pomp that stands between us two!
Here my sweet arms and my soft lips await.
Here is the delicate rosebud of my soul.
So come to me for what you crave.
Discover in my flesh, entranced,
A sleeping mystery!"

W.K.J.

JUAN E. O'LEARY
1879–   Paraguay

The Romanticist O'Leary was one of the earliest of
Paraguay's twentieth-century generation of poets. In
his lines, he celebrated some of the national figures,
wrote romantically about the downtrodden Indians,
then turned to more personal themes. But poetry was
his second choice. He is better known as an outstanding
historian.

THE SAVAGE

Into the entrails of the selva, wrapped
In the sleep of centuries, sunlight rarely comes—
This final resting place of haughty race—
    The Indian brave.

Those nights of darkness of his gloomy past
Are concentrated in his pupils, black,
Brooding, and with a gleam most sinister,
    And full of hate.

The many woes of his indomitable race
Vibrate with every word he speaks, his tone
Is bitter, filled with his age-long reproach
    And heartfelt moan.

But there he makes his way through ungrateful brush
Across the pampas, desolate and sad.
Forever fleeing, in unceasing search
    For kindly light.

Oh, Wandering Jew, pariah vagabond,
Oh, lonely orphan there imploring love,

Like weeping father who from children hears
    A mocking laugh!

Dearly he's paid. Upon the goodly earth
He's spilled his burning blood. He's sacrificed
His courage. He has even cast aside
    His language, too.

Of all his noble past, nothing is left
Except the implacable, crushing memory
That with the sadness of his bitter life
    Still tortures him.

Resign yourself, Oh, Savage, crude, impure!
You are no man like all the other men.
For you no Jesus opened wide his arms
    Upon the cross.

Wrapped in your hatred, you will die some day
Like deer pierced by the arrow that you speed.
Then will the black crow glut his appetite
    On your dead flesh.

You are no man like all the other men.
You are unworthy of the love of Christ.
Perish in rage, because your sons refuse
    To boast your blood.

You with your painted face, your tangled hair,
Your body naked and your bow in hand,
How can you ever hope you might receive
    Baptism now?

How luckier far than you, the wild beast
Who roams the woods, clad in his colored skin,
While you, lashed by your pain, go naked there,
    Dirty and bronzed!

Do not approach those once belovéd shores
Washed by your country's river. Not for you,
Nor for your race will ever Christian cross
      Pour forth its rays.

In holy temple there's no room for you,
Even though merchants raise the Host aloft.
Resign yourself forevermore to be
      An Indian brave!

                                                W.K.J.

ELOY FARIÑA NÚÑEZ
1885–1925   Paraguay

   While an exile in Buenos Aires, Fariña Núñez produced epics in blank verse about his country, like *Canto* .
secular ("Worldly Song") that showed his classical
training. At the same time, in such poems as "Pata de
gallo" ("Rooster's Foot"), he reveals the influence of
his friends who were editing the Modernist *Nosotros*.
One volume, *Cármenes* ("Songs") (1922) contains all
his poetic output, but he also left plays, short stories,
and philosophic essays.

THE SERPENT

This heart of mine, like some vast bonfire red,
Crackles and glows and casts a brilliant light.
The flames erupt in torrents, gleaming bright
Like the sun's glory, shining overhead.
The fire leaps up with loud reverberation,
The flames, corrosive, serpentine, rise high
To fill with scarlet splendor all the sky,
Then sink to steady, devilish conflagration.

Upon my heart, dear, place your gentle hand,
And feel it, like a hot volcano, burning,
And something of its beating understand.
Since you're the virtuous cause of all this fire,
Perhaps there at your feet, though pulsing, turning,
May lie that cursed serpent of desire.

W.K.J.

ALEJANDRO GUANES

1872–1925   Paraguay

Important among Paraguayan poets, Guanes filled a
period of transition, without belonging strictly to any
school, though he did admire the poetry of Poe, whom
he translated. His poetry was not collected until after
his death, when *De paso por la vida* ("Passing Through
Life") appeared. His romantic tendencies are seen in
"La hora de lágrimas," here translated.

THE HOUR OF TEARS

Heaven now dulls the clear blue of the sky.
The trembling flowers curl up their petals bright.
The evening dew sheds tears on foliage dry.
From the perfumed bosom of the woods nearby
Silent and clothed in shadows comes the night.

The sleepy thrush falls silent in the broom;
The swooping swallows to the rafters go.
Funereal shadows wrap the world in gloom
So sinister and sullen there's no room
Within my soul for anything but woe.

Moved by the kisses of the sobbing breeze
Comes a warm flood of liquid pearls that sears

The eyes of weeping, silent night. One sees
Tears. Oh, how many fall! What quantities!
For who is there who has no need for tears?

W.K.J.

GUILLERMO MOLINAS ROLÓN
1892–1947   Paraguay

From Misiones came Molinas Rolón to Asunción in
1913 when Pablo Max Insfrán, Leopoldo Centurión,
and Roque Capece Faraone were bringing new life to
Paraguayan letters with their magazine *Crónica*. A
lover of nature, Molinas wrote voluminously for a
while, then joined the drinking, drug-taking literary
circle. Being still further upset by his study of magic,
symbols, and spells, he returned to his home and his
death. His poetry is only now being collected and an
appreciation of his high place in Paraguayan poetry is
developing.

SPRING

It's time for Life and Love to come. Arise!
Your passing tribulations all have fled.
Awake! The honey suckle you thought dead
Now bursts with flowers that sweetest perfume make.
All through the woods you hear the call of Spring
And every bird on every leafy tree
Greets the new world with full-throat melody,
And to our door to greet us comes awing.

I see a vision in your lovely eyes
Full of the glorious iridescence Phoebus knew,
And in your hair, softness of twilight skies.
Come, darling, come, and let my kiss for you

Be a luminous seal upon your brow. Arise!
Immortal Spring is here! Give thanks anew!

W.K.J.

HERIB CAMPOS CERVERA
1905–1953   Paraguay

Though Campos Cervera left only one published volume, *Ceniza redimida* ("Liberated Ashes") (1950) he
wrote Surrealistic poetry that influenced Augusto Roa
Bastos, Elvio Romero, and others. Basically a melancholic poet, though he wrote of politics, war, the social
problems of his country, and his personal fear of death,
his best works, which rank him among the greatest of
his nation, express his longing for friends and country,
and were the product of his life in exile. One is "Un
puñado de tierra," here translated.

A HANDFUL OF EARTH

I

A handful of earth
From your profound expanse,
From your level of eternal solitude,
From your forehead of clay,
Impregnated by your germinal sobbing.

A handful of earth
With the simple affection of your minerals
And the helpless sweetness of roots;
A handful of earth that carries on its lips
The smiles and blood of your dead.

A handful of earth
To shelter in its warm multiplicity
All the chill that comes at thoughts of death,
And whatever shade remains in your woods
To guard my eyelids in sleep.

I sought of you a night of orange blossoms.
I sought your warm and wooded meridian,
And I sought the forest of your heart.
I sought the minerals residing
Deep within your buried body.
All that I sought of you,
Land of my happiness and my sorrow.
All that I sought of you!

II

And now I ask again,
Naked and desolate,
On a cliff of memories;
Lost amid the confused memories,
Naked and desolate,
Far from the firm symbol of your blood.

No longer do I see the far-off jasmine of your stars,
Nor the nightly harassment of your selvas;
Nothing! Neither your days of guitars and knives
Nor the forgetful clearness of your evening sky.

Alone, like a rock or a moan,
I call to you, and when I seek
To return to the stature of your name,
I know that the rock is rock, and that the water of the river
Flows from your overwhelmed girdle, and the birds
Make use of the lofty shelter of the humiliated tree
As a precipice of their song and their winds.

III

But walking like this under different clouds,
Amid the artificial profiles of other cities,
Suddenly I find you again.
Amid unconquered solitudes
Or blind roads of music and wheat fields,
I discover you at my side, stretched out
With your crown of martyrdom
And your limpid memory of Guaraníes and oranges.

You are in me; you walk in my step;
You speak through my throat; you arise with me,
And you die each night, when I die.
All your banners are part of me,
And your honest hands of a laborer,
And your small, irremediable moon.

Inevitably—
As constant as the constellations in their orbits—
There come to me, ever present and earthy,
Your torrential hair of showers,
The nostalgia of your sea;
The immense grief of your thirst plains.

You dwell in me and I in you,
Submerged in your wounds
I watch your forehead that, dying, lives again.
I am at peace with you.
Neither the crows nor the hatred
Can separate me from your side.
I carry your root and your sun
On the mountain peaks of my shoulders.

A handful of earth
That did I seek from you,
That do I have from you.

W.K.J.

JOSEFINA PLA
1907–   Paraguay

Josefina Pla came from the Canary Islands and published her first sensitive volume of poetry, *El precio de
los sueños* ("The Price of Dreams") (1934), at a bad
time. Following a literary surge headed by the magazine
Juventud, and by the short-lived Heriberto Fernández
(1903–1927) had come the Chaco War that brought
out newspaper verse more patriotic than poetic. So her
work took a long time to shock writers out of their ruts.
Meanwhile she continued writing, experimenting, introducing Surrealism to the Paraguayans, and being regarded as more Paraguayan than many Paraguayans.
Now recognized as the nation's greatest poetess, she
continues producing poetry, along with dramas and
criticisms. The second of the translated poems is a
product of 1960.

TRIPTYCH OF REBIRTH
IN SHADOW

I

Say not: 'T is ashes!
From the very ash
To prove you're lying,
The foliage will grow green again.
Say not: 'T was foam
Against a shallow reef!
For foam is water, too,
And once again you'll be a wave.

II

Through mortal landscape
Of dreams without a dawn,

Your compass must be guide
To useless tenderness.

Love. Though unwounded,
Having neither veins nor knife,
Blood gushes out.
(A bewitched stream
Where die the birds,
 And moon is blotted out.)

Love, Love! The four
Arms of a cross
To bear anew upon one's shoulder.
Love! Who has named it?
Who is awakened by its kiss?
My heart, a steed
Madly in flight.
All time stands still.

Over my tired eyes
Drift in slow voyages
The shipwrecked sails
Of many wounded dreams.

They pass, not to return
Toward the hushed shore
Where end in silence all
My aspirations born
Under unlucky signs,

Shore bathed in sleepy waves
And muted winds, like hooded monks.
There is no mourning there
Since waves themselves are tears.
There moaning is forbidden
Because the rocks suffer.

> And high above the coast
> Like a dark, distant bird,
> A fluttering banner bears
> The words:
>> Forever more!

W.K.J.

FOREVER

Any drop of dew whatever,
The ephemeral drop on the tip of a leaf,
Containing in its liquid pupil the secret of light and shadow,
A drop with its neophyte spark
That tries tirelessly, again and again, to be
A purer diamond, a clearer star . . .
So has it always been.

Lips creating honey and embers
Around a kiss, always widowed; lips
Like twin skiffs, with sleeping oarsmen, sail
Aimlesssly toward the dull and misty pool
Of boredom . . .
So has it always been.

A cry, a golondrina of knives, cutting its way
Through the perpetually virgin and ignorant wind,
A meteor wounding with its spurs the lungs of air
From the depth of the heart
To beyond all hearing,
A cry without beginning or end
Coming from a dotted line of cries,
An interminable dagger with an edge of hot obscurity,
Its point of terror
Its hilt of presentiment . . .
So has it always been.

A leaf freed from its languid equilibrium
In search of dreams, shattered into a thousand vigils;
A leaf facing the sun, falling toward the shadows
Tired of being so distant, tired of its height, tired
Of being the cutting edge of the wind,
Of being a wing that cannot fly,
Of being a song without echo, without accompaniment,
A leaf falling wearily from its height
And from its solitude among a thousand leaves
All with the same song, chained when they would take
    flight . . .
So it will be forever.

                                                            W.K.J.

AUGUSTO ROA BASTOS

1918–   Paraguay

Perhaps because of the violent criticism that greeted
his first book of verse, *El ruiseñor de la aurora* ("Night-
ingale of Dawn"), as well as the greater success of his
fiction, *El trueno entre las hojas* ("Thunder Among
the Leaves"), Roa Bastos did not complete his *El
naranjal ardiente* ("The Ardent Orange Grove") till
1960. The poems printed separately from it show this
disciple of Josefina Pla to be a poet of deep feeling and
excellent technique.

TRIPTYCH FROM THE
FOUR ELEMENTS

I

The fire forgets its face within the embers.
The waters on the earth find chill and sadness.
The wind illuminated by its madness,

Its wing amid the breeze no more remembers.
Only what won't endure can be eternal,
And what endures is full of promised death.
As I grow old with pulsing heart and breath
I see a mound of ashes, heat infernal.

I'm part of that same fire that snuffs me out,
Thirst of the sand that on my forehead feeds,
Face in the water, wound in the air about.
A thread of motionless dust, wind-blown, astray,
With its four elements completes my needs
And, unfelt, builds my nothingness each day.

II

Upon the water once my name I traced.
The instant it remained stretched endlessly.
My terror made it seem eternity
Before the moving flood that name erased.
Letters of silver in the chilly blue
Written with calmness, yet deliberate rage,
As my reflected image in the watery page
Watched all I did and kept me full in view.

III

My writing finger rose. I seemed to sense
Life's voice. I closed my eyes. My hand pressed tight
My ribs, as though I felt a wound intense.
Then in that instant always to abide
Within my memory, a piece of night.
A childhood light of life fell at my side . . .

W.K.J.

ELVIO ROMERO
1927–   Paraguay

Romero, a follower of Campos Cervera, is a poet of the
people and one of the important figures in today's
Paraguayan poetry. Love of the land is characteristic,
even though sometimes weakened by touches of Romanticism and a nostalgic view of his country. He
has published four volumes of forceful verse with three
more ready for the printer. This "Guitara pueblera" is
from his *El sol bajo las raíces* ("The Sun Under the
Roots") (1956).

THE GUITAR OF THE PEOPLE

The guitar of the common folks
Bleeds and weeps,
Bleeds and weeps in pain.
Its wood becomes excited,
Its pegs resonate,
Its body is covered with ashes
And the guitar clothes itself
With sad and beautiful shadows.
Fettered and foreign
Is the guitar of common folks.

Dense, strange guitar,
Poor, poor,
Cold, obstinate body.
Black night rests on top
Of its strings, copper
Chained to the wind,
Tangled in the air.
We draw near its whiteness,
Guitar of common folks.

When it bleeds,
The wood seeks to rise.
A laborer is its lowest string
With no abode and none to mourn.
Its neck a sweaty ploughtail,
A farmer's glance
That does not see his harvest,
Spoils of the dawn,
Guitar of common folks.

But a banner, too,
When the people want it;
A restorer of health
From their wounds and their sterile existence;
A seed for sowing,
Fugitive, dazzling,
Oh, the song and the resonance
Of the guitar of the common folks!

W.K.J.

LEOPOLDO LUGONES

1874–1939   Argentina

Lugones, most famous of Argentine Modernists, tried his hand at every sort of poetry, and even made somewhat of a reputation with a kind of poetic prose, written at the encouragement of his friend Horacio Quiroga. Under the influence of Walt Whitman and Victor Hugo, he published his first volume of verse, *Montañas de oro* ("Mountains of Gold") (1897), in unrhymed free verse separated only by dashes, and printed like prose. It was generally disregarded. Eight years later appeared *Crepúsculos del jardín* ("Twilights in the Garden") (1905), using some of the devices of the Parnassians, but also containing "El solterón" ("The Bachelor"), which marks his beginning of realism, as a reminiscing old man catalogues his bed-room. It ended Lugones' strident period and indicated his quest for novelty in comparisons. Carrying his search even farther, *Lunario sentimental* ("Sentimenal Calendar") (1909), while a "lunar almanac including about all that anyone ever wrote about the moon," according to one critic, drew heavily on science and medicine for its figures, and was probably the most influential of his volumes.

The demand of the centenary of Argentine Independence ended this phase of artificiality as Lugones wrote the patriotic *Odas seculares*. In later volumes, *Libro de los paisajes* ("Book of Landscapes") (1917) and *Poemas solariegos* ("Ancestral Poems") (1928), he returned to some of his earlier styles and showed that when this modern Góngora wrote with precision and polish, few of his contemporaries could equal him.

In his kaleidoscopic career, Lugones followed many models: Poe, Baudelaire, Herrera y Reissig, and many others, but managed always to add his own personal touch. A socialist, nationalist, general enemy of Spain and admirer of the United States and France, he brought his career to an end by suicide.

THE GIFT OF DAY

Amid the glory of the sun, the world
　　A-tremble lifts in tossing clouds and blue
Melodious architraves, with towers unfurled
　　Like festal banners to the daylight's view.

Afar prophetic sounds the cock's loud call
　　Hierophant before the gates of light;
Amid his radiant canticle stirs all
　　His emerald plumage in its joyous might.

And every little pebble shines with gold;
　　The harvest fields exhale their fragrant heat;

Swept are the woods with waves of shadows old;—
Day is like bread, a blessing clean and sweet.

Garret Strange

A MESSAGE

Dove, if you're flying to the bower
Beyond the land and sea
Where my love lies, take her from me,
My message in a flower.

With swift wings you will not be long,
Then on her roof take rest
And let the passion in my breast
Thrill through your sweetest song.

Come quickly back should she receive
My message with a sigh.
But if disdain is in her eye,
You need not haste to leave.

Should you sometime come back to me,
Say nothing, nor abide.
You'll find me lying dead beside
A mournful cypress tree.

W.K.J.

JOURNEY

I met upon the road
A woman and a man,
And a tree that genuflected
Before the wind;
Farther on, a browsing burro;

And still farther, a heap of stones.
And in three thousand leagues of my spirit
There was nothing more than these:
A tree, a stone, a burro,
A woman and a man.

Muna Lee

DROPS OF GOLD

Mystery.
With creeping strides,
As a panther might,
From the forest glides
The starry night.

Autumn Poem.
Slow gold from the poplar rains
Over the lake of blue.
Nothing is there but the swan
And you.

Blot.
The moon is tilted on the brink,
An inkwell alabaster pale;
It spills a flood upon its trail,
A shining blot of golden ink.

Dawn.
At the quiet edge of the world,
Night in a starry gown
Lifts her azure urn
And turns it upside down.
Two, three golden drops still fall
That its shadowy depths were keeping . . .

Over her cool white arm
The light of dawn comes peeping.

Danger.
A love that laughs
You may freely flout;
A love that sings
You may easily doubt.

But never mock
Love silent, still;
This, like grief,
    Can kill.

Alice J. McVan

THE CULT OF THE FLOWER

"Nothing important," said the renowned philosopher, "nothing important do we do in our life without flowers. This, perchance, is the most characteristic note of civilization. By bringing flowers into his daily life, man began to be loveable.

"And woman sentimental," he added with a complimentary smile for the beautiful Andrea, on whose bosom a snowflake of jasmine posited a poetic contradiction to the sweet fire of the twin doves nestling beneath.

"Hear, for example, how the first bohemian came to be: The savage youths who loved in the primitive forests paid their court by means of presents: the choicest fruits and the firstlings of the chase. One of them sallied forth upon a day, with his arrow and his fish-hook, in search of the well-known present.

"The river offered him, as always, the sure promise of the silver fish which he wished to have more beautiful than ever. While, however, the hook, left to the movement of the current, tempted with its bait, the fisherman began to think how beautiful would be the feet of his beloved, wading in the brook that rippled over the shining pebbles: little feet that the water would surround with crystal.

"This distracted him so much that the longed-for fish came, took the bait, began to pull . . . oh, little feet of maidens in the limpid water . . . pulled harder and harder . . . and carried away the hook!

"Then the savage youth went hunting. Soon he found a beautiful bird on the tip of a *hugeous* tree. To see it and let fly an arrow was one and the same thing. But his arrow missed, not without his being aware that there was, in the brief flight of his dart, a likeness to the glance of his sweet love. This impression, however, was so vague that, in order to make sure, he sent another arrow, and another, and another . .

"When he had exhausted his quiver, he thought with terror that it was now impossible to hunt any more this day. Then he betook himself to an old apple tree where there was an apple, just one, but the most beautiful ever seen. Only that, when he had it in his hands, he felt the cheeks of his darling so near that he could do no less than kiss them on the fruit; and since from kissing to biting is but a step when it comes to tempting objects, behold the savage youth suddenly converted his apple into an unsolvable problem! He ate it up.

"Defeated in all his plans as a prudent lover, he was returning sadly across the meadow. He was not carrying to his dear one either the silver fish or the firstling of the chase, or his usual gift of fruit. Suddenly it occurred to him to notice the flowers he was trampling under foot.

"The first of love's nosegays was rejected by the object of his worship. It was not the fashion. But the first bohemian had come into being, by culling the flowers of infinite misery; the flowers with which life is beautified, even when there is no bread.

"Another day I shall tell you how the oracle of the daisy originated."

Anon. (Inter-America, Vol. 1)

ENRIQUE BANCHS
1888–   Argentina

Argentina's first great poet after Lugones was Banchs,
whose literary career covered only four years. He began
with *Las barcas* ("Ships") (1907), and the excellent *El
cascabel del halcón* ("The Falcon's Bell") (1909).
After *La urna* ("The Urn") (1911) he gave up writing, yet he had produced enough to establish his reputation. In simple verse with humble themes, his ballads
clothed the Golden Age in modern spirit. In their repetition of words and phrases, they suggest Scotch ballads. The repetition of the original is followed in this
translation of "Balbuceo." In sonnets, Banchs could be
profound and subtle, like Petrarch, to whom he dedicated his sonnet "Thou Gallant Spirit." His mastery of
technique allowed full play for delicacy of expression
and creation of emotion.

BABBLING

Melancholy is our household,
Lonely, too, be it confessed.
Since you went, there's left but little
Of your warmth within the nest.

Since you went, I, too, am lonely.
That's a truth to be confessed.
But I know you'll be returning
Some day soon, back to the nest.

If you only knew how greatly
Both the house and I love you!
Some day when again you enter
You will see how we love you.

Never could I tell you fully
All the love we feel for you.
Like a heap of stars a-twinkle
Is the love we feel for you.

If you never planned returning,
Better far that I should die,
But I feel you'd be unwilling,
Never wanting me to die.

Well-beloved, who went and left us,
Won't you say that you'll return?
So that we don't mourn forever,
Won't you say that you'll return?

W.K.J.

TIGER (IRIDESCENT FLANKS)

The tiger's flank turns like a golden flower,
Sinuous his walk and suave as flowing verse.
Malignant hate has burnished to brilliance terse
The gleaming topaz of his eyes' fierce power.
With muscles taut and limbs that treacherous cower,
With tawny thighs, both languid and perverse,
He crouches low. The falling leaves disperse
Upon his still repose a bright-hued shower.

In the silence of the jungle, where at rest
With flat-nosed head between his paws he spies,
His pupils motionless, intrepid wait.
Beating his curling tail with nervous zest,
He flays the fennels which about him rise,
Restrained in deadly ambush—such my hate.

Elizabeth du Gue Trapier

ALFONSINA STORNI
1892–1938   Argentina

A pagan full of the pain of living was Miss Storni, one
of Latin America's great women poets. Love of nature
in all its sensual forms, together with a desire to be
loved unstintingly, characterized her poetry. Death and
the transmigration of the soul also gradually crept into
her verses. With *El dulce daño* ("Sweet Danger")
(1918), her first important volume, she began her feud
against men and against conformity and materialism.
By her poem "Cuadros y ángulos," she anticipated the
modern scorn of Squares.

"I am superior to the average man about me," she
wrote. "But physically as a woman, I am his slave, his
clay to be molded. I cannot love freely; I have too much
pride to submit to man."

With *Mundo de siete pozos* ("World of Seven
Wells") (1934), she gave up her erotic poetry for a style
full of Symbolism. The title refers to the seven openings
in the skull. It was followed by a collection of unrhymed sonnets, *Mascarilla y trébol* ("Mask and
Trefoil") (1938), whose chilly reception convinced
her that she was written out, so, on October 24, 1938,
she wrote the unrhymed "Voy a dormir" ("I Am Going
to Sleep") and cast herself into the ocean.

SQUARES AND ANGLES

Houses in a line, in a line,
In a line there,
Squares, squares, squares,
In a line there.
Even people now have square souls,
Ideas in file, I declare,

And on their shoulders, angles wear.
Just yesterday I shed a tear and it
Oh, God, was square!

W.K.J.

LITTLE MAN

Little man, O little man,
Your canary wants freedom, so let it fly free,
O little man, I am that captive bird.
Let go of me!

I was caged, O little man,
By your strong bars all surrounded, little man.
I call you small, since me you have not fathomed,
And never can.

Nor do I fathom you,
So open the cage door and let me fly free.
Once, little man, I loved you half an hour.
Ask no more of me!

W.K.J.

INHERITANCE

You said to me: "My father did not weep,
Nor my grandfather weep." I heard you say:
"No man of all my race has ever wept;
Of steel were they."

And thus upon my trembling mouth I felt
The poison of your bitter teardrop fall,
Worse potion than my lips have ever quaffed
From a cup so small.

Weak woman, born all grief to comprehend,
I drank the pain of ages infinite;
But oh, my wretched soul cannot support
The weight of it!

Jessie Read Wendell

SHE WHO UNDERSTANDS

Her dark head fallen forward in her grief,
The beauteous woman kneels in suppliant fashion—
A woman past her youth; the dying Christ
From the stern rood looks on her with compassion.

A burden of vast sadness in her eyes,
Beneath her heart a child, a burden human.
Before the white Christ bleeding there she prays:
"Lord, do not let my child be born a woman!"

Alice Stone Blackwell

LIGHTHOUSE IN THE NIGHT

A black sphere is the heavens:
A black disk is the sea;
The lighthouse on the coast
Casts its light-fan far and free.

For whom is it searching,
Whirling unceasingly?
If in my heart it is seeking
The living heart of me,

Let it look on the black rock
Where perceived it will be.

There's no blood, though a raven
Pecks it eternally.

W.K.J.

I AM GOING TO SLEEP

Oh, kindly nurse, you with the teeth of flowers,
With hair of dew and open hands of grass,
Lend me, I beg, some earthy sheets and quilt
Of plucked-out moss, in place of eiderdown.
For I would sleep, dear nurse. Put me to bed
And at my head gently set down as lamp
A constellation. Any one will do.
They're all so lovely. Turn it down a bit.

Leave me alone where I can hear things grow.—
"A heavenly foot will rock you to and fro.
A bird will sing a constant lullabye
So you'll forget."—Oh, thanks! One more request:
If he should telephone to me again,
Tell him not to persist. I have gone out.

W.K.J.

JORGE LUIS BORGES
1899–   Argentina

One of Argentina's leading intellectuals of today is
Borges, who studied in Switzerland during World
War I, then went to Spain, where he was associated
with Rafael Casinos Assens in the Ultraist movement
that he introduced into Argentina in 1921. Through
magazines, like *Prisma* and *Proa*, which he founded
with Güiraldes in 1924, he influenced younger Argentines, while he himself was writing both semi-
Surrealistic and mystic poetry, and translating Faulkner,

Joyce, Virginia Wolff, Gide, and Kafka. He published
several volumes of realistic, though not naturalistic, poetry, with romantic symbolism and daring and unusual
metaphors, in which emotion was more important than
meter. Also he tried to picture in verse the beauty he
saw in Argentine streets and houses. They contained in-
tellectual symbols of universal philosophy. He could
be a poet and a metaphysicist at the same time. Some
critics say he voices the Americanism of which Darío
dreamed and to which Chocano aspired. Eventually,
however, he gradually abandoned verse for short stories.

TO RAFAEL CASINOS ASSENS

A last long walk over the exciting heights
Of the viaduct's span.
At our feet, the wind seeks sails, and the stars—
Hearts of God—throb intensity.
How pleasing night's taste pierced by shadows,
Night, once more a habit of our flesh!
The last night of our conversation before there come
Between us leagues of distance.
Still we share the silence where, like meadows,
Voices are resplendent.
Still is dawn a bird lost in the vileness,
In the uttermost parts of the world.
Our last night, protected from the great wind of absence.
Delightful home of the heart, that grip of the fiery horseman
Who knows how to rein in an agile tomorrow.
How tragic the inward goodbye, like that of every event
Of which time is a part.
It is hard to realize that we shall not even have the stars in com-
  mon.
When afternoon is quietness in my patio, from your manu-
  scripts,
Morning will surge.

The shadow of my summer will be your winter.
And your daylight will be the glory of my shade.
Still we persist together;
Still our two voices blend in agreement,
Like intensity and tenderness in the setting sun.

W.K.J.

LATE AFTERNOON

The viol
no longer tells its love upon your lap.
Silence that lives in mirrors
    has formed its cell.
Darkness is the blood
    of wounded things.
In the puny sundown,
    mutilated eve
prays a "Hail Mary" in technicolor.

Chesley M. Hutchings

A PATIO

As afternoon declines
The two or three colors of the patio become tired.
The great frankness of the moon no longer fills
With enthusiasm, its usual firmament.
Today, since the sky is overcast,
Diviners will say that a little angel has died.
The patio, a sky with boundaries.
The patio is the window
Through which God looks at souls.
The patio is the hillside
Through which the sky spills down into the house.
Serene,

Eternity awaits in the labyrinth of stars.
Pleasant it is to live in the obscure friendship
Of a vestibule, an overhanging roof, or a pool.

W.K.J.

BUTCHERSHOP

More vile than any bawdy house,
The butchershop leaves its insulting mark on the street;
Above the entrance
A sculptured cow's head
With its sightless stare and stretching horns,
Is master of a witch's revelry
Of coarse meat and eternal marble,
With the impassive majesty of an idol
Or the impassible firmness
Of the written word next to one spoken.

W.K.J.

CÉSAR TIEMPO
1906–   Argentina

Under the pen name of "César Tiempo," a Russian
Jew, Israel Zeitlin, born in the Ukraine, became an important figure in Argentine literature. Not only did he
edit the newspapers *Crítica* and *El Sol*, but he wrote
poems, prize-winning plays like *Pan criollo* ("Creole
Bread") (1937), and essays. He served as secretary of
the Argentine Society of Authors. Beginning with
Versos de una . . . , he wrote about his people in
Libro para la pausa del sábado ("Book for the Saturday
Pause") (1930), *Sabatión argentino* ("Argentine Sabbath") (1933) and *Sabadomingo* ("Saturday-Sunday")
(1938). In bitter protests in Biblical language, he offers

his social criticism with no racial distinction, unless perhaps the Jews are most severely criticized.

HARANGUE ON THE DEATH OF CHAYIM NACHMAN BIALIK

What other interest than that of the present moment can a people have which must drag itself through the shadows and the abysses? BIALIK

On July 5 the Associated Press gave the news to the world:
Chayim Nachman Bialik had died in Vienna.

Twenty days later, and in the same city,
they put an end to Dollfuss, the "millimetternich."

Look out for poets
whose fists pound on the desks of hangmen!

The world's dailies were able
to publish the item on the Society Page,
next to the account of the party
with which the Barabanchik family
celebrated the circumcision of their offspring.

I have a violent heart
and a harsh voice.
I walk the streets of the Jewish Quarter
weighed down by my anger and my grief.

Brothers of Buenos Aires,
our proudest poet is dead.
As in the Psalms,
God guided him with strength and made straight his way.

Minkowski was plaintive,
Bialik an imprecation.

And both will rot under the earth,
facing the blind eyes of tremendous night.
A shirtsleeve sky runs over the roofs.
The peddlers in the *Pilsen* are at their endless game of dominoes.
Girls who want to get married don't walk under scaffolding.

You bourgeois who break all the Commandments
and spend your Sabbaths over your books bound in black,
stroking the spines of the figures
in order to make them stretch out like cats,
I have seen you in your glittering temples—
ranged like thoroughbreds in sumptuous stalls—
and your round lifeless little eyes,
with your formal tall hats and your pure silk prayer-shawls,
trying to bribe God
who knows you better than your employees.

Chayim Nachman Bialik is dead.

There's gefüllte fish today in "The International,"
and a good stock of doctors for your poor drooping daughters.

Who remembers the massacres in the Ukraine,
the raving storm of the pogroms,
where hooligans raped your mothers
and you were trembling in your cellars, useless
as a ray of light striking a mirror?

Bialik shouted, he thundered across the black waters,
and his angry laughter ran through the villages like a wild wind.
"The people are withered grass,
they have gone dry as timber."

And there were youths who shook themselves like wolf cubs
and their sharp teeth tore our shame to shreds.

Chayim Nachman Bialik is dead.

The old-clothes dealers smile in the doorways of their pande-
    moniums.
The Lacroze trolleys are greener than ever.

Cast thy bread upon the water, says Ecclestiastes.

How nice to hear Mischa Elman from a soft orchestra seat
at the Colón.
Gorki said that with Bialik the Jewish race gave a new Homer
    to the world.

Would the Bank of Israel give him credit on just one signature?

Voices:
"Tonight when the store's closed and I'm dunking my toast in
    a glass of tea, I'm going to ask my Missus to read me
    The Bird and *The Garden*, and after supper we're going
    to the Ombú Theatre; if you want to get on the 'Com-
    mittee,' you've got to be on your toes."

Chayim Nachman Bialik is dead.

"Ma, will I wash my hair with kerosene and put on my sky-blue
    satin dress to go to the Library?"—"All right, darling, and
    mind you get yourself a young man, like the rest of the
    girls: it's about time."

Chayim Nachman Bialik is dead.

At the door of the People's Kitchen, our brothers, the ones who
    haven't the courage to starve to death, are waiting for their
    rations.

Our legs drag through the deepest marshes of the night and
above our heads shines a pure light.

In Tel-Aviv there was a poet.
And now?

Donald D. Walsh

JULIO HERRERA Y REISSIG
1875–1910   Uruguay

Many Latin Americans combine politics and letters.
Herrera y Reissig, though nephew of an Uruguayan
president, preferred to concentrate on poetry in his
Tower of Panoramas, the attic of his father's house,
decorated with Doré drawings. During ten years he ex-
changed ideas with a group of bohemian friends and
published a book of verse every two years: *Pascuas del
tiempo* ("Dawn's Festival") (1900), *Los maitines de
la noche* ("Night's Matins") (1902), *Los éxtasis de
la montaña* ("Ecstasies of the Mountains") (1904),
etc., then died of an overdose of morphine.

Herrera was an outstanding Symbolist of the Modernist group, and laid the foundations for the acceptance of Ultraism, that fleeting, though powerful
movement of the 20's that developed a new Gongorism
and freshened poetic language. González Martínez and
Huidobro, the exponent of Creationism, acknowledged
their debt to him. At his death, the Uruguayan government broke precedent by sponsoring a five-volume edition of his complete works.

Said Herrera of Symbolism: "Once you combine the
soul of harmony and the soul of the idea, there is released . . . a strange wave of sound, the intimate echo
of the mind . . . a psychic X for each to solve in his
own way." In contrast to Darío's early cult of the artificial, Herrera wrote of ordinary things, but because of
his horror of the commonplace, he used exuberant

vocabulary and striking figures that sometimes resulted in obscurity. Yet at the same time, his realistic treatment of rural life, often in sonnet form, exemplified in "Los carros" ("The Carts") (1904, pub. 1910), anticipated the work of Lugones.

When critics made fun of some of his extravagant poetry, Herrera bought advertising space in a newspaper for:

A DECREE

I HATE THE ABOMINATION OF BEING CATALOGUED. I AM MYSELF ALONE. I HEREBY PROCLAIM THE IMMUNITY OF MY PERSON. I AM EMPEROR. IT BOTHERS ME TO HAVE CERTAIN BARBAROUS CRITICS TRY TO TRIM MY BEARD. LET THE GODS ALONE.
                      (Signed) I, JULIO

THE CARTS

Long ere the noisy barnyard sounds, or ere
The dusky smithy strikes the morning lay,—
Ere chemist wakes or barber starts his day,
A single lamp burns,—lightless on the square.
Athwart the melancholy dawning fare
The oxen throwing up their furrow way;
Beneath the gloom of the unsettled gray
The plowman mutters rustic curses there.

Meantime the lordly manor dreams.—The jet
Through its old marble speaks the fountain's soul;
And where the tranquil shepherd's star is set,
Waking the lone path's yearning for its goal
Of old, slow breathing airs in echo roll
From tinkling carts the daybreaks ne'er forget.

                                        Thomas Walsh

THE PRIEST

He is the *cura*. Long the silent peaks
Have watched him breast his hardships on his knees,—
Risking the passes when the winters freeze,—
Taking the lonely routes the moonlight seeks.
As though by magic, 'neath his blessing hand
A plenteous harvest its responses speaks;
His very mule indulgenced graces leaks
That lift the parish to a heavenly land.

From his asperges to his clogs and hook
He turns in readiness to drain his brook
Of mountain gold to deck his altar crude;
His preaching through a breath of basil sounds,—
A nephew is his only turpitude—
His piety with cowlike airs abounds.

Thomas Walsh

THE PARISH CHURCH

In blessed silence vegetates the place;
The wax-faced Virgins sleep in their attire
Of livid velvets and discolored wire,
And Gabriel's trumpet wearies on his face.
A marble yawn the dried-up font would trace;
There sneezes an old woman in the choir;
And in the sun-shaft dust the flies aspire,
As though 't were Jacob's ladder for their grace.

The good old soul is starting at her chores;
She shakes the poor-box, and in reverence pores
To find how the Saint Vincent alms are going;
Then here and there her feather duster hies;

While through the vestry doorway come the cries
From out the barnyard and the gallant crowing.

Thomas Walsh

THE QUARREL

It happened thus: lilac and heliotrope beguiled
Your window, wafted on the evening air.
Night within your dusky pupils smiled
As if she your better sister were.
My trembling lip and your fresh countenance took
A halting air of uneasiness profound;
You through the open lattice feigned to look;
I, to dream to the far-off sheep-bell's sound.

Vibrated the whip-lash of a sharp farewell.
A swaying blade in the wind you seemed to stand.
And just as I, emboldened, began to dwell
Upon the sovereign rhythms of my theme,
Unsheathing it suddenly from a glove of cream,
Like a dagger you presented me your hand.

Muna Lee

JUANA IBARBOUROU
1895–　　　　　　　　　　　　　　　　　　　　Uruguay

Educator, poet, and great soul, Miss Ibarbourou of Uruguay has been called *"Juana of America"* because of the
way she has spoken for the continent in her many books
of verse. Chiefly, however, this "Poet Laureate of Spanish America" speaks for women, beginning as a pagan
about the temptations of the flesh in her earliest *Las
lenguas de díamantes* ("Diamond Tongues") (1918).
Later she wrote of happy family life and the beauties of

the landscape. During one phase she turned to the
Bible and produced the mystical *Estampas de la Biblia,
poemas en prosa* ("Bible Scenes: Poems in Prose")
(1938). But whatever the theme, she is a master crafts-
man, writing beautiful verse, simple in structure but
with rich imagery and delicate feminine sensitivity.

MARCH TWILIGHT

The afternoon goes climbing toward the night,
A river opulant and warm
With perfume of peaches and grapes,
With murmur of laughter and tears,
With the gasp of fear,
With a spiraling song,
A full-rigged ship it is that wafts me
Toward the lofty, mysterious shadow,
With no one to clasp my waist
In strong, protective arm.

I am erect, with neither voice nor smile.
White in the night's immense solitude;
With the red coals of poetry in my throat,
And in my breast a thirst for adventure.

The last magnolias of Summer
Provide a cool resting place for my weariness:
The fading flame of twilight
Still dimly lives
In the secret net of arteries;
I go to meet the Three Marys.

Oh, how sad, how calm and brave,
That woman who mounts toward the night
Without a tremor, as if she were
The only sleepless traveler!

She knows of the encounter with phantoms
In the burning files of memory,
And the anguish of human sorrow,
A splitting wail in the silence.

Tomorrow she will reach the new dawn
Exhausted by suffering,
As if she had been in the foundry
Where clamor and prayers are fused.

And she will disembark weeping
Because she could not see heaven clearly.

W.K.J.

FLEETING RESTLESSNESS

I have eaten apples and have kissed your lips.
I have embraced the dark and resinous pines,
In flowing waters plunged my restless hands.
I have penetrated the dim cedar forest,
A dull-hued snake across the level plain;
My feet have raced along the rocky paths
Which bind the mountain as a sash is bound.

O love, be not angry with my restlessness.
O love, do not complain because I laugh and sing.
A day will come when I'm forever still,
Ay, ever and forever,
With my hands crossed and my eyes closed,
With my ears deafened and my mouth dumb,
With my feet that were roving, now in still repose
In the black earth
And the crystal vase of my clear laughter broken
In the obstinate crevices of my closed lips.

Then, though you say, "Go!" I shall not go.
And though you say, "Sing!" I shall not sing.
I shall be crumbling in cold silence
Beneath the black earth,
And over me life buzzing
Like a drunken bee.

Oh, let me enjoy the sweetness
Of the fleeting hour.
Oh, let the naked rose of my mouth
Weigh down your lips.

Afterwards I shall be ashes beneath the black earth.

Elizabeth du Gue Trapier

LULLABIES

The Morning Star grew angry,
The Moon began to weep,
Because my little darling
Refused to go to sleep.

So go to sleep, Natacha,
And make the Moon so glad
That he will bring you olives,
The best you've ever had.

. . . .

The mama wolf went shopping
To buy her little brat
A pair of silken breeches
To match his pretty hat.

The mama wolf went walking
Looking so gay and coy,

And close behind her trotted
Her ugly little boy.

The mama wolf is coming
And she will soon appear
If you, my baby darling,
Don't go to sleep—you hear!

————

The sandman wanders somewhere,
I know, in search of me.
Run quickly, little mousey,
And see where he can be.

"Oh, mistress, I must tell you,
I saw him dancing there
With two blonde lovely ladies
Upon the palace stair."

Please tell him that Natacha
Now wants to sleep awhile.
She's like a little angel,
So good she'll make him smile.

Go, tell the sandman: Hurry!
And he'll get a surprise:
A silver necklace and some fruit,
And then she'll close her eyes.

Paul T. Manchester

IN PRAISE OF THE
SPANISH LANGUAGE

Oh, language of war and singing!
  Oh, tongue of old romancers!

Teresa the Mystic spoke you,
    And you gave my love his answers.

The language my mother prays in,
    In which I murmured: "I love you,"
In that bright American midnight
    With millions of stars above you.

Oh, language of richness and beauty,
    So haughty and gallant,—sustaining
Most fitly the haunting music
    Of the sweet guitar's complaining.

Read Bain and *W.K.J.*

LIKE THE SPRINGTIME

Like a black wing did I spread my hair
        Over my knees.
Closing thine eyes thou didst breathe in its perfume
        Saying to me the while:
"Art wont to sleep on moss-covered stones?
With twigs of willow dost bind thy tresses?
Is thy pillow of clover? Are thy locks so black
Because perhaps into them thou has pressed the juice
Dark and thick, of the woodsy blackberries?
What fresh, strange perfume enfolds thee?
Thou smellest of brooklets, of the earth and of forests.
What perfume dost thou use?" And smiling I said:
        "Not any! Not any!
I love thee and I am young. 'T is the smell of Springtime.
This odor thou notest is that of firm flesh.
Of clear cheeks and new blood.
I love thee and I am young; hence it is I have
The same fragrance as the Springtime."

Anon. (*Inter-America, Vol. 5*)

FERNÁN SILVA VALDÉS
1887–   Uruguay

In Montevideo, Uruguay, in 1921, appeared the volume
Agua del tiempo ("Water of Time") with its first section titled *"Poemas Nativos."* This began the Nativist
school of poetry. It was the intention of its author,
Silva Valdés, to recreate the Creole world more ar-
tistically than in the earlier crude poetry like *Martín
Fierro* and *Santos Vega.* Silva Valdés described the
gaucho, his life and enemies, with many unusual metaphors: "His dagger was a compass needle with the
heart as its North Pole," and "The horseman sheathed
himself in the darkness." Simple and local vocabulary
and irregular meter marked the poems. Contemporary
critics hailed him as an innovator, and young poets imitated him.

THE GAUCHO TROUBADOUR

I. EVOCATION

Troubadour, with your mane like the Nazarene,
Poet of the desert vast,
Not yet does paint or stone your glory immortalize,
In your progress through the world you've reached America at
    last.
Your race first saw the light in far Provence,
And in the Pampas finally closed its eyes.

II. NORTH

Lord of the four-fold compass points,
Adventure-loving, free of habitat,
You used to wander aimlessly,

Yet one by one all routes would finally sweep
Beneath the wide brim of your ragged hat.

III. LIKE THE BIRDS

You did not need much urging to display your art:
A drink, a rival (if he sang well, you'd rejoice).
As birds have song bubbling in their throats,
You used to have your verse ready in your voice.

IV. THE GUITAR

Your guitar in your arms was like a daughter,
  Tiny and motherless,
And you would croon to it so drowsily.
Your guitar in your arms was like a mother
Whose milk, seeping through warm arteries,
Has come even to me!

V. SINGING

Your hat, pushed back with pride upon your head,
Pulled tight against your jaw its leather thong,
And where your beard against your moustache pressed,
Each time you raised your voice in song
Your lips peeped out like a cardinal in its nest.
The whitened skull of cattle used to serve you as a throne,
Or if you'd rise about the earth, a counter was your seat;
An unsophisticated audience squatting on its heels
Would sit around you solemnly in speechlessness complete,
Though from the hitching post outside
A chorus of bridle rings was your accompaniment,
With the metallic tinkle of their beat.

VI. REWARD

No matter where you sang, trailed merriment a-wing.
You used to pass, with festive gayness at your back

And afterward lay silence over the countryside,
Harmonious as a copper kettle, used and black.

Unheeded beauty girt you which you never knew.
Nature, being blind, mingles the good with the bad.
Its showers, wetting you, dirtied your skies, it's true,
Yet reared a rainbow arch of triumph over you.

W.K.J.

THE INDIAN

He came
Who knows from where
With headband like a *benteveo* bird,
And crested like a cardinal.

Little he knew of native land, although he loved his home.
The Spaniards found him rooted deep
Fishing in rivers, hunting in forests, ranging wide.

His ringing war cry served to keep
Eternal obstacles, eternal checks between them and
The vast horizon's sweep.

Molded in clay of stubbornness his slim, sly body passed
Swift as a naked shadow, ever on the run,
Along his well-known hillside steeps,
Its color, copper fused with red; its brawn surpassed by none.
At noise of war, his sharpened instincts tensed,
And in his veins, instead of blood, ran liquid sun.

Instinctive slave of beauty he;
Upon his face he traced a mass of brilliant hues, none pale.
His plumed war bonnet made him no more Indian,
Yet more of color made him more the male.

Master of all the region,
Over trifling hunting quarrel with some neighboring chief
He'd brandish in the wind his courage, keen-edged as a sword;
Like Uruguayan trees he, too, was tough,—trunk, stem, and leaf,
Within, without; his only softness was his uttered word.
The heart of him, as in the hardiest *pitanga* tree,
A sweet and trembling flower seemed to be.

How often his canoe would cut the streams;
One was he with the wildest animal
As he would roam for months on end,
Lured by the never-reached horizon's call,—
His copper hide tanned by the elements;
Reddened by sun or soaked by rainy splash,—
Through those hot, dreary days when locusts chirp,
Or through the long nights bright with lightning's flash.

The Spanish conquest checked his wanderings,
And tribes who widely roamed in any weather
Came clustering in a bunch about a chief,
Boleadora like, going round together.

He had no skill at laughter or at tears;
The puma-bellow at the killing was his only cry,
And when his end came, he passed on without a sound,
His feathers trembling, dying as the wild birds die.

W.K.J.

GASTÓN FIGUEIRA
1905–   Uruguay

Son of the Uruguayan McGuffey whose textbooks
taught generations of Uruguayan children to read, the
present-day Figueira is teaching the children of the
continent to sing. Slim, short, and full of abounding
energy, he is author of thirty volumes of verse that

make him the Pan-American spokesman for human brotherhood and peace. His first book, *Dulces visiones* ("Sweet Visions") (1919), published when he was only fourteen, brought an enthusiastic review by Alfonsina Storni hailing his "deep feeling and originality of theme."

In 1928 appeared *Para los niños de América* ("For the Children of America"), that included verses in English and Portuguese intended to instil in the children of the three Americas a pride in their birthright. That year Figueira also embarked on the ambitious project of a twenty-volume series to include each Pan-American country. The first book of *Maravillosa América* ("Marvelous America,") that appeared in 1931, was dedicated to Brazil. Mexico followed. Several of the poems here translated come from Vol. V, hymning northeast Brazil.

Figueira's poetic creed appears in his *Huyendo del hastío* ("Fleeing Boredom"): "The true artist discovers beauty in every aspect of life however insignificant and humble it may appear, provided he knows how to relate it to that which is infinite."

BALLAD OF LIFE

Life said to me: "Come, now! Your dreams surrender."
To life my dreams I tender.

Life said to me: "Give me your gaiety."
I did, immediately.

Life said to me: "And all your tears I need."
Now am I poor indeed.

Return again!—I'm tired of strife.
And ask for one thing more: my life.

W.K.J.

PRAYER TO THE MOON
OF THE TROPICS

O Moon, our mother, in the heavens thou art.
  Bring us thy kingdom for our consolation.
Each night put bread of dreams into our heart,
              And resignation.

Forgive defects by which we're daily cursed,
  As daily we forgive men's scorn; then soon,
Though wounded oftentimes by beauty-thirst,
  From all blaspheming free us, Moon.   Amen.

                                             W.K.J.

MARACATU   (*an Afro-Brazilian street dance*)

New Orleans, Virginia, Cuba, and Martinique,
Jamaica, Borinquén, immense Brazil . . .
A black nostalgia lurking everywhere,
The same black stridency is everywhere,
Beside green forests, beneath the gleam
Of a sky that indigo shadows fill!
Sugar plantations, fields of coffee and of cotton
Where our ancestors, deprived of hope,
Shed burning tears, forgotten.
Come, let us dance, though eyes be wet,
Oh, oh, uh, uh!
Let us forget! Let us forget!

The blues, the rumba, and the *maracatú*
Are kin.
The sorrows of our ancestors,
Transformed into rhythm, lurk within.

Mornings crazy with birds. Ardent sunshine.
Early evening with timidly pulsating stars.
Peace of a colonial Sabbath.
Gambling shacks, and on the hill
An ancient chapel, on its altar keeping
A Negro saint who hears them weeping.
White and beautiful is the Great Lord's child.
Hard is her heart, and cruel and wild,
Blacker than coal, black and defiled.

Come, let us dance and never stop.
Oh, oh, uh, uh.
We must forget, although we drop.
The blues, the rumba, and the *maracatú*
To the same family belong.
The woes of our ancestors
Converted into song.

Tropical phantoms of palms
Beating out in incessant rhythm, Pocema, Orichá, Mandinga.*
The black heart sings. The black heart weeps.
The black heart is vibrant.
Silhouetted against the diaphanous horizon, the crazy dance
Seems etched in india ink.

Waters of the Amazon, waters of the Mississippi,
That secretly bear out to sea
More tears than you think . . .
The blues, the rumba, and the *maracatú*
One blood possess,
The sorrows of our ancestors
They transform into loveliness.

So let us dance and never cease,
eh, eh, oh, oh, uh, uh,
Forgetfulness will bring us peace.

W.K.J.

* *Gods and voodoos of the Brazilian blacks.*

THE SOUTHERN CROSS

(For the children of the United States and Canada)

When in the tranquil sky of night
Thine arms of light I see,
O thou mysterious Southern Cross,
What joy thou givest me!
Sometimes I think thou sayest: "Come
To this blue land and bright,
And with thy sisters play and sport,
The daughters of the light.
Come to this vast, unbounded realm,
And in mine arms repose.
And thou from here will see the earth,
At play through space she goes.
With beauty and with kindliness,
'Twill make thy spirit burn,
And then to give thy brothers aid,
To earth thou shalt return."
To me the magic Southern Cross
Speaks thus each calm, clear night,
When in the heaven's depth profound
I see its arms of light.
And every night I go away
To those far, starry skies
While sleep my mother woos to me
With lulling melodies,
And a new world of stars I seem
To see within her eyes.

Alice Stone Blackwell

THE PINEAPPLE

(From *For the Children of America*)

With my green, feathered plume
And my pock-marked face, all browned,
I'm an Indian in ambush
On the ground.

W.K.J.

II

FICTION

ALCIDES ARGUEDAS
1879–1946   Bolivia

Arguedas' talent for writing showed itself while he was still a student in La Paz. His first published work was *Pisagua* (1902), based on anecdotes of the War of the Pacific (1879–1883), related by his father. Arguedas then turned his attention to the Bolivian Indians in the novel *Wuata—Wuara* (1904), which was well received. While studying in Paris, he wrote his sociological work, *Pueblo enfermo* ("A Sick People") (1904), about the Indians and their exploitation by society. Despite its critical approach, the work won him appointment from the Bolivian government and a contract to write the section on Bolivia for a French history of South America. Now recognized as an important historian, he also represented his country as a diplomat in Paris, London, and elsewhere.

Arguedas' *Raza de bronce* ("Race of Bronze") (1919) firmly established his reputation as one of the best Bolivian novelists. It opens with a long journey by the Aymará Indians across streams from the *altiplano* or upland to the valley, to sell their products. It goes on to show the mistreatment of this enslaved "Race of Bronze" by the whites who profit by their labor. Here is one section from the novel.

THE FUNERAL OF THE INDIAN

When the Indian died, they dressed him in his best clothes; in the new world to which he was going, he must present himself so as not to deserve anyone's scorn. They put on him his new hemp-sole shoes to prevent his suffering on the long journey ahead; beneath his cap was a handful of grass to absorb the sweat of his fatigue; they fastened on one side of his belt a pouch full of coca and corn—on the other hip was a purse pierced by a needle so he would not suffer hunger or fatigue, and could keep safely the wealth he acquired and repair any clothes torn by the thorns along the way; he had his *quena* and his *zampoña*, the two musical instruments so that he could break the monotony of the journey by playing the tunes he had learned to play as a child; finally they put into his hands some tools so that once at his destination, he could go on working as he had in his old country, and would keep on working forever.

The widow provided abundantly all sorts of food and drink. For this one time, to offer a big banquet for all the friends and relatives of her deceased husband who would stay for the long burial ceremony, she had a little heifer and some sheep and chickens slaughtered, and she herself worked diligently and serenely to get them ready. . .

For two days the corpse was left on a stretcher in the patio and it was watched over by almost all the laborers of the village, none of whom left the house during this time, and so the widow had to supply them all with food and drink.

On the morning of the third day, a funeral procession was formed. This was the hour of enormous satisfaction for the widow because each one of her many friends appeared with a black flag adorned with bells and with white tears made of metal, and the number of mourners testified to the esteem in which the deceased had lived and the many favors he had done. This was the significance of the banners that preceded the stretcher on which the Indian was to be carried to the cemetery.

Men and women were dressed in mourning. The women covered their heads and part of their faces with black mantillas. The widow was completely swathed in a black cloak. All that could be seen of her was her nose and her eyes.

Four strong boys lifted the stretcher. That was the signal for all women to launch a tremendous outcry that provoked from the dogs of the vicinity a long, pitiful howl.

The dark, drunken group, first trotting, then running, followed the stretcher to the cemetery so that the soul of the dead man might arrive at his immortal destination with the same speed that his body had come to the site of his eternal repose.

It raced at a lamentable speed down the long, dry road, providing a dreadful spectacle, because the head and the feet of the dead man were exposed. When the four boys trotted, the rigid feet swung and the head hung facing the sun.

Two obligatory rests were made on the way to the cemetery so that the carriers of the stretcher could empty a cup of brandy apiece and be replaced by other bearers. And, as was traditional after the third stop, which brought them close to the cemetery, the widow began to bewail her loss.

At this stop, they put the stretcher on the ground and the group squatted down around the corpse, their eyes fixed on the face of the now half-decayed body. Its huge eyes were sunken in the head, the nose was tapered, and the lips had turned black.

The helpers, sent there ahead of time, began to distribute cups of liquor and handfuls of coca which the attendants accepted without saying a word. The widow gave a prolonged sigh, the near relatives sighed, and finally all the others sighed ostentatiously; they drank another cup of brandy while other friends hoisted the stretcher on their shoulders to cover the final stage of the route. Then the widow burst into a series of humming moans that were stretched out in sustained, monotonous notes, occasionally interrupted by brief phrases: "Hi . . . hiii . . . My   husband! . . . hiii . . . hii . . . he was so good! . . . hii . . . hii . . . he has left me. . . . hi . . . hii . . . forever!"

The moans grew stronger and the phrases were lengthened until finally it turned into a sorrowful monologue. The mourners stood silently listening to the cries of the widow so they would know when their acts of sympathy for the dead should start. In a monotonous voice the lamenting widow told the history of her loves, pains, and disappointments. It was a kind of public confession . . . including a final account of her husband's doings and wanderings; a dolorous review of his private life with even the most intimate details: "How good! How good my husband was! He beat me sometimes, but just because he loved me. He had a mistress, but he never went out of the house without leaving us money. . . . He drank a lot, but he was so quiet about his drunkenness."

The whole story was told by the time they reached the cemetery. Immediately afterward, a desperate cry came from the women when the first shovelful of dirt was dropped on the body of the dead man.

After the body was buried came the drinking, which lasted until late in the afternoon, at which time they started down the road home.

They left in separate groups and all were completely intoxicated. The men sang their laments and the women wailed, their faces hidden by their black mantillas. On the treeless plain, the howling and chanting resounded till the innumerable birds that lived on the shore of the lake rose into flight.

With the departure of the afternoon, the sunset illuminated the sky; the far-off hills were sometimes silhouetted against the bright horizon, sometimes hidden by the huge gray clouds that were slowly covering the vast brilliant sky: one might say a curtain was drawn.

Elizabeth Turner

JORGE ICAZA
1902–   Ecuador

Icaza started first as a dramatist while still a university student in Quito. Then, disgusted by censorship, he turned to novel writing with *Huasipungo* (1934), about the mistreatment of his country's Indians by church and state. Now twenty-five years old, this novel has had twelve Spanish editions and ten translations. Croatians, Poles, Chinese, and Jews can read it in their own language. An English version was published in a Russian magazine, but the novelist declared it not worth using and personally selected three sections of his novel for inclusion here.

The novel comprises loosely woven episodes about Alfonso Pereira's efforts to get rich by marketing the lumber on his estate. With the help of the village priest, Padre Lomas, he persuades his Indians to build a road, then tries to drive them from their *huasipungo*, the land they had received in return for working for their master. Their vain attempt at rebellion ends the novel.

Earlier, one laborer, Andrés Chiliquinga, digs up a tainted cow for his hungry companions. His wife Cunshi dies, poisoned by it. A description of her funeral wake is one of the parts here translated.

HUASIPUNGO

Through the valley and the village, hunger threaded its way among houses, huts, and *huasipungos*. It was not the hunger of rebels who are allowed to die in jail, but the hunger of slaves who are killed. It was not the hunger of jobless people; it was the hunger of overworked Indians. It was not an unproductive hunger, but hunger that had raided the mountain granaries to bring pride to city-dwelling aristocrats. A hunger that seemed to find harp strings to pluck in the ribs of the children and in the stray dogs, hunger that can be cured by prescriptions of begging, prostitution, and robbery. Hunger that gnawed the humble guts of the Indians, that spread through the muddy streets, personified in beggars, paralytics, anemic children, through the muddy streets of the town of Tomachi, where an old Indian woman, seated in the doorway of her hut, was nursing a baby from exhausted, pendent, empty breasts, and the *chola* women who passed were making comments:

"Why don't you feed him barley broth?"

"Th'ain't none, ma'am."

"Then goats' milk?"

"Th'ain't none, ma'am."

"Cow, then?"

"Not a chance, ma'am."

"The poor baby will die."

"I know, but what're you goin' to do, ma'am?"

"He's been hexed by hunger."

"The baby won't nurse, ma'am."

"You're bleeding."

"I know, ma'am."

"The baby of the Indian Encarnación died, too."

"My nephew, too, ma'am."

"Ave Maria!"

"An epidemic, looks like."

"And epidemics pick on the children first."

The epidemic also attacked Mono, wrapped in his black muffler, and with his head sunk onto his shoulders, Mono whom Teresa and Pancha found stiff one day at Jacinta's store, with a thread of blood-stained saliva dripping from his mouth.

The epidemic sent Indians scurrying, under cloak of night, among houses and gardens of the village in search of something to satisfy their hunger. And every morning it brought consternation among the *chola* women.

"Hey, neighbor, is my small hen over there?"

"No, and mine has disappeared, too."

"Hey, Teodora, do you think somebody got into the garden last night? Look, every one of the onions has been pulled up."

"Somebody stole my black pig!"

"Old friend, will you look around your yard for my gray rooster?"

"What for, friend? How could it get over a wall this high?"

"It won't do any harm to look, will it?"

"That new poncho that Carlos left on the line last night, now where is it?"

"Must be those thieves."

"My boy Juan said he saw some Indians sneaking around here the other night."

II

(*Getting news of Cunshi's sickness, Andrés ran away from his work and found her dead.*)

In the afternoon, Policarpio, the overseer, came in search of the Indian who had left his job. At the *huasipungo* fence, he shouted:

"Andrés! Andrés Chiliquinga!"

Getting no reply, the overseer entered the yard and got off his mule. The youngster and the dog—especially the dog that had often felt the pain of the hobble—had hidden in the pigsty. The *cholo* stared from the door of the hut. When his eyes got accustomed to the gloom of the hovel and could make out the dead body of Cunshi on the floor, the only thing he could think of was a reprimand, his eternal reproach:

"A fine thing, damn it! That's what you get for stealing, and being such a no-good. You ate the dead cow. Maybe you think I didn't know. It's the punishment of the good God, damn it! The Indian José Risco is making his last kicks in his hut, too. Now what?"

Andrés, as if coming to life at the sympathetic question of the *cholo*, replied, putting into each word the compelling entreaty of desperation:

"Please . . . Please, good overseer, please have pity! Help me. Please ask the master for some money for the funeral."

"I'll see if he won't contribute something," the overseer agreed, interested in the request, perhaps, because of the prospect of the liquor that would be provided.

Policarpio spread the news through the countryside. The relatives and friends of dead Cunshi began arriving at Andrés's house, full of sad comments and tears. At nightfall, the Indian musicians, with flute and drum, took their places at the head of the dead woman as she lay among four candles that flickered in holders of baked clay. From the time the musicians got there, the hut was filled with the monotonous and depressing rhythm of *sanjuanitos*, and Andrés, as the nearest relative, sat at her feet, huddled in his poncho to take part in the wake and bewail his grief and to the rhythm of the music to empty himself of all the choking bitterness at the solitude caused by the loss of Cunshi. With eyes and nose dripping, his words poured out.

"Alas, Cunshi, *sha*,
Alas, darling, *sha*,
Who will take care of the pigs?
Why have you gone without taking me with you?
Alas, Cunshi, *sha*,
Alas, darling, *sha*.
Leaving me all alone,
Who will do the sowing in the *huasipungo?*
Who will take care of the baby?
Poor, lonely baby, alas!
Alas, Cunshi, *sha*,
Alas, darling, *sha*.
Who is going to see if the hen has laid an egg?
Who is going to heat the broth?
Who is going to light the fire on a cold night?
Alas, Cunshi, *sha*,
Alas, darling, *sha!*"

(*This tender and poetic lament continues for two pages.*)

With dry lips, burning eyes, hoarse throat and broken heart, the Indian kept listing the good qualities of Cunshi, his memories of the Indian woman, his wishes about the Indian woman, the very life of the Indian woman. In the silence of the hut, surrounded by drunken and weeping companions, he could say anything, shout anything. When his friends and relatives noticed his exhaustion, being voiceless and with tears dried up, they dragged him into a corner where he reclined groaning for the rest of the night. Then another of Cunshi's family took his place in the mourning ceremony. So relatives and friends came and went in an unending series of lamentations. The monotonous music of the *sanjuanitos* and the barrels of rum charged at Jacinta's store encouraged the chorus of lamentations and memories that grew more intense as time passed. The Indians give the name of *chasquibay* to that outcry in the midst of the indifference and callousness of the hour.

III

By midafternoon the rebels, milling around, were surprised by rifle and machine-gun shots. The fear of gunfire scattered the crowd over the hillside. Patrols of soldiers, sneaking closer under protection of gullies, ravines, and ditches, gave chase to the rebellious Indians who tried to conceal their crime in every hiding place imaginable, the caves, the grasses of the swamps, the underbrush, the overhanging rocks, the openings of canyons.

The soldiers had no fear as they advanced, continually improving their aim.

"Look, chum! There's an Indian in that thicket."

"You're right. He's hiding from the patrol that should be going along the road."

"Watch what good aim I have."

A shot sounded and the Indian discussed by the soldiers broke violently from the underbrush of the slope, grabbed his chest, and tried to scream, but a second shot ended the Indian and his cry.

At the other side of the hill, other soldiers were talking.

"Hush a minute, chum. There's an Indian in that tree."

"He's not moving."

"You'll see how I drop him with one bullet."

"Damn, that won't be easy!"

"You said it."

At the first shot, tumbling and getting his poncho tangled in the branches of the tree, an Indian fell to the ground.

The fury of victory in the hunt fanned the cruelty of the soldiers. They killed the Indians as they might kill rats, with the same diligence, the same gesture of disgust and repugnance as they destroyed them, with the same frenzy and desire to be rid of their presence. Let them die, all of them!

The children had taken refuge with the women under some trees whose branches overhung the muddy water of an enormous pool. One blast of machine-gun fire, with its precise chat-tering, sank the women and children forever in the roiled water, from which clouds of bloody bubbles rose to the surface.

Much later in the afternoon, the sun seemed to be sinking in cotton soaked in the blood of the pool. All was quiet again on the hillside, but a group of Indians, strong and stubborn, kept up their resistance in the strategically-located hut of Andrés Chiliquinga, protected by the cliff of the big gorge.

"We'll have to attack soon, or the damn Indians will sneak away when it gets dark. That's a steep slope, but——" The leader remarked among the soldiers, but before he could com-plete his sentence, he had to dash to safety to escape a huge rock that came bounding down the hill like a wild bull.

"Damn it, if I hadn't been quick, those bastard Indians would have got me!" the officer exclaimed, leaving his shelter and gazing with hate and defiance toward the top of the slope where Andrés's cabin looked menacingly down.

"Damn Indians!" the soldiers agreed.

"Don't let them get away. Otherwise they'll join up with the others in the Republic and there'll be hell to pay."

Hidden in an open ditch, a short distance from the hut of Andrés Chiliquinga, the last of the rebels kept hurling rocks down the hill, and one of them, the oldest, took occasional shots with a bird gun.

Suddenly some of the soldiers began climbing the slope in open file, and started mounting their machine guns on flat surfaces. Stones, rolled down on them by daring Indian women and children who left the protection of the gulley, left them stretched out forever on the hillside. Their cries and groans could be heard everywhere. But others kept on.

Suddenly to the surprise of the few rebellious Indians that remained, the lower jaw of the ditch seemed to grow bayonet teeth. Their refuge became transformed into a macerating beast.

"Here, dad," insisted the son of Chiliquinga, pulling at his father's poncho and guiding him toward a gulley. Several other Indians who heard the boy's words, followed. On all fours, and guided by the youngster, they made their way to Andrés's hut. Instinctively they barricaded the door with everything that might serve as protection. They occupied the brief pause given to them in what they thought was a safe refuge by wiping their muddy faces, spitting, cursing, scratching their heads and glaring suspiciously with that same superstitious and vengeful hatred at Chiliquinga that they had expressed just before killing Cabascango. But events were developing much more rapidly than their evil intentions. Outside, the groans of the people and the terrifying sounds of the guns had stopped for a few seconds. This joyful silence was suddenly broken by a machine-gun blast that passed through the straw roof into the crowded hut. Andrés's son, who up to now had kept up the courage of his elders by means of his easy-going attitude, gasped and shuddered and grabbed his father's leg.

"Daddy! Daddy!" he whispered.

"Shut up, you ornery devil. Don't be a sissy!" Chiliquinga muttered, choking back his tears and sheltering his child under his ragged cloak.

It did not take long for the straw to catch fire, and the rafters to start burning. The hut burst into flames. Amid the choking smoke, black and sooty, the moan of the boy, the coughs that tore at chest and throat, the shower of sparks, the acrid odor that irritated eyes, amid all this, the groans and curses of the Indians no longer visible rose shrilly as they groped about.

"Damn it!"

"Papa!"

"To die, roasted like a rabbit!"

"Like a devil in hell!"

"Open the door!"

"Where is the door?"

"Open up, damn it!"

Overwhelmed by desperation, asphyxiation, by the dying boy beside him, the Indian Chiliquinga groped toward the door that was beginning to burn. Behind him, was the gully; above, the fire; and facing him, the rifles.

"Open, for God's sake!"

Andrés hurriedly pulled aside the barricade, seized the boy under his arm, and opening the door, cried:

"Come on. Let's go!"

The afternoon breeze blew coolly on his eyes and face. He again looked at life squarely. But he advanced into the open air, with his boy under his cloak. He bit down on a curse, then shouted, in words that bit deeper than the bullets:

"*Ñucanchic huasipungo!* (Our own bit of land!) Damn it!"

He ran forward desperately as if to smother the rifles, hearing behind him the cries of his fellow Indians:

"*Ñucanchic huasipungo!*"

Finally everything became silent. The hut stopped burning. The sun finally sank amid cotton soaked in the blood of the pool. Over the bitter protest fluttered the national flag of the glorious battalion, with fiery, sarcastic laughter. What next? The gringos!

At dawn amid the ruins of huts, the ashes, the corpses still warm, a nightmare-like vision took form, made up of emaciated arms resembling new shoots of barley that, as the chill winds of America's highest plateau blew over them, seemed to scream with the piercing sound of a drill:

"*Ñucanchic huasipungo!*"

"*Ñucanchic huasipungo!*"

W.K.J.

CIRO ALEGRÍA
1909–   Peru

An adventurer whose crusade for good government brought him imprisonment and exile, Alegría was a friend of the Indians from his boyhood days and has written of their problems in several novels. *Los perros hambrientos* ("The Hungry Dogs") (1939) tells of the simple life of the upland Indians who found sympa-

thetic masters but had to fight nature for a living. It was
followed by *El mundo es ancho y ajeno* ("Broad and
Alien is the World") (1941), the prize winner in an
international competition for the best Latin-American
novel. It has been translated into English, but the
earlier novel about Indians and their hungry dogs who
live in harmony till a severe drought causes a struggle
between them, has never been fully translated. Here is
one abbreviated chapter.

A SMALL PLACE IN THE WORLD

The old Indian Mashe and fifty others—men, women, and children—pleaded with Don Cipriano in the hallway of his farm
house:

"Please take us, dear master. Please listen to us . . ."

"What can we do here? Don't you see that everything is
ruined . . . ?" His voice reflected irritation, and actually he had
been very worried for some days now. At first, when the rains
began and water fell by bucketfuls and for an entire week beat
upon his land, Cipriano, the owner, was very happy, and he
repeated the old agricultural proverb: "After a great drought,
there finally comes a great drenching." The green freshness of
the planting appeared in the fields of the landowner as well as
in the fields of his tenants. The young plants rose out of the
soil with the happy impulse and easy adaptability of youth. But
suddenly the water became scarcer. . . .

"Will it keep on raining?" Don Cipriano asked Don Rómulo each day; and to this Rómulo answered: "Sir, always it
has!"

If the preceding year the water was scarce, it seemed this
year that they would receive even less. And while he himself
was in the midst of such tribulation, here came fifty Indians
asking for shelter! They were moaning under their ragged
shawls and dusty ponchos. They had come before Don Cipriano like a flock of harassed animals, but their human quality

was expressed by their imploring hands, and it shone in their pleading, hungry eyes.

"Please take us, dear master!"

They had come from the ghost town of Huaira. After some years of legal proceedings, Don Juvencio Rosas, a prominant landholder, had proved his unchallenged right to possess the lands of a tribe whose tenacious existence had maintained itself since the Inca period, through the colonial and national period, in spite of many misfortunes. Then Don Juvencio appeared one fine day in Huaira accompanied by soldiers and by his own henchmen to take possession of this land. The Indians, in a final and desperate attempt, tried to resist. Some fell, before the impressive voice of the guns made them understand soon enough the small value of bush knives and slings. Many of those who had stood up for their rights were put on trial for treason.

Mashe, whose name in a "Christian language" was Marcelino, possessed a dark, beardless, yet wrinkled face.

"What shall we do, dear master?" he said in a pitiable voice, now learning for the first time to beg. Up to now, he had enjoyed the use of communal property, and so he usually spoke in the full raised voice of a landowner.

Don Cipriano looked at the group of Indians, thinking of the drought, but also of the fact that he would be needing strong arms for the daily tasks around the farms, and here were a lot of them.

"Very well," he finally told them. "Remain and choose whichever tenant lands you wish, as long as you don't infringe upon the property of other tenant farmers already established. . . . Of course I guarantee nothing. Do you see the sky? You understand that if it doesn't rain, well . . ."

The sky at the moment was cloudless. The Indians knew too well what that meant, especially old Mashe, who because of his age had had abundant experience. The wind blew like some evil bird which flaps its wings strongly and loudly caws. The bleak region raised its tall and dark peaks in an attitude of watchful waiting toward the north, the south, the west and the east. Nowhere was visible any promise of life—not even one dark overhanging cloud. The few wisps that rapidly crossed the sky were as thin as the rags of the exiled Indians.

"Dear master, we don't wish to bother you, but give us some place, any place no matter how small. . . ."

Don Cipriano ended the discussion:

"Well, for now you may seek shelter in the houses of the tenant farmers; they will give you shelter . . . at least I am fairly certain they will give it to you."

The Indians remained motionless. Only old Mashe dared to beg:

"Boss, we would also like a little bit to eat, even if it's just some barley . . . and perhaps a few seeds to sow."

The landowner knitted his eyebrows before this new problem. But it was evident that these men needed food and, being his tenant farmers, it was his duty to provide them with nourishment.

"Very well," he finally said. "Don Rómulo, give them a half-bushel of barley apiece and a bushel of wheat. There isn't enough for more. You will have to plant some of it to obtain more nourishment. . . . Now, go away."

The Indians dragged themselves away after receiving a bit of grain to ease their misery.

Don Cipriano stood for a moment thinking of the tragedy of the Indians and of the other, even greater dilemma that faced all of them: Would it rain soon? And then he remembered the old proverb: "First sow the crop and you'll get your money."

"Bah!" he laughed, "ten days more of drought and it won't be worth while to sow."

Simon was seated on the stone fence of his hut, chewing coca leaves. The wind was playing with his long grayed mustache and his goatee. His wrinkled face showed as much sadness as the dry land. Mashe was passing by, looking for a resting place, and seeing Simon he stopped.

"Good afternoon, sir. Could you allow us a small resting

place?" Mashe was accompanied by his elderly wife and two daughters. Simon gazed upon all of them as he thought of the scarcity of his food supply. But finally he said:

"Why not? Come on in."

The elderly, bearded mestizo extended his hospitality to the old beardless Indian. He would not have done it perhaps for a white man, but the fact was that their copper skin made them brothers, linked by the sentiments of the race and the distant land from which they both had come, which in spite of everything, they loved, and which was their end and destiny.

After lunch, Mashe explained the Indians' sad plight, to which Simon replied:

"I used to have an abundance of land when I came here; yet today it no longer belongs to me, nor is it even mine to sow. One looks for his small place in the world and there is none, or else it is simply loaned to him. And it is so little, such a tiny place in the world."

The men chewed their coca for a long while. Simon finally added:

"They are smart, aren't they? But then, what happened to the white fox may happen to them."

Knowing his natural ability as a storyteller, the group became silent with expectant curiosity.

"At this particular time the foxes were starving, and the leader of the pack saw they could not endure much longer. Unfortunately the sheepfolds were surrounded by high walls and by many dogs. Finally one fox said:

" 'This is no time to be stupid: one has to be alert.' So he went to the nearby mill and taking advantage of the absence of the miller, he began rolling around in the flour until he became whitened by it. That night he crept alongside a sheepfold.

" 'Bah, Bah!' he bleated like a sheep. The shepherdess came out and saw the white, shadowy form in the night:

" 'Oh, one of our little lambs has been left outside,' she thought, and she opened the door, allowing the disguised fox to enter the fold. The dogs were barking, and the fox said to himself:

" 'I will wait until they are sleeping as soundly as the sheep. Then I will look for the fattest little lamb . . . and crunch! with one bite I will kill it and eat it. At dawn they will open the door and I will begin to run. Who can overtake me?'

"But the fox did not plan for showers. And that very night it began to rain, washing away his protective covering of flour. A certain sheep that was standing behind him noticed the white ground and thought:

" 'What kind of sheep is this that loses his color?'

"Looking closer and realizing that this fading object was a fox, he began to bleat. The rest also saw it then, and they began bleating. Soon the dogs came, and with a couple of vicious bites they turned the fox into jerked meat.

"This is what I have to say: there is always something that is not within the reckoning of even the most alert. Now let's draw our conclusion. The long drought will hurt all of us and Don Cipriano, and old and young alike. However, these foxes are going to suffer from lack of rain, whereas we poor Indians continually suffer drought of justice and a drought of the human heart. . . ."

Afterwards Mashe, who had agreed completely, inquired painfully: "I wish to take land over there where you see those elder trees. What do you think?"

"All right, although now that land is both good and bad, but if it rains, everything will come out all right."

Before long they went to sleep. The newcomers yielded to their weariness on the ground in the hallway of the farmhouse, huddled together beneath their few tattered blankets and those which the tenant farmers supplied them. Even now sleep did not come easily, for late into the night they continued to hear the howling of the hungry dogs and the relentless wind.

As the novel progresses, the situation grows worse. There is no food. The Indians are finally driven to eating the sheep killed by the hungry dogs; some even eat snakes. At last Mashe steals wheat from the church for his family. The consciousness of his wrongdoing kills him. Only after he is buried does he get his "own small place" that no one can take away from him.

Finally in November, the rains come and the cycle of life begins again.

Elaine Schaefer

DEMETRIO AGUILERA MALTA
1909–   Ecuador

After publishing one volume of prose and another of verse about the blacks who clear the swamps around Guayaquil, Aguilera Malta joined with two other young writers, Joaquín Gallegos Lara and Enrique Gil Gilbert, to produce the volume *Los que se van* ("Those Who Go Away") (1930), short stories about the *cholos* and the *montuvios*, the half-breeds and woodcutters. It was one of the most important books ever published in Ecuador because of its encouragement for aspiring authors. Twelve outstanding novels by various Ecuadorean writers followed in the next five years, making Ecuador a rival of Brazil in the field of important fiction. Aguilera Malta himself went on to write separately *Don Goyo* (1933), set in Guayaquil and the coast, and *Canal Zone* (1934) about the North Americans on the Isthmus. It was with *La isla virgen* ("The Virgin Island") (1942), however, that he really reached his full powers as a novelist. The first pages, translated here, give an idea of his poetic style and feeling for atmosphere, his sympathy for the workers, and the realism that extends to his use of regional words not in dictionaries. Since the appearance of his novel, Aguilera Malta has written other novels and a number of plays and has become a leading literary figure of Ecuador.

THE VIRGIN ISLAND

Chapter 1

Clearing the Land

The earth trembles.

Over the hills and the flat spaces men swarm like ants, clearing the selvas. The continuous noise of the ax blows becomes louder and stronger. The trees fall, one after another. One sees them seeming to leap unbelievably, their flexible branches waving, their fan-shaped clusters of leaves agitated. By the intensity of their movements upon falling, one can tell what kind they are: the tough and age-old ceibos, the iron-hard *carcoles*, the willowy carobs, sinewy *cabo de hachas*, brittle *colorados*. The maneuver of the laborers has been the signal for their extinction.

The sky darkens as swift birds weave a gigantic spiderweb of feathers. Shrill cries of terror come from their frightened bills. Parrots, ducks, *colembas*, wild peacocks, *cagonas*, and a dozen other sorts of fowl seem shot out of the ground. For just an instant they hesitate. Then with fluttering wings they start their strident flight, an absurd mingling of sizes and colors. The dense net of the jungle seems to break. Like an ocean overflowing its bank, surges a formless phalanx of animals and serpents. And (an unheard-of thing!) one sees the bone-tail snake beside a leaping deer, a hungry and treacherous puma alongside squirrels and iguanas, catamounts and wild donkeys. There is constant movement among the slender trees, the underbrush, and the lianas. The intricate tangle of bushes is covered with dust. The gray labyrinth of the low shrubs is slashed in a thousand pieces. The ground is covered with a variety of tracks. All nature trembles and roars.

In terror the men watch the parade, silently. Many would probably like to say something, do something, but the ax, flashing dizzily in their hands, holds them captive. They are in the midst of their jungle clearing.

Only this morning they began, when the sun was just showing its head, like a golden crustacean, above the slopes of the island to the east. Now that same sun is beating down on them, and although a few trees not yet uprooted furnish a sort of shade, they feel, nevertheless, the foetal blows of its pitiless heat.

There are twenty in the clearance gang, almost all from "down below," from San Manuel del Morro, from the boundary islands, even from as far away as the distant seacoast. Only the

overseer and the black half-breed, Aguayo, are from "up there."
There is even one from the mountains, Don José Domingo
Carrillo.

The white man, Don Nestor, always says: "It's never a good
idea to take everybody from the same region."

They have naked, strong bodies, of the color of mahogany
patent leather. The sweat runs down them like rivers, over their
knotted muscles. They don't stop working for an instant because when this does happen through some misfortune, the
gruff, deep voice of the old overseer can be heard from nearby:
"I'm going to take your hide off if you start loafing on the job!"

"I was just going to brush off a horsefly, Don Guayamabe."

"The devil with horseflies! You get paid for working, not
for shirking!"

"O.K., boss."

The first thing is to use their machetes on the underbrush
around the foot of the tree. They form a circle around it, big
or little according to the size of the tree. Then they figure in
which direction they want it to drop. After that, they begin
chopping. Some, like the half-breed Negro Aguayo, specialists in
felling trees, produce a special and peculiar sound. It is a continuous and musical hammering that makes everybody who
hears it, regardless of how far away they are, declare:

"There's Aguayo chopping! That *zambo* is a wizard when he
gets his hands around an ax!"

"He sure doesn't waste any time!"

"You said it." And the chips fly.

The first chips are big and thick, chopped out of the wound
just opened in the trunk. But little by little the angle of the
wound becomes sharper, and then the chips are smaller and
harder to get out. But the ax keeps on flying.

The chopper burns with excitement. "That's the end of
you!"

After a little while, he tries with his hands to push over the
wounded giant. Sometimes it still resists and he has to swing
the ax a little longer. But most of the time it sways a little and

then, unable to remain erect, comes crashing down. Its fall is a catastrophe. This colossus of the earth crushes hundreds of saplings, reducing them to a thousand bits. Its branches raise a dust. Its own trunk, where it is slender, also breaks into fragments. And amid all this, sounds a fantastic roar, like an earthquake shaking the mountain.

The laborers view its fall impassively. As soon as this monster of the selva comes to rest, they clamber over it, beginning to clear away the branches, to chop away the lianas and the vines that have twined around it.

The mosquitos are the only creatures, except for the men, that have not fled in terror. As they close in, they seem to have been excited, too. They settle on shoulders, legs, and arms. Only the faces are protected by the inevitable cigar.

The sun keeps on biting the laborers. Sometimes they take on the color of fire. Indeed, in the clearings, the sun's flame seems even nearer. The men sweat and sweat. The backs of some of them ache from bending so much.

"I swear to God it's easier to clear the hillsides. There you work standing up, with a shovel in front of you, the way a man fights. Here, bent over, chewed by mosquitos, damned if I see any fun in it for me!"

Once in a while, puffs of wind from the south fan them. Then they half-raise their heads. How badly they want to stop a minute! But instantly from behind them comes the growl of the boss, the implacable Guayamabe: "Quit that loafing. This is no time to shirk!"

The soil is hot. The thorn bushes turn red. The thorns seem to curve even more, ready to catch the bare foot of the shoeless laborers. They try to walk on tiptoe to avoid contact with the earth. From time to time, one after another starts bleeding.

"Damn it, a thorn got me!"

They would like to pull it out and put something on the wound so it wouldn't get inflamed, even if it were only cigar ashes and spit. But there is Don Guayamabe. And he won't put up with any stopping of their work.

"We're all going to quit pretty soon. The devil with thorns!
What are you men for? And if you aren't men, why do you
want to work? Why do you want to do what men do? Complain as much as you want. But nothing very serious has happened to you. All you want is to be slackers. The devil with
thorns! Any deer gets rid of them by scratching its belly! Quit
loafing!"

                                                        W.K.J.

JOSÉ EUSTACIO RIVERA
1889–1928   Colombia

Of all the "Green Hell" novels, *La vorágine* ("The
Vortex, or Whirlpool") (1924), by the Colombian
writer Rivera, is the one in which nature plays the
greatest role. Its author regarded the jungles as mankind's mortal enemy, from which there was no escape.
The book is the outcome of Rivera's experiences in the
South American jungles as a member of the commis-
sion to establish the frontier between his country and
Venezuela, as well as to investigate accounts of cruelty
to the rubber gatherers. The descriptions, therefore, are
authentic. Even some of its most villainous characters
come into it under their real names. Arturo Cova, the
narrator, disillusioned about himself yet determined to
guard his honor and defend his fellow man, has no real-
life prototype, unless it be some old conquistador.

The novel is a curious blend of romanticism and realism. The tropical jungle is the vortex, alive and cruel,
and the novelist sees its horrors with poetic vision,
though perhaps the overtones seem exaggerated to
Anglo-Saxon tastes. Yet its universal acceptance as one
of the greatest of Latin-American novels proves that it
spoke for many people.

This is Rivera's only novel. A few years after completing it, he died of some mysterious tropical fever.

THE VORTEX

*In Part I, Arthur Cova who tells the story, falls in love with
Alicia, and when her family opposes their marriage, they run
off to the jungles. Here they meet all sorts of unfortunate people, held captive by the selvas, as a whirlpool sucks in everything that comes within its grasp. While each of them has an
interesting story of passion, jealousy, and crime, the greatness
of the book lies in its pictures of the many phases of rubber
collecting and the fight against cruel and encroaching nature.*

*The poetic yet melancholic apostrophe to the Jungle, which
opens Part II, sets the tone.*

Oh, jungle, wedded to silence, mother of solitude and mists!
What malignant fate imprisoned me within your green walls?
Your foliage, like an immense vault, is between my hopes and
the clear skies, of which I see only glimpses, when the twilight
breeze stirs your lofty tops. Where is the loved star that walks
the hills at evening? Where are those cloud-sweeps of gold and
purple? How often have I sighed as I pictured the sun—far
beyond your tangled labyrinths—steeping the distant spaces
in purple, there where my native land lies, where the unforget-
table plains stretch, where rise mountains on whose foothills
I could feel as high above the world as their white-crowned
peaks.

Where is the moon hanging her silver lantern? You stole
from me the dreams that spring from the broad horizons. You
offer my eyes nothing but the dull monotony of your green
roof. Over it flows the peaceful dawn, but never lighting the
depths of your humid bosom.

You are a cathedral of sorrows. Unknown gods speak in
hushed voices, whispering of long life to your majestic trees,
trees that were the contemporaries of paradise, old when the
first tribes appeared on the face of the earth, and which impassively await the sinking of future centuries. Your vegetation is

a family that never betrays itself. The embrace your boughs cannot give is carried by creepers and lianas. You share even in the pain of the leaf that falls. Your multisonous voices rise like a chorus bewailing the giants that crash to earth; and in every breach that is made, new germ cells hasten their gestation.

You possess the austerity of a cosmic force. You embody the mysteries of creation. Nevertheless, my spirit, bearing the weight of your eternity, yearns now only for what is fleeting; and so, instead of loving the stout and rugged oak, I have learned to love the languid orchid, because it is ephemeral, like man, because it fades, like his dreams.

Let me flee, oh, jungle, from your sickly shadows, formed by the breath of beings who have died in the abandonment of your majesty. You yourself seem but an enormous cemetery, where you decay and are reborn. I want to return to the places where there are no secrets to frighten, where slavery is impossible, where the eye can reach out into the distance, where the spirit rises in light that is free! I want the heat of the sand dunes, the sparkle of stars, the vibrating air of the open pampas. Let me return to the land from which I came. Let me unwalk that path of tears and blood, which I entered on an evil day, when, on the trail of a woman, I plunged into jungle and wilderness, seeking Vengeance, the implacable goddess who smiles only over tombs!

Entering the jungle, Cova describes his impressions.

Before descending the steep bank that separated us from the dugout, I turned again to gaze at the furthermost fringes of the plains. A soft haze hid the horizon, but distant palm-fronds nodded a farewell. Those vast spaces had injured me; yet I wanted to embrace them. They had been decisive factors in my existence. They had become part of my being. I know that in my dying moments the images I most clearly bear within me will blur in glassy eyes; but I know, too, that in the eternal atmosphere through which my spirit must rise, I shall find anew the half-tones of those tender twilights, for with brush-strokes of opal and rose they have already shown me on friendly skies the path that the soul is to follow.

The dugout, like a floating coffin, moved down the river in the afternoon hours when shadows are lengthening. From the center of the wide stream we watched the parallel banks, of somber vegetation and hostile insect plagues. That river, waveless, foamless, was still, sullenly still like a thing of ill omen. It seemed a darkening road that moved towards the vortex of nothingness.

As we floated along in silence, the earth began to lament the passing of the sun, the last rays of which were fading on the sandy river shores. But it seemed that it was my sadness, like an opaque lens, that was causing dusk to fall on all things. Upon the evening scene my disconsolateness was spreading like the deepening twilight, and slowly one shadow darkened the outlines of the ecstatic forest, the long ribbon of motionless water, the silhouettes of the paddlers. . . .

We landed at the foot of a steep bank, its precipitous slope broken by crude steps cut into the soil. A number of dugouts floated listlessly in the backwaters of the stream. Over a muddy trail that lost itself in the underbrush, we pushed our way, until we reached a clearing of felled trees, and a rude reed-thatched shelter. The place was so deserted that we hesitated to go in, fearful of an ambuscade. Pipa, however, after some agitated conversation with our native companions, explained to us that the inhabitants of the hut had fled on seeing the mastiffs. Our guides, he also said, sought permission to pass the night in the dugouts.

And when they were gone, Fidel ordered Correa to sleep with Pipa on the spilt-reed table, in order to prevent any attempt to betray us that night. He also took the collars off the dogs, and, under cover of darkness, moved the animals from the place where we had tied them to the side of our hammocks.

With my carbine at my side, I gave myself to sleep.

One of the tribes with which he stayed briefly gave a dance exhibition in Cova's honor.

More than fifty Indians, of both sexes and every age, came to the dance, daubed with paint, licentious, and squatted on the moonlit stretch of river beach, drinking the pungent wine they carried in their calabashes. Early that afternoon some had started gathering *mojojoyes*, thick grubs girded by hairy rings, that live curled up in rotting trunks. These they decapitated with their teeth, as a smoker bites his cigar, and sucked the buttery contents, afterwards rubbing the empty shells of the insects over their hair, to give it luster. The hair of the young girls, the *pollonas* of proud breasts, shone like polished patent leather glistening between their headgear of parrot feathers and the black seed and scarlet cornelian necklaces.

The chief had smeared his face with yellowish-red *annotto* dye and honey. He snuffed enormous quantities of the intoxicating *yopo*, taking it into his nostrils through little hollow canes, until soon he was staggering around as if suffering from delirium tremens, pursuing and embracing the girls like a restless buck, but impotent. Sometimes, gibbering, he came over to congratulate me, because I, according to our guide Pipa, was like him, an enemy of the cowboys and had burnt their ranches, deeds that made me worthy of an excellently-fashioned wooden saber, flint-edged, or a new bow.

Throughout their orgiastic carousal the atrocious liquor ran like water, and the cries of the women and children added to the bacchanalian turmoil. At length the men began to circle slowly on the sands, shaking the left foot every three steps. It seemed more the sluggish plodding of fettered prisoners than a dance,—prisoners in slow-paced rotation around the fire, forced to tread an only path, eyes on the ground, shackled by the mournful wail of the *chirimía* flute and the grave throbbing of the drums. Now only the music was heard, and the sonorous padding of the feet of the dancers, dancers sad as the rounded moon, silent as the river that tolerated them on its shores.

But of a sudden the women, until then hushed within the circle, grasped the bodies of their lovers and paced along with the same step, swinging as in a stupor; until with slow unburdening of spirit there rose from every throat a growing lamentation that quivered through the muted jungles like the doleful tolling of a bell: A-a-a-a-h-y . . . O-h-é-é . . . !

Coming upon Clemente Silva who, in search of his lost son, had toiled unrewarded for sixteen years collecting rubber, they learn how the rubber plantations are managed.

"What are those sores due to?" I asked after greeting him. And then sitting down, I added. "Tell us how you got them."

"Ah, señor, it seems incredible—leeches. We are tortured to death by them when in the swamps picking latex; and while the rubber tapper bleeds the trees, the leeches bleed him. The jungle protects itself against its opponents, and at length it is man who's defeated."

"Judging by you, the struggle is one to the death," I observed, interested in learning of the rubber world we were entering.

"And in addition the mosquitoes and ants," Silva went on. "The *veinticuatro* ant and the *tambocha* ant are like scorpions. Something even worse: the jungles change men. The most inhuman instincts are developed; cruelty pricks like a thorn, invades souls; covetousness burns like a fever. It's the thirst for wealth that sustains the weakening body, and the smell of rubber produces the 'madness of millions.' Every peon suffers and works with the hope of some day being an independent producer, so that he can go to the cities to spend the rubber he takes with him, to enjoy white women, to be drunk for months at a stretch, knowing that in the jungles there are thousands of slaves who are giving their lives to provide him with those pleasures, toiling as he himself had toiled for his master.

"But reality travels slower than ambition, and beriberi is a bad friend. On remote trails in the solitude of the jungle, they succumb to fever, embracing the tree from which the latex oozes. Lacking water, they stick their thirsty mouths to the bark, that the liquid rubber may calm their fever; and there they rot like leaves, gnawed as they die by rats and ants—the only millions that ever come to them.

"A few, by dint of shrewdness and cruelty, become overseers. Every night, notebook in hand, they credit the returning peons with the latex they have gathered. They never are satis-

fied with the work the peon has done—the lash makes that
evident to the worker. They put down five for the one who has
brought ten liters, and in this way they swell their contraband
stores. This stolen rubber is sold secretly to the manager of
some other region; or it is buried to exchange it for liquors and
merchandise with the first peddler who happens to visit the
rubber groves. Some of the rubber gatherers can play the same
game. The jungle arms them to destroy them; and they steal
and murder, favored by their environment, for the trees never
speak of the tragedies they cause."

"And why do you tolerate such abuses?" I asked indignant.

"Ay, señor, misfortune makes a nobody of one."

"And why don't you return to your country? What can we
do to free you? We must cure your sores. Let me see them."

And although the old fellow, astonished, protested, I knelt
down to examine him.

"Fidel, are you blind? There are worms in these ulcers!"

"Worms? Worms?"

"Yes, we must look for some *otaba* to kill them."

The old man began to moan.

"Can it be possible?" he said. "What humiliation! Worms!
Worms! Worms! I suppose it was the day I fell asleep and
those flies got me."

As we led him back to the hut, he repeated:

"Wormy, wormy, while yet alive!"

And eventually Cova sees it for himself.

For the first time, I saw the inhuman jungle in all its horror,
saw the pitiless struggle for existence. Deformed trees were held
imprisoned by creepers. Lianas bound them together in a death
grip. Stretched from tree to palm in long elastic curves, like
carelessly hung nets, they caught falling leaves, branches, and
fruits, held them for years until they sagged and burst like rotten bags, scattering blind reptiles, rusty salamanders, hairy
spiders, and decayed vegetable matter over the underbrush.

Everywhere the *matapalo*—the pulpy creeper of the forests

—sticks its tentacles on the tree-trunks, twisting and strangling them, injecting itself into them, and fusing with them in a painful metempsychosis. The *bachaqueros* vomit forth trillions of devastating ants. These mow down the mantle of the jungles and return to their tunnels over the wide swaths they cut, carrying leaves aloft like the banners of an army of extinction. The *comején* grub gnaws at the trees like quick-spreading syphilis, boring unseen from within, rotting tissue and pulverizing bark, until the weight of branches that are still living brings the giant crashing to the ground.

Meanwhile the earth continues its successive renovations: at the foot of the colossus that falls, new germs are budding; pollen is flying in the midst of miasmas; everywhere is the reek of fermentation, steaming shadows, the sopor of death, the enervating process of procreation. Where is that solitude poets sing of? Where are those butterflies like translucent flowers, the magic birds, those singing streams? Poor phantasies of those who know only domesticated retreats!

No cooing nightingales here, no Versaillian gardens or sentimental vistas! Instead the croaking of dropsical frogs, the tangled misanthropic undergrowth, the stagnant backwaters and swamps. Here the aphrodisiac parasite that covers the ground with dead insects; the disgusting blooms that throb with sensual palpitations, their sticky smell intoxicating as a drug; the malignant liana, the hairs of which blind animals; the *pringamosa* that irritates the skin; the berry of the *curujú*, a rainbow-hued globe that holds only a caustic ash; the purging grape; the bitter nut of the *corojo* palm.

At night, unknown voices, phantasmagoric lights, funereal silences. It is death that passes giving life. Fruits fall, and on falling give promise of new seed. Leaves come to earth with a faint sighing, to become fertilizer for the roots of the parent tree. Crunching jaws are heard, devouring with the fear of being devoured. Warning whistles, dying wails, beasts belching. And when dawn showers its tragic glory over the jungles, the clamor of survivors again begins: the zoom of the shrieking *guan*; the wild boar crashing through the underbrush; the laughter of ridiculous monkeys. All for the brief joy of a few more hours of life!

This sadistic and virgin jungle casts premonitions of coming danger over one's spirit. Vegetable life is a sensitive thing, the psychology of which we ignore. In these desolate places only our presentiments understand the language it speaks. Under its influence, man's nerves become taut and ready to attack, are ready for treachery and ambush. Our senses confuse their tasks: the eye feels, the back sees, the nose explores, the legs calculate, and the blood cries out: "Flee! Flee!"

And yet, it is civilized man who is the champion of destruction. There is something magnificent in the story of these pirates who enslave their peons, exploit the environment, and struggle with the jungle. Buffeted by misfortune, they leave the anonymity of cities to plunge into the wilderness, seeking a purpose for their sterile life. Delirious from malaria, they loose themselves of their conscience, and adapt themselves to the environment; and with no arms but the rifle and the machete, they suffer the most atrocious needs, while longing for pleasure and plenty. They live exposed to the elements, always ravenous, even naked, for here clothes rot on one's body.

Then some day, on the rock of some river, they build their thatched hut and appoint themselves "masters of the enterprise." Although the jungle is their enemy, they don't know whom to fight; so they fall upon one another and kill and subdue their own king during intervals in their onslaught on the forests; and at times their trail is like that left by an avalanche. Every year the rubber workers in Colombia destroy millions of trees, while in Venezuela the *balatá* rubber tree has disappeared. In this way they defraud the coming generations.

At the end, Cova has become as cruel as the rest, but he does kill El Cayeno, the overseer most responsible for the cruel treatment of the Indians, and wounds the contractor of laborers, Barrera, who had stolen Alicia, and leaves him to be devoured by piranha fish. Reunited with Alicia, Cova tries to escape his pursuers by hiding in the jungles till the consul of his coun-

*try could arrive to protect him, but as the epilogue proclaims,
he disappears, swallowed by the jungle.*

E. K. James

RÓMULO GALLEGOS
1884–   Venezuela

A leader in Venezuelan politics and president from
1947 till overthrown by a military dictatorship ten
months later, Gallegos has been a teacher and school
administrator, as well as author of nearly a dozen novels
about his country. One of the earliest and best known
is *Doña Bárbara* (1929), widely recognized in its combination of reality and symbolism as a historical, economic, social, and political interpretation of Venezuela.
It has gone into forty editions, with ten translations into
foreign languages and a movie in 1943. Some critics,
however, prefer his *Canaima* (1935), in which the
hostile selva is even more the chief character, and
which gets its title from the jungle god who conquers
and devours men. It narrates the adventures of Marcos
Vargas. *Cantaclaro* (1931) deals with the native min-
strels of Venezuela. A complete edition of Gallegos'
works published in 1959 in honor of his seventy-fifth
birthday had ten volumes.

Doña Bárbara concerns a beautiful but unscrupulous
mestiza and her schemes to acquire territory in the
wildest section of the Arauca River basin of Venezuela.
It is one of the earliest of the "Green Hell" stories.

The Altamira ranch had been divided, with the
Barquero section in the possession of the mistress of
its owner. The part owned by the Luzardo branch had
deteriorated since the owners lived in Caracas, and an
overseer was managing it and letting Barbara steal
part of it. Santos Luzardo, the lawyer-owner, arrived to
see about putting his share in condition to sell. One of
his first acts was to round up the stray cattle and see
which belonged to him. Antonio, María Nieves, and

Pajarote were in charge of the rodeo. This is the way
Gallegos describes it, in Chapter XII.

DOÑA BÁRBARA

María Nieves was doing a giant's work at his task of leading
the herd across the fords of the wide streams where death lay in
hiding; exposing himself to the deadly teeth of the alligators,
with nothing but a goad in his hand and a song on his lips.

The corrals at Algarrobo Pass were full. A part of the herd
was to be taken over the Arauca, and the horsemen were already in place along the barriers to defend them against the
assault of the trampling cattle. María Nieves was now in readiness to lead them across to the other side, to guide them swim-
ming. He was the best "waterman" in the Apure country and
was never so happy as when he was in the stream up to his
neck, with the scarcely visible horns of the flocks behind him
as he guided them across the ford and on, far over there on the
other bank, for the river was wide.

Already in the water, riding his horse bareback, he carried
on a shouted conversation with the canoers who paddled by
the side of the herd to keep it from scattering downstream. The
shouting of the peons driving the cattle could be heard in the
corrals. Now the steers were coming down the barrier, with the
troop of greenhorns behind them. María Nieves burst into song
and jumped into the water, for his horse would just serve him
as a buoy to be held with his left hand while he swung the
right, grasping the goad to defend himself from the alligators.
Then the trained leaders flung themselves in and commenced
to swim, with their horns and noses barely above water.

"Hold on! Hold on!" the cowboys shouted. The horses
shoved and the steers tumbled into the river; they roared in
fright, and some tried to turn around, while others were borne
away by the current, but the men on the bank and the boatmen
in the canoes in midstream held them back and forced them
into line. A tangle of horns indicated the oblique path of the

ford, with María Nieves' head in the lead, next to that of his horse. His song could be heard from the middle of the wide river, in whose muddy waters were lurking the treacherous alligator, the electric eel, the ray, and voracious schools of caribs, with the vultures hovering overhead.

At last the herd reached the opposite bank, hundreds of meters away. One by one the steers were dragging themselves out of the water, giving piteous cries. They stood dejectedly on the bank, huddled together, while the guide went back into the river to fetch another lot.

The corrals at the Pass had been emptied, and on the other side of the Arauca, on a dismal, dry bank, under a sky the color of slate, rose the mournful wailing of hundreds of jostling cattle—to be taken to Caracas, across leagues and leagues of flooded savannah, step by step, to the tune of the drivers' songs.

> Come, come, my little bulls
> Follow in your leader's tracks,
> Count your steps to where the butcher's
> Waiting for you with the axe.

As many more had been sent in a different direction towards the Cordilleras, as if it were the heyday of the old Luzardos, when Altamira was the richest ranch in the Arauca basin.

This was the beautiful and vigorous life of the wide streams and vast savannahs, where man always goes singing in the face of danger; the Epic itself, the Plain under its most imposing aspect: the winter demanding the last bit of patience and daring, the floods making the risks a hundred fold greater, and making the immensity of the desert all the more apparent from the stretches of high land above the sea of water; but also accenting the immensity of man's stature and the powers in attendance upon him, when, unable to hope for anything from anyone, he resolves to confront what may come.

To increase their wages, some of the Plainsmen, the "llaneros," collected and sold heron plumes, and one part of the novel deals with the arrival of the birds in the spring.

It rained, and rained, and rained. For days nothing else happened. The cattlemen who had been outside their houses had returned to them, for the creeks and streams would overflow into the prairie and there would soon be no negotiable path. Nor any need to travel one. It was time for "quid, cup, and hammock," and beneath his palm thatch with these three things, the Plainsman is happy, while out-of-doors the clouds are falling in an endless pouring rain.

The return of the wild herons began with the first days of rain. They appeared in the south—whence they migrate in the winter, though no one knows where they go—and the numberless flocks were still arriving. Wearied by their long flight, they rested, swaying on the flexible branches of the forest trees, or, being thirsty, flew to the rim of the marsh, so that the woods and waters were covered with white.

The wild ducks, the scarlet flamingos, the blue herons, the *cotuas*, the *gavanes* and the wild blue chickens, none of whom had migrated, flew up to greet the travellers, in other numberless flocks coming from the four corners of the sky. The cranes had also returned and were telling of their voyage.

The marsh was full to overflowing, for the winter had set in with a will. One day the black snout of a crocodile rose to the surface, and soon there would be alligators too, for the creeks were rapidly filling and they could travel all over the prairie. The alligators came from far away, many of them from the Orinoco; but they tell nothing of their journeys, for they pass the entire day sleeping or pretending to be asleep. And it was a good thing they were silent, for they could have related nothing but crimes.

The moulting commenced. The home of the herons was a snowy forest. In the trees, in the nests built in them, and around the pools, was the whiteness of thousands and thousands of the herons; while on every side, in the branches, in the shoals floating over the muddy water of the swamp, lay the white frost of feathers shed during the night.

At dawn the collecting began. The pickers start out in canoes, but end up by jumping into the water; up to their waists in it, they defy death in a dozen hidden forms, shouting and

singing, for the Plainsman never works in silence. If he does
not yell, he sings.

Rain, rain, rain! The creeks had overflowed and the pools
were full. The human beings began to fall ill, stricken by
malaria, shivering with cold, their teeth chattering. They became pale, and then green, and crosses began to spring up in
the Altamira cemetery, which was no more than a small rec-
tangular plot with a barbed wire fence, in the middle of the
prairie, for the Plainsman, even after death, is content if he
may lie in the midst of his plains.

But the rivers commenced to go down at last, and the
ponds on the river banks to dry up; the alligators began to
abandon the creeks, some for the Arauca, some for the Orinoco,
from wherever they had come, to gorge themselves on the
Altamira cattle. The fever was dying out, and the guitars and
rattles, the ballads and stories could be heard once more; the
wild, merry soul of the Plainsman singing his loves and his
work and his trickery.

"Where does the Plainsman get the strength, when he's
so anaemic?" exclaimed Santos. "He stands a whole day's hard
work on horseback, riding after cattle, or in water up to his
waist."

*With the beauty of nature were combined superstition and
treachery. Marisela, the illegitimate daughter of Doña Barbara
and Lorenzo Barquero, her lover whom she had debauched and
driven from his own ranch, witnessed the spells cast by her
mother, at her ranch, fittingly named El Miedo (Fear), to attract Santos. Chaper XIII describes her reactions.*

Towards nightfall, as she was going to the kitchen to prepare supper for Santos, who was already entering, Marisela
heard what Eufrasia, the Indian woman, was saying to Casilda.

"Why should Juan Primito insist on finding out exactly
how tall the señor is? Who could it interest, unless it's Doña
Barbara. Everybody says she's in love with the master."

"And you believe there's something in it, sister?" Casilda
inquired.

"I should say I do believe it! Don't you think I've seen proof

of it? The woman that ties a man's length around her waist
can do what she likes with him. That Indian, Justina, tied
Dominguito's length around her waist, and made a fool of
him; Dominguito who came from Chicuacal. She measured
him with a piece of cord, and tied it to her girdle. And that
was the end of Dominguito!"

"Woman!" exclaimed Casilda, "and if you believe that,
why didn't you tell the Doctor not to let Juan Primito measure
him?"

"I did think of it, but since the Doctor won't believe in
these things and was so much amused over the booby's antics,
I didn't dare say anything. My idea was to take the string away
from Juan Primito, but he threw dust in my eyes, as they say,
and when I went to look for him, I couldn't even see the dust.
He must be way off now, although that was just a little while
ago. When he gets going, nobody can follow him."

This was the most ordinary and primitive practice of witchcraft conceivable, but Marisela felt herself grow tense when she
heard about it. In spite of the persistent pains Santos had
taken to combat her belief in these frauds, and although she
herself declared that she didn't give any credit to them, superstition was deeply seated in her soul. Besides, the words of the
kitchen maids, which she had heard with bated breath and with
her heart ready to leap out of her breast, had changed into certainty the horrible suspicions that had often crossed her mind:
Her mother was in love with the man *she* loved.

She choked back the exclamation of horror that was about
to escape her, clapping a trembling hand to her mouth, and
forgot her purpose in coming to the kitchen. She crossed the
patio towards the house, turned, retraced her steps, and went
back again, as though the horrible ideas in her head, rejected
by her conscience, were changing themselves into involuntary
movements.

At that moment she saw Pajarote coming. She went out to
meet him, and asked:

"Haven't you seen Juan Primito on your way in?"

"I passed him on the other side of the cork-trees. He must

be near El Miedo now, because he was going like the devil with a soul in his bag."

She thought a moment, and then said:

"I've got to ride right now to El Miedo. Will you go with me?"

"And the Doctor?" Pajarote objected. "Isn't he here?"

"Yes. He's in the house. But he mustn't know about it. I'm going secretly. Saddle Catira for me, without letting anybody know about it."

"But Marisela, my child—" Pajarote demurred.

"No. That's no use, Pajarote. Don't waste your time trying to make me give up the idea. I've got to go to El Miedo right now. If you're afraid—"

"Don't say any more. Wait for me behind the banana tree; there no one will see you going."

Pajarote decided that something very important was in the wind, and because of this and because Marisela had said, "If you're afraid," he made up his mind to go with her without any more question. No one had yet been born who could say: "Pajarote doesn't dare to do this."

Hidden by the banana tree, they rode away from the house unperceived, as night was coming on. The desire to avoid seeing her mother face to face made Marisela ask:

"Do you think, if we hurry, we might catch up with Juan Primito before he gets there?"

"We won't catch up with him even if we ruin the horses," answered Pajarote. "With the start he has, and the length of his stride, if he isn't there yet he's pretty near to it."

As a matter of fact, Juan Primito was at that moment arriving at El Miedo. He found Doña Barbara at the table, alone, for it had been some days since Balbino Paiba had allowed himself to be seen there, fearing, as he did, that his presence would provoke the rupture that was imminent.

"Here's what you sent me for," said Juan, taking the roll of string from his pocket and putting it on the table. "It's not a hair's breadth long or short." And he told her how he had contrived to take Luzardo's measurement.

"Good," said Doña Barbara. "You may go. Get anything you want from the commissary."

She remained seated in thoughtful contemplation of that bit of greasy cord which held something of Luzardo and was to bring him to her arms, according to one of her most deeply-rooted convictions. Desire had changed into passion, and since the longed-for man who was to give himself up to her "with eager steps" was not directing them towards her, the grim determination to secure possession of him through sorcery had risen from the turbid depths of her superstitious, witchcraft-ridden soul.

Doña Barbara had just risen from the table and gone into the next room when Marisela put her head in the door. She took one step, another, and then another, silently, looking behind her. The beating of her heart made the blood pound in her temples, but she was no longer afraid.

In the little room she used for her magic, before the shelf full of holy pictures and rude amulets on which a lamp, just lighted, was burning, Doña Barbara stood gazing at the cord while she mumbled the incantation:

"With two I gaze upon thee, with three I bind thee: With The Father, Son, and Holy Ghost. Man! I shall see thee before me, more humble than Christ before Pilate." And untying the roll of cord, she prepared to wind the string around her waist, when it was suddenly snatched out of her hands. She turned swiftly and stood there, petrified with surprise.

It was the first time mother and daughter had met face to face since Lorenzo Barquero had been obliged to leave the house. Doña Barbara well knew that Marisela had become quite another person since she had been living at Altamira; but her surprise at the girl's unexpected appearance united with the effect produced on her by her daughter's beauty, and she was for a moment unable to fling herself upon Marisela. She was about to do it, as soon as the moment of disconcerting surprise had passed, when Marisela swung around to prevent her, seizing the cord, exclaiming:

"Witch!"

The conflict in Doña Barbara's heart, when she heard from her own daughter the insulting epithet no one had ever dared pronounce in her presence, was like the collision of two masses hurtling together and falling shattered in ruins. The consciousness of wickedness and ardent desire, what she was and what she wanted to be, so that Luzardo would love her, crashed, in a formless confusion of primitive emotion. Marisela, meanwhile, had darted to the shelf and had swept to the floor, with a single movement of her arm, all the horrible confusion of holy pictures, Indian fetiches and amulets resting on it, the taper burning before the image and the chimney of the little lamp. She was shrieking,

"Witch! Witch!"

Doña Barbara, infuriated, seized the girl and tried to take the cord away from her. Marisela resisted, struggling in the grasp of the powerful, man-like hands that were tearing her blouse, baring her virginal breast, as they fought; when suddenly a vigorous calm voice ordered:

"Let her go!"

It was Santos Luzardo who had just appeared on the threshold.

Doña Barbara obeyed, and tried, with a superhuman effort at dissimulation, to transform her sinister expression into one of affability. But instead of a smile, there appeared on her face a hideous, forlorn grimace at the failure of her attempt.

To ruin Santos, Doña Barbara sent some of her cowboys to kill his llaneros as they took the feathers to market. The failure of the authorities to do anything about it enraged the lawyer and sent him to avenge his men as the Green Hell began working its spell on him.

He thought his shot killed Melquiades, the Wizard, and in Chapter XXI he said as much to Marisela, as she sat beside her dead father, in his squalid hut.

"You, too, Santos Luzardo! You've heard the call, too?"

Lorenzo had already succumbed, a victim of the ogress, which was not so much Doña Barbara as the implacable land,

the wild land, with its brutalizing isolation, the quagmire where
the pride of the Barqueros had wallowed; and now he too had
begun to sink in that other quagmire, that of barbarism which
never releases those who throw themselves into it. He, too, was
now a victim of the ogress. Lorenzo had ended his subjugation;
he was just beginning.

"Santos Luzardo, look at me! This land never relents!"

He looked at the sunken face, covered with the clayey patina
of death, replacing, in his imagination, his own features for
those of Lorenzo and saying to himself:

"Soon I shall begin to pass my days in drunkenness to forget, and soon I shall be like this, with hideous death drawn on
my face, the death of a man's spectre, the death of a living
corpse."

And having taken Lorenzo's place in this way, he was surprised that Marisela spoke to him as to a living being.

"They tell me you've been very strange these days, doing
things that you weren't meant to do . . ."

"They haven't told you anything yet. I killed a man tonight."

"You? . . . No! It can't be."

"What's odd about it? All the Luzardos have been murderers."

"It isn't possible," Marisela replied. "Tell me about it. Tell
me."

When he had told her about the evil event, as he saw it in
his excited imagination—as it had happened, but badly interpreted in his confused mental state, she repeated:

"Don't you see that it wasn't possible? If the thing happened as you tell it, it was Pajarote who killed the Wizard.
Didn't you say that he was on your right, face to face with you,
and that the wound was in the left breast? Then no one but
Pajarote could have shot him on that side."

The presence of the scene before his imagination for hours,
and persistent reflection over all its details had not sufficed to
make Santos take account of what Marisela had inferred in

an instant; and he sat and looked at her with the hopeful be-
wilderment of a man lost in the depths of a dark cave who sees
the salvation of a light coming towards him.

It was the light he himself had set burning in Marisela's
spirit, the clarity of intuition in the intelligence he had bright-
ened, the spark of goodness directing her judgment to carry
comforting words to his troubled soul. It was his work, his real
accomplishment, for his was not to crush out evil with blood
and fire, but to discover, here and there, the hidden springs of
goodness in his people and in his land. It was his work, unfinished, and abandoned in a discouraged moment, which was returning good for good, restoring his self-esteem—not because
the material fact that it had been Pajarote's bullet and not
his own which had killed the Wizard altered the situation, so
that his spirit had reacted against the confusion violence had
done to it; but because coming from Marisela, the comforting
persuasion of those words had sprung from her confidence in
him, and that confidence was part of him, the best part, sown
in another heart.

He accepted the gift of peace, and gave in exchange a word
of love. And that night, light came down into the depths of
the cave for Marisela, too.

*So on Santos the jungle had not worked its will. He was
still a human being. And his example helped Doña Barbara, too,
because at the end she returned the feathers, left him documents giving him possession of the entire ranch, and agreed to
his marriage to Marisela. Then she went away, and the novel
concludes:*

The name of El Miedo disappeared from the Arauca and
all the land once more became known as Altamira.

Robert Malloy

CÉSAR URIBE PIEDRAHITA
1897–   Colombia

Doctor Uribe is not a professional writer. He is one of the most famous scientists of his country, and an authority on tropical diseases. However during his youth, while studying and traveling in the jungles, he gathered data and local color that he set down in his only novel, *Toá* ("The Flame Girl") (1933), which is based on the experiences of Dr. Antonio de Orrantia, who investigated the slave labor of the rubber plantations. It is full of violence and terror and horror, with wild animals and mad, vengeful Indians, but at the same time it shows Colombia's attempt to regulate the conquest of one of its riches, rubber. The language varies between grotesque exaggeration and lyrical and almost Biblical beauty as the trip of the doctor, the guide Tomás Muñoz, and "*La Niña Toá*" make it one of the most important "Green Hell" novels. It was republished in Buenos Aires in 1942, but the author has been too busy as head of his laboratory in Bogotá to write more, or even arrange the reprinting of two excellent volumes of short stories, *Relato de caucherías* ("Tales of the Rubber Gatherers") and *Mancha de aceite* ("Oil Stain").

TOÁ

The Anaconda Hunt

It was raining without pause over the immensity of the Amazonian plain. The rivers were swollen. The channels and tributaries overflowed their banks and spread through the forest until all the land was covered for thousands of miles along the width and length of the flatlands. And still the waters rose. The rivers intermingled. There were no river beds, nor banks, nor pools, nor swamps, nor rivers. It was one vast sea, hidden under the dark roof of the forest, turbulent, still, and deep. The beasts of the jungle took refuge on the little islands that the water respected. Prisoners on the islands, they lived in a confused flock: jaguars, pumas, deer, and rabbits. The ground was infested with snakes. The water kept rising slowly in proportion as the rivers carried down from the mountains enormous liquid masses, sticks, leaves, and drowned animals.

Life in the lowlands, favorable to the production of the cursed rubber tree, was almost impossible. Days and nights passed without the recession of the rivers or the drying of basins, lagoons, or channels.

In the small settlement of Churo only one of the houses remained. The rest, chewed by termites and destroyed by dampness, had collapsed.

But as Tony and his friends painfully made their way up the Senseya River, the waters were beginning to diminish in volume, and were depositing muddy soil mixed with leaves torn from the trees along the river. Everything smelled bad on the river.

"Are you very tired, Toá?" asked Tony.

"No, sir, I'm all right."

"Listen, doctor," said the pilot. "Tonight we will arrive at the town of Faustino's. Now you certainly must rest and forget all your trouble, since it's all over."

At dusk, they arrived at the village of the Siona Indians. The town was peaceful. The children were playing with their humming tops. At the arrival of the strangers, the chief and his officials came out to meet them. After long talks between Faustino and Tomás, the chief extended his hand to the doctor and his friends, and offered them the ample hospitality of his village.

Serafín, the chief, was descended from the ancient race of the Pirangas, former chiefs of the tribes that dwelt along the Senseya, from the headwaters of the Putumayo in the vicinity of Sucombíos to the Cochas del Cuyabeno. He was old but still retained a manly and frank appearance that pleased the newcomers.

"You go to the chief's house, doctor," said Tomás. "They'll give Niña a hammock in the house of the old women."

The chief's big house was built over the clean and dry ground of the ravine rim. It was just one large room with entrances at both ends. Lined up on each side of the room were the curtained quarters of the attendant couples and the distinguished people of the tribe. In one of the apartments, Faustino lived with his wife and his two children.

Tony, pleased with the hospitality of Piranga, ate with a hearty appetite and without hesitation drank the nippy *chicha* that the chief offered personally to his guest. The women peeped through the cracks in the walls and laughed shrilly like mice. Tony's red hair and beard caused great admiration and were, from then on, the basis of his fame as the great wizard, the witch doctor with white man's medicines.

The days passed calmly in the village of Piranga. Tony recovered from his illnesses and began to forget the nightmare of the time spent in the rubber regions. Diligently he studied the aboriginal language. He liked to play with the children and fish in the river with Tomás and Faustino.

"Doctor!" Toá said to him one day. "I wonder whether you'd like to go with the Indians to hunt an anaconda in the lagoon up there. What a huge anaconda! He has swallowed many dogs and they even say that last year he swallowed an Indian child. Don't you respect him? I have never seen this animal, but I've always respected him. . . . Tonight they're tying a rabbit in his feeding place, and early tomorrow they're going to hunt him down. Do you want to go?"

"Of course. Let's all go and see whether an anaconda falls into the trap or whether we come up with a water witch," said Tony smiling.

"Don't tell me, doctor, that a water witch might appear. . . . Really? I'm plenty afraid of those old ones of the water."

Tony watched them enclose the victim in a bamboo cage.

The rabbit was a poor little beast with a broken paw and a deep wound in his nose. He uttered weak, pitiable cries.

"Around this bunny they will fasten crosswise some flint-pointed spikes and then tie it to a stake that will have a ball of string attached. The anaconda arrives, swallows it, and goes back to his pond to digest it. He keeps unwinding the cord and finally tears up the stake which stays floating or tangled in the patch of rushes. That's why one must use good strong string. You'll see it all. Won't you be scared when they pull out that creature?"

"I feel sorry for the poor rabbit."

Soon dawn broke. In the warm air of the early morning floated a milky, thin mist that obliterated everything with its tenuous opaqueness. The men arrived, accompanied by Tony and Toá. The anaconda had swallowed the bait, and there amid the rushes floated the telltale buoy.

"He swallowed the rabbit!" cried Tomás, slapping the doctor on the shoulder.

The natives launched their narrow canoes and paddled out to form an angle opening toward the middle of the pond. On the bank, some men slowly hauled in the cord. There was the prisoner! The cord was tight. They tried to drag out the captured victim, but they had to let out slack when they felt the enormous pull that the serpent gave.

"He is a monster!" said Tomás, looking at the lake with wide open eyes.

The maneuver of hauling in was repeated several times. Everyone was watching the bubbles that rose from the bottom of the dirty pond. Again . . . Suddenly, without warning, the serpent turned in the water and made the canoes bounce about. The natives on the bank fell in the mud, climbed back quickly, and kept on pulling the cord. The dirty water churned, and a cloud of black and decayed muck appeared on the surface. An enormous ring rose into the air and gyrated like an enormous wheel covered with mud. The maneuver of the natives continued. Little by little the cord was being hauled in. The canoes closed the angle and the hunters got ready their harpoons and bows. Suddenly the whole pond moved in whirlpools. Mud flew into the air, and there appeared a spiral that turned like a monstrous screw. The water re-echoed under the blow of the infuriated beast. Twenty harpoons, discharged from the canoes, disappeared into the churning, scummy water. The whirlwind approached the rushes on the bank, the harpoons fell like rain on the powerful moving spiral that tore out the reeds and water plants by their roots. The enormous tail came out of the water and lashed about. A canoe upset. The head, wrapped in weeds and twisted in the cord, struggled in the mud of the bank. The men in the canoes hurried to make ready their chonta and bamboo lances. Everyone shouted to the noise of the tumultuous boiling of the swamps and the splash of the tail and head of the anaconda that were gyrating like fantastic propellers.

Tony looked on enthusiastically at the tremendous beauty of the primitive scene. In this lagoon bristling with dead tree trunks and covered with slimy weeds, he felt he was watching a scene back in the age of the reptiles. The naked savages might have been hunting a gigantic plesiosaurus or a prehistoric lizard. . .

The group formed by the doctor, the guide, and Toá, stood motionless in their intense watchfulness.

One effort more by the men and the reptile came out onto the bank, writhing in huge loops and perilous rings. It pulverized the reeds but pushed the darts still farther into its flesh. Faustino landed a tremendous blow with his machete on the serpent's head. The monster writhed and coiled, then stretched his dying body over the mud. The tail kept on beating the water. Little by little it became motionless, stretched over the mud of the bank.

At the moment when the enormous anaconda became quiet, Tony came back to reality.

"That really is an anaconda!" said Tomás. "It was right to have had so much respect for him. He is at least forty-five feet long . . . Maybe more."

Linda Wilson

EDUARDO ACEVEDO DÍAZ
1851–1924   Uruguay

Acevedo Díaz, the first Uruguayan nationalist writer, created the novel of his country with a series of brutal, realistic books that provided the model for Carlos Reyles, Javier de Viana, and Justino Zavala Muniz. They even repeated some of his episodes. His masterpiece, *Soledad* (1894) from which this description of a prairie fire is taken, is the story of the revenge of Pablo Luna against the society that ostracized him. He had been secretly meeting Soledad, daughter of a wealthy rancher. This novel was preceded by Acevedo Díaz's "Hymn of Blood" trilogy: *Ismael* (1888), *Nativa* (1890), and *Grito de Gloria* ("Shout of Glory") (1894), that fictionalize some of Uruguay's civil wars.

THE PRAIRIE FIRE

The tall grasses and wild rushes were burning far and wide, filling the sky with a bright glow. In the section bounded by rocky hills, huge tongues of flame licked upward, and there where the *totora* grass was thickest, dazzling flowers seemed to take form amid the loud crackling and the shower of sparks.

Through terrifying paths of ashes, the fleeing cattle milled, as though attacked by madness. The feet of the herd churned up the embers, kicking them behind them like a whirlwind of burning ashes. Many bulls, with their hair and hide singed, bellowing and forcing their way through the rest of the cattle, crowded into the fatal paths where the grating of their interlocked horns mingled with the crackle of tree-trunks bursting apart from the pressure of their boiling sap.

To the formidable pressure of the frightened cattle, forced closer by the flames on all sides, were added the lesser animals that had not been able to escape in time to the waters of the ditches. The odor of burning wool, combined with that of horse-hair, along with all the refuse consumed by the voracious flames, rolled skyward in coils of black smoke shot through with flashes of red.

The slopes of the mountain, usually so dull in color, now seemed clad in blood-red velvet, speckled with ashen patches of gases that floated in dense clouds over the abysses. And in the midst of that choking atmosphere, full of smoke, noise, and flying stars, loud bellowing and whinnying, could still be heard the shouts of men, all shrilly combined in the heroic struggle against the prairie fire.

The cultivated cornfield, like the center of a battle line, con-tributed to the noise as the kernels on its ears popped open in rosettes.

In one corner of the valley, a herd of wild mares, formed in a semicircle facing away from the fire, were kicking back at the flames that came on swiftly and irresistibly. With flying manes and frightened eyes, with nostrils distended and sweat and foam standing out on their skins, their escape was blocked by jagged rocks that were covered with harpoon-like spiny bushes.

Dry and combustible, these branches had by now been showered by burning cinders, driven like projectiles from a distance. The thicket was already crackling as one serpent of flame after another crawled, amid puffs of smoke, through the doomed underbrush.

Ferrets and lizzards scurried swiftly in all directions, hunting safety, darting dizzily in and out of their crevices. Swift groups of bats uttered their shrill cries through the smoke. From the dark entrances of other caves, more winged creatures flew out to collide with their fellows in flight, and fall in piles in the path of the fire.

Pablo Luna, from his shack above where the mares had collected, saw a couple of caretakers appear suddenly. Scorning the danger, they tossed a lasso over the nearest mare and brought her to earth. They killed her at once, with a knife slash from neck to belly, so that the guts began spilling out. With

their woven lassos, one looped a front foot of the carcass and
the other a hind leg. Then spurring their horses, they started
dragging the body over the burning grass. Widely separated,
they rode across part of the field not yet dominated by the
flames so that the bloody corpse that formed a sort of vertex
of a triangle was dragged over the flames, extinguishing them
in places, in others spreading them without being able to
quench their violence. Behind this lugubrious train remained
strips and black islands encircled by flames.

Looking at their hopeless effort, which he watched without
emotion, the gaucho muttered: "It's useless. You can't capture
the wind by the legs the way you can a horse!"

In reality, the Northeaster was blowing furiously, driving
the flames toward the grape arbor and the garden, only a short
distance from the house. Pablo Luna had chosen a fine time to
carry out his work of destruction. Complete disaster seemed inevitable in that field of high grass and dry thistles, of boneset
rushes and cattails. Everything burned like tinder.

With his dishevelled head between his hands, the livid
gaucho kept his bloodshot eyes focused on the scene. Only
when the fire, driven by the wind, was close to the houses did
he jump on his pony, and with a lash of his whip and the cry of
a wild animal, he departed on a gallop for the woods, on his way
to the Witch's Gorge.

W.K.J.

HUGO WAST
1883–   Argentina

"The American Pereda" is one name for Argentina's
most fertile novelist, Gustavo Martínez Zuviría, who
transposed the letters of his first name into his signature to more than thirty exciting novels of history, adventure and local customs, besides some dealing with
rural and urban social problems. Some have sold more
than 100,000 copies, with a total of a million and a

half copies in 290 Spanish and 70 translated editions in eleven languages. His *Valle negro* ("Black Valley") (1918), scorned in a local competition as unworthy of consideration, became his best seller and received a gold medal from the Spanish Academy. *Pata de zorra* ("Fox's Paw") (1924) deals with a fortuneteller who helped a student pass his examination in Roman law. *Flor de durazno* ("Peach Blossom") (1911) about unmarried love, made a hit movie. *Desierto de piedra* ("Stone Desert") (1925) the first novel that satisfied its author, and *Casa de los cuervos* ("House of the Ravens") (1916) are classics of the mountainous regions of Argentina, and remind one that their author taught economics and sociology at the University of Santa Fe before his books made him wealthy. *La mano que faltó*, part of which is here translated, was written for the magazine *Caras y caretas* ("Faces and Masks") of Buenos Aires in 1925, and is a sample of Wast's themes and technique, with abundance of detail, strong emotions, and a suspenseful plot.

THE MISSING HAND

Down the long hill at the siesta hour, along the shady road, between rows of tall poplars, came a man at whom the dogs of the huts he was leaving behind barked without approaching him. His thick boots stamped unfamiliar tracks in the white dust, and his blouse of blue cloth also added a strange note to the local scene.

He moved with a slow, weary step, carrying on his shoulder a sack-cloth bag hung from a club steadied by his left hand. He stopped to take a breath, dropping the bundle, and then, as the right sleeve was drawn up, it was possible to observe the reddish, hairy stump of a wrist cut off at the root. He had neither a mustache nor beard, and his lips were parched, as if he were dying of thirst. He inhaled deeply the sweet air that swayed the tops of the trees, and again took up his bundle and resumed his journey, divining, perhaps, that a brook flowed at the base of the hill.

However, thirst overcame him. He approached one of the straw-thatched clay huts that could be seen through the opening between the trees on the border of an alfalfa field. The dogs did not permit him to come as far as the patio, where some hens were pecking and where a little motherless lamb was nibbling the grass that grew in the shade of the wall. He dropped his bag and knocked two or three times on the palisade with his stick.

The barking of the dogs redoubled; a woman's voice shouted from the interior of the hut, "Who is it?" and two timid little girls appeared holding hands, suspicious in the presence of the visitor. "What will you have?"

"A drink of water, for the love of God."

The man made a gesture, and the children noticed that he lacked a hand and fled in terror.

"Mamma, the man of the missing hand!"

The door of the hut closed with a bang, and outside were left only the infuriated dogs, the startled lamb, and the indifferent hens that were pecking crumbs of bread near the beehive-shaped oven. The man waited awhile, then smiled with disdain and bitterness, caught up his bag, and continued on his way.

The woodland ended at the beginning of the slope, which was stony and arid because the rains had denuded the surface, carrying away all the vegetable mold into the valley. There flowed a limpid, inexhaustible brook between cresses and reeds, beneath the shelter of aged willows, the shade of which refreshed its waters. On one of the banks could be seen the ruins of two mills that had given to the town its name.

The man with the missing hand dropped to his knees and drank greedily of that purest of water, which was so clear that the sands at the bottom and thousands of tiny silvery fish were visible; and then he seated himself on the red stone, bound by a hoop of iron, that half a century earlier had been moved by the current of that same brook to grind the grain for the village bread. Amid the song of the birds, he began to drowse, with his head resting on his bag, his face covered by the sleeve of his blue blouse. Suddenly the noise of the snapping of twigs roused him.

Half a dozen urchins were gazing at him with curiosity and fear, and down the hillside came others to look at him, as if he were a savage animal trapped by a hunter. As he sat up, they uttered cries of terror and scampered away.

"The man of the missing hand!"

In a moment they all disappeared, some up the hill, others over the hurdles of thorny branches, others along the brook which half a league below emptied into the broad tranquil Río Segundo. The man of the missing hand shook his head wearily, settled himself again, hiding his face, and once more he slumbered.

When he awoke, he saw an old man seated on the same stone, looking at him as if waiting for him to open his eyes. Between the foliage, which was beginning to darken with the approach of night, were visible white patches and restless forms, a sign that other people were awaiting the result of the conference that was going to take place between the two men.

The old man was pale, he had a discolored beard, he was dressed in black, and he wore spectacles with frames of brass.

"Obviously you are a stranger," he began, but the man with the missing hand interrupted him with a question.

"Yes, I am a stranger . . . But do you always receive strangers like this?"

The man regained his composure and continued: "I am the village schoolteacher. It is evident that you have never been in this place."

The man of the missing hand looked at him curiously.

"Why is it evident?"

"Because you approached a hut to ask for water when you had this brook here."

"True! You are very sagacious."

The teacher smiled, flattered.

"Maybe you do not even know the name of this town."

"Yes, I know it. They told me yesterday in the neighboring village. I am a bird of passage."

"You are passing through? All the better. You could not live in this place for even two days."

"Are your neighbors such savages?"

"It is not that. You see, they . . . they have been waiting for many years for a man . . . a man who has lost a hand . . . as you have."

"Why are they waiting for him?"

"It is believed that inevitably he will come some day or other to seek the hand that he lost here."

"How curious!" exclaimed the unknown, getting to his feet with the use of the heavy stick, as if he needed it for support or defense. He kept silent for a moment during which only the fresh song of the brook could be heard. "To seek his hand? Where would he find it?"

"In the cemetery. In the coffin of a dead woman, buried more than twenty years ago."

"In the coffin of a dead woman? Your neighbors must be crazy. What was her name?"

"Panchita Montiel. She was the *sacristana* of the church."

The dark man, with his skin burned by the sun and the wind, turned pale when he heard that name. The cudgel slipped from his hand. He bent to pick it up, but said nothing till he had regained his seat beside the teacher, who repeated: "You are not from here. Therefore you did not know this."

The schoolteacher then invites the stranger to spend the night at his house where he will explain. The villagers keep spying on them, and the teacher's sister will not even sit at the table with the man with the missing hand. After supper the two men sit down and the teacher tells the story.

Panchita was the oldest child of the town's most important citizens. She had only one surviving brother, Diego, all the others having died during childhood. Diego had a bad reputation for pranks, but she looked after him, and also kept the church dusted and neat. Diego, with no education and no job, could not marry Polonia, the daughter of a poor widow. She was also being courted by one of the rich boys, but had told Diego she would run away with him if he got some money so they could go to the city.

Shepherds from the mountains, driving their flocks to market, asked Panchita's permission to pasture the animals in the church yard. She overheard their plans to steal the treasures from the church, so she hurried home, roused Diego, and told him to run to the police station for help to save the altar pieces which "would bring lots of money in the city."

Diego hurried off, then began thinking of the possibilities of getting that money for himself. He thought of Polonia. He knew how he could enlarge a crack in the door to release the bolt.

Meantime Panchita had seized an ax and run over to defend the church till help came. She heard a noise at the big door. She saw a knife enlarge the slit.

She saw the hand slip through softly, a hand that was accustomed to things and showed its familiarity with the arrangements by unhesitatingly seizing the bolt. Panchita lifted her ax and came down with a ferocious blow on that hand.

A frightful howl was the response to her blow; an accent that pierced as the blade of that knife would have done. She stood petrified, looking at that hand that had fallen to the floor and that lay there at her feet, a hand a thousand times dead . . . dead to its owner and to God.

She bent lower and lower till her eyes could contemplate it from very near, and as the dim light was still not strong enough and she needed more light in order to see it, she dropped the ax and picked up the cold, viscous hand.

XI

"Poor woman!" exclaimed the teacher. "On the following day they found her dead under the lamp of the *sagrario*, holding to her breast that hand that they were unable to take away from her. It would have been necessary to break her arm and fingers, so they decided to bury her with it. No one ever heard anything more of her brother or of the drovers that had spent the night there. They disappeared as though the mountains had swallowed them, and the people were left in doubt about the ownership of the hand that Panchita bore to her sepulcher; but since in the Day of Judgment we must all gather with our bones, the legend started that some day or other the owner of the hand will come in search of it. The peasants want to see him when he arrives, and find out for certain who he is."

"It is a stupid legend!" brusquely announced the man with the missing hand. "Whoever it was that the woman mutilated with the ax, he will take good care not to return here. And if I had known of this story, I wouldn't have come either, because I don't like to have people stare at me as your neighbors have stared at me today."

The teacher agreed, then, rising, he led his guest to one of the vacant rooms where there was a lighted candle at the head of a cot. The stranger put his bundle in the corner and after saying good night, closed the door.

XII

Neither the teacher nor his sister ventured to knock at the door when daylight came.

"We shall let him sleep? He arrived so tired that he could sleep all day."

However at about nine, when the teacher was in the midst of explaining the lesson, one of his pupils who always came late because he lived at a great distance, practically fell off his trotting donkey, then burst out with what he has just seen over the wall of the cemetery.

"Last night some foxes dug into a grave, pulled out the coffin of some dead person and scattered the bones all around!"

"Where was the grave?" asked the school master.

"Just as you enter, on the left, in the corner."

"That was no fox!" The teacher went to the guest room and jerked open the door. The room was empty.

"That was no fox," he repeated. "It was he who came in search of his hand." They sent parties to search for the stranger who had violated the grave of Panchita, but the mountains have a thousand paths, and no tracker was able to find him.

Anon. (*Inter-America*, Vol. 8)

RICARDO GÜIRALDES
1886–1927   Argentina

Güiraldes was a wealthy aristocrat, born on a ranch in the pampas of Argentina, but of a family whose father was once mayor of Buenos Aires, with money enough to permit Ricardo to take a two-year tour of the world. Paris was his second home, and looking back with nostalgia from there, he wrote in poetic prose about the easy life on the range. First came *Raucho* (1917) containing many of the elements of his later masterpiece. Then afflicted by Ultraism, he wrote several volumes, including *Xaimaca* (1923) that caught the fancy of some critics. *Don Segundo Sombra*, however, written in 1926 in a more tempered style, is a better book in its revelation of traditions and ideals. Many of the author's own experiences are retold in the story of a fourteen-year-old gaucho, the illegitimate son of a ranch owner, who is literary kin of the North American Tom Sawyer.

Scorned by his father, the gaucho attaches himself to Don Segundo Sombra, a figure whom the novelist modeled after a gaucho on his father's ranch, a man who not only teaches the boy the craft of a cowboy, but becomes a sort of spiritual father.

DON SEGUNDO SOMBRA

Chapter II. Description of the gaucho.

I looked the man over. He was really not so huge. What made him seem as he appears to me, even today, was the sense of power flowing from his body. His chest was enormous, and his joints big-boned like those of a horse. His feet were short and high-arched; the hands thick and leathery like the scales of an armadillo. His skin was copper-hued and the small eyes slanted slightly upward. Talking, he pushed his narrow-brimmed hat from his forehead showing bangs cut like a horse's, just above his eyebrows. He was dressed like any poor gaucho. A plain pigskin belt girded his waist. The short blouse fell over the bone-handled knife from which swung a rough plaited quirt, dark with much use. His *chiripá* was long and coarse, and a black kerchief was knotted around his neck. with the ends across his shoulders. He had split his *alpargatas* at the instep to make room for the fleshy foot.

The boy's warning saved the gaucho's life and eventually when Segundo Sombra came to tame horses at the ranch where the boy worked, he took him on as a sort of apprentice. In Chapter X, the narrator tells what he had learned.

Five years, and we had not parted from each other a single day of the hard herder's life! Five years, of the kind that make a gaucho of a lad if he has the luck to spend them with a man like the man I called godfather. It was he who had guided me with care toward all the wisdom of the pampa. He had taught me the knowledge of the herder, the cunning of the buster; he showed me how to use the lasso, and the *bolas*, the difficult art of training a horse to cut in on a stampeding herd and stop it, how to train a string of ponies to stand in line at a word on the open pampa, so that you could catch them whenever and wherever you wanted. Watching him, I had learned the ways of thongs and straps, learned to make my own bridles, reins, cinches, saddle pads, how to twist lassos, how to place the rings and the buckles.

Under him, I became physician to my ponies: I cured sore hoofs by turning the horse on his track, distemper by the dog method or by means of a halter pieced from ears of corn, weak kidneys with a plaster of putrid mud, lameness by tying a hair from the tail on the sound leg, hoof growths with a hot whetstone, boils and other ills by ways too numerous to mention.

And he taught me how to live: courage and fairness in the fight, love of one's fate whatever it might be, strength of character in affairs of the heart, caution with women and liquor, reserve among strangers, faith to friends.

I even learned from him how to have a good time: from him, and none other, how to strum the guitar and shake a light foot in the dance. From the store of his memory I took songs to sing alone or with a partner; and by watching him learned to manage the intricate steps of the *gato*, the *triunfo*, and other gaucho dances. He was overflowing with verses and stories, enough to make a hundred halfbreed girls crimson with joy or with shame.

Yet all this was nothing but a spark from the fire of the man; and my wonder at him grew with every day. He had ridden everywhere! In every ranch he had friends who admired him, loved him, although he was always on the move. His authority with the country folk was such that his bare word untangled the knottiest problem. But he did not exploit his popularity; it seemed rather to bore him. "I can't stay long on any ranch," he said, "because first thing you know I'm wanting to be more boss than the owner." What a *caudillo* he would have made! But more than everything, Don Segundo loved his freedom. His was the lone, anarchic spirit which droops in any prolonged intercourse with men. The action he loved best was the endless ride; the talk he loved best was the soliloquy.

One virtue of my godfather flowered best in the easeful talks around the evening fire. He was a great teller of stories,

and this gift added luster to his fame. I think his tales changed
my life. By day I was always the tough, sturdy pampa boy, fearless in the dangers of my work; but my nights now became
peopled with eerie shapes: a will-o'-the-wisp, a strange shadow,
a cry, was enough to fill my mind with scenes of magic, black
or white. My imagination began to thrive and to grow potent
with thought; a new creative gladness transfigured the vague
reverie of the pampa.

*Occasionally they had relaxation, such as a country gather-
ing in Chapter XI, where they danced the traditional gato.*

The leader clapped his hand:
"Now then, folks, let's have a *gato* sung like it should be
and danced by them that know their steps!"
The accordion player made room for the guitarist who was
going to sing. Two couples took their place near the musicians.
The women kept their eyes on the ground and the men turned
up the hat brims from their faces. The guitars began to strum.
Flexible wrists swayed and balanced above the strings; sharp
twangs gave the accent, cutting the rhythmic murmur of the
strum like a knife. The intermittent lash of the measure, like
a drum roll, began to irradiate daring in the air. The dancers
stood, until the vibrant fires of the music became the very
soul of their long-fibered muscles, of their lithe, slow backs,
of their eager shoulders.
Gradually, the room was drenched in the song. The white
walls shutting in the tumult were steeped in the song.
The door cut four rigid lines into a night made of infinitude
and stars above fields that cared only to sleep. The candles
trembled like old grandmothers. The floor tiles rang with the
feet of the dancers. Everything had succumbed to the proud
male strum of the music!
The singer bespoke his tenderness in tense tones:

"All I need is a ladder of love.
All I need is a ladder of love
To reach the heaven of your throat, my life."

The two women and the two men began to dance. The men moved agile and insistent, like amorous cocks flapping their wings. The women kept inside the prescribed circle and sent discreet glances over their shoulders. The four made a turn; and the singer continued:

> "Fly, unhappy one, fly, I'm going to sea
> In a little boat, my life, in a little boat."

The women picked up their skirts with careful fingers and opened them fanwise, as to receive a gift or defend something. Shadows flickered on the walls, touched the roof, and fell like rags to be trod on by gallant steps. Haste suddenly roused the two male bodies. Their boots rustled and shuffled a prelude; heels and soles clicked a multiplying rhythm that caught the guitars' accent to mark it and make it hurry. The moving folds of the *chiripás* sounded like faint waters. But the dance steps grew vigorous as a broncho's leaps, complementing in resonant counterpoint the melodious strings.

Several of the women pursed their lips in disdain at these country dances, trying to ignore them. But a wild gladness mastered us all, for we felt that here was the pantomime of our true loves and delights.

I took part in one dance with Don Segundo and my girl.

However all was not pleasure. The work of a cowboy had its perils, like the stampede in Chapter XXIV. They took on a job to drive six hundred yearlings to the city pens, a trip of about twelve days.

The afternoon we started was hot and sultry; just to saddle made us sweat. Every pampa creature, every blade of grass, was thirsting for one of those storms that lay the pampa flat in their fury and then set it straight again, like sprouting wheat. Even before we had started, we were drenched by a couple of slanting squalls that spotted the soft dirt of the corrals and roads like chickenpox. But the body of the storm was still up there, watching for us in a great pile of cloud to the southward. It threatened to turn chilly later, and we prepared for a hard march.

We had already supped, and it was dark, when a strong wind blew from a sudden spell of heat. Lightning for some time had been streaking the black clouds on the southern horizon. The herd was nervous, and getting worse. The horses neighed, feeling, as we did, the panic in the air. It was a perfect night for losing animals! Every flash revealed, livid, the imperturbable landside and the uneasy herd moving upon it, hemmed in by us men. An ominous, formless weight hung overhead. Things stood out in the flickering light with uncanny clearness: the white steers and the spots on the calves seemed to pierce the eye. The next instant we were lost in the black night, the swift vision branded on our minds like scars on hide; and we groped toward another flash. After the wind came a hush, as suddenly. In the sky were great ponds and silvery rivers, against the thick, black background. And tatters of gray cloud scurried across in wild confusion, like mustangs flying before a prairie fire.

The head man warned us to keep close to the steers who were milling around in fear. Lightning struck the earth with a dry crack that seemed to tear our flesh. The wind, I thought, was coming from underground. The herd crumbled apart like limestone in water. We remembered that we had to cross the bed of a deep gulch and we galloped hard to prevent the menace of falling beasts breaking their legs and getting mired. I was blinded. The ends of my handkerchief flew in my face, my hat brim flapped in my eyes; the wind kept me from guiding my horse but he ran on, perhaps because he could not stop and had lost his bearings like the cattle.

I sensed a dark mass running before me: probably a horse that had broken loose from some carriage overwhelmed by the wind. Men, women? Whoever they were, God help them. I dashed ahead until I was abreast of a bunch of steers. By now, the rain was pouring in torrents and tempering the wind. I heard one of the men yell and made in the direction of his call. The two of us stood against the opening of the gulch and battled to hold the beasts. My horse's hind feet slipped and I went down, as though hell had swallowed me. By luck, the slide stopped before my horse fell on me. Down on his haunches, he tried to get up, and I saw him trampling a calf. I could not hold him. Terror was riding him, and he fell on his right side, vising my leg against a mound in the gully. Then, laboriously, he got to his feet, slipped, and fell again on his haunches. Again and again. At last, his body tense with will, he gave a mighty upward lurch and we made it.

The storm had left the animals nervous, and we had to ride round them by fours. The night was still sultry. The cloudburst with its lightning and its whirlwinds had done us no good.

Dawn was dull, and we followed the trail after the head drover had counted the steaming beasts. All that day we stopped only to eat. The bad start had depressed us, and the animals were still rebellious and kept us going hard to wear them down and quiet them. Again and yet again, we made the round.

All that night we kept the trail, but so bad was our luck that we ran into two other herds and had to stand watch for the third time!

We were really beginning to get tired! And I was no amateur. But I knew that if you stand a lot because your body is hardened, you stand a lot more because your will won't give in. The body suffers only at first; then it grows numb and goes wherever you carry it like a load. Later your thoughts begin to cloud; you don't know how near you are to the goal, you don't know if you will ever reach it. Later still, your thoughts and facts get mixed into something so unreal that you grow indifferent and watch it dimly moving beyond your ken. Finally, all that is left is the strength to keep on without welching: to keep on forever. For this, and by this, you live: all else has vanished. And you win at the end (at least so it had been with me) after winning itself has become a matter of indifference. Your body falls asleep only because your will has left it.

Six days more we moved through cold and drench, standing watch every night, always on the alert, mastering swamps and mudflats, piling fatigue on fatigue. My reserve horse gave me a whole day's work; at the slightest chance, when I was driving or roping, he was up to his tricks. So I gave him the quirt, thong and handle, without stopping, till I had him tamed.

Maybe I would kill him? I had no time for standing on cere-mony.

We looked like a band of pampa Indians, ragged, muddied, sullen. Demetrio, the biggest and strongest of the herders, seemed annihilated by fatigue. And which of us would take oath he was any better? At last we came to a place that prom-ised a rest. There was a small enclosed pasture where the herd could be left without risk, and for us there was a shed where we could sleep! We got there early in the afternoon, drove in the herd, and walked our horses slowly toward the shed. De-metrio rode in front. When he reached the hitching post, his horse shied. Demetrio fell like a sack of *mate* and lay without moving. He had struck his head. Had the sudden terrible fall broken his neck? We rushed up. He was breathing like a child. Don Segundo laughed:

"He was a little tired . . . the fall rocked him to sleep."

We unsaddled his horse, stretched his outfit in the shade and placed him on it. He lay, unaware of how sleep had tricked him; but perhaps he was feeling the bliss of letting this body go, of wanting nothing in the world.

The rest of us sat around a while, drinking *mate*. We were sure of the still night ahead and this made us happy and talka-tive. We watered our ponies, rubbed them down. We looked over our outfits, mending a strap, sewing a pair of hobbles, ad-justing a saddle or a halter. We waited calmly for the night to take us: a being great and gentle upon which we could softly float away as on a river within whose banks flows the joy of oblivion. . . .

At the end, the boy's father died, and left his possessions to the boy he had abandoned all his life. It was Segundo Sombra who made him see it was his duty to take care of the ranch and the people dependent on it. So their companionship came to an end and the book ends:

I turned my horse about and set forth slowly toward the ranch. My going was like life-blood flowing away.

Harriet De Onís

ALBERTO BLEST GANA
1831–1920   Chile

Blest Gana, son of an Irish doctor and a Valparaiso
beauty, began his writing career at the middle of the
past century, with *Martín Rivas* (1862), an epic of the
Chilean civil war. *Durante la reconquista* (1897), one
of the most vigorous novels of Spanish America, from
which the translated excerpt is taken, deals with an
earlier period, the colonists' first attempt at independence, repulsed by the Spaniards at Rancagua, in 1814.
Its 1,000 pages are the epic of colonial Chile.

Though eighty-four Chilean authors wrote more than
150 novels between 1846 and 1900, none equalled the
work of the "Chilean Balzac," Blest Gana, in historical interest, naturalness, and spontaneity. Though sometimes not deeply studied, his novels abound in life and
color, and all concern some moment in Chile's history,
from the colonial patriots to the twentieth century
"transplanted Chileans" who, like the author, betook
themselves to France. Besides containing exciting plots,
they express the patriotism of their author who ran
away from school at fourteen to enlist in the army and
fight for his country.

DURING THE RECONQUEST

Camara's Fight

"Summary judgment" was an invention of Camara, adopted
by Major Robles on his own responsibility. In the Hispanic-
American conflict, the fury of the struggle had developed a
blind racial hatred between the armies. The Spanish government troops were scorned by the colonists as "Goths," while
the Chileans were regarded as "insurgent dogs" by the Spaniards. Exterminating each other rather than a noble aspira-

tion toward victory alone mattered. All practices of civilized warfare, scarce as they were, were in the eyes of the fighters only a philosophic fiction applicable to international struggles. Here death alone could assure a victory. Prisoners would only be a bother who might later fight again in the alternation of victory and defeat that marked each campaign.

In one of the final skirmishes before the defeat of Rancagua, Major Robles found himself with four prisoners at a moment when retreat was necessary before the superior Spanish army.

"If I were you, Major," Camara remarked, "I'd shoot all who are Goths. Any Chileans will surely want to throw in with us."

"All four will say they're Chileans," the perplexed major pointed out.

Then Camara proposed a test surer than any oath: "Make them say 'Francisco,' Major, and any one who pronounces it like a Goth gets a bullet."

This is what the major later termed "summary judgment." Without making up his mind to take the final steps, Robles tested the prisoners.

"Come here, you!" he ordered, seating himself at a table on which candles were burning. The men advanced slowly on account of their shackles. "All right. Let's hear you say, Francisco."

He first addressed a soldier who had surrendered without resistance. Since the man did not understand the unusual order, the major had to repeat it.

"Fransisco," said the soldier, using the "s" of the Chilean pronunciation.

The next prisoner, given the same test, pronounced it with a Castilian "th": "Franthisco."

"He's a Goth! Notice his accent!" cried Camara, sure that the major would condemn him to death on the spot. However, in old Robles, a conflict was waging between his hatred of the victors of Rancagua and a feeling of war chivalry. But the prisoner forced the decision. As a European, he looked with scorn at the colonists.

"If I weren't tied," he told Camara, "you'd be more respectful. You captured me by treachery."

"Let me prove to him, Major," Camara begged, "that I'm not afraid of him."

The major nodded, his blood heated at the insults of a Goth. So Camara slashed the bonds on the Spaniard's hands and feet, and tossed a sabre onto the ground in front of him.

"Now you'll see what a patriot is like," he shouted. "I have it in for you and all your rascally Goths!"

The Spanish soldier picked up the sabre and put himself on guard. In front of him, with his left arm wrapped in a poncho, and a dagger in his right hand, the Chilean *roto* prepared for the duel. His sharp eyes seemed searching for the target for his tricky knife. Motionless, the major watched as he would have witnessed a cock fight.

Camara took the offensive, though the combat was waged with equal fury by both. Without the protection of the poncho, the *roto* would have received a furious side swipe because in a desperate effort to end it quickly, as he had done in other dagger fights, Camara had attacked too hastily without protecting his head, and the sabre-point had scratched his forehead.

After that, he became more careful and trusted to agility instead of frontal attacks. He realized that his adversary was worthy of him. The Spaniard found himself defending himself against stabs from every direction, so he backed up against the wall. Otherwise that mad *roto* with the agility of a cat would certainly have killed him.

By now, on account of the tension of that life and death struggle, rather than the length of it, both combatants were wearied. But the Spaniard saw a ray of hope. The door to the hallway was open. If he could reach it, his legs would carry him to safety, since the *roto*, weary with his leaping, could never overtake him. Step by step, never letting down on his defense, he sidled toward the door. Several times the tip of Camara's dagger had lightly touched him.

By now, Camara had understood what the enemy was doing

and instead of preventing it, was helping it. And so, more easily than he had expected, the Spaniard reached the open door. But the moment he turned, Camara was on him and sank his knife in the Spaniard's back, through to the lungs.

"There goes one!" the *roto* exclaimed as the Spaniard fell to the ground and a spurt of blood stained the bricks. Then satisfied, he cleaned his dagger on a handkerchief he found in the Spaniard's pocket.

The major, calm and serious, made his report to his leader as if it was an ordinary barracks incident. General Rodríguez in a friendly tone commented that it was an imprudence that had better not be repeated.

"It's one Goth less, sir!" Camara told him. "Better tell them to send another one from 'Gothland,' to replace this one who's useless now!"

W.K.J.

ENRIQUE RODRÍGUEZ LARRETA
1875–1961   Argentina

Though an Argentine, Rodríguez Larreta used European more frequently than South American subjects for his novels. *Artemisa* (1903) deals with the glories of classical Greece and *La gloria de don Ramiro* (1908) fictionalizes the activities of the Inquisition during the time of Philip II of Spain. *Zogoibi* (1926), which some critics consider his best novel, deals with Argentine gauchos of the past. In his dramas, like *El linyero* ("The Wandering Cowboy"), Larreta strikes a more national note, but his most famous work, and the one which best reveals his Classic style, reminiscent of Valle-Inclán, is *The Glory of Don Ramiro*, the epilogue of which, set in Lima, Peru, and dealing with Santa Rosa, is translated here.

THE GLORY OF DON RAMIRO

Epilogue

In Peru, the year of 1605, in the City of the Kings. It is a night toward the end of October. The city sleeps under the brightness of stars and its belfries rise here and there, dark against the shadows. Fireflies and glowworms shine in thousands amid the orchards and the shadowy trees. The damp air is heavy with perfumes, and in the silence of the fields, the concert of crickets and frogs is broken only by the voice of the night watchman and the steps of a night owl homeward bound from the gambling house.

Gradually the hills of San Cristobal and Amancaes take on the rosy glow of dawn. A soft, languid breeze blows from the sea. The roosters have not yet roused.

Not far from the Plaza Mayor, in the small garden of a humble dwelling, a woman whose white dress shines in the darkness walks back and forth like a restless ghost. It is Rosa, the youngest daughter of Gaspar Flores and María de Oliva. Every morning before dawn, she gathers piously from the garden cultivated by her, the flowers that a little later she will take to the Virgin of the Rosary, in the nearby Church of Santo Domingo.

Even in the deepest gloom, her eyes can recognize the flowers that are fully in bloom and she feels they clamor with mystic voices, eager to die on the altar.

In one corner of the garden, the little door of a tiny, whitewashed cell reveals the golden splendor of a burning candle. It is the domestic hermitage constructed by Rosa in which to give herself over to contemplation and penance, without leaving her parents and brothers and sisters. She has not been driven into this life by remorse or sorrows. She is a born saint with miraculous powers from the cradle. . . .

Early she has come to understand that suffering and poverty

are, in the eyes of God, the worthiest things in life; and she continually visits the hospitals; she enters the hovels of the *cholos* and the Indians, looking for those suffering with fevers, ulcers, leprosy. She shelters in her oratory the old women who pick over the garbage piles in search of food. With her own hands she looks after the plague victims abandoned by their relatives . . .

Today Rosa opens the garden door carefully so as not to rouse those who are sleeping, and leaves the house, pressing to her bosom the flowers she will offer the Virgin. She walks slowly, hardly moving the folds of her garb. One might say the heavy fragrance occasionally causes her to swoon.

A soft glow of opal dawn tints the house tops. One after another, doors open. Through the grating passes the scent of incense in the convents. Occasionally a bare arm through the lattice waters the pots of basil. The humming of the slaves, scrubbing the patios and vestibules, reaches her ears.

Rosa enters the church, reverently treading the dark tiles. Two wax tapers burn in the distance, near the main altar. Their flickering light allows her to catch a glimpse within a black coffin of the crossed hands of a dead man and the yellowed garb in which the corpse is clad. Not a flower, not a prayer, not a mortuary cloth. The girl approaches the black box.

A Dominican friar, bearded and without tonsure, is dozing on a stool a few feet from the casket. Rosa nears him. The novice opens his eyes and murmurs, frightened:

"Heavens! I was dreaming about her and I saw her coming in that very robe, that veil and those flowers!"

Then suppressing his astonishment, he adds:

"God brings you here, holy maiden! What lips could more fittingly make the last prayers for the soul of this dead man than yours?"

"Who was he?" Rosa asks, observing the face of the dead man.

"I don't know exactly," replied the friar. "I met him about six years ago at Huancavelica. Men called him the Tragic Cavalier, and said that the strange story of his repentance should be told as an example to sinners. He had a gang of bandits which by the will of the Devil, I joined. . . . Later we came to Lima to spend on vices the fruit of our crimes."

Rosa sighed, and the novice, passing his hand across his face, went on with his story.

"One day he came to me to take communion. He saw you come out through the door of the sacristy, and leaving me, he followed you. Learning later of your piety and avoidance of the vanities and passions of the world, still he made up his mind to seduce you or steal and violate you by force. For that purpose, one morning, he made me bring a litter to your house while he prepared to jump over your garden wall.

"An hour later he came back, his expression changed. When he reached me, he threw his arms around my neck and exclaimed: 'She is a saint, a bride of Christ, and He speaks through her lips,' and he groaned like a man who dares not draw from his breast the dart by which he has just been wounded . . . From then on he began to watch you from afar as he saw you scattering everywhere your Christian bounty. He, too, abandoned his life of luxury, and bestowed his jewels and money upon the needy. I could never imagine remorse so profound. May God forgive his sins and grant me time to purge my own in this holy monastery!"

"How did he die?" asked the maiden, timidly and anxiously.

"His death," replied the novice, "gives further proof of his contrition. An Indian whom he was treating for a disease of the bones was being forced to work in the mine of Huancavelica that is called 'The Fetid.' So the Tragic Cavalier disguised himself as an Indian and took his place, more than five hours a day in the bowels of the earth. In less than a week he contracted a severe fever that left him helpless. I brought him to this monastery, where he died last night, with his last breath mingling your name, O holy maiden, with the name of Christ and Our Lady."

Rosa approached the coffin. There was no doubt of it! This was the man who, one morning, had scaled the wall of her garden, and before he could utter a word, she had spoken to him of the divine and true love, with words doubtless inspired by Heaven.

She gazed upon the emaciated face, and seeing the joy that bathed his eyelids, she understood that before his death he had seen a dazzling vision of paradise. Upon his chest she dropped a flower.

The light of dawn through the windows was illuminating the altar, and the ancient cloud of incense drowsing in the naves was pierced for a moment as if angels hovered about it. Rosa de Santa María dropped piously to her knees and murmured a prayer for the soul of that dead man.

And this was the glory of Don Ramiro.

W.K.J.

MARIANO AZUELA
1873–1952   Mexico

Doctor Azuela, trained in medicine at the University of Guadalajara, Mexico, opened an office in Jalisco, then began writing novels while waiting for patients. Among his early attempts, *Mala yerba* ("Marcela") (1909) written before the revolution that ended the corrupt period of Dictator Porfirio Díaz, sympathized with the position of the peons who were like serfs under the oppression of wealthy landowners.

Azuela showed his admiration for Madero in the novel *Andrés Pérez, maderista* (1911), but Madero's defeat and the approach of Carranza, another of the "preservers" and pillagers of the Mexican nation, sent the novelist fleeing to join Pancho Villa and his "Golden Boys." It was while serving him as army doctor that Azuela put *Los de abajo* ("The Underdogs") onto paper. It was serialized in a Texas newspaper in 1915, but attracted little attention. Not till its reprinting in a Mexican newspaper in 1925 was its greatness appreciated. Then it was acclaimed the novel of the Mexican Revolution and translated into many languages. Like all Azuela's novels, it is concise, almost skeleton-like, resembling a doctor's case history in the transformation of the ordinary Mexican under the impact of revolution. There is no artificial adornment or falsification of events, but it captures the dynamic aspects of these stirring times. All his work shows the influence of Galdós and to some extent of Azorín.

The Underdogs is not a pretty story. Reacting against centuries of slavery and injustice, the lower-class Mexicans saw in the revolution an opportunity to get some of the wealth so long denied them. Under petty leaders who eventually united in powerful armies, they committed every sort of crime. Azuela, marching with them, set down this epic of men fighting for a variety of motives. Its disunited, episodic form and impressionistic writing is supremely fitted to the subject.

Azuela wrote about many other phases of the revolution, but only *Los caciques* (1917) and especially *Las tribulaciones de una familia decente* (1919) even approach in power his greatest novel.

THE UNDERDOGS

Demetrio Macías, an illiterate rancher, became a revolutionist because of the abuses of the caciques and the Federal troops. Angered because they had burned his home, he collected twenty followers and attacked a force of five hundred Federal troops in a ravine. His bravery and skill in leadership attracted others, including Luis Cervantes, a medical student and journalist, who deserted the government through admiration for the revolution. He explained to Demetrio why they should join General Natera who was trying to take Zacatecas.

"As I was saying," Luis Cervantes resumed, "When the revolution is over, everything is over. Too bad that so many people have been killed, too bad there are so many widows and orphans, too bad there was so much bloodshed.

"Of course, you are not selfish; you say to yourself: 'All I

want to do is go back home.' But I ask you, is it fair to deprive
your wife and kids of a fortune which God himself places within
reach of your hand? Is it fair to abandon your Motherland in
this most solemn moment when she needs the self-sacrifice of
her sons, when she most needs her humble sons to save her
from falling again into the clutches of her eternal oppressors,
executioners, and *caciques?* You must not forget that the thing
a man holds most sacred on earth is his Motherland."

Macías smiled, his eyes shining.

"Will it be all right if we go with Natera?"

"Not only all right," Venancio said insinuatingly, "but I
think it absolutely necessary."

"Now, Chief," Cervantes pursued, "I took a fancy to you the
first time I laid eyes on you and I like you more and more every
day because I realize what you are worth. Please let me be ut-
terly frank. You do not yet realize your lofty noble function.
You are a modest man without ambitions, you do not wish
to realize the exceedingly important role you are destined to
play in the revolution. It is not true that you took up arms
simply because of Señor Mónico. You are under arms to protest against the evils of all the *caciques* who are overruning the
whole nation. We are the elements of a social movement which
will not rest until it has enlarged the destinies of our Motherland. We are the tools Destiny makes use of to reclaim the
sacred rights of the people. We are fighting against tyranny
itself. What moves us is what men call ideals; our action is
what men call fighting for a principle. A principle! That's why
Villa and Natera and Carranza are fighting; that's why we,
every man of us, are fighting."

"Yes . . . yes . . . exactly what I've been thinking myself," said Venancio in a climax of enthusiasm.

"Hey, there, Pancracio," Macías called, "pull down two more
beers."

*One of Natera's officers, Solís, meeting Cervantes, wanted
to know how he retained his enthusiasm, and confessed his own
disillusionment with the revolution.*

"I tell you honestly: I have been converted," Cervantes answered.

"Are you absolutely convinced?"

Solís sighed, filled the glasses; they drank.

"What about you? Are you tired of the revolution?" asked Cervantes sharply.

"Tired? My dear fellow, I'm twenty-five years old and I'm fit as a fiddle! But am I disappointed? Perhaps!"

"You must have sound reasons for feeling that way."

"I hoped to find a meadow at the end of the road, I found a swamp. Facts are bitter; so are men. That bitterness eats your heart out; it is poison, dry-rot. Enthusiasm, hope, ideals, happiness—vain dreams, vain dreams. . . . When that's over, you have a choice. Either you turn bandit, like the rest, or the time-servers will swamp you . . ."

Cervantes writhed at his friend's words; his argument was quite out of place . . . painful. . . . To avoid being forced to take issue, he invited Solís to cite the circumstances that had destroyed his illusions.

"Circumstances? No—it's far less important that that. It's a host of silly, insignificant things that no one notices except yourself . . . a change of expression, eyes shining—lips curled in a sneer—the deep import of a phrase that is lost! Yet take these things together and they compose the mask of our race . . . terrible . . . grotesque . . . a race that awaits redemption!"

He drained another glass. After a long pause, he continued:

"You ask me why I am still a rebel? Well, the revolution is like a hurricane: if you're in it, you're not a man . . . you're a leaf, a dead leaf, blown by the wind."

Demetrio reappeared. Seeing him, Solís relapsed in silence.

"Come along," Demetrio said to Cervantes. "Come with me."

Unctuously, Solís congratulated Demetrio on the feats that had won him fame and the notice of Pancho Villa's Northern division.

Demetrio warmed to his praise. Gratefully, he heard his

prowess vaunted, though at times he found it difficult to believe
he was the hero of the exploits the other narrated. But Solís'
story proved so charming, so convincing, that before long he
found himself repeating it as gospel truth.

"Natera is a genius!" Luis Cervantes said when they had
returned to the hotel. "But Captain Solís is a nobody . . . a
time-server."

*In the midst of battle, Solís told Cervantes some of its de-
tails.*

"A number of men from Moya's brigade who went down to
the meadow decided to attack the enemy's trenches the first
chance they got. The bullets whizzed about us, the battle raged
on all sides. For a time they stopped firing, so we thought they
were being attacked from behind. We stormed their trenches
—look, partner, look at that meadow! It's thick with corpses!
Their machine guns did for us. They mowed us down like
wheat; only a handful escaped. Those god-damned officers went
white as a sheet; even though we had re-enforcements, they
were afraid to order a new charge. That was when Demetrio
Macías plunged in. Did he wait for orders? Not he! He just
shouted:

" 'Come on, boys! Let's go for them!'

" 'Damn fool!' I thought. 'What the hell does he think he's
doing!'

"The officers, surprised, said nothing. Demetrio's horse
seemed to wear eagle's claws instead of hoofs, it soared so
swiftly over the rocks. 'Come on! Come on!' his men shouted,
following him like wild deer, horses and men welded into a
mad stampede. Only one young fellow stepped wild and fell
headlong into the pit. In a few seconds the others appeared
at the top of the hill, storming the trenches and killing the
Federals by the thousand. With his rope, Demetrio lassoed the
machine guns and carried them off, like a bull herder throwing
a steer. Yet his success could not last much longer, for the
Federals were far stronger in numbers and could easily have
destroyed Demetrio and his men. But we took advantage of

their confusion, we rushed upon them and they soon cleared out of their position. That chief of yours is a wonderful soldier!"

Standing on the crest of the hill, they could easily sight one side of the Bufa peak. Its highest crag spread out like the feathered head of a proud Aztec king. The three hundred foot slope was literally covered with dead, their hair matted, their clothes clotted with grime and blood. A host of ragged women, vultures of prey, ranged over the tepid bodies of the dead, stripping one man bare, despoiling another, robbing from a third his dearest possession.

Amid clouds of white rifle smoke and the dense black vapors of flaming buildings, houses, with wide doors and windows bolted, shone in the sunlight. The streets seemed to be piled upon one another, or wound picturesquely about fantastic corners, or set to scale the hills nearby. Above the graceful cluster of houses, rose the lithe columns of a warehouse and the towers and cupola of the church.

"How beautiful the revolution! Even in its most barbarous aspect it is beautiful," Solís said with deep feeling. Then a vague melancholy seized him, and speaking low:

"A pity what remains to do won't be as beautiful! We must wait a while, until there are no men left to fight on either side, until no sound of shot rings through the air save from the mob as carrion-like it falls upon the booty; we must wait until the psychology of our race, condensed into two words, shines clear and luminous as a drop of water: Robbery! Murder! What a colossal failure we would make of it, friend, if we, who offer our enthusiasm and lives to crush a wretched tyrant, became the builders of a monstrous edifice holding one hundred or two hundred thousand monsters of exactly the same sort. People without ideals! A tyrant folk! Vain bloodshed!"

Large groups of Federals pushed up the hill, fleeing from the "high hats." A bullet whistled past them, singing as it sped. After his speech, Alberto Solís stood lost in thought, his arms crossed. Suddenly, he took fright.

"I'll be damned if I like these plaguey mosquitoes!" he said, "Let's get away from here!"

So scornfully Luis Cervantes smiled that Solís sat down on a rock quite calm, bewildered. He smiled. His gaze roved as he watched the spirals of smoke from the rifles, the dust of roofs crumbling from houses as they fell before the artillery. He believed he discerned the symbol of the revolution in these clouds of dust and smoke that climbed upwards together, met at the crest of the hill and, a moment after, were lost. . . .

"By heaven, now I see what it all means!"

He sketched a vast gesture, pointing to the station. Locomotives belched huge clouds of black dense smoke rising in columns; the trains were overloaded with fugitives who had barely managed to escape from the captured town.

Suddenly he felt a sharp blow in the stomach. As though his legs were putty, he rolled off the rock. His ears buzzed. . . . Then darkness . . . silence. . . . Eternity. . . .

As Demetrio won skirmishes, his fame and the number of his followers increased. Many were political prisoners, others were criminals, all released by him from the jails. Prostitutes like War Paint made a play for him but he preferred a simple girl Camilla, who had looked after him when he was wounded in his first battle. She, however, was taken with Luis. Now called General Macías, Demetrio captured Moyahua. He tried to prevent looting, but remembering how his own house was burned, he ordered the house of the Cacique Mónico set afire. His soldiers garrisoned the town.

They established themselves in a large gloomy house, which likewise belonged to the *cacique* of Moyahua. The previous occupants had already left strong evidences in the patio, which had been converted into a manure pile. The walls, once whitewashed, were now faded and cracked, revealing the bare unbaked adobe; the floor had been torn up by the hoofs of animals; the orchard was littered with rotted branches and dead leaves. From the entrance one stumbled over broken bits of chairs and other furniture covered with dirt.

By ten o'clock, Luis Cervantes yawned with boredom, said good-night to Blondie and War Paint who were downing endless drinks on a bench in the square, and made for the barracks.

The drawing-room was alone furnished. As he entered, Demetrio, lying on the floor with his eyes wide open, trying to
count the beams, gazed at him.

"It's you, eh? What's new? Come on, sit down."

Luis Cervantes first went over to trim the candle, then drew
up a chair without a back, a coarse rag doing the duty of a
wicker bottom. The legs of the chair squeaked. War Paint's
black horse snorted and whirled its crupper in wide circles.
Luis Cervantes sank into his seat.

"General, I wish to make my report. Here you have . . ."

"Look here, man, I didn't really want this done, you know.
Moyahua is almost like my native town. They'll say this is why
we've been fighting!" Demetrio said, looking at the bulging
sack of money Cervantes was passing to him. Cervantes left
his seat to squat down by Demetrio's side.

He stretched a blanket over the floor and into it poured the
ten-peso pieces, shining, burning gold.

"First of all, General, only you and I know about this. . . .
Secondly, you know well enough that if the sun shines, you
should open the window. It's shining in our faces now, but
what about tomorrow? You should always look ahead. A bullet,
a bolting horse, even a wretched cold in the head, and then
there are a widow and orphans left in absolute want! . . . The
Government? Ha! Ha! . . . Just go see Carranza or Villa or
any of the big chiefs and try and tell them about your family.
. . . If they answer with a kick you know where, they'll say
they're giving you a handful of jewels. And they're right; we
did not rise up in arms to make some Carranza or Villa President of our Republic. No—we fought to defend the sacred
rights of the people against the tyranny of some vile *cacique*.
And so, just as Villa or Carranza aren't going to ask our con-
sent to the payment they're getting for the services they're
rendering the country, we for our part don't have to ask anybody's permission about anything, either."

Demetrio half stood up, grasped a bottle that stood nearby,
drained it, then spat out the liquor, swelling out his cheeks.

"By God, my boy, you've certainly got the gift of gab!"

Luis felt dizzy, faint. The spattered beer seemed to intensify the stench of the refuse on which they sat; a carpet of orange and banana peels, fleshlike slices of water-melon, mouldy masses of mangoes and sugar cane, all mixed up with corn husks from tamales and human offal.

Demetrio's calloused hands shuffled through the brilliant coins, counting and counting. Recovering from his nausea, Luis Cervantes pulled out a small box for Fallieres phosphate and poured forth rings, brooches, pendants, and countless valuable jewels.

"Look here, General, if this mess doesn't blow over, (and it doesn't look as though it would), if the revolution keeps on, there's enough here already for us to live on abroad quite comfortably."

Demetrio shook his head.

"You wouldn't do that!"

"Why not? What are we staying on for? . . . What cause are we defending now?"

"That's something I can't explain, tenderfoot. But I'm thinking it wouldn't show much guts."

"Take your choice, General," said Luis Cervantes, pointing to the jewels which he had set in a row.

"Oh, you keep it all . . . Certainly! . . . You know, I don't really care for money at all. I'll tell you the truth! I'm the happiest man in the world, so long as there's always something to drink and a nice little wench that catches my eye . . ."

"Ha! Ha! You make the funniest jokes, General. Why do you stand for that snake of a War Paint, then?"

"I'll tell you, tenderfoot, I'm fed up with her. But I'm like that: I just can't tell her so. I'm not brave enough to tell her to go plumb to hell. That's the way I am, see? When I like a woman, I get plain silly; and if she doesn't start something, I've not got the courage to do anything myself." He sighed. "There's Camilla at the ranch for instance . . . Now she's not much on looks, I know, but there's a woman I'd like to have. . . ."

"Well, General, we'll go and get her any day you like."

Demetrio winked maliciously.

"I promise you I'll do it."

"Are you sure? Do you really mean it? Look here, if you pull that off for me, I'll give you the watch and chain you're hankering after."

Luis Cervantes' eyes shone. He took the phosphate box, heavy with its contents, and stood up smiling.

"I'll see you tomorrow," he said. "Good night, General! Sleep well."

Evil days came upon the army. Cervantes fled to Texas. One of the other soldiers brought bad news:

"It's very serious. A terrible mess! Villa was beaten at Celaya by Obregón, and Carranza is winning all along the line! We're done for!"

Valderrama's gesture was disdainful and solemn as an emperor's. "Villa? Obregón? Carranza? What's the difference? I love the revolution like a volcano in eruption; I love the volcano, because it's a volcano, the revolution, because it's the revolution!"

But the others did not agree with the poet, and gradually drifted away. So the few survivors started homeward.

They entered the streets of Juchipila as the church bells rang, loud and joyfully, with that peculiar tone that thrills every mountaineer.

"It makes me think we are back in the days when the revolution was just beginning, when the bells rang like mad in every town we entered and everybody came out with music, flags, cheers and fireworks to welcome us," said Anastasio Montáñez.

"They don't like us no more," Demetrio returned.

"Of course. We're crawling back like a dog with its tail between its legs," Auail remarked.

"It ain't that, I guess. They don't give a whoop for the other side, either."

"But why should they like us?"

They spoke no more.

Presently they reached the city square and stopped in front of an octagonal, rough, massive church, reminiscent of the colonial period. At one time the square must have been a garden, judging from the bare, stunted orange trees planted between iron and wooden benches. The sonorous, joyful bells rang again. From within the church, the honeyed voices of a female chorus rose melancholy and grave. To the strains of a guitar, the young girls of the town sang the Mysteries.

"What's the fiesta, lady?" Venancio asked of an old woman who was running toward the church.

"The Sacred Heart of Jesus!" answered the pious woman, panting.

They remembered that one year ago they had captured Zacatecas. They grow sadder still.

Juchipila, like the other towns they had passed through on their way from Tepic, by way of Jalisco, Aguascalientes, and Zacatecas, was in ruins. The black trail of the incendiaries showed in the roofless houses, in the burnt arcades. Almost all the houses were closed, yet, here and there, those still open offered, in ironic contrast, portals gaunt and bare as the white skeletons of horses scattered over the roads. The terrible pangs of hunger seemed to speak from every face; hunger on every dusty cheek, in their dusty countenances; in the hectic flame of their eyes, which, when they met a soldier, blazed with hatred. In vain the soldiers scoured the streets in search of food, biting their lips in anger. A single lunch room was open; at once they filled it. No beans, no *tortillas*, only *chile* and tomato sauce. In vain the officers showed their pocketbooks stuffed with bills or used threats.

"Yea, you've got paper all right! That's all you've brought! Try and eat them, will you?" said the owner, an insolent old shrew with an enormous scar on her cheek, who told them she had already lain with a dead man, "to cure her from ever feeling frightened again."

Despite the melancholy and desolation of the town, while

the women sang in the church, birds sang in the foliage, and the thrushes piped their lyrical strain on the withered branches of the orange trees.

However Demetrio could not stop fighting. He explained why to his wife when he rejoined her after an absence of almost two years.

"Why do you keep on fighting, Demetrio?"

Demetrio frowned deeply. Picking up a stone absentmindedly, he threw it to the bottom of the canyon. Then he stared pensively into the abyss, watching the arch of its flight.

"Look at that stone; how it keeps on going . . ."

It was a heavenly morning. It had rained all night, the sky awakened covered with white clouds. Young wild colts trotted on the summit of the sierra, with tense manes and waving hair, proud as the peaks lifting their heads to the clouds.

The soldiers stepped among the huge rocks, buoyed up by the happiness of the morning. None for a moment dreamed of the treacherous bullet that might be awaiting him ahead; the unforeseen provides man with his greatest joy. The soldiers sang, laughed and chattered away. The spirit of nomadic tribes stirred their souls. What matters it whither you go and whence you come? All that matters is to walk, to walk endlessly, without ever stopping; to possess the valley, the heights of the sierra, far as the eye can read.

Trees, brush, and cactus shone fresh after rain. Heavy drops of limpid water fell from rocks, ochre in hue as rusty armor.

Demetrio Macías' men grew silent for a moment. They believed they heard the familiar rumor of firing in the distance. A few minutes elapsed but the sound was not repeated.

"In this same sierra," Demetrio said, "with but twenty men I killed five hundred Federals. Remember, Anastasio?"

As Demetrio began to tell that famous exploit, the men realized the danger they were facing. What if the enemy, instead of being two days away, was hiding somewhere among the underbrush on the terrible hill through whose gorge they now advanced? None dared show the slightest fear. Not one of Demetrio Macías' men dared say, "I shall not move another inch!"

So, when firing began in the distance where the vanguard was marching, no one felt surprised. The recruits turned back hurriedly, retreating in shameful flight searching for a way out of the canyon.

A curse broke from Demetrio's parched lips.

"Fire at 'em. Shoot any man who runs away!"

"Storm the hill!" he thundered like a wild beast.

But the enemy, lying in ambush by the thousand, opened up its machine gun fire. Demetrio's men fell like wheat under the sickle.

Tears of rage and pain rise to Demetrio's eyes as Anastasio slowly slides from his horse without a sound, and lies outstretched, motionless. Venancio falls close beside him, his chest riddled with bullets. Meco hurtles over the precipice, bounding from rock to rock.

Suddenly, Demetrio finds himself alone. Bullets whizz past his ears like hail. He dismounts and crawls over the rocks, until he finds a parapet; he lays down a stone to protect his head and, lying flat on the ground, begins to shoot.

The enemy scatter in all directions, pursuing the few fugitives hiding in the brush. Demetrio. aims; he does not waste a single shot.

His famous marksmanship fills him with joy. Where he settles his glance, he settles a bullet. He loads his gun once more . . takes aim. . . .

The smoke of the guns hang thick in the air. Locusts chant their mysterious, imperturbable song. Doves coo lyrically in the crannies of the rocks. The cows graze placidly.

The sierra is clad in gala colors. Over its inaccessible peaks the opalescent fog settles like a snowy veil on the forehead of a bride.

At the foot of a hollow, sumptuous and huge as the portico of an old cathedral, Demetrio Macías, his eyes levelled in an

eternal glance, continues to point the barrel of his
gun. . . . . . .

The End.

E. Munguía, Jr.

MARTÍN LUIS GUZMÁN
1887–   Mexico

Guzmán wrote historical fiction about the early days
of Mexico's revolution which, as a journalist attached
to Villa's Army of the North, he himself had witnessed.
Later he served as Villa's secretary and even briefly as
Minister of War till the defeat of his side sent him into
exile, first in New York and later in Spain. Returning
briefly to Mexico to found the newspaper *El Mundo*,
he was again exiled by his one-time friend Obregón.

El águila y la serpiente ("The Eagle and the Serpent") (1928), from which part of a chapter is here
translated, is a rugged, expressive series of episodes in
journalistic style, dealing with the wrangles among
Huerta, Carranza, Villa, and others between 1913 and
1915: They reveal how the author's original admiration
for Villa had changed to disgust and fear. Though
Guzmán wrote other books, balanced between realism
and romanticism, neither *La sombra del caudillo* ("The
Shadow of the Leader") (1929) about the corruption
of the Calles administration, nor *Mina el mozo*
("Young Mina") (1932) equals in freshness and vigor
the earlier work.

THE EAGLE AND THE SERPENT

Chapter X. The Bullet Party

That battle, completely successful, had ended, leaving in Villa's
hands no less than five hundred prisoners. Villa ordered them
separated into two groups: in one the volunteer followers of

Orozco, who were called "Colorados"; and in the other the Federales. And since he finally felt secure enough for grand gestures, he decided to make an example of the first group, while showing generosity to the second. He would execute the Colorados before dark; and would allow the Federales to chose between joining the revolutionary troops, or returning home. . . . Rodolfo Fierro, as was expected, took charge of the execution.

He arrived at the corral where they had enclosed, like a herd of cattle, the three hundred prisoners condemned to die, and stopped for a moment to look over the boards of the fence. From their appearance, those three hundred followers of Huerta had been through other revolutions. They were of the fine race of Chihuahua: tall bodies, lean muscles, robust necks, well formed shoulders, and vigorous and flexible backs. Fierro considered at a glance the small imprisoned army, he appraised it as worthy and brave soldiers and he felt a strange pulsation, a shudder that went down from his heart, or from his forehead, up to the forefinger of his right hand. Without thinking, the palm of that hand settled on the butt of his pistol.

"Quite a battle" he thought.

Fierro advanced to the corral gate; he shouted to a soldier, who came and pushed aside the bars, and he entered. . . . He got off his horse. His legs were stiff from fatigue and cold; he stretched them. He adjusted his two pistols. He then began deliberately to observe the layout of the prison and its various parts. . . . He released his horse, removed from the saddlebags something that he put inside the pockets of his coat, and crossed the corral close to the prisoners.

There were three divisions of the corral that joined each other through narrow passageways. Fierro walked by, sliding half his body through the crossbars of the gate. And then, to the other one. There he halted. His figure, tall and handsome, radiated a strange glow, something superior, authoritative, and at the same time fitting for the sad state of the corral. Through the fence, the prisoners saw him, from a distance, with his back toward them. His legs made a huge, gleaming compass as the leather of the leggings shone in the afternoon light.

About a hundred meters away was the chief of the troop in charge of the prisoners. Fierro saw him and signaled him to approach. They talked. As he talked, Fierro was pointing out different spots in the corral where he stood and in the next corral. Then he described, with motions of his hand, a series of maneuvers that the official repeated as though for better understanding . . . The official, sure of his orders, galloped toward the corral of the prisoners.

Then Fierro returned to the center of the corral, once again studying the position of the walls and other details. The corral had, on two of its sides, doors leading to the field. The other side had a gate that opened into the adjacent corral. And the last side, in short, was not a simple partition of boards, but a mud wall of adobe, at least ten feet high. The mud wall measured some sixty meters in length, of which twenty served as the back of a shelter or shed, whose roof went down to the wall and rested on it, one part, on the posts, extending from one end of the walls that bordered on the field, and the other, on the wall, also of adobe, that extended perpendicularly from the mud wall and ran a matter of fifteen meters toward the middle of the corral. And so, between the shelter and the near corral wall remained a space closed on two of the sides by thick walls. In that corner the afternoon wind was piling up the rubbish and making sounds in a wild rhythm, as it blew an iron pail against the curbstone of a well. . . .

A soldier jumped over the wall, inside the corral. He was Fierro's assistant. He walked toward his master. Without turning his face, Fierro asked:

"Have they come with you? If they don't come soon, there won't be time."

"Looks like they're coming over there," answered the aide.

"Then join them there right away. By the way, what pistol did you bring?"

"The one that you gave me, chief. The Smith and Wesson."

"Give it to me, then, and take these boxes of 'ammo.' How many rounds do you have?"

"About fifteen dozen with those that I have collected today, my chief. The others found a lot, but not me."

"Fifteen dozen? I said the other day that if you sold any more ammunition in order to buy drink I was going to put a bullet in your belly . . ."

"No, my chief."

"No, my chief, what?"

"I did get drunk, my chief, but I didn't sell the ammunition."

"Well, be very careful, because you know me. And now get going so that this venture turns out well for me. I'll fire and you reload the pistols. And listen well to what I am about to order: if on your account even one Colorado escapes, you will lie with them."

"Oh, but general!"

"You heard me."

The aide spread his blanket upon the ground and emptied out the boxes of cartridges that Fierro had just given him. Then he began to extract, one by one, the shells that he carried in the cartridge loop of his belt. In his hurry he took that much longer. He was nervous; his fingers got all tangled up.

"What a chief!" he kept thinking to himself.

Meanwhile, behind the fence that enclosed the nearest corral, the escort of soldiers began appearing. Mounted on horseback, only heads and shoulders rose above the top of the fence. Many others distributed themselves along the two remaining walls.

The leader of the escort rode through the gate that opened into the neighboring corral, and said:

"I have a list of the first ten. Shall I let them go?"

Answered Fierro:

"Yes, but first tell them how you are going to handle it: As soon as they appear at the gate, I will begin to shoot them; those that make it to the top of the wall and jump over go free. If someone doesn't want to enter, you shoot him yourself."

The officer returned to where he had come, and Fierro, gun in hand, remained attentive, his eyes fixed on the narrow space through which the prisoners were going to burst in. He had situated himself near enough to the dividing wall so that, when he fired, the bullets would not reach the Colorados that still might be on the other side: he wanted to keep his promise. But he was far enough away from the planks of the fence that the prisoners, as soon as he would begin the execution, would discover, the moment they came through the door, the pistol pointed at them from twenty paces. Behind Fierro, the setting sun converted the sky to a luminous red. The wind began blowing. . . .

It wasn't very easy to force those destined for mass killing from one corral to the next. The fate that threatened them made them break out in hysterical shouts. The escort yelled and occasional gun shots sounded like the cracking of a whip. From the first prisoners that arrived at the intermediate corral, a group of soldiers selected ten. They drove their horses upon the prisoners in order to make them go; they pushed the barrels of their carbines against the bodies.

"Traitors! Now we are going to see how they run and jump! Over there, traitors!"

In this manner they were made to advance up to the doorway beyond which waited Fierro and his aide. . . .

As soon as they appeared within his vision, Fierro greeted them with a strange sentence—a sentence both friendly and cruel, containing both irony and hope:

"Come on, boys: I'm the only one and I'm a bad shot!"

They jumped like goats. The first tried to dash at Fierro, but he had not taken three steps before he fell, riddled by bullets from the soldiers disposed along the wall. The others ran headlong toward the top of the wall—their mad race would seem like a dream. Upon seeing the curb of the well, one prisoner sought refuge there, a bullet from Fierro reached him first. The rest continued fleeing; but one by one they were falling; in less than ten seconds Fierro shot eight times. . . .

Another group of ten came, and then another, and another, and another. Fierro's three guns—his two, the other his aide's —alternated in the murderer's hand in perfect rhythm. Each one fired six times—six times without aiming, six times on the unarmed prisoners—and dropped onto the aide's blanket. The latter removed the hot shells and put in new ones. Then, without changing position, he handed the pistol to Fierro, who took it as he let another fall. The aide's fingers touched the bullets that seconds later would kill some prisoner; but he didn't raise his eyes in order to see those that fell. . . . Above, over his head, sounded the shots as his chief gave himself over to the delight of target shooting.

The slaughter lasted two hours. Not for an instant did Fierro lose his steadiness or his serenity. He fired at moving human targets, that leaped and stumbled among the bloody pools, but shot without any more emotion than that of missing or hitting. . . .

The last group to be executed was not of ten victims, but of twelve. . . . Not a shot missed, with sinister precision one hit followed another. . . . One of them, nevertheless, the last remaining alive, succeeded in getting to the top of the same wall and vaulted it. The fire suddenly ceased and the throng of soldiers crowded together in the corner of the near corral in order to see the fugitive. . . .

The afternoon was wearing away. In the twilight, things were no longer clear. But then, far away, in the vastness of the plain, partly in shadow, everyone could make out a moving dot, somebody running.

A soldier pointed:

"He's pretty hard to see," he said, and shot.

The report was lost in the twilight wind. The dot continued on its course.

"Unsaddle and make my bed," ordered Fierro; "I'm too tired to go on."

"Here in this corral, my chief? Here. . . ?"

"Yes, here. Why not?"

For several hours they slept in that grisly place. The moon at last illuminated the scene.

From the bottom of one of the mountains of corpses came a distant voice. It seemed to murmur:

"Oh . . . Oh . . !"

Fierro stirred in his bed . . .

"Please . . . , water . . ." came the voice.

Fierro awoke and heard . . .

"Please . . . , water . . ."

Then Fierro kicked his aide with his foot.

"Hey, you! Didn't you hear? One of the dead is asking for water."

"My chief?"

"Get up and go shoot the fellow that's moaning. See if you can let me sleep!"

"Shoot who, my chief?"

"That man who asked for water, imbecile! Understand?"

"Water, please," repeated the voice.

The aide took the pistol from under the saddle, and, grasping it, got up and left the shed in search of the corpses. He was trembling from fear and cold.

In the light of the moon he searched. All the bodies he touched were lifeless. He halted without knowing what to do. Then he shot at the spot from where appeared to come the voice; the voice was heard again. The aide fired again; the voice was silent.

The moon was sailing across the limitless sea of blue. Under the roof of the shed, Fierro slept on.

Robert Alan Goldberg

RUFINO BLANCO FOMBONA
1874–1944   Venezuela

As a supporter of Dictator Cipriano Castro, Blanco Fombona was appointed governor of Amazonas. The dictator's overthrow by Gómez in 1908 brought him imprisonment and exile to Paris, where he wrote poetry and prose and helped edit *Revista de América*. His earliest important novel was *Hombre de hierro* ("Man of Iron") (1906), an ironical picture of a weakling amid revolution. Other fiction included *Hombre de*

oro ("Man of Gold") (1916), about backstage manipu-
lating of an elderly and corrupt money lender; and *La
mitra en la mano* ("With Mitre in Hand") (1927),
satirizing churchly corruption. While not a great novelist, Blanco Fombona impressed readers by the very fury
of his attack. This translated story, "Redentores de la
patria," somewhat abbreviated, is a sort of summary of
Hombre de hierro.

REDEEMERS OF THE
FATHERLAND

Crispín Luz, Mary his wife, and Juanita Pérez, half friend, half
servant of the couple, had gone to spend some weeks in their
country estate. They hoped that Crispín, victim of pulmonary
tuberculosis, would benefit from the fresh, invigorating climate
among the mountains.

Early one morning Joaquín Luz, Crispín's older brother and
manager of the estate, appeared very much upset, and shouting
excitedly:

"María! Crispín!"

"What is it? What's going on?"

"You must get ready to leave at once."

"To leave? But, why?"

"The war is about to begin. General Hache began gathering
his forces for rebellion last night in Guarico."

"But why should we leave?" asked Crispín, bewildered by
the attitude of his brother. "Certainly everything is quiet around
here and it will remain this way for a long while."

"Crispín, my God! You don't know what you're saying.
Listen," he continued dropping his voice almost to a whisper,
"I just received a communication and definite orders from the
revolutionary committee in Caracas. Tomorrow at dawn, I myself will establish rebel headquarters here."

"You? Here at the estate? But, are you crazy? What about
your wife and your children?"

And because Crispín had noticed the red, ripened berries of coffee and the fertile harvest, he could not comprehend this abandonment of the estate, so with his practical sense alarmed, he rebuked his brother.

"It's a crime, Joaquín! Your crops, your home, all of this will be lost! Just when we might pull ourselves out of debt with the sale of the coffee and a little economy . . . Now we'll be ruined. What lunacy!"

"Nevertheless, you will have to prepare to flee immediately. My own family leave today for Caracas."

Then lowering his voice again into a confiding whisper, he added:

"I should have begun the uprising this morning: those are the orders. But it is impossible to gather together all the people. It will be tonight or at dawn. Well, then, get ready to leave this afternoon by train."

Joaquín showed them the proclamation by the revolutionary chief published in Caracas and circulating certainly by now over the whole nation: an impressive, bombastic proclamation like all good subversive documents, in which one swore to demolish the tyranny, to save the country and to spread happiness by means of the purifying bayonet. It invited the Venezuelans with all the high-sounding eloquence of our eloquent political language to carry out the tremendous work of redemption: all Venezuelans, no matter what their political faction. The rebels called themselves "redeemers," and the revolution was grotesquely entitled the "Revolution of Redemption."

That evening at dusk, these "redeemers" began arriving. They were unfortunate peons and neighboring farmers, improvised cannon fodder; future victims, some scarcely able to decipher the proclamation of war. They stole up secretly, one by one or in groups, like stage conspirators.

At the first signs of dawn, they began slaughtering and cutting up cattle, and three hundred mountaineers began barbecuing chunks of meat on the fire. Most were dressed in trousers and a smock; on their heads they wore a palm straw hat and on their feet, sandals. Others wore shirts, and some, a jacket.

From each broad belt in its protective sheath hung a bush knife. Every one carried his blanket and machete, the indispensable protection and weapon of these Venezuelan peasants.

Joaquín appeared finally upon his spirited steed, followed by eight or ten horsemen displaying their swords and Winchesters. Joaquín Luz was certainly a distinguished leader, characterized by his virile, erect figure and his ease of gesture. His jovial conversation, his frank grin, and finally his carefully trimmed black beard won him the good will of his neighbors.

"Boys," he said, "I suppose all of you will go willingly. I want no one to volunteer who does it against his will. Anyone who doesn't want to accompany me, I advise him to remain behind."

Those nearest the impromptu leader responded:

"Yes, we want to go."

Someone then shouted:

"Long live our chief!"

"Hurrah, Hurrah!" replied the chorus.

Enthused by the ovation and by the compliance of his followers, Joaquín rose high in the stirrups to make a speech.

"Good companions, let us leave for the war. Our cause demands it; our country requires it. Let us abandon our homes; let us make the sacrifice of our lives in order to stamp out the tyranny and to impose law and justice. The enemy has arms. Let's take them away from those devils. Hurrah for the Revolution!"

The reply sounded like one ardent and sonorous shout:

"Hurrah! Hurrah! Hurrah!"

The leader had spurred his horse and now was lost among the trees, followed by horsemen and peons.

"Poor Joaquín!" sighed his wife.

"Poor Venezuela!" Crispín corrected her. "Joaquín is happy. Didn't you notice how this crowd follows him wherever he leads them? He seems like a feudal lord."

About two hours later they heard the noise of the government troops from the city of Teques. Having just learned of Joaquín's insurrection, they were now hurrying to quell it. The commander of the force, an alert and respectful person, quieted the frightened family. There was no need for alarm. He was not an executioner. But he recommended that they leave for Caracas as soon as possible, since evildoers increased during times of war.

While the soldiers were carefully searching the grounds of the estate, the inhabitants remained huddled together, and Crispín swore about the war in general.

Suddenly, a crackling and a flaming light in the distance drew their attention. The soldiers had set on fire a nearby straw-thatched hut. Soon they came into view dragging a body. It was Juan, a young servant who had attempted to flee. His dying body was now shot full of bullets. His poor mother, the old cook, on seeing her son bleeding and unconscious, broke into hysterical sobs.

"This is nothing, old lady," said one soldier.

"Assassins!" she cried in her grief.

Another soldier, looking at the dying boy as if he was in the mood for jokes, said with an idiotic smile:

"Buck up, my fine young lad, so you can serve your country."

"The country! Damn the country!" cried the old woman.

The soldiers finally left, each one carrying away a hen, clothes, pots from the kitchen, anything they could lay their hands on.

As they left, they brutally shook the small coffee trees. The fragrant, red, ripe grains fell to the ground, useless, like a futile shower of round flaming corals.

Elaine Schaefer

RAFAEL ARÉVALO MARTÍNEZ
1884–   Guatemala

Fifty years after the publication of his first work, a prize-winning short story, *Mujer y niños* ("Woman and Children"), February, 1909, Dr. Arévalo Martínez was honored by the University of Guatemala on his

"*Golden Wedding with Literature*" by the publication of a 500-page volume of his selected works.

After completing school, Don Rafael entered banking, only to become a teacher of grammar and history in 1908 and, since then, the outstanding figure of Guatemalan letters. Though having written in many fields, including philosophy with his *Concept of the Cosmos, Viaje a Ipanda* ("Journey to Ipanda") (1939) and *Embajador de Torlania* ("Ambassador from Torlania") (1960) he is most widely known for his psycho-zoological story *El hombre que parecía un caballo* ("The Man Who Resembled a Horse"), first published in 1914. It was based on fact, having been inspired by an actual poet of Colombia, one of whose pen names was "Porfirio Barba Jacob." This writer, creator of beauty and lover of precious stones, seemed to Arévalo Martínez to be sometimes transformed by basic instincts into a beast. Later along the same lines, Arévalo Martínez wrote *El hombre que parecía un tigre*, about the tiger-like Dictator Ubico, and another story about a man who resembled an elephant. The story here translated is slightly condensed at the author's suggestion. A poem by Arévalo having a similar concept is also included.

THE MAN WHO RESEMBLED
A HORSE

At the moment when they introduced us, he was at the end of the room, with his head tilted, as horses usually are, and with an air of not noticing what was going on around him. He had sturdy, long and lean arms and legs, strangely attached, like one of those figures in an English illustration for *Gulliver's Travels*. But my impression that that man in some mysterious way resembled a horse was then only subconscious and might never have chanced to reach my level of consciousness if my abnormal contact with the hero of this story had not been prolonged.

In that very first introduction, Señor Aretal began to extend himself, by giving to us one of those translucent necklaces of opals, amethysts, emeralds, and carbuncles that constituted his personal treasure. In puzzlement, I expanded and extended myself like a large white sheet, in order to make my surface of contact as wide as possible with the generous donor. The antennae of my soul unfolded, touched him and trembled and vibrated to send me the good news: "This is the man you were waiting for; this is the man for whom you looked among so many unknown people, because your intuition had already assured you that one day you would be enriched by the arrival of this unique being. The eagerness with which you accepted, tested, and discarded the people who had made themselves desirable and then defrauded your hope, will today be amply satisfied; bend down and drink of this water."

And when he got up to leave, I followed as if bound to him, fastened like a lamb that the shepherdess had tied with a rope of roses. When I entered the room of my new friend, he came to life, hardly had we passed the door that led into his habitual surroundings. He became dazzling and dramatic like the horse of an emperor in a military parade. His swinging coat tails had a vague resemblance to the trappings of a charger of the Middle Ages, bedecked for a tournament. They fell below his skinny buttocks, caressing his fine and elegant legs. And his theatrical performance began.

.   .   .   .   .   .

Then suddenly, this transparent angel, Señor Aretal, began to take the shape of an almost nebulous dark cloud. It was the shadow thrown ahead of it by a horse that was approaching. Had my noble friend frequented the barroom of the hotel in which he was living? Who was coming? An obscure being, possessor of some horribly broadened nose and of some thin lips. If the line of his nose had been straight, his soul also would have been straight. If his lips had been thicker, his sincerity would have been increased. But no. Señor Aretal became a fester. There he was . . . And my soul, which in that instant had the power of discernment, understood clearly that that creature, whom until then I had believed a man because one day I saw his cheeks redden with shame, was nothing but a homunculus. With those nostrils, he couldn't be sincere.

·   ·   ·   ·   ·   ·

One day, Señor Aretal found his setting. A number of us were his listeners; in the room enchanted by his customary creations, he recited poetry. And suddenly, in the midst of one of the most beautiful of all, as before a trumpet blast, our noble host arose, pawing and prancing. And then and there, I had my first vision: Señor Aretal was stretching his neck like a horse.

·   ·   ·   ·   ·   ·

Afterward, the second vision, the same day. I went out for a walk. Suddenly I noticed, I noticed Señor Aretal fall just like a horse. His left foot gave way and his flank almost touched the ground like a lame horse. He recovered rapidly but he had already left me with the sensation.

Later the third vision, a few days afterward. Señor Aretal was seated in front of his gold coins and suddenly I saw his arms moving like the legs of a thoroughbred horse, extending outward the tip of his arms in that beautiful series of movements that so many times you have observed when a competent horseman, in a crowded path, checks the advance of the splendid dancing horse.

Afterward, another vision: Señor Aretal peered about like a horse. When his own words got him drunk, as a noble steed seems drunk with his own generous blood, I saw Señor Aretal trembling like a leaf, like all those lifelike forms of nervous and fine intertwined roots. He bent his head, tilted his head, and looked around, while his arms were moving about in the air as the hoofs of a horse would.

And a hundred other visions later. Señor Aretal approached

women like a horse. In the luxurious parlors, he couldn't remain quiet. He would approach a beautiful woman, to whom he had just been introduced, with easy springy motions and, lowering and tossing his head, would seem to prance about her.

And then, finally, a question of mine, formulated long ago, appeared on the physical plane: Which one is the true spirit of Señor Aretal? And I answered it right away. Señor Aretal, who had a high mentality, did not have any spirit, he was amoral. He was amoral as a horse and was allowing himself to be ridden by any spirit. . . .

I posed the problem to the excellent mind of my friend. He made a confession to me: "I show the best part of myself to you who love me. I show you my internal God. It is painful to confess it, but when I am between two human spirits I tend to take on the color of the lower one."

.   .   .   .   .   .

"You are beyond morals," I told him, "you are beneath morals. But the horse and the angel have much in common, and on that account you seem to me divine. Saint Francis of Assisi loved all beings and all things, as you do; but he loved them after the circle, not before the circle, the way you do."

.   .   .   .   .   .

I left my friend of the precious stones, and a few days later marked the end of our relationship. Señor Aretal felt that my handclasp was not too firm, that it stretched out to him wretchedly and cowardly, and the nobility of the brute rose in protest. With a rapid gesture he hurled me away from himself. I felt his hoofs against my forehead. Later a swift and martial gallop raised the sand of the desert. I turned my eyes toward where the Sphinx rested in her eternal, mysterious repose, and I didn't see her. The Sphinx was Señor Aretal, who had revealed his secret to me, that he himself was the Centaur!

It was Señor Aretal who was moving away in his swift gallop, with his human face and his body of a beast.

Sheila Toye and W.K.J.

THE WOLF MEN

At first I called them "brothers" and reached out to clasp their
    hands,
But later from among my sheep, they tried their thievery.
And then my heart forgot that I had ever thought them friends.
I drew still nearer, watching them, and each a wolf was he.

What could be happening in my soul that used to walk so
    blindly,
My poor, sad soul that dreamed and overflowed with friendly
    feeling?
Why had I not seen in their stride a beast's fleet-footedness?
Why had I overlooked their eyes, their savage lust revealing?

Then later I became a wolf, the right pathway forsaking,
Fated, a wolf like all of them, in unknown mud to fall.
And everywhere, in each of them, I found I had a brother,
And I drew nearer, watching them. Men were they one and all.

                      B. Jane Johnson and *W.K.J.*

GREGORIO LÓPEZ Y FUENTES
1897–   Mexico

López y Fuentes taught school among the Indians till
he left for the capital to become a journalist and poet.
While still young, he had witnessed the beginnings of
the Mexican Revolution, whose aims provided him with
themes for his novels: agrarian reforms and betterment
of the Indians. First came *Campamiento* (1931), followed by *Tierra* (1932), *Mi general* (1933) and his
masterpiece, *El Indio* (1935), which shows the pathetic
efforts of the upland Indians to cope with the oncoming
civilization.

More recently, López y Fuentes wrote *Cuentos*

campesinos de México ("Rural Tales of Mexico") (1940), based on Indian customs and folklore. Typical of his work with its poetic touches, sentiment, and expression of the Indian's love of his land, superstition and faith, and distrust of the white man, is his short story here given in its entirety, "Una carta a Dios."

A LETTER TO GOD

The house, which stood alone in all the valley, was on top of a small hill. Nearby a river could be seen, and next to the corral, a field of ripe corn and blossoming kidney beans gave promise of a good crop.

The only thing that the land needed was a good rain, or at least a heavy shower that would drench the fields. To doubt that it was going to rain would be to stop believing in the experience and the wisdom of the old ones of the village.

All morning long, Lencho, who knew the country thoroughly and believed strongly in the old customs of his people, had done nothing but search the sky toward the northeast.

"Now the rain *is* coming, old girl!" he exclaimed.

And his wife, who was preparing the meal, replied, "God grant it!"

The older children pulled up weeds in the sowed field while the smaller ones played near the house, until their mother called them: "Come and eat. . . ."

During the meal, as Lencho had predicted, big drops of water began falling. Large banks of clouds could be seen advancing in the northeast. The air was fresh and sweet.

The man went out alone to look for something in the corral in order to give himself the pleasure of feeling the rain on his body. Coming back to the house, he exclaimed: "These are not drops of water that fall from heaven; they are new coins. The large drops are ten centavos and the small ones are five centavos."

He feasted his eyes upon the field of ripe corn with the

blossoms of the beans entwined among the stalks, all covered with a transparent curtain of rain. But, all of a sudden, a strong wind began blowing, and large hailstones began falling with the rain. Those *did* look like new silver coins. The children, bare-headed, ran out to pick up the ice-pearls.

"This really *is* bad!" exclaimed Lencho. "I hope it's soon over!"

It was not soon over. For an hour, hailstones fell on the house, the garden, the mountain, the corn, and all the valley. The field looked white, as if it were covered with salt. The trees were stripped bare of leaves, and the bean plants lost all their blossoms. Lencho's soul was filled with sadness at the sight. When the storm passed, he said to his children:

"A cloud of locusts would have left more than this. . . . The hail has not left anything—we won't have any corn or beans this year."

The night was filled with their lamentations:

"All our work—ruined!"

"There is nobody who will help us!"

"This year we'll go hungry!"

But in the hearts of all those who lived in that house standing alone in the middle of the valley, there was one hope—the help of God.

"Don't feel so bad," Lencho comforted his family. "Even though our misfortune is great, remember that nobody dies of hunger! That's what they say: 'Nobody dies of hunger.' "

By dawn, Lencho had thought a great deal about something he had often seen in the village church on Sundays: a carving of a triangle with an eye inside, which, according to the explanation he had been given, was God's eye within the Trinity. It saw everything, even those ideas which lie in the depth of the conscience.

Lencho was a simple man who worked like an animal in the fields, but he knew how to write. With the light of day, taking advantage of the fact that it was Sunday, he began to write a letter that he himself would take to town to mail. It was nothing less than a letter to God.

"God," he wrote, "if You do not help me, my family and I will go hungry this year. I need a hundred pesos to buy seed again and to live on while the new crop comes up, because the hail . . ."

He wrote "To God" on the envelope, inserted the letter, and, still full of worries, went to town. In the post office, he stamped the letter and dropped it into the mailbox.

The clerk, who was the mailman and general helper in the office, laughed heartily as he went to the postmaster and showed him the letter addressed to God. The postmaster, who was fat and good-natured, also began to laugh, but very quickly he became serious. As he tapped the table with the letter, he said:

"Such faith! If only I had the faith of the man who wrote this letter! To believe what he believes! To hope with the confidence with which he hopes! To start writing letters to God!"

To prevent the disillusionment of that paragon of faith, since it was impossible to deliver the letter, the postmaster had an idea: to answer the letter himself. But when he opened it, is was evident that more would be needed to answer it than good will, paper, and ink. However, he persisted with his plan: he asked his clerk for money, gave part of his own salary, and asked some friends for something "for a work of charity."

It was impossible, however, for him to collect the one hundred pesos Lencho had asked for. He was able to send only a little more than half. He inserted the money in an envelope addressed to Lencho along with a letter containing only one word—"God."

The following Sunday, Lencho came to inquire, much earlier than usual, if there was a letter for him. The mailman himself gave him the letter, while the postmaster, with the happiness that comes from doing a good deed, watched through the door of his office.

Lencho did not show the least surprise when he saw the money—so great was his faith—but he got angry when he counted it. . . . God couldn't have made a mistake, and He wouldn't have sent Lencho less than he asked for!

At once Lencho went over to the post office window to ask for paper and ink. On the table provided for the use of the public he began to write, scowling in his efforts to express himself. When he had finished, he went to ask for a stamp, moistened it with his tongue, and then affixed it with a blow of his fist.

As soon as the letter fell into the mailbox, the postmaster went to open it. It said:

"God: the money which You sent me amounted to only sixty pesos, by my counting. Send me the rest, because I have great need for it; but don't send it to me through the post office, because the clerks are a bunch of thieves.

Lencho."

Susan Louise Shelby

MARTA BRUNET
1901–   Chile

Best of Chile's woman short-story writers is Miss Brunet, who went as a child (1911–1914) to Europe, but completed her education in Santiago. Only Latorre, among the creolists, can compete with her in stories of the country people of Chile; and in her realism she has no trace of the romanticism of Latorre. *Montaña adentro* ("In the Mountains") (1925) was her first and perhaps her best novel. *Reloj de sol* ("Sun Dial") (1930) the collection from which "Francina" was taken, contains the gem "Doña Santitos" also involving the philosophy, rather than actions, of its chief character.

Some of her books were published in Buenos Aires where she represented Chile in consular or ambassadorial duties between 1939 and 1951, when she returned permanently to Chile. *Aguas abajo* ("Downstream") (1943) a book of short stories won prizes in both countries. *Raíz de sueños* ("The Root of Dreams") (1949) is her most recent collection.

FRANCINA

The daughter of an invalid mother, with her father always gone on extensive business trips, Francina lived capriciously in the enormous house, poorly looked after by a governess.

Tall, strong, with arms as long as a monkey's, an apple-shaped face, tightly-curled hair, and sparkling eyes—much too ecstatic—the girl thought only of one thing: reading.

She devoured everything except textbooks. Newspapers, magazines, stories, novels—she was crazy about them. The other stuff, that "Mademoiselle" wanted to force her to read—that did not interest her. That the earth is round, that in such and such a year the Goths devastated Europe, that water is chemically written H_2O, that the trail which a moving point leaves is a line—why should she know this?

She liked the extraordinary, that which did not have any possible explanations, except in the power of mysterious beings or forces. And since she could not find that miraculous thing in her life as a middle-class girl, she withdrew from that, in order to live the adventures of as many books as she was able to read.

Stretched out face downward on the carpeted floor, when the cold weather kept her inside—or on the grass when the heat drove her into the yard of the big house—Francina read with complete concentration, an alert sensitiveness, and as though drugged, projecting herself into each character: with steel-like muscles, a penetrating frown, and a valorous soul, when in battle a hero excited her; full of deep sympathy for an unfortunate lover; feeling her heart brim with hatred and with a bitter expression on her face for an envious wretch; all tenderness at the sighing of a marvelously beautiful captive; uttering ringing challenges through the mouth of the conquering warrior; fearless with the pirates upon boarding their ship; all the lives described in all the books that a youngster could read, Francina read fascinated.

After reading came a period of relaxation, in which she was lost in her own illusions. But with the passing of time she began taking pleasure in acting out what she had read and imagined, and since she hit upon this new whim the hours were filled with riding a broomstick horse; with enveloping herself in a quilt, with a soup-tureen lid on her head and a feather duster in her hand; with saying "virtuous little twig" to any stick that she found in her path; with reserving the hour of midnight for going to see the elves leave their flowers; with adorning herself with strips of paper and with great leaps dancing the religious ceremonies of savages; with looking anxiously beneath all the rough stones searching for the gnome guardian of treasures.

She did not shrink from reality; rather, she never saw it. So great was her imagination that everything she was imagining became real, and so the broomstick became a spirited horse which made her gasp; and the quilt, the most beautiful of ermine capes; the soup-tureen lid, a crown of pearls; the feather duster, a golden sceptre; the magic twig granted her anything for which she asked; and at midnight she saw the elves dancing mad whirls with the fairies; and the sacred rite left her with a fetichism that caused her to worship anything, from the sun to an unusual type of root; and the gnomes used to bring her magnificent jewels.

Such was Francina's life.

At times the governess protested and would go complaining to the sickly mother or to the father on one of his short stays in the home. The mother was able to excuse the child, looking for motives of pardon and tolerance in her own great affection. The father, with his imperious voice, thundered threats and reprimands upon the child, who listened soberly, wide-eyed, with her thoughts far away. She would say to herself, "He seems like Blue Beard. But, no, with his whiskers bristling, he looks like King Almaviva, the one with the golden elephants."

And she gave no signs of repentance, nor did she promise to change. Her mother's caresses and her father's scoldings made no impression. The "Mademoiselle" finally became weary and left the girl to her pleasure.

At the age of fourteen, unco-ordinated due to normal child development, ugly, and unattractive, Francina had the soul of a child in the body of a woman. She remained an outcast from life, a dreamer clinging firmly to what was miraculous.

The great crisis of puberty passed without any anxiety; man existed for her only as a chimera. She did not bother about making herself pretty. She liked to wear a sack dress that gave her complete freedom, and in the evening, for the informal meals which were always the same—the mother was still sick and the father traveling—the only sign of coquetry shown was a ribbon tied around her neck, a ribbon that she thought might belong to a pet cat, perhaps that of Mucifuz, a pirate.

Accustomed to imaginary beings, flesh and blood people frightened her. No sooner had she spoken to them than she would hide. She only knew how to speak through the lips of her heroes. . . . The confusion of the streets terrified her. One time she was taken to the movies and they made such an impression that she came down with a nervous fever, and her mother, frightened, never allowed her to go to the theater again. Music was her delight, giving her trances which were almost ecstasy. But she continued to find her most complete happiness in books.

Then one day Francina met Marcial Luco and her life changed.

She was in the park, hurling stones at some imaginary monkeys which were bothering good old Robinson Crusoe on his island. She was Robinson. Suddenly, at her shoulder, a voice called, "Francina . . ."

She turned, startled.

Nearby, wearing a riding habit, a tall, dark-haired man with pearly teeth in a youthful mouth, and attentive, kindly eyes, was watching her. It was Prince Floridor . . . Of course! Prince Floridor! How exquisitely he walked! And he clapped his hands and smiled and gave a courtly salute, just like those that Princess Corysanda made.

"Sir," she said, "welcome to my island. You are speaking to Robinson."

Surprised, the youth looked at her.

"Child, don't you remember me? I am your Uncle Marcial, your father's cousin. Don't look at me with that frightened expression."

Francina began to remember . . . and terrified, she tried to flee, because she was so ashamed of having spoken as she did. But the young man anticipated her action and, resting a hand on her shoulder, stopped her.

"Were you playing?" he asked.

"Yes . . . No . . . The fact is—" and she could not say anything else, choked by fear and sorrow.

She wanted to hide, she wanted to flee, she wanted to kill herself rather than keep feeling the youth's hand still resting on her shoulder or seeing his eyes looking inquisitively at her.

And since she could not think of any way to avoid that examination, she covered her face with her hands and burst out crying inconsolably.

"Don't cry, little one . . . Have I frightened you?"

His serious voice made her nerves tingles. Was it true then that someone, anyone could possess such a voice—a voice she had thought the privilege of her legendary heroes? Could a man approach her and cause such a ripple of warmth that made her flush at an unknown pleasure?

"Have I frightened you?" insisted the youth.

"No . . . No . . ." She went on crying, in spite of the happiness that she felt, because it was another pleasure to see him through the tears, upset and trying to console her.

"What are you denying? Your fear? Or is it that you do not want me to see your tear-streaked face? Is that it? Come! Run, wash your eyes and put on a little powder. I am eating lunch with you. While you are fixing yourself up, I'll stay here, smoking. Don't be long! I'll be waiting."

He withdrew his hand from her shoulder, withdrew his hand which was petting her head. He moved farther into the park. The girl watched him go. He was not the hero Prince Floridor of her dreams: he was her flesh and blood uncle, Marcial. He was not a chimera: he was a reality.

What had he said? Fix herself up? Powder her nose? Waiting for her? Oh!

She examined her hands, covered with scratches. She examined her lanky legs and her feet, looking so enormous in tennis shoes. She looked at the unwashed, sail-cloth sack dress. And she was ashamed of herself. An impulse made her run home, with her heart still bewildering her by its dull pounding, under its emotion. She reached her room gasping, her body trembling, her cheeks burning, her eyes shining.

She searched through her wardrobe, turned over everything in the bureau, opened drawers, upset boxes, rushed back and forth feverishly until she got together a dress, shoes, stockings, and a large ribbon to wear. Then with keen anxiety, she stared into the mirror to study herself.

Francina the child there met Francina the woman.

Marilyn Bauman

EDUARDO MALLEA

1903–   Argentina

Existentialism, derived from Kierkegaard with its attempt to evaluate human existence as a being or factor in the world, inspired Mallea, whose literary career began with *Cuentos para una inglesa desesperada* ("Stories for a Desperate Englishwoman") (1926). It was followed by ten years of silence till, being tormented by a feeling of responsibility, he started writing again, first some novels with autobiographical elements. Then he attacked national problems, with *La ciudad junto al río inmóvil* ("The City Beside the Motionless River") (1936) a psychological study of Buenos Aires, comprising sketches full of realistic details, one chapter of which is translated here. *Fiesta en noviembre* (1938) was more of a novel. *La bahía de silencio* ("The Bay of Silence") (1940), a Kafka-like self-analysis with lyrical philosophizing to interrupt the story, helped increase Mallea's reputation.

THE CITY BESIDE THE
MOTIONLESS RIVER

Conversation

He did not answer. They went into the bar. He ordered a whisky, she a whisky and water. He looked at her—she wore a black velvet cap that was pressed tightly round her small head, her eyes opened, dark, out of a region of blue. She noticed his red tie with its dirty white dots and untidy knot. Through the window could be seen the front of a cleaner's shop, beside whose door a child was playing; the pavement revealed a gaping mouth through which—almost incredibly— surged the thick trunk of a chestnut tree; the street was very wide.

The waiter came with the bottle and two large glasses and ice. "Cigarettes?" he said. "Maspero?" The waiter took the order without moving his head, flicked his cloth over the stained surface of the table, and then placed glasses on it.

Nearly all the tables in the saloon were empty; behind an enormous desk the owner was writing in the leaves of a ledger. At a table in the far corner two men were speaking, their heads uncovered, one with a thick, trimmed mustache, the other clean-shaven, repugnant, bald, and yellowish. For a moment, not even the stirring of a fly could be heard in the saloon, but soon the younger of the men in the far corner was heard to speak hurriedly and to make abrupt pauses. The owner would lift his eyes and look at the speaker as if to listen better to this coarse and irregular manner of speaking, and then would bury himself once more in his figures. It was seven o'clock.

He helped her to some whisky, about two centimetres of it, and then helped her to some ice; then he helped himself and immediately took a short, energetic gulp. He lit a cigarette, which remained dangling from the corner of his mouth, and he had to half-close his eyes against the smoke in order to look at her; she had her eyes fixed on the child playing by the cleaner's. The cleaner's name was written in the color of silver; and the C, which had been a pretentious baroque capital, now had its two ends broken; and instead of the embellishments, there remained two stains which were much lighter than the homogeneous background of the board on which many years had gathered their dust. His voice was authoritative, virile, dry.

"You do not wear your white dress any more," he said.

"No," she answered.

"It suited you better than this one does," he said.

"It probably did."

"Much better."

"Yes."

"Do you want to make yourself some clothes?"

"Later on," she said.

"The eternal 'later on,'" he said. "We no longer live now. We don't live within the passing and living moment. Everything is 'later on.'"

She said nothing; the taste of the whisky was pleasant, fresh, and with a barely perceptible bitterness.

The saloon served as a refuge from the evening rush. A man entered, dressed in a white linen suit and dark shirt, with a handkerchief with brown dots peeping out of the jacket pocket. He looked around him and sat near the counter, and the owner lifted his eyes and looked at him. The waiter came and flicked his cloth over the table and listened to the man's order and then repeated it. One of the men in the far corner turned his slow, heavy eyes toward the patron who had just entered. A sleeping cat was stretched out on the balustrade of dark oak which separated the two sections of the saloon, starting from the window where you could read the inscription reversed: Café de la Legalidad.

She thought: Why should it be called Café de la Legalidad? Once she had seen, in port, a ship called *Causalidad*; what did *causalidad* mean? Why had the owner thought of the word *causalidad*? What would a dingy man of the sea know about causality unless he might be a man of letters out of his element?

Perhaps that same word *causalidad* had had something to do
with his personal disaster; or he might have meant to put
casualidad, coincidence—that is to say, it might mean the opposite, this word, put there through possible ignorance.

Next door to the cleaner's, the doors were already closed,
but the showcases displayed an orderly accumulation of gray,
white, and yellow title pages of books, and the heads of photo-
genic intellectuals, and advertisements written in large black
letters.

"This is not good whisky," he said.

"Isn't it?" she asked.

"It has a peculiar taste."

She had not noticed any peculiar taste; it was true, however, that she took whisky very seldom. Neither did he take it
often. Sometimes, when he came home fatigued, he had about
half a tumbler full before the evening meal. He usually took
other alcoholic drinks in preference, but hardly ever alone,
only with friends, at midday; but those few bouts of drinking
were not responsible for the greenish color which spread down
from his forehead over the bony meager face up to the chin—
it was not a sickly color, but neither was it an indication of
health. None of the standard remedies had been able to transform this lusterless color, which sometimes even approached
a livid tone. He asked:

"What are you looking at? What's wrong with me?"

"Nothing," she said.

"For once and for all, shall we be going tomorrow to the
Leites'?"

"Yes," she said, "of course, if you want to. Didn't we tell
them we would go?"

"That doesn't mean a thing," he said.

"I know it's beside the point, but if we didn't intend going,
we should have let them know."

"All right, we'll go."

There was a pause.

"Why do you say we will go in that manner?" she asked.

"In what manner?"

"Yes, with a resigned air. As if you did not like going."

"I'm not fond of gadding about."

There was a pause.

"Yes. You always say that. And yet, when you are there——"

"When I am there, what?" he asked.

"When you are there, you seem to like it and to like it in a special way."

"I don't understand," he said.

"Well, you like it in a special way, that's all. For instance, when you talk to Ema, it seems to be a sort of relief to you, something refreshing—and you change. . . ."

"Don't be silly."

"You change," she said. "At least, I think you change. Oh, I don't know. Anyhow, don't deny that you wouldn't take a step to see her husband."

"He's an insignificant, dingy man, but I suppose I'm indebted to him," he said.

"Yes. But I don't know about that; I still think that a word from Ema uplifts you, does you good."

"Please don't be silly," he said. "She also bores me."

"Why pretend that she bores you? Why say the opposite of what really is?"

"I have no reason for saying the opposite of what really is. You're stubborn. Leites bores me and Ema bores me and all that surrounds them and that they touch bores me."

"All that surrounds them annoys you," she said. "But there is another thing."

"What other thing?"

"You cannot bear the idea of an extravagant creature like Ema being united to a man so inferior, so trivial."

"But what you are saying is absurd. What's put it into your head? Each one of us forms his relationships according to his needs. If Ema lives with Leites, it is not through some divine ruling or a law of fate, but simply because she does not see beyond him. So don't be ridiculous!"

There was another pause. The man in the white suit went out of the bar.

"I am not ridiculous," she said.

She had meant to add something else, to say something more significant, to throw light on all those cryptic sentences they had been exchanging, but she did not, would not say it. She looked at the letters in the word "Cleaners." The owner of the bar called the waiter and gave him an order in a low voice and the waiter went and spoke to one of the men sitting in the far corner. She swallowed the last drop of the amber spirits.

"At bottom, Ema is a woman who is quite contented with her fortune," he said.

She did not answer.

"A cold-hearted woman," he said.

She did not answer.

"Don't you think so?" he questioned.

"Perhaps," she said at last.

"And you insist on saying such absolutely fantastic things."

She did not say anything.

"What do you think might interest me in Ema?" he went on. "What do you think?"

"But why return to the same subject?" she said. "It was a passing remark. Simply a passing remark."

They were silent. He looked at her. She looked outside at the street which was gradually thickening with shadows, the street where night moved forward by degrees. The asphalt once whitish, now gray, would soon be dark, dark with a certain deep bluish reflection shining on its surface; automobiles passed swiftly by, a bus or two, full. Suddenly a bell was heard—from where did that strange toll come? The voice of a boy was heard, distantly, announcing the evening papers, the fifth edition which had appeared.

The man ordered another whisky for himself; she never drank more than one. The waiter turned his back on their table and shouted the order in the stentorian and emphatic voice with which hirelings of a tyrannical master give themselves the pleasure of assuming some authority for themselves. The man knocked on the window and the boy who was running past with his load of papers entered the saloon. The man bought a paper, unfolded it and started to read the headlines. She fixed her attention on two or three photographs on the back page and saw the young woman of the aristocracy who would shortly be married and the manufacturer of British cars who had just arrived in Argentina on a business trip. The cat had got up from the balustrade and was playing with one paw with an earthenware vase, moving the stalks of the lifeless flowers. She asked the man if there was any important news and the man hesitated before answering, and then said:

"The same old thing. The Russians don't agree with the Germans. The Germans don't agree with the French. The French don't agree with the English. Nobody understands each other. Neither is anything understood. It looks as though everything will go to the devil at one moment or another. Or things might remain as they are: the world steeped in misunderstanding and the planet continuing to revolve."

He moved the paper to his side, filled his glass with a little whisky and then a lump of ice and some water.

"It is better not to stir it," he ruminated. "Those who know how to drink it say it is better not to stir it."

"Will there be war, do you think?" she asked him.

"Who can say yes, who can say no? Not even they who are involved themselves; that is what I think. Not even themselves . . ."

"It will last two weeks, the war, with all those inventions . . ."

"It was the same with the other one; they said the same about it lasting two weeks."

"It was different . . ."

"It was the same. It is always the same. Would the sacrifice of more grams of blood or more thousands detain man? It's like the miser and his money. Nothing satisfies the love of money for money. And so no amount of hate will satisfy the hate of man for man."

"Nobody wants to be massacred," she said. "That desire is stronger than all hates."

"What?" he exclaimed. "A general blindness obscures it all. In war, the ghastly fulfillment of killing is greater than the fear of death."

She was silenced. She thought of what he had said and then was about to answer but decided not to say anything; she thought it was not worth while. A young woman with graying hair appeared on the sidewalk outside and with the aid of a long iron rod began pulling down the metal shutters of the cleaner's shop; the shutters fell thunderously. The electric lights in the street appeared to be dim and the traffic had thinned somewhat, but people continued to pass at intervals.

"You make me furious every time you touch that Ema question," he said suddenly.

She did not say anything.

"Women should sometimes be silent," he said, feeling that he must continue.

She did not say anything. The clean-shaven man with the yellow skin said good-by to his friend, walked between the tables and left the bar; the owner lifted his eyes toward him and then lowered them.

"Do you want to go out somewhere to dinner?" he asked bitterly.

"I don't know," she said. "As you like."

When a minute had passed she said: "If only one could give life some purpose."

He was silent.

They stayed a little longer and then went out. In the temperate night air they roamed those streets of solitude and poverty. Between them a mood had established itself, an ominous mood which seemingly challenged the mild air. They walked a few blocks, to the central district where the galvanic arches glowed, and then entered a restaurant.

And here there was laughter, clatter, and the babble of tongues; the ten-piece orchestra sustained a strange rhythm. They ate in silence. From time to time a question and an answer would stir between them. They did not have anything more than fruit and coffee after the cold turkey. The orchestra ceased now and then for short intervals.

When they went out, when the night air and the city received them again, they walked aimlessly as if hypnotized by the blazing neons of the cinemas. He was absent-minded, exacerbated, and she was looking pointlessly at the pink and yellow posters. She would like to have said many, many things, but it was not worth it and so she was silent, silent.

"Let's go home," he said. "There is really nowhere to go."

"Yes, let's go home," she said. "What else can we do?"

Hugo Manning

HORACIO QUIROGA
1878–1937   Uruguay

Though born in Uruguay, Quiroga exiled himself to Argentina for most of his life, and spent many years on the Upper Paraná River. From the jungles, where he witnessed the struggle between man and elemental nature; he drew much of the inspiration for his stories. Many are cruel, telling of disease, alcoholism, superstitious fears, and death. He was a master of the emotional effects of terror and horror. But having studied both Poe and Kipling, he also fused the aesthetic and naturalistic qualities in stories of humanized animals, and gave philosophic interpretation to their struggle in such collections as *Cuentos de la selva* ("South American Jungle Tales") (1918). Situations, rather than plot or character, is the forte of this writer whom most critics consider the best short-story writer of the continent. "Anaconda" ("The Return of Anaconda") (1921), about the clash of poisonous and non-poisonous serpents, is the greatest of his animal stories. "El hijo" ("The Son") is a sample of his dynamic emotional appeal, and "Las medias de los flamencos" shows wild creatures with credible human traits.

THE FLAMINGOS' STOCKINGS

Once upon a time the vipers gave a big dance. They invited the frogs and the toads, the flamingos, and the alligators and the fish. Each alligator, in order to dress up, had put a banana necklace around its neck and came smoking Paraguayan cigars.

The frogs had perfumed their whole bodies, and they arrived on two feet. Besides that, each one wore a firefly hanging like a lamp and swinging back and forth. And the most splendid of all were the coral snakes, who arrived wearing long filmy dresses of red, white, and black, and when they danced they looked like variegated streamers.

Only the flamingos, who at that time had white legs, were sad. They had so little intelligence that they didn't know how to make themselves look pretty. They envied the dresses of all the rest and especially those of the coral snakes. Each time a snake passed in front of them coquetting and swirling her sheer skirt, the flamingos nearly died of envy. Then one flamingo said:

"I know what we should do. Let's put on red, black, and white stockings, and the coral snakes will fall in love with us."

Flying off together, they crossed the river and went knocking at the door of a store in town.

"Knock-knock!" sounded their feet on the wood.

"Who is it?" asked the storekeeper.

"We are the flamingos. Do you have any red, black, and white colored stockings?"

The storekeeper answered:

"What are you talking about? Red, black, and white? There aren't any stockings like that anywhere. Who are you?"

"We're flamingos," they replied.

And the man said:

"Then for sure you're crazy flamingos." And the man chased them away with a broom.

The flamingos went to all of the stores, and everywhere people thought they were crazy.

Then an armadillo that had gone to the river for a drink of water, wanted to play a joke on the flamingos, so he said, with a sweeping bow:

"Good evening, distinguished flamingos! I know what you're looking for. You won't find stockings like that in any store around here. Maybe there are some in Buenos Aires, but you would have to have them shipped here by parcel post. My sister-in-law, the barn owl, has stockings like that. Ask her, and she'll provide you with red, black, and white stockings, I'm sure."

The flamingos thanked him, and they flew away to the cave of the barn owl. There they told her:

"Good evening, barn owl! We've come to ask you for some red, black, and white stockings. Today is the big snake ball, and if we wear pretty stockings like those, the coral snakes will fall in love with us."

"I'll be glad to help you!" said the barn owl. "Wait a second and I'll be back right away."

She flew away and left the flamingos alone. And soon she returned with the stockings. Only they were not stockings. They were beautiful skins from coral snakes that the barn owl had recently caught.

"Here are your stockings," the barn owl told them. "You have only one thing to worry about: Be sure to dance all night, and don't stop for a minute, for if you do, you'll be crying instead of dancing."

But the flamingos, being so stupid, didn't realize their great danger, and crazy with happiness they put their legs through the tubes of the coral snake skins, like stockings. And they went flying off happily to the dance.

When those at the dance saw the flamingos arrive wearing their beautiful stockings, they were full of envy. All the snakes wanted to dance just with them, and since the flamingos kept their legs in motion all the time, the snakes couldn't very well see what those beautiful stockings were made of.

The coral snakes especially were very upset. They did not

take their eyes off the stockings. They squatted almost to the floor in their efforts to get a good look, and tried to touch the legs of the flamingos with their tongues, because a snake's tongue is like the hand of a person. But the flamingos danced and danced, and never stopped even though they were so tired that they could hardly move.

Realizing this, the coral snakes immediately begged the frogs for flashlights, the fireflies they wore around their necks. And they all waited together until the flamingos should drop from exhaustion. As a matter of fact, a moment later, a flamingo that couldn't dance any longer staggered and fell down. Instantly the coral snakes rushed up with their lamps, and got a good look at the legs of the flamingos. They saw what the stockings really were, and they hissed so loudly that it was heard all the way across the Paraná River.

"They aren't stockings," screamed the snakes. "We know what they are! The flamingos have killed our sisters, and are wearing their skins for stockings."

On hearing that, the flamingos, frightened at being discovered, tried to fly away, but they were so tired they couldn't even lift one leg. So the coral snakes attacked them. Wrapping themselves around the legs of the flamingos, they tried to chew off the stockings. Furiously they tore them off in pieces, at the same time biting the legs of the birds and trying to kill them.

The flamingos, crazy with pain, jumped back and forth trying to shake off the coiled coral snakes. Finally, seeing that there wasn't a single piece of stocking left, the snakes let the flamingos go, being exhausted themselves. They went away smoothing out the sheer fabric of their dresses. Besides, the coral snakes were sure that the flamingos would die, because half, at least, of the coral snakes that had bitten them were of the poisonous variety.

But the flamingos did not die. They dashed into the water, as a relief for their extreme pain. They screamed with agony. Their legs, that had been white, were now crimsoned by the venom of the snakes. They spent day after day standing in the water, continually suffering from the terrible pain in their legs, which were now blood red because of the snake poison.

That was a long time ago, and yet even today the flamingos spend most of the day with their red legs immersed in water, trying to ease the burning pain. Occasionally they leave the water's edge, and walk a few steps onto the ground in order to see how they feel. But the pain of the poison soon returns and they hurry back into the water. At times the agony that they feel is so great that they raise one leg and stay that way for hours, because they can't extend it.

This is the story of the flamingos, who used to have white legs, but now they are red.

W. P. *Negron* and W.K.J.

THE SON

It is a magnificent summer day in Misiones, with all the sun, heat, and calm that the season can offer. Nature seems satisfied with itself.

Like the sun, the heat, and the calm atmosphere, the father also opens his heart to nature.

"Be careful, youngster," he says to his son, summarizing in that remark all his observations and advice, and his son understands perfectly.

"Yes, papa," the child replies, while he takes his rifle and loads his shirt pockets with cartridges.

"Come back by lunch time," his father adds.

"Yes, papa," repeats the boy. He balances the rifle in his hand, smiles at his father, kisses him on the forehead, and off he goes.

His father follows him a short distance with his eyes and then returns to his task for that day, happy because of his little son's joy.

He knows that his son, brought up since his tenderest childhood to take precaution against danger, can use a rifle and hunt anything. Although he is very tall for his age, he is only thirteen years old. And he would seem to be younger, judging by the clearness of his blue eyes, still naive with childish astonishment.

The father doesn't need to raise his eyes from his task to follow his son's progress in his mind. By now the boy has crossed the red trail and is walking across the clearing straight toward the forest full of birds.

To hunt fur-bearing game in the forest requires more patience than his small son possesses. After crossing that isolated section of forest, his son will go along the cactus border as far as the swamp, looking for doves, toucans, or perhaps a couple of herons like those his friend John discovered a few days before.

Alone now, the father smiles faintly at the thought of the two boys' passion for hunting. Sometimes they hunt only a *yacútoro* bird or a *surucuá* that is still smaller, and return triumphant, John to his hut with the 9 mm. rifle that he gave him, and his son to the house on the hill with a large sixteen calibre St. Etienne shotgun with a quadruple lock and white gunpowder.

He had been the same way. At thirteen, he would have given his life to possess a shotgun. His son, at that same age, owns one and the father smiles. It is not easy for a father who has lost his wife, to bring up a son. Danger is always at hand for a man, but even more if he has always to depend on himself. It has been a constant worry. Sometimes he has even suffered hallucinations like the fright he once had because of his weak vision, seeing the boy hammering on a bullet at the workshop bench when really he was polishing the buckle of his hunting belt.

Suddenly, at no great distance, he hears a gunshot.

"The St. Etienne!" thinks the father, recognizing the report. "Two less doves in the forest."

Without paying any more attention to the unimportant incident, the man concentrates again on his task.

The sun, already very high, continues ascending. Wherever one looks, at the rocks, the land, or the trees, the air, rarefied as in a furnace, vibrates with the heat. The father glances at his watch; it is noon. He raises his eyes toward the forest.

His son ought to be returning. In the mutual confidence that they place in each other, the father with silvery temples and the son of thirteen, they never deceive each other. When his son answers, "Yes, papa," he will do what he promises. He said that he would return before twelve, and the father smiled upon seeing him depart.

And the boy has not returned yet. Suddenly he realizes that for three hours he has heard no more shooting. A shot, a single shot has sounded, long ago. Since then, the father has heard no other sound, has seen no bird.

Bareheaded and without his machete, the father runs out. He cuts across the clearing, enters the forest, and hurries along the cactus border without finding the least trace of his son. By the time he has covered the game trail and explored the swamp in vain, he is sure that every step is taking him fatally and helplessly toward the spot where he will find the body of his son, killed while crawling through a fence.

"Son!" he suddenly exclaims. If the voice of a man of character is capable of weeping, let us cover our ears in pity in the presence of the anxiety apparent in that voice.

No one has replied. Nothing! Along the trail red in the sunlight, aged ten years hurries the father, looking for his son who has just died.

"Son! Oh, son!" he shouts, with a surge of affection that rises from the depths of his soul.

Once before, in the midst of complete happiness and peace, the father had suffered the hallucination of seeing his son, fallen with his forehead pierced by a bullet of chrome nickel. Now, in every dark corner of the forest he sees flashes of wire; and at the foot of a post, with his musket discharged near-by, he sees his . . .

"Sonny! . . . My son! . . ."

The strength of a poor father subjected to such a frightful hallucination has its limits, and the father in our story feels he is approaching his, when suddenly he sees his son coming abruptly out of a side path.

The sight, even at a distance of fifty meters, of his father, distraught and unarmed is enough to make a child of thirteen hasten his steps.

"My little boy!" murmurs the man. And exhausted, he drops onto the white, sandy soil, throwing his arms around the youngster's leg.

The child remains standing, with his father's arm around his knees, and as he understands his father's anguish, he slowly strokes his head:

"Poor papa!" . . .

By then, time has passed. It is already going on three. Together now, father and son start back to the house.

"How did it happen that you didn't notice the sun and see how late it was?" murmurs the father again.

"I did notice, papa . . . But when I started to return, I saw John's herons and followed them . . ."

"What anxiety you caused me, my boy!"

"Papa!" also murmurs the young boy. After a long silence:

"What about the herons? Did you kill them?" asks the father.

"No . . ."

That really doesn't matter, after all. Under the blue sky and the shimmering heat, through the clearing, the man returns home with his son, over whose shoulders, almost on a level with his own, rests the happy father's arm. He gets back drenched with perspiration and although upset in body and soul, he smiles happily. . . .

He smiles with a happy hallucination. . . . The father is walking alone. He has found no one and his arm encompasses empty space. Because behind him, at the foot of the post with his legs in the air, entangled in barbed wire, his beloved son lies in the sun, dead since ten o'clock that morning.

Linda Wilson and W.K.J.

CARMEN LIRA
1888–1949   Costa Rica

> Under the pen name of "Carmen Lira," a Costa Rican
> teacher, María Isabel Carvajal, published one of the
> best collections of folklore in Spanish America, *Los
> cuentos de mi tia Panchita* ("My Aunt Panchita's
> Stories") (1920), told by the Central-American equiva-
> lent of Uncle Remus. In fact, one story is called "Brer
> Rabbit," though unrelated to the Joel Chandler Harris
> version. Others have Kiplingesque titles like *Por qué
> el tío Conejo tiene las orejas tan largas* ("Why Uncle
> Rabbit Has such Long Ears"). All are written charm-
> ingly and with local color and language like this one
> which, against a religious background, combines humor
> with the lesson of casting one's bread on the water.

UVIETA

Well, sir, once upon a time there was a poor old man named
Uvieta who lived all alone in a small house. One day he suddenly got the idea of going traveling and no sooner said than
done. He went to the bakery and spent on bread the last ten-
cent piece that was loose in his pocket. They gave him some
big three-for-a-dime rolls, none of those hard shoestrings they
sell nowadays that break your jaws when you bite them, but
buns well baked outside and soft inside.

He went home and started to pack his rags when—knock-
knock! Someone at the door. He went to see who it was and
found a trembling old man in a pitiful state, who was begging
for alms, so Uvieta gave him a roll.

He was just packing the other two buns in his knapsack
when—knock-knock! at the door again. He opened it and there
stood a decrepit old woman whose face looked as though she

were starving. When she asked for alms, he gave her another of his buns.

He looked once more around his house and had just put his knapsack on his shoulder and was just leaving when— knock-knock! at the door again. This time it was a little boy with a dirty face and dressed in rags, and skinny as a tapeworm. There was nothing to do but give him the last roll. "What the deuce! At least everybody has God!"

Now without any food for himself, Uvieta took to the road and started on his travels. After walking a long time, he came to a brook. The poor man had the healthy hunger that is a gift of God, but since he had nothing to eat he went to the brook and tried to fool his stomach by filling it with water.

Just then the little old man who had come begging appeared all of a sudden and said to him: "Uvieta, Our Lord sent me to ask you what you wanted. You may have whatever you like. He is greatly pleased with you because you gave us help. You see, the three of us who came begging were Jesus, Mary, and Joseph. I'm Joseph. So tell me. Whatever you say, Uvieta, here, there, anywhere, anything."

Uvieta started to think what to ask for, and finally he said: "Very well, go and tell Him that I'd like a sack that will hold whatever I want."

Saint Joseph was off like a skyrocket toward Heaven, and in an instant he was back with the sack. Uvieta threw it over his shoulder and continued on his way.

As he was walking, he passed a woman carrying on her head a tray loaded with cheese-filled buns. Uvieta exclaimed: "Let those cheese sandwiches come into my bag."

They ended up there, so he sat down along the road and ate them all up and wished for more. But he took to the road again. Some distance farther on, he came upon the old woman who had begged alms. She said to him: "Uvieta, Our Lord, my son, sent me to say if you need anything, just ask for it."

Since Uvieta wasn't at all grasping, he shook his head. "No, thanks, Mary. Tell Him thanks, but I have enough with my sack. 'Belly full, heart content,' you know. What more could I want?"

The Virgin began to plead. "For Heaven's sake, Uvieta, don't be unfair. Don't scorn me. You asked Joseph for something back there, but nothing from me."

Since Uvieta realized that it wasn't very nice to scorn Our Lady, he finally told Her: "Very well. As truly as my name is Uvieta, I'd like to have you plant a grape arbor at my house just for my use, and if anybody else climbs it, he can't get down without my permission."

The Virgin told him he could consider it done, and left him.

Later Joseph appeared again and told him that Jesus wanted to reward him but was too busy to come and see what he wanted. After argument, Uvieta was persuaded to ask that he might be given permission to choose the hour of his death. Then, curious to see the grapes, he went home and was so delighted with them that God feared he was more interested in earthly than in heavenly things, so he sent Death to fetch him. Uvieta protested. He pointed out that he had been given the gift of deciding when he wanted to leave the earth, and was not yet ready. But Death was insistent, so Uvieta invited him into the patio to wait while he packed his things. There Death saw the grapes and wanting to taste them, he climbed into the arbor.

"Now let's see you get down till I'm good and ready," Uvieta laughed at him.

Death tried vainly to climb down, but there he stuck, and the years passed and nobody died. And there wasn't room on earth for all the people, and there were a lot of doddering old people roaming around everywhere, and God sent one messenger after another to Uvieta. One day he sent the gigantic Saint Christopher, and another day King Louis, and the following day the Archangel Michael with his sword. "Look here, Uvieta, Our Lord orders you to release Death from your grape arbor or you'll see what's going to happen to you."

But the messages went in one ear and out the other, and Uvieta kept repeating: "I'd be a fool to let him come down."

Finally Grandfather God sent word that if Uvieta would let Death come down, Death wouldn't take him away. So Uvieta let him come down, and he disappeared in a flash to put himself at God's command.

God was still angry with Uvieta so he sent the Devil after him, but when Uvieta recognized him, he made the wish that he had the Devil in his sack, and there he kept him a prisoner, beating him till God came down to release him promising no retributions against the old man. Then God sent Death secretly at night to seize him and deposit him at the gates of heaven. However, because of the trouble Uvieta had caused God, Saint Peter would not admit him, but persuaded him to go down to hell.

The Devil was walking outside and saw Uvieta coming. He fled inside and barred the gate. Then he called all the devils to bring everything they could find to barricade the entrance, because outside was that man Uvieta who had beaten him to a pulp.

Uvieta approached, calling the way people used to shout in colonial times when they entered a house: "Ave María Purísima!" And you can imagine how upset the Devil was when he heard those words. But Uvieta remained there for three days, knocking at the door and shouting: "Ave María Purísima!"

Since they wouldn't let him in, he went back to heaven. As he reached the gates, Saint Peter exclaimed: "What's all this? Are you still wandering around?"

"Well, what do you want me to do? I was down there for three days, knocking at the door and they wouldn't open it."

"Why not? What did you tell them?"

"Me? I said Ave María Purísima. Ave María Purísima."

The Virgin was in the patio feeding some chickens that had beaks and feet of gold and laid golden eggs. Hearing the cry: "Ave María Purísima," she stuck her head out, thinking somebody was calling her. When she saw Uvieta, she was delighted. "What has God done to you, Uvieta? Come right in."

Since Saint Peter did not dare contradict Mary, Uvieta came pompously into paradise and I come in one hole and out another so you can tell me another story.

Astrid S. Hasbrouck

FROYLÁN TURCIOS
1877–1943   Honduras

(See the poetry section for discussion of him.)

THE VAMPIRE

Padre Felix is the villain of El Vampiro (1912) a ghost novel that went through several editions. Told by Rogerio in the first person, it described a room in the house locked according to the will of Grandfather Humberto because his mistress had died and been buried there. Rogerio's father, following his archaeological interests, had discovered a valuable granite image in the Church of the Concepción, the Church of Padre Felix. He had almost died when hit by a stone while examining it. No one ever discovered the attacker. After a period of suffering, the father entered the room, an act that hastened his death. Felix tried to seduce Rogerio's sweetheart Luz, and finally killed her, so he had probably killed the rest of Humberto's family.

VIII

I examined the room. . . . Except for a frightful odor, there was nothing in the place that would inspire horror. Nothing! I dropped onto a sofa musing over the respected legend inspired by that room, devoid of all fantastic appearances.

It is a deserted chamber, I thought. That is all.

How did the ban imposed by my grandfather originate? What was there that had so tragically surprised my father? I reasoned that my father had become crazy, not by visiting this room, but from a blow that he received on the head while he was guarding his archaeological discovery in the debris of the church.

And to think that such a room had robbed me of sleep! And that it had come to obsess me with its fiendish and ghostly vision! . . .

An almost unconscious joy came over me, that was mixed with an ironic amusement when I thought how carelessly we had given importance to such a ridiculous, absurd idea. . . . I began to improvise, in the middle of the room, a poem which seemed especially fitting.

He dared to rebuke his grandfather for including in his will the clause that no one should enter the room.

But, what was happening? I couldn't recognize my own tone! Was it I who laughed? Was that my voice? Was I crazy?

A distant, yet near, cry attracted my attention.

It was one of those anguished moans that dogs, enveloped in the shadows, make on gloomy nights. That howl, like the futile cry for help of a prisoner, prolonging itself in space, rose and fell, started again and was extinguished in my own heart. I remembered, as in a frightful nightmare, the funereal words of Genaro: "When the dogs howl like this, in the dark, it is because they see Death or the Devil."

The dreary moaning ceased, and almost at the same moment, I heard a dull clamor coming along the corridor. Scarcely had I invented a faulty explanation of its cause when I saw Bravonel, the dog, bound into the room. Upon seeing me, he stopped and fixed on me his flashing eyes, in which I thought I observed a human and terrifying look. He stuck his head into a purple curtain that hung from the ceiling to the clothes closet, and I heard the harsh scratch of his claws upon a hidden board. I advanced, with the lantern in my left hand, and raising the heavy curtain, I discovered a low, narrow door! Until this moment I hadn't realized that the room where I was, was so very small in proportion to its apparent size from outside. There existed, then, another chamber, and it was Bravonel who showed me the door. Without trying to understand such a mystery, I pushed the door wide open. What a foul and deadly smell came out! At the impact I almost fainted. The dog whined. What did I fear, then, in my heart? Nothing! My heart remained calm; only my body trembled.

At first I saw only a dark bedroom, in which stood a black bed; an enormous, old bed with carved posts; it was one of those large double beds made of exquisite wood, in which lived and died our ancestors. Disordered sheets on it contained large blackish stains, easily identified as blood. Over the broad headboard, I saw a faded, time-worn woman's dress, with the same bloodstained traces. Beside a lounge I made out a low shoe, with a black ribbon; and, further away, an old comb of gold and tortoise shell.

But the pestilential odor was suffocating me and I was about to turn back when my eyes stopped on a horrible pit, opened in a part of the floor. The carpet was destroyed in this place and the bricks were mixed with the earth. It was a shadowy opening; as I bent over in order to examine it, I finally realized that I had found the horrible cause of that terrifying odor. I reached my right arm into the hole. My hand touched a hard round object: a small skull. I picked it up. From it spilled a reddish powder before it fell from my fingers and rolled dryly across the carpet, hitting the dog, that jumped backward. Inside the pit I would certainly find other bones.

I was turning back again, poisoned by the putrid atmosphere, when a horrible noise, brother of those foul vapors, resounded in the bedroom. Where did it come from? From the bed or the wide folds in the drapery? From the ceiling or from the wardrobe against the wall? It was a muffled, threatening noise, that came from that very grave. Where else could be heard again after many years, that infernal muttering, that harsh and gloomy murmur like a hoarse death rattle? Where? Where? Ah! Yes! I finally remembered it.

I retreated with feverish temples and angry heart?

"Damned, impure priest!" I shouted. "Damned! Damned!"

From the gloomy hole suddenly escaped a gigantic bat, that hurled itself against me. I struggled with it, violently waving the lantern that filled the room with shadows and sudden brilliance. The dog leaped to my defense, snapping at the black creature. But the bat, flying above him, attacked me furiously. Three times I felt the poisoned wind of its wings upon my face, as many times I succeeded in driving it back. But suddenly, the lantern rolled across the floor and went out.

A shudder shook my shoulders. A frightful quiet fell. Icy threads ran through my heart. . . .

I heard, as if from Eternity, twelve strokes of the bell in a distant church. At the same time could be heard the funereal death rattle, and vaguely I began to hear again that ominous beat of wings in the room.

The dog ran around desolately, growling mournfully. I grabbed the curtain, attempting to pass. But I suddenly felt something like a violent dagger thrust in my neck. I raised my hands and seized the loathsome monster. It seemed to me enormous, sickening, and gelatinous. I squeezed it with brute strength, and it struggled in an incredible manner, trying to escape. Hearing its rasping horrid cries, I was convinced that it was no ordinary bat. It sucked greedily at one of my fingers; but I felt the loud cracking of its membranes in my grip. With relentless rage, I tightened my pressure on its head that emitted, for the last time, the hoarse death rattle. Then, in the darkness, I hunted for the dog's mouth and put into it the horrible prey. And as I stood motionless in the dismal den, I heard the horrid, hair-raising crack of Bravonel's jaws tearing the hairy animal to pieces, though it still emitted its nauseating, corpselike odor.

I groped my way out of the sinister rooms, followed by the dog. In the hall I noticed a stream of blood flowing from my neck. A deathly weakness invaded my limbs. Dragging my way along the floor, supporting myself by the walls, I made my way to my room, and fainting, I fell face downward on the carpet.

Much later, strange murmurs woke me for a moment; noises of pacing and of sobbing in the next room, the shutting of doors, distant voices. Near me, in the gleam of a lamp, I saw some shadows, moving like apparitions. Then my being lost itself again in nothingness. Formless dreams of fantastic fathomless vagueness crossed my imagination, preying on my weakness.

In one of those fantastic shadowy worlds, in an unknown region of ice and silence, I saw, for a second, an angelic virgin, wrapped in a spectral whiteness, with her neck encircled by a collar of drops of blood.

Many hours passed. . . .

Although motionless because of my extreme weakness, and with burning eyes covered by leaden eyelids, I realized that I had returned to life, by hearing some words from those that surrounded me and listening to the striking of the hour by a distant clock. There was an incredible subtlety in the profound chaos of my brain, in which existed no memory.

I submerged myself little by little in the vague debility from which I was awakened by the tolling of the bells of several churches. Then I vaguely heard a brief dialogue in a whisper near my bed;

"It is time for the burial of the Padre," said one of the strange voices. "Did you find out how he died?"

"Yes. A telegram arrived from the parish priest. In it he states that last night at midnight, in Alta Verapaz, Padre Felix died of strangulation."

How did I feel upon hearing these words? How is it possible to explain all the bitter sensations that surged through my being upon hearing such words?

My memory came back for an instant and I remembered. And remembering, I lapsed back into the darkness.

I opened my eyes in the stillness of the night. My mother was nodding in an easy chair, at my bedside. . . .

With a portentous impulse, I sat up and dressed quickly; and without making the slightest noise, I left my room and went down the corridor. . . . The spirit dragging my miserable body stopped at the threshold of the Sombra. In my head only one recollection glittered, an image, and one name, the only name in the universe of my anguish, vibrated in my heart with each beat.

On entering the oratory, I stood paralyzed.

On a white bier, covered with white roses, among four enormous wax tapers, I saw death. A black curl fell over that palid face. On the snow of that bare neck glittered a tiny spot of blood.

"Luz!" I cried, from my mad soul, a sound that seemed to come from beyond the horizon of life, impelled by a tragic unearthly breath.

And I toppled, as though struck by lightning, to the floor.

Robert A. Goldberg

RAFAEL MALUENDA LABARCA
1885– Chile

Many Latin Americans try to write romantic and senti-mental prose. Rafael Maluenda Labarca a Chilean newspaperman and dramatist who several times served his country on diplomatic missions, has succeeded in a story about a typical Chilean cowboy sport, the *Topeadura,* in which *huasos* try out their horses in a sort of wrestling match. One cowboy puts the neck of his horse over the hitching post in front of a bar or *cantina.* Another horseman tries to push both away. If the horses are about equal, as in this story *Como Dios quiere* ("As God Wills") from Maluenda's sec-ond volume of short stories *Los ciegos* ("The Blind Ones") (1913) the skill of the rider is what counts. It has been somewhat condensed by the omission of some paragraphs of description and conversation.

AS GOD WILLS

"We have arrived almost together, boss," Hilario says to me. "I am glad to see you; I hope you're feeling better."

"Thank you. It's really nothing. And what's new around here?"

"Nothing, I guess"; and turning toward my mother, he tells her: "I'll bet you're happy he's here."

She does not respond; but once again, on that afternoon of my arrival, her two thin arms encircle my neck.

"And for how long is the boss going to be here, if I may ask?" continues Hilario.

"Until we make him well, Hilario," my mother smilingly suggests. "The country does wonders for a person's troubles. I hope he stays here forever."

"Me, here? Oh, no! There are some things you can get only in the city, Hilario: glory, triumph, recognition, all that I really want, I can find only there."

The white head that rests on my shoulder shakes sadly.

"Glory!" says my mother with sweet reproach. "But you have brought from the city only a sick soul."

The farmer smiles in agreement with his employer's words. Carelessly he leans against one of the pillars of the porch; a large dark poncho covers his long body. His beard and the hair that frames his brown face are black; under the narrow forehead shine clear green eyes. And there is, in his neatness and in his speech, something so full of strength that I say to him:

"Time stands still for you, Hilario. You're always the same, never a gray hair."

"You're always joking, sir!" he says and moves slightly to stare out over the countryside where the afternoon shadows are gathering.

Once again, a bird of passage in my own land, I have come in search of health; nothing has changed on my family estate; only my mother's arm around my neck has become weaker. Then suddenly remembering, I ask him:

"What about Florinda, Hilario?"

"She got married," Hilario declares. "She married Ramón Pérez, the mule driver of Peartree Ranch. They now live on a farm called Cortada Ranch."

"When was all that?"

"A year and a half ago, sir. They have a child now. Ever since . . ."

"But didn't you sort of plan to——"

"Me?" he interrupts, and he begins to smile. "Ever since I got here, Florinda liked me . . . But between liking and loving . . . She's been engaged ever so long. She married Ramón Pérez, and we've gone on being friends. . . ."

He sits down and is quiet for a moment; then he goes on talking to me about memories so deep-seated that, as I listen, I seem to guess the pains and anguishes of a loneliness never eased by talk.

"And Florinda has been very unhappy, sir. That man treats her bad. Things like that make me sad and angry at the same time!"

"That's the way life is, Hilario. It seems fated that a man always suffers for a woman."

II

The following Sunday, Hilario came with an invitation for me.

"Two very famous horses are going to have a kind of wrestling match, sir, and you'll feel better if you come along with me and watch them."

Half an hour later, we were galloping along the road, and it was not long before his usually unexpressive brown face was aglow.

"Do you see her?" he asked me.

"Who?"

"Florinda . . . over there with her children . . . Do you see her? The one in the pink dress . . . Don't you agree that she's changed a lot? But she still has that something in her face and body."

"What about the muleteer?"

"He just arrived. . . . There he is. . . . he's the man without a beard, and wearing that green cloak."

At four o'clock that afternoon, the *Tòpeadura* match took

place, amid the laughter and comments of the horsemen. One after another put his horse in position at the bar and each one in his turn tried out the skill of his horse.

Suddenly the man in the green cape detached himself from the group and approached the rail. No one seemed to notice him, but with a lash of the whip, he placed his horse and shouted:

"Move him, whoever wants to try!"

There were various *huasos* who offered to compete with him. The man ignored those who approached, however, and over the shoulders of the men who surrounded him, he looked at us, repeating:

"Isn't there anyone willing to risk it?"

I remembered my old days on horseback, and as the muleteer kept on looking our way, I spurred my horse forward. But Hilario stopped me.

"What are you going to do? Hold on, sir. Don't you see that I'm the one he's waiting for?"

And with a decisive movement, he approached the hitching rail, taking off his cloak and tightening the stirrups. Then he rode up to the rail and set his horse in position. For an instant both riders patted the neck of their horses, then someone shouted: "Go!"

The muleteer lifted the reins and spurred his horse . . . but the animals did not move. To the eye, they seemed to be making no efforts. From a distance one could believe them standing quietly against the rail; but the trembling that shook the flanks of Ramón's horse and the rhythmic rocking of Hilario's horse made the rail sway as if under a terrific pressure.

Those two work horses were no animals for feats of that kind; and understandably the cowboys predicted that the most expert horseman would win.

The muleteer encouraged his horse with hoarse shouts and sudden pushes while Hilario tried only to maintain his position and keep his horse from being pushed away. Imperceptibly he was pushing the animal forward, taking advantage of the exasperated movements of the muleteer until he could manage to press his horse down against the rail, so that he might push the other horse away . . . one pace, an instant of immobility, a pat . . . another pace, accompanied by a swift clicking of his tongue.

Suddenly Hilario caught up his reins and with a vigorous push, shoved the muleteer to the end of the rail. The audience applauded . . . the muleteer, exasperated, beat Hilario's horse, making it rear up on its hind legs . . . What an uproar! . . . Angry voices were shouting . . . I saw a pale, disheveled figure in a pink dress run toward us . . . trying to prevent the fight. Some of the men knocked the woman down.

Enraged, I shouted:

"Leave them alone!"

"No, Hilario, for God's sake!" the woman cried, and two hands stretched toward him over the horses.

The men hesitated and then stopped.

"Please, for my sake!" she begged in that pitiable tone.

Suddenly calmed, Hilario left the group, his aggressive air lost. Calmly he approached me.

"I'm doing it for her, sir. I had promised to leave before he came, but I stayed. But now I've got to go so she won't worry. Excuse me for leaving you, sir." And he rode off with an air of satisfaction and contentment that filled me with pity.

The other horsemen, again smiling, began to dismount, and one after another went toward the arbor.

With clownish gestures, the man in the green cloak strutted among them, while from an obscure corner, two dark eyes full of tenderness looked toward the horizon where a horseman rode slowly away in a cloud of dust.

III

The darkness of the moonless night made it impossible to recognize the horseman who was slowly approaching the Cortada Ranch. He seemed to be looking over the hedge that bordered the road.

When ruddy reflections among the branches announced the

buildings of Cortada Ranch, the horseman drew rein and waited. . . . Very slightly the leaves moved on the other side of the blackberry hedge . . . the man dismounted, looked for an opening between the branches and then passed inside. . . .

"Did you come here on horseback? Be careful."

And an instant later, the woman, in the same tone, which perhaps the puffs of wind made tremulous, added quickly:

"I wanted to see you in order to thank you for what you did Sunday."

The wind played with those voices; it carried them away and brought them back; it made them tremble; it unified them; at times it drowned them out; at times it lent them sonority. . . . The voice of the woman spoke of sufferings, of fatality, of resignation. The accents of the man expressed hopes, consolation, memories. . . . One might say that under the shadows of the branches the muted murmur was a sad prayer that the wind spun out.

"And now," declared the man; "now that I have said it all, I can leave contented. I love you now and forever, and although I may never return . . ."

"Please come back!"

And that was the last sound uttered by that trembling voice.

IV

Beaten by life and filled with melancholy, one evening I approached my old family estate along the road of the poplar trees. The peace of the countryside was friendly; the quietness that enveloped the land was restful; the musical murmur of the wind cheered me up.

Beaten by life and filled with melancholy, I slowly approached the old estate. Behind me, far away, I had left the city with its torments and its anxieties, with my hopes and with my faith. Tired, exhausted, hurt, it seemed to me that that journey had lasted for twenty-four years and that from my rich inheritance, lost along the rough road, there remained to me only fatigue of the journey and a handful of longings in my heart.

In the distant city, none mourned my departure; here, too, in my house no one watched for me: with the leaves and flowers fleeing from a cold winter, the two weak trembling arms had also fled and the voice that called me "son" was stilled.

Everything had changed, everything!

Thirsty and looking for a drink, I drew near to the house along the road. At the sound of my footsteps, a man came out to meet me.

"What do you want?"

"A drink if I may."

The man came closer . . . he looked at me for an instant.

"Why, it's you, sir!"

"Hilario, you?"

"It certainly is. Here, come in! Nobody knew that you would be coming."

With keen curiosity, two youngsters crowded around me. Hilario called:

"Florinda!"

The woman appeared in the doorway. Tall, erect, still young, I saw her smile, as she tried to pull the children back.

"And how have things gone, Hilario, how have they gone?" I asked him.

He hesitated as though remembering, and then he replied:

"As God willed, sir."

And it couldn't have been truer, according to the account that he gave me of the suffering, of four years of waiting, the death of the muleteer in a fight, his return to the farm, and at last that marriage that had been desired for such a long time. There was nothing more he could tell me than his simple conviction: he had suffered, he had waited, and God had finally willed it.

"I'm glad, Hilario, I'm very glad."

An hour later, when saying good-by to him, and seeing him determined to accompany me, I begged him:

"No, Hilario. Let me go alone. . . . I want to reach there alone. Later, you must come to see me with the children, with Florinda."

"Are you going to stay for awhile, sir?"

"Forever, Hilario, forever . . . I couldn't live in the city. I couldn't . . . One has to have ability and no heart."

And that rude farmer agreed with me.

"You're right. You can't live there."

"Good-by, Hilario."

"Until I see you again, sir."

I left for the road. Slowly the moon arose and it seemed to me that its soft light moving over the branches made more vital and sweet that little white cottage. How immense is the peace of the country! Tired from its daily labor, enjoying the same tranquil repose, slept the land, the men, and the trees. Nothing disturbed that soothing quietness. Only the wind, saturated with perfumes, continued singing a song of hope in the ears of that traveler, who slowly approached the old estate of his ancestors.

Elaine Schaefer

JOSÉ ENRIQUE RODÓ
1872–1917   Uruguay

Three small volumes published under the general title of *La vida nueva* ("The New Life") made the Uruguayan Rodó an Olympian figure, removed from the pride and self-glory of so many writers. The title, possibly derived from *Vita nuova* of the Italian patriot Dante, covered: *El que vendrá* ("He Who Is to Come") and *La novela nueva* ("The New Novel") (1897), *Rubén Darío* (1899), and *Ariel* (1900). The last, directed to *"La juventud de América"* ("The Youth of America") contained an idealistic and patriotic appeal to them to combine the noblest elements of Latin America in a struggle against the current turn-of-the-century Positivism and Utilitarianism, for which Rodó blamed the commercial tendencies of the United States. This "gospel intermediate between Plato and Renan, between the Christian and the Hellenic," as one critic described it, made its author the idol of young people all over the continent. "A universal handbook for Latin America," it was called. It revealed Rodó as a master of Spanish style, full of imagery, poetical figures, and noble feeling. Some see a resemblance to Walter Pater of English letters. In writing it, he drew for examples upon his wide reading in European philosophy. He upheld the Greek ideals of civilization against the Anglo-Saxon concept and expressed the belief that democracy can be achieved by leading the life beautiful with time to indulge in the purest activities of the mind. Equality was not nature's way. A democracy should be built on natural selection with superior people liberated from the abstract tyranny of the state.

Later Rodó wrote *Los motivos de Proteo* ("Motives of Proteus") (1909), which he considered his best book, but it lacks the directness and charm of *Ariel*. Here are its opening pages.

ARIEL

That afternoon the venerable old professor, nicknamed Prospero after the wise magician of Shakespeare's *Tempest*, was saying farewell to his young students who, after a year of study, were once more grouped around him. They had come to the vast study where taste, not less delicate than severe, had tried to honor the noble presence of the books that were Prospero's faithful companions.

Dominating the room, like the deity of its serene surroundings, was the beautifully modeled bronze statue of Ariel of *The Tempest*. Customarily the professor sat beside it and that was why he had been given the name of the magician who is served and loved by the fantastic creature depicted by the sculptor. Perhaps in a more profound sense, however, there was more reason for his nickname in his teaching and his character.

Ariel, the genius of air, represents in the symbolism of Shakespeare's drama the noble and winged part of the spirit.

Ariel embodies the mastery of reason and feeling over the base stimulus of irrationality. It is the generous enthusiasm, the lofty and unselfish motive of action, the spirituality of culture, the vivacity and grace of intelligence, the ideal end to which human selection aspires, cleansing the superior man of the tenacious traces of Caliban, that symbol of sensuality and stupidity . . .

Prospero stroked the forehead of the statue thoughtfully . . . Then as his students regarded him with affectionate attention, he began to speak:

"Near this statue where you have seen me preside every afternoon over our friendly discussions—discussions from which I have tried to remove any formality—I am going to speak to you once more, so that our last class meeting may be like the seal stamped on our compact of feeling and ideas. . . .

"I call upon Ariel as my deity. I wish for my words today the most gentle and persuasive reception they have ever had. I think that speaking to youth about noble and elevated motives, whatever they are, is a kind of sacred oratory. I also think that the spirit of youth is a generous soil where the sowing of an opportune word may in a short time produce the fruits of an immortal ·harvest . . . If, concerning individual liberty, Goethe could say profoundly that the only one worthy of liberty and life is he who can conquer them for himself day after day, with even more reason can it be said that the honor of every human generation demands that it conquer by the continuing activity of its thinking, by its own effort, its faith in the determined manifestation of its ideals, and its place in the evolution of all ideas . . . I say to you with Renan: 'Youth is the discovery of that immense horizon which is life.'

"Greece is the soul of the young . . . Greece achieved mighty deeds because it had the gaiety of youth which is the atmosphere of action, and enthusiasm which is the all-powerful lever.

"Be then conscious possessors of the blessed power which you contain within yourselves. But always remember that it can quickly weaken and disappear, like any unused power. From

Nature comes this precious gift, but on your ideas depends whether it will be fruitful or wasted . . .

"Will you who are about to pass, like workmen into a factory, through the portals of a new century, will you bestow upon knowledge, brighter and more glorious images than those left behind by us? If those divine times in which young souls gave inspiration to the radiant dialogs of Plato were possible in the brief springtime of the world, if Forquias of the second part of *Faust* could instruct the chorus of captives 'not to think about the gods,' may we not also be permitted to dream of the appearance of a human generation that will bring back to life a sense of the ideal, a grand enthusiasm in which feeling will regain its place, in which a vigorous resurrection of the power of the will may, with shouts of victory, expell from the depths of the soul all moral cowardice that feeds on deception and doubt? Shall youth again be a reality in collective life as it is in individuals? . . .

"I believe that there is no doubt that he who has learned to distinguish the delicate from the common, the ugly from the beautiful, has made half the journey to where he can distinguish the evil from the good. Good taste is not, as some moral dilettante might wish, the only criterion of human actions, but even less should it be considered, as the strict ascetic does, as a temptation to err and a hidden peril . . . As Humanity progresses, it perceives more clearly that moral law is beauty of conduct. It will flee from wrong and evil as from a discord; it will seek good in which it finds the pleasure of harmony . . .

"Even more than for these words of mine, I beg that you retain the sweet and indelible memory of my statue of Ariel. I would that this light and graceful statue of bronze impress itself on the depths of your spirit. I remember once seeing in a museum an ancient gold coin bearing the almost obliterated inscription: 'Hope.' I meditated on the influence this word may have had. Who knows what active and noble part to attribute to it in the formation of the character and the lives of generations of human beings who handled it? How many fainting spirits did it revive, how may generous impulses did it develop,

how many despairing resolutions prevent, as eyes fell on the
encouraging word? So may the image of this statue, graven on
your hearts, play in your lives an unnoted but determining
role! In the dark hours of discouragement, may it renew in
your conscience the enthusiasm for an ideal that has been slip-
ping away. May it return to your hearts the warmth of a lost
hope. Ariel, first established behind the bulwark of your inner
lives, will sally forth to conquer new souls. I see the spirit in
the future smiling at you in gratitude even though your own
spirit is merged in shadows. And I have faith in your will and
in your strength, but even more in those to whom you will pass
on your life and your works. I can dream happily of the day
when actual achievement will convince the world that the
Cordillera that rises above the soil of America has been carved
to become the pedestal of this statue, to be the immutable
altar of the cult of Ariel."

                                                        W.K.J.

EDUARDO BARRIOS
1884–   Chile

When French Naturalism was influencing all Latin
America, Barrios made his only experiment in that field
with *Del natural* (1907). He also attempted drama in
1913 with two plays, and later a short skit, *Papá y
mamá*. But psychology proved more appealing, and in
1915 he published *El niño que enloqueció de amor*
("The Boy Driven Mad by Love") one of the continent's great novelettes, about a schoolboy who fell in
love with an older woman. Later came *El hermano
asno* ("Brother Ass") (1922), another outstanding
novelette, set in the mind of Fray Lázaro, who punished
his animal body for his unpriestly feelings toward a
girl. Some of the greatest beauty and deepest aesthetic
emotion to be found in any Latin-American prose is to
be found in it, along with a mysticism like that of

Anatole France. The musicality of its phrases, the simplicity yet deep irony, are hard to match in the literature of the continent.

After critics had declared him written out, Barrios began with a series of novels about different periods of Chile's life, including *Tamarugal* (1944) about abuses in the nitrate fields, that won him a national prize, *El gran señor y rajadiablos* (1948), a picaresque novel, and *Los hombres del hombre* ("The Man's Men") (1950), under the influence of Gide. In them all he reveals himself as one of Latin America's most brilliant stylists.

BROTHER ASS (*a fragment*)

I return from lecturing to the novices on Franciscan History and find my cell cleaned. That does not surprise me; Fray Rufino has got me accustomed to this morning present. He feels closer bonds with me than with anyone else in the monastery because neither of us has been ordained. We remain deacons; I, because of scruples about my sinful earlier history in the world and the vacillating purification of my soul; he, because his life of penitence kept him from concluding his studies.

The morning is cool, bright, and pure, like the voice of a bird. I have opened my window and my door wide, and early morning smells come in that I breathe into the depth of my soul. I have nothing to do, no unfinished business, no feeling in my heart. There's nothing I want. I see the clean air . . . the atmosphere as far as the blue of the sky; the garden is clean where everything shines young and gay. My cell is clean. So are my senses, my conscience, and my feelings.

Therefore I am happy.

This is happiness, Lord, a cleanness inside and out, a feeling in my soul of coolness and transparency, as if it were a fine crystal, to which gentle sensations come gently, like delightful beings who appear unexpectedly and with their faces bright and smiling.

I am going out. The garden calls me at such moments. I want to walk, to bask in light under a benigned sun, and get my sandals covered with dark spongy earth, and peer down into the well and see the water that reflects the sky like an innocent, humble, and silent soul.

. . . . .

That's where I went. There is no fragrance of flowers in the garden; there is a green smell of vegetables.

Among them, I have taken a seat amidst the cabbages, and for a long time have caressed a gray cabbage that shines as if silverplated, a hard, bursting cabbage with life in its body.

Everything enters new into my clean and avid senses.

Fray Bernardo has hung in his doorframe a bamboo-birdcage where a thrush hops on its perch.

A white dove flutters down from an old olive tree, rests on the well curb and starts drinking the water held in its worm-eaten wood, never noticing Brother John who pulls up the bucket to fill an earthen pitcher.

Finally I get up, open my hands, close my eyes, and lift my face to the sky: the sun spills its warmth between my fingers, scatters it across my motionless face, passes through my eyelids, and takes possession of my veins like a favoring deity.

I understand, Lord, the pleasure that Your divine favor reserved for blind people.

Suddenly I opened my eyes instinctively and saw Brother John beside me. He was carrying the earthenware pitcher and I asked him for a drink. Lord, that thin, pure water entered my mouth, bathed my lungs and reached clear to my heart.

"Did you hear, Father Lazarus?" Brother John asked me later, "A miracle! A true miracle. Fray Rufino . . . we just saw him . . . put a plate of scraps in his cell, and like good friends, the cats and rats came together to eat it."

"Really? God be praised, brother!"

I had to exaggerate my astonishment. With their blinking and raised eyebrows, the blue eyes of Brother John demanded it.

"Yes, Father. And what do you think he said when he saw us so amazed? That it was nothing. That a century ago in Lima a Dominican had been able to bring it about, and so he had prayed for a miracle in our monastery. To think he said it was nothing! A Miracle! But we persisted, he got upset and advised us not to talk about it."

"I suppose you've told the whole community by now."

"In praise of our Lord, you've always got to talk about such things. Let it be known for a century. Oh, but there's something else: he was talking to them while they ate; talking to rats and cats, Father Lazarus! I could imagine I was hearing part of *The Little Flowers* where Saint Frances was speaking to the birds. 'From now on,' he was telling them, 'you've got to stop being enemies, because it is contrary to God's love to have His creatures hate and devour each other.' Isn't he a saint? And he has a soft place in his heart for plants, too. See this shoot that the jasmine is growing? Well, he saw the other day that it was half broken off, and he spliced it and covered it with mud to heal it. Who knows what miracle may come out of this?"

Yes, brother John, this whole morning was a miracle.

W.K.J.

PEDRO PRADO
1886–1950   Chile

For the most part, Pedro Prado's literary work has been poetry composed between the years 1908 and 1950. Even in his three novels, *La reina de Rapa Nui* ("The Queen of Rapa Nui") (1914), *Un juez rural* ("A Rural Judge") (1924), and *Alsino* (1920), he remains, essentially, a poet. The last work, undoubtedly his masterpiece, has earned him a reputation as one of the greatest stylists in Spanish-American literature. Alsino is a Chilean peasant boy who longs to fly, and in an abortive attempt falls from a tree. From the fall he develops a hunchback which eventually grows into wings. After lyrical flights over the Chilean countryside, Alsino is captured and abused, but he later regains his freedom and suffers death by fire as he hurtles like a meteor from an enormous height. The novel is at once lyrical, symbolic, philosophical and realistic, standing alone as a thing of beauty.

ALSINO

Chapter XX. The Storm (*fragment*)

In the tragic silence of a contained anxiety, free and unbridled, from the very bowels of the earth, there arose a deep, rumbling sound, and, muffled, powerful and interminable, continued to swell, to the point of wrath, in depth and terrifying power. The earth oscillated, quivering. As if beneath it passed the waves of the sea, in violent undulations of serpents in flight, the mountains, previously quiet, danced in confusion like ships anchored in an unsafe harbor.

A crimson colored light, like the reflection of a distant fire, stained the cloudy sky. Below, the harsh clashing of the branches of the trees put to flight the tiny birds that fluttered urgently about, crying out with brief, shrill whistles.

As if eager hands were rocking them in order to bring to earth the inaccessible fruit, the trees of the forest were shaken with continual momentum by the tremor. Dry snapping sounds, penetrating crackling, and the shattered branches fell in the fray. And while some trees, fully grown at the edge of the ravines, tumbled down with a thunderous crash, dragging with them the clods of earth and the stones which their roots tore away, from every quivering grove, in a soft, soothing rain, the countless leaves were loosened.

An indefinite period of time passed in extension; the earth ceased to move. Still restless, the animals scourged their flanks with their tails, nervous and panting. The birds continued to fly over the mountains, like horseflies waiting for their victim's back to settle down.

Distant and lost, a clap of thunder, born in the north, caused all eyes to turn in that direction. The silence which followed was amplified by the stillness lying in wait. A sharp flash of lightning darted against the dark clouds in a zigzag of fire. For a fleeting moment the entire valley, as perceived from the summit, was brightly lighted by its greenish, spectral radiance. More somber, after its blinding light, the night was left an ash-colored red. In the silence, another clap of thunder rolled resoundingly, arrogant, accentuating its rough, resonant quality, prolonged and deep. Far off, numerous flashes of lightning flared with brilliant light, and minor thunder claps followed close upon them, like the sounds of battle. A sudden wind of warm, dry gusts began to blow. With it that strange fetor which announced the storm was intensified. Slowly the clouds began to scatter. Some of them, low, white and torn in shreds, passed quickly, creating the illusion that the others, higher and darker, were moving in an opposite direction. One, two, three clear spots were created among the highest thunderheads, and patches of sky, of a serene and pure blue, opened up in the reaches.

Alsino saw fall the first drops of a passing rain. Scattered drops that left no trace, dried by the burning breath of the hurricane which was being unleashed. Invisible, in frenzied gusts, the wind, heralded by its howling voice as it advanced, deadened the bellowing of the bulls in flight and the strange sounds of the wild animals. Rash and clamorous birds among a shower of leaves, fly rapidly toward the south, pregnant with their own wings.

While the trees moan, whistling like the strakes of warships, and whirlwinds of dust twist about in giddy gyrations, Alsino, his eyes burning, his lips dry, his wavy hair trembling like a black flame, restless now his enormous wings which half-

spread drag him aloft, unable to contain any longer the trembling madness that shakes him, obedient to the unbridled desires which within him free a tumultuous force, crying aloud
with frenzied screams and longing for the terrible gladness
which, when given free rein, gives impetus to life, spreads his
wings and effortlessly surrenders himself like the loosened rocks
and dust of the earth to the invisible torrent of the wind of the
storm.

Easy as a downhill road, stirred by the ever more rushing
onslaught of the hurricane, Alsino feels the rapture of falling
into unconsciousness. There remains in his heart only a wild
and unchained gladness, unlocked to the greatest yearnings,
which, humble and overwhelmed, now offer themselves to him.

With a voice no longer human, but strange and hoarse, he
shouts:

"I am coming; yes, I am coming! Farther and farther! Outside myself! Mature as the pod that bursts and tosses its wise
seeds to the wind, my eager spirit breaks forth from its jail!
Infinite and scattered flight! Thou art quick to seek out every
boundary. Hail, O divine wind! Thou movest and dost oblige
all ships to cut the cable, and all men. Thou fillest their lives
with terrible passion, which they receive from no other emis-
sary. Who awakens and quickens the ecstasy with this fury?
Come forth, divine presence. Thou alone art capable of this
holy fire. From wings supreme, in flight, thou art born!"

Swiftly the dreadful wind drags him, lifts him up, drops him,
takes him in hand again and, irate, tosses him. It scrapes and
chews at his feathers, and, roaring, strives to tear away his wings.
Beneath its claws his wings vibrate and groan like great harps!

The turbid day becomes darker and darker. Suddenly a torrential rain lets loose. Alsino accepts it joyfully and sings.

"Eager for thee, naked and dancing in the highest winds,
thou findest me, O bountiful baptism! Anoint my body: my
head, my back, my breast, my wings, my arms, my legs! Spill
thy waters upon my lips. Neither cup nor hollow hand to mingle
them. My mouth doth drink them in direct. It is a thirst never
to be quenched. Though I receive ten drops my thirst remains!"

The ill-tempered rain persists. The warmth that was now becomes cold and cutting. The drops fall like pins of ice that prick Alsino's naked flesh. His warm body evaporates the rain. The water blinds flight and causes his wings to feel heavy. He crushes and conquers the wind. A cloak of hail falls thunder-like. Alsino descends, wounded by the hailstones. On the top of a hill a white halo of mist engulfs him, issuing from his weary body soaked with rain. He watches with uncertain gaze, the falling of the water. It is a curtain which becomes more and more impervious. A veil which recedes from the far-away high sierras, from the deep, dark plains to nearby rocks; and all of that with a crackling in crescendo which sustains itself for hours on end to the point of startling the soul.

Threads of wriggling water form, and little creeks that receive them and swell and tumble down, lowing, in torrents, pawing deep fissures in the slopes. The thick, reddish water is flung into sounding cataracts.

Robert Scott

AMADO NERVO
1870–1919   Mexico

Nervo, among the contemporary Spanish-American poets, stands in prose as in poetry an influential figure in Modernism. In poetry, he carried on the powerful French influence that helped revivify Spanish poetry on both sides of the Atlantic, without becoming a victim to its less artistic forms. His Mysticism is especially evident in his prose.

His real name should have been Ruiz de Nervo, but his father called himself Amado Nervo and passed on the name to his son, who began to write poetry secretly, at an early age. Destined for the church, he broke away to become a writer, though his writings contain many contradictory religious thoughts, as well as paganism and Buddhism. He had a wavering attitude toward life and death, ending with a kind of poetic Nirvanism that considered silence the best poem of all.

LEAH AND RACHEL

There were two sisters, the two sisters of all stories, and like
the two sisters of all stories, one was fair, the other dark; only
here the light-haired girl was beautiful and the brunette ugly
and malformed. The blonde was the pride of the family, the
one for whom the clothes and jewels were bought, the one
whom the parents took to the theatre and to make calls, while
they told the other, "You don't want to go, do you? You must
be tired."

The dark-haired daughter was a true Cinderella, the unattractive Cinderella of this uninteresting story, a Cinderella
whose feet would never be sought by the wonderful prince
desiring to clad them in the glass slipper found by the roadside.

She was timid, as malformed women generally are, and her
eyes seemed to beg pardon of all the world for daring to shine,
pardon for the disrespect of looking like the others (those eyes
so beautiful and lovely) at the gay color of a morning rose,
the golden hours of noon, the severe richness of the afternoon,
the feasts of leaves and flowers in the valleys and the majesty
of the cedars in the mountains, the trembling shimmer of the
lakes and the blue of the heavens.

The ugly girl (she whom we shall call Leah in memory of
Rachel's sister of the tender eyes whom Labin with shameful
craft put in Jacob's bed as reward for seven years of toil) this
ugly girl knew how to do thousands of useful things; she was,
like those mighty queens who, on their wheels, spun their
clothes and their dreams, a real magician from whose fingers
came miracles made with the thread of the Virgin itself, or
with the substance of her illusions. What dishes fit for the tables
of an emperor she could cook! And together with this useful
knowledge, hers was a charming and gentle touch upon the
piano and the harp.

Leah had early learned that it was necessary to conceal her
ugliness, to cover it somewhat that it might be less repellent

before the eyes of men, and she had clothed it with intelligence, with kindness, and love. Her soul was a precious stone whose greatest merit consisted in an incalculable instinct for sacrifice.

Leah was one of those beings full of pity and self-sacrifice who always give up their part of life and return to Eternity more naked, if possible, than the others. Truly such people abound in the Latin-American family; in almost every house there is a Cinderella who gives her share to the others and feels happy for having given it. Rare souls which are born with a mysterious hunger for serving, divine thirsters who never tire of sacrificing; Leah was like these.

If she had cooked one of those savory and delightful dishes which are the joy of a table, she would not taste it because it was her pleasure that all might enjoy it, promising herself to eat what remained, and usually that was nothing.

She always came late to receive the good things, like the poet of the story who presented himself before Jove when the distribution of the gifts of earth had already been made.

If her sister, after having wasted her own possessions, wanted them, there were the treasures of Leah. If her sister, whom we shall call Rachel to hasten the Biblical simile which we used at the beginning, committed an error, Leah took upon herself the blame and received without protest the fitting punishment. It was Leah who broke all the plates, who lost the thimbles and scissors, who first wore out her dresses, who scorched the milk of the desserts, who let herself be robbed by the servants. Leah was always to blame; that was a principle established in the house.

And it was Leah also who slept on the floor on a mat unknown to her parents when unexpected guests arrived and a bed was lacking. It was Leah who was up at dawn, fixing everything, going through the house like a benediction while the others idled between sheets, enjoying their interrupted morning naps.

But one day this soul, naked of everything, even of desires, realized that steps were approaching its door, and the pale thing trembled: he who thus knocked was Love.

Among the crowd of men who were courting her sister,

wonderfully beautiful, and whom Rachel was treating collectively with a friendly and coquettish disdain, one of them, Charles, guided, perhaps by a secret instinct, had little by little been withdrawing from the beauty to approach Leah, poor little Leah, so quiet, so ugly, so pale, and so melancholy, divining, it may be, the precious jewel of her spirit.

Charles was a silent lad, also, and thoughtful, probably an idealist, a poet, a sentimental being who started by mistaking love for pity.

Leah was afraid at the beginning of being deceived, then following her unwavering tendency to sacrifice, looked around the sphere of her existence to see if any of those who passed, needing affection, should ask it of Charles, that it might be given to them. But no one appeared in sight, nobody took note that Leah was the possessor of a great affection, a very great affection; and so the poor girl (as a little beggar girl who stumbles upon a plaything in the street turns her glances timidly all around for fear some rich girl will claim the discovery and will hit her, and seeing that no one pursues her, seizes the treasure rejoicing) began to run with her love hidden in the most holy recesses of her heart. To the corner most apart from her life she carried that love recently born on her lips, and she would kiss it tenderly, very sweetly at first, afterward like a madman in an unforeseen awakening of life, overcome by a powerful conflagration of sighs, fears, and hopes.

Did Charles love her? Oh yes, without doubt. In all the world there is no being bad enough to mock an ugly little girl up to the point of storming with deceit the hushed virginity, the hermetically sealed modesty of her soul. Charles was not bad, and Charles had said that he loved her as she was—dark, very dark, small, very small, ill-formed, decrepit, and miserable. Yet she had the fawnlike fear that it would be found out, a fear and a sense of modesty, and she did not cease imploring her generous Charles, "Don't tell anybody, don't let anyone know," and she would add as the collect, "If they should know that I have this treasure, and should come to ask me for it, I would have to give it to them."

But no one knew, though even in spite of the dissimulation of both, methodical and careful, it was easy to discover it with only a glance at the tender eyes of Leah, those eyes now so full of happiness, and which were proclaiming it so openly through the whole house, and through the whole city, and through her whole life.

What happened was different and monstrous, even amid the usual monstrosity of existence; it came about that Rachel began to fall in love with Charles. Why? For a very simple reason. Charles was the only one who resisted her charms, the only one who, through causes unknown to herself, refused her due homage, and—this is and always has been a human trait—there was born in her, as in so many other similar cases, a whim of the disdained conqueror which took up the struggle with the arsenal of all her charms; which laid hands on all her resources. The onslaught of her beauty smashed before the indifference of Charles. Then the whim turned to love.

At first Charles took no account of the sentiments which he was inspiring. He was serenely wrapped up in the soul of Leah. But at last the blue eyes of Rachel began to trouble him. Nor had Leah noticed anything; she loved in the full store of her memory, and in absolute ecstasy. Finally, the growing coldness fell like snow upon her spirit, the slowly growing, imperceptible conquest of Charles. One day after many months in which Rachel's eyes had been accomplishing their task, and in which the very difficulty and slowness of it had ended by making the stubborn beauty madly in love, she let out a turbulent cry.

"Sister, sister, I am suffering so much. I am in love with Charles!"

Leah upon hearing the moan felt, like the child of the simile when they demanded the plaything which she had found, a quick and sad conviction that might be translated into these or similar words: "It's true. How could I have thought so beautiful a thing mine? For, have I ever had anything in my life?"

She asked this last in her own mind naturally, and without the least shadow of indignation; for the innate instinct of sacrifice, the peculiar tendency to give, had been blotting out from her mind all ideas of her own rights and possessions—almost all idea of individuality.

However, it must be confessed, Leah defended herself this time. She had an impulse (her only one!) to rebel. Not so easily can there be uprooted from the heart that which is its life, its light, its vital substance. "No," replied Leah, "you do not love Charles." And she was just going to add: "Charles loves me. He told me so!" But she did not say it. Rachel, embracing her as she always did when she wanted to get something from her, flooded her with words.

"Yes, I love him, little sister. He is the only man I have ever loved in my life; you must help me, help me with father, with mother, with Charles himself. Won't you? You don't know how much I love him!"

Leah took refuge in her last hope, a weak and feeble thing. "But has Charles told you anything?"

No, Charles hadn't said anything at all. Charles was filled with shame and anguish. Charles was noble at heart (like all traitors and deserters); but if he had come to Leah in the first place it was because, looked upon from the beginning with a certain disdain by Rachel surrounded by suitors, he saw no chance of being loved by her; and then because Leah was so lonely and weak, and of such little account in the world that his compassion was turned to affection. But now Rachel was coming toward him displaying all her charm. "Fair as the moon, clear as the sun, and terrible as an army with banners." How could he resist her.

· · · · · ·

"I adore him, sister mine. Help me."

Leah was dumb for a few seconds, the seconds which she needed to prepare an offering, and then she kissed Rachel, a soft kiss, whispering in her ear, "Yes, dear sister, I'll help you."

The next day Charles received these few lines:

"Charles: My sister loves you and you love my sister; for my part I thought I loved you, but I was deceived. I loved you only in place of Rachel and while she was coming. Do you want to please me? Then make her happy."

.   .   .   .   .   .

This to which I refer took place years ago. Rachel married Charles and today is a grandmother. Leah, after having been a true mother to Rachel's children for whom she sacrificed herself always, was a second grandmother for the grandchildren for whom she was also beginning to sacrifice herself.

But last Spring pneumonia took her to her grave, and the night we watched by the corpse, observing with sadness that not even Death itself, which is a great beautifier, had succeeded in making her lovely, an old friend of the family, a Catholic, led me to the window to tell me with pious accents, "There as you see her, it is very likely that this saintly Leah is at this very moment in Hell."

"Why?" I asked, surprised.

"Ah," he answered me, smoothing his beard, a characteristic gesture, "Because if on the road of Death she came upon a damned soul, she is very likely to have ceded to him her salvation, and to have descended in his place to dwell in Hell throughout all Eternity."

W.K.J.

JORGE LUIS BORGES
1899–   Argentina

(See the poetry section for a discussion.)

THE GARDEN OF FORKING PATHS

On Page 252 of Liddell Hart's *History of World War I*, you will read that an attack against the Serre-Montauban line by thirteen British divisions (supported by 1,400 artillery pieces), planned for the 24th of June, 1916, had to be postponed until the morning of the 29th. The torrential rains, Captain Liddell Hart comments, caused this delay, an insignificant one, to be sure.

The following statement, dictated, reread and signed by Dr. Yu Tsun, former professor of English at the *Hochschule* at Tsingtao, throws an unsuspected light over the whole affair. The first two pages of the document are missing.

*   *   *   *   *   *

. . . and I hung up the receiver. Immediately afterwards, I recognized the voice that had answered in German. It was that of Captain Richard Madden. Madden's presence in Viktor Runeberg's apartment meant the end of our anxieties and— but this seemed, or should have seemed, very secondary to me —also the end of our lives. It meant that Runeberg had been arrested or murdered.*

Before the sun set on that day, I would encounter the same fate. Madden was implacable. Or rather, he was obliged to be so. An Irishman at the service of England, a man accused of laxity and perhaps of treason, how could he fail to seize and be thankful for such a miraculous opportunity: the discovery, capture, maybe even the death of two agents of the German Reich?

I went up to my room; absurdly I locked the door and threw myself on my back on the narrow iron cot. Through the window I saw the familiar roofs and the cloud-shaded six o'clock sun. It seemed incredible to me that that day without premonitions or symbols should be the one of my inexorable death. In spite of my dead father, in spite of having been a child in a symmetrical garden of Hai Feng, was I—now—going to die?

Then I reflected that everything happens to a man precisely *now*. Centuries of centuries and only in the present do things

---

* An hypothesis both hateful and queer. The Prussian spy Hans Rabner, alias Viktor Runeberg, attacked with drawn automatic the bearer of the warrant for his arrest, Captain Richard Madden. The latter, in self-defense, inflicted the wounds which brought about Runeberg's death. *Editor's note.*

happen; countless men in the air, on the face of the earth and the sea, and all that really is happening is happening to me. . . . The almost intolerable recollection of Madden's horselike face banished these wanderings. In the midst of my hatred and terror (it means nothing to me now to speak of terror, now that I have mocked Richard Madden, now that my throat yearns for the noose), it occurred to me that that tumultuous and doubtless happy warrior did not suspect that I possessed the Secret: the name of the exact location of the new British artillery installation of the English Channel. A bird streaked across the grey sky, and blindly I translated it into an airplane and that airplane into many (against the French sky) annihilating the artillery station with vertical shells. If only my mouth, before a bullet silenced it, could cry out that secret name so it could be heard in Germany. . . . My human voice was very weak. How might I make it carry to the ear of the Chief? To the ear of that sick and hateful man who knew nothing of Runeberg and me save that we were in Staffordshire and that he was waiting for our report in his arid office in Berlin, endlessly examining newspapers. . . .

I said out loud: *I must flee.* I sat up noiselessly, in a useless perfection of silence, as if Madden were already lying in wait for me. Something—perhaps the mere vain ostentation of proving my resources were nil—made me look through my pockets. I found what I knew I would find. The American watch, the nickel chain and the square coin, the key ring with the incriminating keys to Runeberg's apartment, the notebook, a letter which I resolved to destroy immediately (and which I did not destroy), a crown, two shillings and a few pence, the red and blue pencil, the handkerchief, the revolver with one bullet. Absurdly, I took it in my hand and weighed it in order to inspire courage within me. Vaguely I thought that a pistol report can be heard at a great distance. In ten minutes my plan was perfected. The telephone book listed the only name capable of transmitting the message; the man I chose lived in a suburb of Fenton, less than a half hour's train ride away.

I am a cowardly man. I say it now, now that I have carried

to its end a plan whose perilous nature no one can deny. I know its execution was terrible. I didn't do it for Germans, no. I care nothing for a barbarous country which imposed upon me the humility of being a spy. Besides, I know of a man from England—a modest man—who for me is nothing less than Goethe. . . . I did it all because I sensed that the Chief feared somewhat those of my race—the innumerable ancestors who merge within me. I wanted to prove to him that a yellow man could save his armies. And, equally as important, I had to flee from Captain Madden. His hands and his voice could call at my door at any moment. I dressed silently, bade farewell to myself in the mirror, went downstairs, scrutinized the peaceful street and went out.

The station was not far from my home, but I judged it wise to take a cab. I argued that in this way I ran less risk of being recognized. The fact is that in the deserted street I felt myself visible and vulnerable, infinitely so. I remember that I told the cab driver to stop a short distance before the main entrance. I got out with voluntary, almost painful slowness; I was going to the village of Ashgrove but I bought a ticket for a more distant station. The train left within a very few minutes, at eight-fifty. I hurried; the next one would leave at nine-thirty. There was hardly a soul on the platform. I went through the coaches; I remember a few workers, a woman dressed in mourning, a young boy who was reading with fervor the *Annals* of Tacitus, a wounded and happy soldier. The coaches jerked forward at last. A man whom I recognized ran in vain to the end of the platform. It was Captain Richard Madden. Shattered, trembling, I shrank into the far corner of the seat, away from the dreaded window.

From this broken state I passed into an almost abject felicity. I told myself that the duel had already begun and that I had won the first encounter by frustrating, even if for forty minutes, even if by a stroke of fate, the attack of my adversary. I argued that this slightest of victories foreshadowed a total victory. I argued that it was not slight, since without the precious edge the train schedule afforded me, I would be imprisoned or dead. I argued (no less sophistically) that my cowardly felicity proved that I was a man capable of carrying out the adventure successfully. From this weakness, I took strength that did not abandon me. I foresee that man will resign himself each day to more atrocious undertakings; soon there will be no one but warriors and brigands. I give you this counsel: THE AUTHOR OF AN ATROCIOUS UNDERTAKING OUGHT TO IMAGINE THAT HE HAS ALREADY ACCOMPLISHED IT, OUGHT TO IMPOSE UPON HIMSELF A FUTURE AS IRREVOCABLE AS THE PAST. Thus I proceeded, as my eyes of a man already dead registered the fluidity of that day, which was perhaps the last, and the diffusion of the night.

The train ran gently along, past ash trees. It stopped, almost in the middle of the fields. No one announced the name of the station. "Ashgrove?" I asked a few lads on the platform. "Ashgrove," they replied. I got off.

A lamp illuminated the platform, but the faces of the boys were in shadow. One questioned me, "Are you going to Dr. Stephen Albert's house?" Without waiting for my answer, another said, "The house is a long way from here, but you won't get lost if you take this road to the left and at every crossroads turn again to your left." I tossed them a coin (my last), descended a few stone steps and started down the solitary road. It went downhill, slowly. It was of elemental earth; overhead the branches were tangled; the low, full moon seemed to accompany me.

For an instant, I thought that Richard Madden in some way had penetrated my desperate plan. Very quickly, I understood that that was impossible. The instructions to turn always to the left reminded me that such was the common procedure for discovering the central point of certain labyrinths. I have some understanding of labyrinths; not in vain am I the great grandson of that Ts'ui Pên who was governor of Yunnan and who renounced worldly power in order to write a novel that might be even more populous than the *Hung Lu Meng* and to

construct a labyrinth in which all men would become lost. Thirteen years he dedicated to these heterogeneous tasks, but the
hand of a stranger murdered him and his novel was incoherent
and no one found the labyrinth.

Beneath English trees I meditated on that lost maze: I imagined it involate and perfect at the secret crest of a mountain;
I imagined it erased by rice fields or beneath the water; I imagined it infinite, no longer composed of octagonal kiosks and
returning paths, but of rivers and provinces and kingdoms. . . .
I thought of a labyrinth of labyrinths of one spreading labyrinth that would encompass the past and the future and in some
way the stars.

Absorbed in these illusory images, I forgot my destiny of
one pursued. I felt myself to be, for an unknown period of time,
an abstract perceiver of the world. The vague, living countryside, the moon, the remains of the day worked on me; as well
as the slope of the road which eliminated any possibility of
weariness. The lateness of the day was intimate, infinite.

The road descended and forked among the obscure meadows. A high-pitched, almost syllabic music approached and
receded in the shifting of the wind, wrapped in leaves and
distance. I thought that a man can be an enemy of other men,
of other moments of other men, but not of a country: not of
fireflies, words, gardens, streams of water, sunsets. Thus I arrived before a tall, rusty gate. Between the iron bars I made
out a poplar grove and a pavilion. I understood immediately
two things, the first trivial, the second almost unbelievable: the
music came from the pavilion, and the music was Chinese. For
precisely that reason I had openly accepted it without paying
it any heed. I do not remember whether there was a bell or
whether I knocked with my hands. The sparkling music continued.

But from the rear of the inner house a lantern approached:
a lantern that the trees sometimes striped and sometimes
eclipsed, a paper lantern that had the form of a drum and the
color of the moon. A tall man bore it. I didn't see his face, for

the light blinded me. He opened the door and said slowly, in my own language: "I see that the pious Hsi P'êng persists in correcting my solitude. You no doubt wish to see the garden?"

I recognized the name of one of our consuls and I replied, disconcerted, "The garden?"

"The Garden of the Forking Paths."

Something stirred in my memory and I uttered with incomprehensible certainty, "The garden of my ancestor Ts'ui Pên."

"Your ancestor? Your illustrious ancestor? Come in."

The damp path zigzagged like those of my childhood. We came to a library of Eastern and Western books. I recognized bound in yellow silk several volumes of the Lost Encyclopedia, edited by the Third Emperor of the Luminous Dynasty but never printed. The disc on the gramophone revolved next to a bronze phoenix. I also recall a vase of the rose family and another, many centuries older, of that color of blue which our craftsmen copied from the potters of Persia . . .

Stephen Albert observed me with a smile. He was, as I have said, very tall, sharp-featured, with grey eyes and a grey beard. There was something of a priest about him and something of a seaman. He told me that he had been a missionary in Tientsin "before aspiring to become a Sinologist."

We sat down; I on a long, low divan, he with his back to the window and a tall circular clock. I calculated that my pursuer, Richard Madden, would not arrive within that hour. My irrevocable determination could wait.

"An astounding fate, that of Ts'ui Pên," Stephen Albert said. "Governor of his native province, learned in astronomy, in astrology and in the tireless interpretation of the canonical books, chess player, famous poet, and calligrapher: he abandoned everything in order to compose a book and a maze. He renounced the pleasures of both tyranny and justice, of his populous couch, of his banquets and even of eruditions—all to close himself up for thirteen years in the Pavilion of the Limpid Solitude. When he died, his heirs found nothing save chaotic manuscripts. His family, as you may be aware, wished to condemn them to the fire; but his executor—a Taoist or Buddhist monk—insisted on their publication."

"We descendants of Ts'ui Pên," I replied, "continue to curse that monk. Their publication was a senseless act. The book is a shapeless heap of contradictory drafts. I examined it once: in the third chapter the hero dies, in the fourth he is alive. As for the other undertaking of Ts'ui Pên, his labyrinth . . ."

"Here is the labyrinth," he said, indicating a tall laquered desk.

"An ivory labyrinth?" I exclaimed. "A minimum labyrinth?"

"A labyrinth of symbols," he corrected. "An invisible labyrinth of time. To me, a barbarous Englishman, has been entrusted the revelation of this diaphanous mystery. After more than a hundred years, the details are irretrievable; but it is not hard to guess what happened. Ts'ui Pên must have said once: I WILL WITHDRAW TO WRITE A BOOK. And another time: I WILL WITHDRAW TO CONSTRUCT A LABYRINTH. Everyone expected two works; to no one did it occur that the book and the maze were one and the same thing. The Pavilion of the Limpid Solitude stood in the center of a garden that was perhaps intricate: that circumstance could have suggested to the heirs a physical maze. Ts'ui Pên died; no one in the vast territories that were his came upon the labyrinth. The confusion of the novel suggested to me that IT was the maze. Two circumstances gave me the correct solution to the problem. One: the curious legend that Ts'ui Pên had planned to create a labyrinth which would be strictly infinite. The other: a fragment of a letter I discovered."

Albert rose. He turned his back on me for a moment and opened a drawer of the black and gold desk. He faced me and in his hands he held a sheet of paper that had once been crimson, but was now pink and tenuous and cross-sectioned. The fame of Ts'ui Pên as an expert penman had been justly won. I read, uncomprehendingly and with fervor, these words written with a minute brush by a man of my own blood: "I leave to the various futures (not to all) my Garden of Forking Paths." Wordlessly, I returned the sheet. Albert continued:

"Before unearthing this letter, I had questioned myself about the ways in which a book can be infinite. I could think of nothing other than a cyclic volume, a circular one. A book whose last page was identical to the first, with the possibility of continuing indefinitely. I remembered too that night which is at the middle of the Thousand and One Nights when Scheherezade (through a magical oversight of the copyist) begins to relate word for word the story of the Thousand and One Nights, establishing the risk of coming once again to the night when she must repeat it, and thus on to infinity. I imagined as well a Platonic hereditary work transmitted from father to son, in which each new individual adds a chapter or corrects with pious care the pages of his elders.

"These conjectures diverted me; but none seemed to correspond, not even remotely, to the contradictory chapters of Ts'ui Pên. In the midst of this perplexity, I received from Oxford the manuscript you have examined. I lingered, naturally, on the sentence: I LEAVE TO THE VARIOUS FUTURES (NOT TO ALL) MY GARDEN OF FORKING PATHS. Almost instantly, I understood: 'the Garden of Forking Paths' was the chaotic novel; the phrase, 'the various futures (not to all)' suggested to me the forking of time, not of space. A broad rereading of the work confirmed the theory. In all fictional works, each time a man is confronted with several alternatives, he chooses one and eliminates the others; in the fiction of Ts'ui Pên, he chooses—simultaneously—all of them. HE CREATES, in this way, diverse futures, diverse times which themselves also proliferate and fork. Here, then, is the explanation of the novel's contradictions.

"Fang, let us say, has a secret; a stranger calls at his door; Fang resolves to kill him. Naturally, there are several possible outcomes: Fang can kill the intruder, the intruder can kill Fang, they both can escape, they both can die, and so forth. In the work of Ts'ui Pên, all possible outcomes occur; each one is the point of departure for other forkings. Sometimes, the paths of this labyrinth converge: for example, you arrive at this house, but in one of the possible pasts you are my enemy, in another, my friend. If you will resign yourself to my incurable pronunciation, we shall read a few pages."

His face, within the vivid circle of the lamplight, was unquestionably that of an old man, but with something unbreakable about it, even immortal. He read with slow precision two versions of the same epic chapter. In the first, an army marches to a battle across a lonely mountain; the horror of the rocks and shadows makes the men undervalue their lives and they gain an easy victory. In the second, the same army traverses a palace where a great festival is taking place; the resplendent battle seems to them a continuation of the celebration and they win the victory. I listened with proper veneration to these ancient narratives, perhaps less admirable in themselves than the fact that they had been created by my blood and were being restored to me by a man of a remote empire, in the course of a desperate adventure, on a Western isle. I remember the last words, repeated in each version like a secret commandment: *"Thus fought the heroes, tranquil their admirable hearts, violent their swords, resigned to kill and to die."*

From that moment on, I felt about me and within my dark body an invisible, intangible swarming. Not the swarming of the divergent, parallel, and finally coalescent armies, but a more inaccessible, more intimate agitation that they in some manner prefigured. Stephen Albert continued:

"I don't believe that your illustrious ancestor played idly with these variations. I don't consider it credible that he would sacrifice thirteen years to the infinite execution of a rhetorical experiment. In your country, the novel is a subsidiary form of literature; in Ts'ui Pên's time it was a despicable form. Ts'ui Pên was a brilliant novelist, but he was also a man of letters who doubtless did not consider himself a mere novelist. The testimony of his contemporaries proclaims—and his life fully confirms—his metaphysical and mystical interests. Philosophic controversy usurps a good part of the novel. I know that of all problems, none disturbed him so greatly nor worked upon him so much as the abysmal problem of time. Now then, the latter is the only problem that does not figure in the pages of the GARDEN. He doesn't even use the word that signifies TIME. How do you explain this voluntary omission?"

I proposed several solutions; all unsatisfactory. We discussed them; finally, Stephen Albert said to me:

"In a riddle whose answer is chess, what is the only prohibited word?"

I thought a moment and replied, "The word *chess*."

"Precisely," said Albert. "*The Garden of Forking Paths* is an enormous riddle, or parable, whose theme is time; this recondite cause prohibits its mention. To omit a word always, to resort to inept metaphors and obvious paraphrases, is perhaps the most emphatic way of stressing it. It is the tortuous method preferred, in each of the meanderings of his indefatigable novel, by the oblique Ts'ui Pên. I have compared hundreds of manuscripts, I have corrected the errors that the negligence of the copyists has introduced, I have guessed the plan of this chaos, I have re-established, I believe, the primordial organization, I have translated the entire work: it is clear to me that not once does he employ the word 'time.' The explanation is obvious: *The Garden of Forking Paths* is an incomplete, but not false, image of the universe as Ts'ui Pên conceived it.

"In contrast to Newton and Schopenhauer, your ancestor did not believe in a uniform, absolute time. He believed in an infinite series of times, in a growing, dizzying net of divergent, convergent, and parallel times. This network of times which approached one another, forked, broke off, or were unaware of one another for centuries, embraces *all* possibilities of time. We do not exist in the majority of these times; in some you exist, and not I; in others I, and not you; in others, both of us. In the present one, which a favorable fate has granted me, you have arrived at my house; in another, while crossing the garden, you found me dead; in still another, I utter these same words, but I am a mistake, a ghost."

"In every one," I pronounced, not without a tremble to my voice, "I am grateful to you and revere you for your re-creation of the garden of Ts'ui Pên."

"Not in all," he murmured with a smile. "Time forks perpetually toward innumerable futures. In one of them I am your enemy."

Once again I felt the swarming sensation of which I spoke. It seemed to me that the humid garden that surrounded the house was infinitely saturated with invisible persons. Those persons were Albert and I, secret, busy, and multiform in other dimensions of time. I raised my eyes and the tenuous nightmare dissolved. In the yellow and black garden there was only one man; but this man was approaching along the path and he was Captain Richard Madden.

"The future already exists," I replied, "but I am your friend. Could I see the letter again?"

Albert rose. Standing tall, he opened the drawer of the tall desk; for a moment his back was to me. I had readied the revolver. I fired with extreme caution; Albert fell uncomplainingly, immediately. I swear his death was instantaneous; a lightning stroke.

The rest is unreal, insignificant. Madden broke in, arrested me. I have been condemned to the gallows. I have won out abominably; I have communicated to Berlin the secret name of the city they must attack. They bombed it yesterday; I read it in the same papers that offered to England the mystery of the learned Sinologist Stephen Albert who was murdered by a stranger, one Yu Tsun. The Chief had deciphered this mystery. He knew my problem was to indicate (through the uproar of the war) the city called Albert, and that I found no other means to do so than to kill a man of that name.

He does not know (no one can know) my infinite contrition and weariness.

Donald A. Yates

JOSÉ ANTONIO CAMPOS
1868–1930   Ecuador

Under the pen name of "Jack the Ripper," a Guayaquil
reporter, Campos, contributed humorous sketches to
El Telégrafo, of which he later became editor. Eventually he collected them in three volumes, *Rayos cató-
dicos* (1906), *Cosas de mi tierra,* and *Cintas alegres.*
Many have political significance. His early novel, *Dos
amores,* is practically forgotten, but the literary group
of Guayaquil, calling him their "Spiritual Grandfather," spread his liberalism, while themselves presenting the gloomy side of the *montuvios,* or coastal dwellers, whose festive side he had displayed. A number of
his short stories appear in translation, in the pages of
Inter-America, 1918–1923, especially, Vol. 6 (1923).
In his more serious moments, he was Ecuador's Minister of Education.

MAMERTO'S MOTHER-IN-LAW

"Tell me, Nicolasa, about something that has been bothering
me during the three weeks of our happy union."

"Speak, dear Mamerto."

"I am a man, am I not? And you are my wife."

"What foolishness is this?"

"None, if we are agreed. Now tell me what is matrimony?"

"It is the union of two beings who love each other, and who
form a home legalized by the state and blessed by the church."

"Oh, two beings, you said. Yet I find in my matrimony that
there are three beings."

"What?"

"What I wish you to explain to me is what whistle your
mother blows in this household."

"What whistle? None! She is at my side because she is my mother."

"Whom I did not marry. It was her daughter."

"How silly you are, Mamerto! You know very well that the poor thing is the widow of Major Leech who died in '83."

"And left her to me?"

"Of course not!"

"I am the one who is saddled with her, it seems to me."

"Do the few loaves she eats in this house hurt you?"

"Would that she ate all the loaves. It is another loaf that pains me."

"I do not understand you."

"Ah, my darling, how happy I would be if the señora would pick up her possessions and light out."

"I should go after her. In what way does my mamma offend you?"

"Only the spoon knows what is the matter with the pot."

"Are you trying to drive me crazy?"

"Him that the shoe pinches is pinched."

"Explain yourself, *por Dios*, Mamerto, if you are saying something sensible."

"Let's see; who rules in this house?"

"You do, naturally, since you are the master of all, including me."

"Well, then, have them cook me for dinner tomorrow the turkey I bought at the market yesterday."

"No, the turkey, no! The cook is fattening him for mother's saint's day."

"So you see I cannot command even domestic animals."

"But man, you take everything in bad part! You ought to have more delicacy. My poor mother!"

"Suppose I wish to invite a friend of my boyhood for dinner tonight."

"That presents difficulties. You know mother does not like to have outsiders here to dine."

"What difference does it make to me what she likes? Am I a zero on the left side here?"

"You are unbearable, that's what you are. If I had only known you were like this!"

"Well, my dear, let's not quarrel. It comes down to the fact that I am going to dine with a friend at the restaurant to-night with a sense of shame that I can't bring him to my home."

(*The old lady, entering*). "What is this I hear? It sounds as if this gentleman (*pointing to Mamerto*) is behaving un-pleasantly to you" (*looking at Nicolasa*).

(*The son-in-law*). "What is happening is that I plan to dine with a friend because you say you do not want me to bring him to the house."

"Certainly not! I would have you know, señor don Ma-merto, that Major Leech—may he rest in peace!—was op-posed to breaking the sacredness of the family circle."

"But what the devil do I have to do with Major Leech?"

"Speak with more respect of the dead, señor don Mamerto. He was a man who loved his home."

"How fortunate! However, I have other feelings about my home."

"Shut your mouth! Ingrate! Revolutionist! You have a pearl of a wife; a mother-in-law who is like a mother to you, and yet you want to leave us and eat with a friend. What do your friends do for you?"

"Señora, do not drive me . . ."

"Brazen, ill-bred creature! Boor with a capital V!"

"No, mother; boor with a capital B."

"It's all the same, daughter. I am not going around with a dictionary just to say that your husband is ill-bred. Poor Nicolasa! How unhappy you would be if you had no mother near you. I never imagined that this man would be a monster in trousers."

"Not could I, either, have supposed that you would be a dragon in petticoats."

(*She*). "How horrible, to insult my mother like that."

(*He*). "My love, what I am doing is only defending my rights as head of this house!"

(*The old lady*). "What would my dear departed Leech say to this if he should rise from the dead?"

(*He*). "Goodbye! . . ." He takes his hat in all haste and departs. In the street he sees his friend and runs to him to pour out his bitter grief.

"Think nothing of it," his friend says, to console him.

"Nothing, you say! What about my rights?"

"There are no rights. It is the same way with nations. For all they are nations, they do not exercise their rights when they are ruled over by despots. With less reason do individuals . . . who have mothers-in-law."

"And autonomy?"

"Your autonomy, dear Mamerto, is like that of some of the Latin American people. Console yourself. In the other world you will have your glory; in this one you must have patience."

". . . But I have none!"

"What difference? Having it or not having it is all the same to a man with a rope around his neck and his feet in the air."

Anon. (*Inter-America*, Vol. 3)

ÁNGEL PINO
1875–1921   Chile

> Humor is not easy to find in Latin-American literature, but one humorist was Joaquín Díaz Garcés, diplomat, journalist and corresponding member of the Royal Spanish Academy. Under the pen name of "Ángel Pino," he contributed to *El Mercurio* of Valparaiso and later of Santiago, which he directed and edited. *Páginas de Ángel Pino* appeared in 1917. Díaz Garcés also owned and edited *Zig-Zag* and the influential *Pacífico* magazine that published Chile's first detective stories, about Román Calvo. In addition, he wrote books about Chilean customs. A light touch, rather than a biting pen, characterized his attack on the foibles of his countrymen.

A CHRISTENING: SCENES FROM DOMESTIC LIFE

A blow on the back brought me up with a start from the profound abstraction in which I was jogging along. It was Andrés, one of those friends who pass years without showing up anywhere but who, nevertheless, are more our friends than some we see every day.

"I invite you to the christening of my latest child," he said.

"From your words, you must have several."

"Seven."

"Seven? You are my age. What have you done to produce so many youngsters?"

"My life is very tranquil. I have been married eight years. I do not go out at night. But you have not replied whether you will come to the christening. Are you afraid you won't fare well?"

"What has eating to do with a christening?" I asked.

"You aristocrats have your christenings dry. We of the people irrigate the ceremony with abundance. You will not eat caviar, but I think you will enjoy yourself."

I assured him that I would come, and we parted with an effusive handshake and his final: "You won't come. I know you. The party is on Sunday. I shall expect you at twelve o'clock. The house is 724 Huemel, which is also yours. But you'll not come."

.   .   .   .   .   .

A christening at twelve o'clock in the morning, I thought to myself, is not a christening at all. It is a breakfast. It will be a stupendous affair. There will be dancing and interminable lunching. They will dine late and then dance some more. I shall try to slip away, but that will be impossible. We shall have supper when day is breaking. I shuddered from head to foot as I repeated all this shocking program.

Having determined to get out of the celebration in spite of my promises, I wrote a facetious letter of excuses. Before I could mail it, Ovalle, the jolliest reporter and the greatest lover of good living in the world, entered my office. He told me he had been invited to the home of Andrés and that he expected to go with me.

"It will be a whole day wasted," I complained.

"Don't be foolish! What is one day? Aren't you an artist? You must observe; you must enjoy life. You have a liking for the national pantry and the national cookery. Well, then; you will have excellent wine, fat turkey, extraordinary olives, sublime cheese, voluptuous spareribs."

.   .   .   .   .   .

Within five minutes of entering the home of Andrés, we felt an extraordinary confidence. The guests were being received in a spacious drawing room, with three doors on the street, and three others opening onto the inner patio. The furniture was rigidly cased in white cloth edged with red braid. There was a row of ancestral pictures on the wall, some done in bromide, others in crayon, and almost all of full-length. At each end was an enormous mirror, while a multitude of bric-a-brac littered the old *boules*.

There were half a dozen señoras built on the same model, of the year '65 one would say. They were short, plump, well-preserved, with black eyes, wide noses, expressive mouths. Each of them wore upon her bosom a medalion with a portrait of her husband. All waddled a little in walking, not with the peculiar limp of ducks, but with the rhythmical swaying of a frigate upon a calm sea.

Hardly had we assembled when the people who had gone with the baby to the parish church, returned. It was easy to see that the baptism was not as important as the "trimmings." The youngster was howling like a bear, and his godmother brought him into the room, escorted by a crowd of boys and

girls. We loosed our tongues in praise of the new-born citizen.
We declared with absolute sincerity that he looked like his
mother, had green eyes, and would be a lawyer . . . There
was a bustle as we passed to the dining room.

The appearance of the dining room took away my breath.
The first thing that attracted attention was a large table in
a room a great deal larger. Upon it were set in a row three
great castles of sweets, on the summit of which a sugar angel
on a spiral wire swayed gently. Around these castles that
marked the backbone of the table were accumulated in disor-
der sugared and ironed hams, trembling gelatines with violets
in each figure, roast turkeys with their feet drawn up and
sprigs of parsley in their bills, fritters of bitter orange dressed
with olives, sweet oranges, sweet limes, bananas, cakes, many
kinds of cheese, bottles of wine of every imaginable brand,
and a profusion of flowers truly anarchical . . .

I was not accustomed to a breakfast beginning at one
o'clock and ending after five in the afternoon. Hard on the
plate of fowl with a rich broth tinted with slivers of unmiti-
gated red peppers, came numerous dishes, among which stood
out gloriously the baked meat pies, spareribs with beans,
macaroni, fish, the inevitable kidneys, salads of divers kinds,
crabs, calves' heads, and finally an omelet of sea-urchins. The
long list of dishes was followed by a longer list of desserts:
cakes, gelatines, pastries, fruits crystallized and in syrup. . . .

When we believed everything concluded, trays appeared
with biscuits and pancakes in syrup. After three or four more
dishes, we were still offered grapes, apples, and sponge cake
with palm syrup. Only then was the breakfast concluded and
we were permitted to go into the patio.

I was dragged away violently by Ovalle to a group of girls
who, he said, were calling me.

"You are too serious," one of them said to me. "And you
ought to be gay." Another plied me for details about the
serial novel that we were publishing in the *Mercurio*. "Tell us
how it ends," they begged.

From this agreeable company, one of the men extracted

me with a solemn gesture. "Come here, journalist." And I fell into the midst of a group of the six husbands of the impressive ladies whom I had noticed upon entering. They began a series of questions and answers about the present economic situation, the board of public instruction, the futility of the work of parliament, and other problems no less grave . . .

Others found other diversions. For two hours, until the lights appeared in the drawing room, the guests divided their attention between an incessant, frantic dance, and the attractions of the punch and other drinks that were being served in the dining room. One of the frigates confided to me her literary inclinations, while she fixed on me a pair of fishy, watery eyes. She read a lot and preferred love stories at 100 degrees in the shade. She longed to write a novel, and for half an hour she told me its plot. I found it pseudo-elegant and indecent, but I encouraged her to go ahead, vowing on my word of honor that it will figure in literary history and that I will publish it in the newspaper as a serial story . . .

A short interruption in the dancing gives opportunity for another of the frigates to approach the piano and sing "Vorrei morir," which moved her husband beyond anything. Then a new polka sounded on the piano and everybody started out in a feverish whirl.

From then on, the hours were passed in the most horrible uproar. Andrés let no one depart. Twice I was caught at the street door and deposited again in the dining room. The punch had made its victims, and every time the lady sang "Vorrei morir," tears flowed. The literary señora altered the last chapter of her first volume making it more highly colored and shoddy than seemed possible.

Though the number of people lessened on the dance floor, worn out by the hard campaign, the piano continued to hammer out waltzes, polkas, and mazurkas. I tried to fall into a chair, but Andrés approached me:

"You must be a man, Ángel. It is still early." So I still had to dance, drink, converse, and even think about different subjects. Finally, when the first faint streaks of dawn appeared, touching the tips of the orange trees, I tiptoed out with my hat.

Andrés caught me at the door, and guided me to a passage that led to the back of the house. With a beaming smile, he declared: "Listen!"

There was a dull sound, like a stone falling on something soft.

"We'll soon have something to eat," he promised. "They are pounding the dried beef to make some Valdiviano stew!"

Anon. (*Inter-America*, Vol. 1)

ENRIQUE MÉNDEZ CALZADA
1898–   Argentina

Méndez Calzada was for a long time director of the literary supplement of *La Nación*. Later, from 1933 till the fall of France, he represented *La Nación* in Paris as well as heading the Latin-American section of *Mercure de France*. Not only has he written several volumes, like *Pro y contra* (1930) from which the satire *El Cristo en Buenos Aires* is taken, but he also translated Stevenson and Dickens for the benefit of Latin Americans.

CHRIST IN BUENOS AIRES

The majority of the citizens were unaware of the arrival of Jesus of Galilee in Buenos Aires. To be sure, the good Rabbi, for reasons of a private nature, was traveling incognito, and the Society Page of the Great Metropolitan Newspapers neglected to insert a notice. Yet this omission is not at all surprising if we bear in mind that He was neither an opulent Argentine merchant nor a wealthy auctioneer nor a desert explorer nor one of his descendants. I am not unaware of Jesus' forty-day sojourn in the desert. But what are forty days, compared to the months, the years spent in the desert by nearly all of our numerous generals? In short, He was an insignificant traveler, a poor, ill-clothed dreamer—a very talented man, but with little baggage. And these are not precisely the prerequisites for figuring prominently in *Social Life*; quite the contrary.

It seems that on arriving in Buenos Aires, Jesus immediately went to an aristocratic hotel—that is, to an expensive hotel—to get a room. But no sooner had He set foot on the thick carpet in the lobby than a bell boy went to meet Him. The bell boy was a tall robust bruiser, distinguished, as is common in his profession, by the quality of his clothes and the poverty of his education. He wore an imposing pill-box cap, with cabalistic letters embroidered in gold thread, and a black uniform embellished with a profusion of buttons and passementerie, also in gold. A single glimpse of the man intimidated Jesus, who took him for a general. Cowed, Jesus did not dare address him. The bell boy, on the other hand, on seeing Jesus' ragged clothes, was seized by a great eloquence. Heatedly, he berated the traveler, using expressions which Jesus had never heard before:

"On your way, bum! No panhandling on the premises. Why don't you look for a job, loafer? C'mon, get t'hell outta here before I call a cop!"

With his customary meekness, Jesus answered that He was not begging for alms, that He merely wanted a room for several days, and that He had a few shekels left with which to pay. Contrary to his usual custom, Jesus did carry a few silver coins, which He had intended to distribute to the poor that He might meet on the road.

While Jesus was speaking, six other employees had gathered around him, and roared with laughter at Jesus' words. Jesus heard a few disconnected phrases above the merriment: "What a nut!" "Loafer!" "What a character!" The good Rabbi was hustled out of the hotel. He could still hear the rude jests and the coarse laughter in the hotel and that strange, perplexing word: "Loafer! Loafer!"

When Jesus was far enough away, He shook the dust from His sandals, as of old, for Jesus had said: "And whosoever shall not receive you, nor hear your words, as ye go forth out of that house of that city, shake off the dust of your feet."

Not knowing where to turn, Jesus wandered aimlessly until He came to the South Side. His haunts were always in the districts of the poor. Jesus walked for a long time until He finally arrived at Riachuelo. There He stopped a while to watch the sailors and the stevedores work. Later He went to a restaurant nearby. A sign over the door read: "The Friendship—Open All Night." The owner, a Jew, agreed to give Jesus room and board once the Galilean had given him some silver coins, which the Jew supposed were Turkish. The Jew said he would have to go to the money-changer's, and expressed his opinion that all money-changers were nothing but thieves. He also complained of "how bad business was," a phrase he always employed with new guests. Jesus proffered some kind words, advising conformity and patience, and then went out into the street once more.

Christ reached the Plaza de Mayo and sat down to rest on a park bench, next to a ragged man with hungry features, who was avidly scanning the ads of La Prensa. After reading a while, the man folded the newspaper and placed it on the bench, saying irritatedly:

"Nothing! No jobs. Another day at bread and water—if I can get bread! Goddamit!" and he swore vociferously.

Then Jesus reprehended him sweetly, with good kind words. The man smiled sceptically, and said:

"Yeh, yeh. I know all that. Everything you say, Christ said it two thousand years ago. And look at me; I tell you, the world's gone to the dogs!"

Christ did not reveal His identity. A few idlers from adjoining benches had gathered round the Nazarene. He spoke:

"Blessed are they that hunger and thirst after righteous-

ness: for they shall be filled. Blessed are they that mourn: for
they shall be comforted. Think not that I came to send peace
on the earth. I came not to send peace, but a sword."

By this time, a mob had gathered around Jesus. Idlers,
clerks, newspaper boys listened to Jesus' words. There was also
a priest and a banker. Jesus continued speaking:

"Beware of the scribes, which desire to walk in long robes,
and to have chief seats in the synagogues; they which devour
widows' houses, and for a pretence make long prayers."

Hearing these words, the priest crossed himself and left
hurriedly. And Jesus, casting a glance at him, continued:

"Seest thou these great buildings? There shall not be left
here one stone upon another, which shall not be thrown
down."

The banker turned pale with anger, for he thought that
Jesus referred to the tall bank in which he kept his money,
and immediately ran to call a policeman.

"See here, officer," he said, "I demand that you arrest this
charlatan at once. Yes, I'll be responsible. He's spreading subversive ideas."

The officer proceeded to do his duty, but several students
in the group stopped him. Then a group of well-dressed men
came to the policeman's rescue. A scuffle ensued. Somebody
asked:

"Who is He? What goes on?"

"He's a Bolshevik, a saboteur!" a man replied. Many in
the mob ran to hide in buildings, for fear of bombs.

"Death to the Russian; kill that Jew!"

Others seized Jesus and started dragging him down the
street. A squad of policemen finally managed to rescue Jesus
and were taking Him to headquarters when a well-dressed
matron, the President of the Sodality of the Sacred Heart of
Jesus, happened along in her car. The melée in the street
stopped the car, and the matron told the chauffeur to find out
what was the matter. The officers told her Jesus was an an-
archist and that they were taking Him to jail. The respectable
lady crossed herself and said:

"Well done! We must exterminate these wretches who want to destroy our holy religion."

Jesus was taken to headquarters for questioning. "So you're a Marxist?" the chief of police asked. And as Jesus remained silent he added:

"Won't talk, huh? We'll soon fix that with a rawhide whip."

Jesus said:

"I have spoken openly to the world; and in secret spake I nothing. Why askest thou me? Ask them that have heard me, what I spake unto them: behold, these know the things which I said."

One of the officers standing by struck Jesus with his hand, saying:

"Mind how you talk to the chief!"

Jesus answered him:

"If I have spoken evil, bear witness of the evil: but if well, why smitest thou me?"

"Clerk," the chief of police said, "take down this fellow's words. We must put down His statements in a report to the judge. He's a disturber of the peace."

A few days later Jesus was placed on board a ship. He was landed at an island. Then He was interned in a sordid building together with many other criminals. Before leaving, an officer who had a list of names with him asked:

"What's your name?"

The good Rabbi answered: "Jesus of Nazareth."

"Jesus! Jesus what? Don't you have a last name? Have you no parents? Oh, I get it; of course, of course!" The officer smiled and said: "I'll write down 'Jesus N., Arab. Occupation: professional agitator.' "

Edmund C. García

III

DRAMA

EDUARDO GUTIÉRREZ 1853–1890

and JOSÉ J. PODESTÁ 1856–1937

Argentina

Gutiérrez was a writer of gaucho adventure novels, one of them, *Juan Moreira*, serialized in *La Patria Argentina* during six weeks of 1879–80. Frank Brown, manager of the Carlo Brothers North American Circus, commissioned him in 1884 to make it into a closing pantomime for their performances, and hired an acrobat and clown, José Podestá, to play Moreira. Two years later the idea of adding dialogue took Brown to Gutiérrez, but he was not interested, so Podestá, with the help of the serialized novel, produced an acting version, whose first performance occurred, April 10, 1886. It is here translated.

JUAN MOREIRA

Act I

Scene 1: *The office of Don Francisco, the rural justice of the peace.*

MAGISTRATE: Mr. Sardetti, you have been summoned here because Juan Moreira says you owe him ten thousand dollars.

SARDETTI: Sir, that's a lie. I don't owe him even one dollar.

MAGISTRATE: Then how come so much lying? Why do you try to collect money that isn't yours, Moreira?

MOREIRA: Sir, I am collecting money that I lent, and I'm collecting it because I need it; this man is trying to rob me if he says he doesn't owe it to me, and so, Mr. Magistrate, I have come here to ask for justice.

MAGISTRATE: The justice I'm going to give you is to lock you up, you thief. The idea! Coming here with such lies!

MOREIRA (*to Sardetti*): Do you mean you don't owe me anything?

SARDETTI: Not a thing.

MOREIRA: And you're not going to make him pay me, Mr. Magistrate?

MAGISTRATE: Naturally not, since he doesn't owe you anything, and since you came here to put something over on us.

MOREIRA: All right, my friend, you've denied the debt after I let you off so many times, but I'll get it back if I have to stab you once for every thousand bucks. And you, Don Francisco, since you've forced me from the straight and narrow path, you'd better keep out of my way. You're going to be the cause of my downfall. I've had enough of your justice.

MAGISTRATE (*turning to the soldiers*): Here! Seize him and put him in the stocks for contempt of court!

(*The soldiers carry out the orders. Moreira is beaten; then the magistrate orders them to let him go, saying:*)

MAGISTRATE: Watch your step the next time, or I might send you to the chain gang on the border.

MOREIRA: I'll be seeing you, Don Francisco.

(*They get on their horses and ride away. The magistrate waves a good-by to Sardetti.*)

Scene 2: *Sardetti's store. Several gauchos are playing cards. Others are grouped around a cowboy with a guitar, singing a popular* milonga.

FIRST GAUCHO: Don Mariano, why don't you start one of those singing contests, and quit all that harmonizing?

MARIANO (*singing*): Come on, my friends, lay down your cards;
               You can sing *milongas* any time.
         Are there any of you gaucho bards

> Who would compete with me in rhyme?
> We've got a crowd, so who will come
>   And have a rhyming duel for fun?
> I'll even bet, and buy you rum
>   If I can't sing down every one.

SECOND GAUCHO: With guys like me of nimble tongue
>   Even the devil can't compete,
> For I have sung since I was young.
>   So start it off, for you're my meat.

MARIANO: That's what I like. I'll sing with you.
>   Do you know counterpoint, I wonder,
> Philosophy, *milongas*, too,
>   Or do you sing like pealing thunder?

SECOND GAUCHO: Don't call me thunder, and don't kid
>   A man whose lightning strikes you
>   double.
> I rained all over one who did.
>   Yes, stupid dolts get into trouble.

MARIANO: So? Does Your Ugliness imply
>   That I'm a dolt? Don't dare, I say,
> Or you'll get what I gave the guy
>   That insulted me the other day.

SECOND GAUCHO: He calls me ugly. Men, he's blind!
>   For ugliness he takes first place.

MARIANO: Not me! An uglier man you'll find—
>   Just gaze on the storekeeper's face!

SECOND GAUCHO: He looks like that because he's sad,
>   And I know why he's peaked and pale.
> Yes, things for him go pretty bad,
>   And Juan Moreira'll pluck his tail.

MARIANO: Sardetti, pardon us our song
                        And all we've said, but, what the devil!
                        As I've been told, you've done him wrong.
                        You haven't acted on the level.

FIRST GAUCHO (*speaking*): By the way, speaking of Moreira,
    did you fellows see what happened at the magistrate's?

THIRD GAUCHO: He sure got it, man, but he's a good Creole,
    and it won't be long before he'll be showing up around here,
    because he has to get even for a lot of dirty tricks they've
    pulled. Hey, bartender, pour a drink before I knock you
    down.

(*Enter Moreira.*)

FIRST GAUCHO (*offering his hand to Moreira*): God bless you,
    pal.

MARIANO: What brings you here, friend?

MOREIRA: Maybe it's trouble, pardner.

SECOND GAUCHO: How goes it, Moreira? We were just talking
    about what happened at the magistrate's. It's a hell of a
    note that a man like you should be put in the stocks and
    beaten to a pulp!

MOREIRA: Yes, they took me for a cow that had to be tied up
    to be milked, but they're going to feel my horns. They beat
    me all right, but this time they're not going to get away
    with it. Hey, bartender, pour a drink! Men, I'll buy the
    next round. Patience isn't gold; it wears out; and mine's
    worn down to a nubbin. Last night the magistrate picked
    on me and he put me in the stocks, but today the cow has
    turned into a bull, and blows don't faze me. You all know,
    friends, that I lent that man at the bar ten thousand dollars,
    and I tried to sue him for it because he hadn't paid me.
    And do you know what he said? Well, he told me I was a
    liar and that he didn't owe me two bits.

SARDETTI: That's true, friend Moreira. I denied that debt be-
    cause I hadn't any money, and if I had owned up, they'd

have sold out my store and everything. But I agree I owe
it to you, and some day I'll pay you.

MOREIRA: They put me in the stocks like a thief; they beat me
when I couldn't defend myself; finally they let me go, with
the brand practically hot on me, saying they were going to
send me to the frontier to fight Indians. And all because of
your lies. Don't I deserve revenge?

FIRST GAUCHO: That's true, Moreira, you're right; but a good
man like you mustn't go to jail for taking revenge on a dirty
dog like this. Besides, think of your child. You wouldn't
want him to suffer for what you did. So, if you won't get
hold of yourself for my sake, do it for your son. Come on.
Let's have a last drink and get going.

MOREIRA: I'm not moving, pardner, without keeping my word
and without finishing what I've got to do. And I won't take
any drink, because I don't want them to say tomorrow that
I did what I did because I was drunk and because I didn't
have the guts to do it cold sober.

FIRST GAUCHO: No, friend, you mustn't do it. Think of your
family.

MOREIRA: Let me alone, pardner. I've got to get even. Well,
let's get it over, because it's getting late. Sardetti, my friend,
I've come to make you pay me my ten thousand dollars,
or to keep my promise.

SARDETTI: I haven't the money, Moreira. Wait a few days, and
I swear by God I'll pay every last dollar.

MOREIRA: Not a minute longer. Fork out the ten thousand or
I'll cut ten mouths in your body so you can talk through
them all and say that Moreira is a man of his word, even
if hell takes him. (*He takes out his dagger.*) Either pay me
the money right away or I'll open you like a hog.

SARDETTI: I haven't any money.

FIRST GAUCHO: Don't let yourself in for trouble, brother. That
man isn't worth it. You'll only have to skip the country.

MOREIRA (*shoves him aside and approaches Sardetti. Then he
stops.*): Why don't you defend yourself? Want me to cut
your throat like a hog?

SARDETTI: I'm not heeled. And even if I had a knife, this would be plain murder.

FIRST GAUCHO: Hold on, brother.

MOREIRA (*tosses a dagger to Sardetti who catches it*): That's the way I want to see you, scoundrel, armed and ready. (*They fight. Sardetti wounds him on the chest.*)

MOREIRA: It'll take more than that to scare me. (*He rushes at Sardetti and kills him.*) Now I'm ready to take what's coming to me.

THIRD GAUCHO: Did you see what happened to the storekeeper, fellows, for being a double dealer?

Act II

Scene 4: *Outside the office of a rural magistrate. Moreira enters on horseback and beats on the door with the end of his whip. A voice answers from inside.*

SOLDIER (*inside*): Who the hell's knocking on that door? This ain't no public inn.

MOREIRA: It's Juan Moreira. I want to die tonight. Call the patrol. This is the chance they've been waiting for.

SOLDIER: Juan Moreira, my eye! Beat it, you fool, before I come out and beat you up.

MOREIRA: Come on out, you soldiers. Come on out or I'll set the jail afire.

SOLDIER: Look here, you, come back tomorrow; the magistrate's gone home and he left orders we wasn't to open up to anybody.

MOREIRA: Go to hell, you big bum! First chance I get I'll let you have it. Yellow-bellies are all the same. When there's just a few, they won't come out; and when there's a lot of them, they kick you around.

(*He leaves. A soldier appears with a gun and then runs back inside, frightened.*)

Scene 5: *A country store. Gauchos appear on horseback, in carriages, and on foot. Some have accordions and guitars.*

Some are throwing dice. A few are sipping mate. Others prepare food. Some are dancing. When Moreira appears, they crowd around, asking him what he has been doing.

MOREIRA: Oh, I just roam about. I can't seem to find a place to settle down quietlike. I spend my time fighting with the police and killing all the sheriffs I can find. You see, it's tangling with the law got me in trouble. The law says I'm an outlaw and goes after me. I guess it can't be helped. You got to take it as it comes. So what! I'm buying. What's yours? Set 'em up, barkeep. They're on me.

ALL: Hurray for Moreira! (*Enter a gaucho. He is startled at seeing Moreira.*)

GAUCHO: How come you're around these parts, Moreira?

MOREIRA: So what, big boy?

GAUCHO: Well, the local patrol went out looking for you this morning. And their orders were to search the whole district and to kill you on sight. The idea was to claim that you were armed and resisted arrest.

MOREIRA: Well, they'll come back skunked. I'll take on any patrol with one hand tied behind me.

GAUCHO: Say, listen! Goyo Navarro, a regular army sergeant's in command of the patrol this time, and he's plenty tough. Tie you up hands and feet and then shoot you, see?

MOREIRA: Forget it, pal. There ain't any patrol'll arrest me. I'm lucky, see? Barkeep, give this gaucho a double whisky. He's got the jitters.

GAUCHO: Make it a double rye.

ALL: Hurray for Moreira!

ANOTHER GAUCHO: How about a *gato*.

ALL: Sure, a *gato*. (*They dance that River Plate folk dance. In the middle of the dance, the Negro Agapito comes up to Moreira.*)

AGAPITO: Say, Moreira, slip me that little dame of yours for a swing around.

MOREIRA: You would show up, wouldn't you? All right, come on. (*To the girl.*) Look, honey, how about dancing with this boy? He steps smoother than I do. The sun took a crack at him, but he's a swell partner, just the same.

(*The dance continues. At the end, they ask Moreira to sing. He takes a guitar and sings a cowboy song. As he finishes, the first Gaucho rushes in, in an agitated manner.*)

GAUCHO: Moreira! Quick! You better scram. There's a gang of at least four hundred soldiers after you.

MOREIRA: Let 'em come! I won't scram. Let 'em come to cut my throat. I feel like fighting. But don't let that tough sergeant leave without sniffing me right. He don't know me yet. (*Moreira mounts his horse. Enter Sergeant Navarro and several soldiers on horseback.*)

NAVARRO: Are you Juan Moreira?

MOREIRA: What's that to you? That's me. And can I help you?

NAVARRO: Well, Moreira, I'm sorry, but I'm here to arrest you. Magistrate's orders. (*Takes hold of the reins of Moreira's horse.*)

MOREIRA: Just a minute. I'm not used to being pushed around. And you won't find any handles on me.

NAVARRO: Cut it out. It's no good. My orders are to arrest you and I'm going to do just that. Might as well come along quietly.

MOREIRA: Is that so? Who do you think you are? God Almighty?

NAVARRO: Arrest him! (*Takes out his saber.*) Be careful not to kill him. I want the bastard alive.

(*Moreira fires. One soldier falls. The others flee.*)

NAVARRO: Don't let him get away. (*He charges at Moreira and the cowboy wounds him in the arm. The sergeant changes his saber to his left hand.*)

MOREIRA: Oh, he's got gaucho spirit. He's tough and that's the way I like 'em.

(*Moreira grabs the saber out of the man's hand. The soldier falls to the ground. Moreira asks the bartender for a cot*) *and tells the gaucho to help lift the wounded man. Moreira revives him on the cot, binds his forehead with a handkerchief, and gives him brandy.*)

MOREIRA: How about it? How do you feel?

NAVARRO: Thanks, pardner. You're a man. Now I'm not surprised at all the things I've heard said about you.

MOREIRA: Well, sergeant, I've got to go, but before I do, we'll have a drink together; you see, we may not meet again. I shan't live forever. They'll get me one of these days.

NAVARRO: If I wasn't able to grab you, nobody else will, unless they catch you asleep.

MOREIRA: Amen, friend. Hope you get better. (*He pays the barkeep for the drinks and mounts his horse.*) Friends, it wasn't much fun today because they busted up our party. Better luck next time. Barkeep, take care of this man so he can tell his story. Good-by, boys.

ALL: Good-by, Moreira.

STOREKEEPER (*to Navarro*): You're lucky, sir, that rat of a gaucho didn't cut your throat. He's got more guts than a horse and he doesn't stop at one knife-sticking more or less.

NAVARRO: Anyone who says that man's a rat is a dirty liar, and I'll settle with him.

STOREKEEPER: All right, friend. (*They all leave.*)

This ends the printed dialogue. For the last two scenes, only summaries were provided since the dramatist probably thought the actors were well enough acquainted with the story to ad lib. *the dialogue.*

In the first scene, set in a dance hall, Moreira enters, with the law in close pursuit, but he takes time for a dance. In the final scene, taking place outside his home, he is trapped by the patrol, without his horse. He tries to leap the high fence and escape, but a soldier fatally stabs him in the back.

Carlos Escudero and W.K.J.

FLORENCIO SÁNCHEZ

1875–1910   Uruguay

First of the Latin-American dramatists to be widely
recognized, and by many critics called the best of them
all, was Florencio Sánchez, born in Uruguay of nomadic
middle-class parents. He began writing plays at a time
when Buenos Aires audiences were tiring of farces and
imported tragedies, and his realistic pictures of their
River Plate neighbors earned him popularity.

Sánchez' first success, *M'hijo el dotor* ("My Son the
Lawyer") (1903), displayed this realism and was one
of twenty plays, long and short, written during the six
years of his productive life. Critics argue whether
La gringa ("The Foreign Girl") (1904) or *Barranca
abajo* ("Down the Gully") (1905) is his best play.
Certainly *The Foreign Girl* is more popular now,
though on opening night the audience thought its
fourth act unnecessary, since its main problem, whether
a native Argentine can run a farm as successfully as an
Italian immigrant can, had been settled at the end of
the third act.

Briefly, it is the story of Cantalicio, the old creole
who loses his farm to the harder working immigrant,
Nicola. Próspero, the son of the Argentine, loves the
foreign girl, Victoria, a situation of which neither family approves.

The first scene, full of local color, and the final scene,
revealing the dramatist's belief that the future of Argentina lies in an amalgamation of the races, are here
offered in translation. *The Foreign Girl* is a comedy.
Sánchez' next play was *Barranca abajo*, the tragedy of
an old Argentine gaucho, bedeviled and deceived by
all the women of his family till he sees no solution except suicide. Following it, he began writing city plays,
some dealing with the upper class, about whom he

knew little. The rest were convincing pictures of the lower class among whom Sánchez had been brought up.

THE FOREIGN GIRL

Act I

Scene: *At the right is the exterior façade of an unplastered house, appearing, if not completely a ruin, at least dirty and badly in need of repair. A door and two windows without gratings; above, along the entire length of the wall, a series of holes of the dovecot, quite dirty. Near the window, downstage, are some earthenware pots containing plants; these are protected against the frost by cloths. To the left is an adobe and thatch building and a long bunkhouse with two doors. Upstage is a large well with a low curb and a drinking trough supplied from the well. Nearby is a bucket with a rope. The background is farm land, showing the black furrows of recent plowing. On the walls of the bunkhouse and the shack hang harness, ropes, tools, an old plow, stools and earthenware pots; on the ground, a wheelbarrow. Near the bunkhouse, center stage, stands an anvil with tools nearby. It is winter. When the curtain rises, the rays of the sun are just beginning to bathe the façade of the house.*

VICTORIA (*in heavy winter clothes, stout boots, her head muffled in a shawl, appears in the door, down left, crosses, stops in the center of the stage, undecided, as though thinking that she has forgotten something*): Ah! (*She goes quickly to the flower pots and begins to uncover them.*) What a frost! What a frost! (*She blows on her stiff fingers.*)

MARIA (*off stage*): Victoria! Victoria! Isn't it time? Is that stuff ready yet? (*These questions and the responses should be given with a Piedmontese dialect, if possible.*)

VICTORIA (*observing the position of the sun*): Yes, it's time.
Shall I put up the signal now?

MARIA: Yes.

(*Victoria takes a sack from the ground, sticks it on a pitch-
fork, and places it on the well curb. Enter Prospero, carrying
a plowshare. He, too, is wearing heavy clothing. His face
is muffled. On his feet are sheepskin overshoes.*)

PROSPERO: About time you put up that sign! The farm hands
from the bottoms are almost here now. Must have been hard
for you to get out of bed!

VICTORIA: Well! What's that to you?

PROSPERO: To me? Nothing. . . . But if you'd been working
since two o'clock this morning in this cold—anyway, good
morning. Say hello to the poor men! Did you sleep well?

(*Victoria makes a face at him and then runs away as Prospero tries to spank her. When she is far enough away, she
stops and thumbs her nose at him, then escapes again,
laughing aloud.*)

PROSPERO (*shouting after her*): You know what they do with
the ox that won't plow. (*He goes toward the anvil and starts
to file the plowshare. Enter Maria with a pail of milk in
her hand.*)

MARIA (*with a marked Italian accent*): Good morning, Prospero. Are you very busy right now? Will you do something
for me . . . afterward? After the men drink their yerba
mate, will you take the black cow to the alfalfa field? (*Prospero goes on with his task.*) Good-for-nothing cow! Look
what a little bit of milk! Hardly a drop! Not worth the
trouble to milk her. And after I give her grain every morning—Victoria, have you made the coffee for the old man
and the boys?

VICTORIA (*with four or five tin cups and spoons in one hand
and a package of hardtack in the other*): I can't do everything at once, mama. Yes, everything is ready. The coffee
. . . the boiling water.

MARIA: Loafer! Just what I was telling you this morning. Get up, I said. Get up. And you? Not a move! If you didn't sleep so much, you'd have time to spare. I'm going to tell your father. Ever since you came back from Rosario, you've been putting on airs.

(*Victoria begins to hum a tune.*)

MARIA: Aren't you ashamed of yourself? Get the food out and then bring me a pail of water. Right away. (*Picks up the pail of milk and goes off left, grumbling to herself.*)

PROSPERO (*amused*): Ho, Ho, Ho! (*With his back to Victoria, he strikes the anvil, as though he were working, and sings some popular song.*) Good enough for you! I'm glad of it!

VICTORIA: Silly! (*Upon one of the benches she lines up some plates, spoons, and hardtack.*)

PROSPERO (*turning toward her*): Talking to me?

VICTORIA: I don't know.

PROSPERO: Why the stormy look?

VICTORIA (*wheeling*): Just for that I'm not going to give you what I brought for you.

PROSPERO (*interested, going toward her*): What is it? . . . Let's see?

VICTORIA (*hiding something behind her back*): Uh huh! . . . Eager, aren't you?

PROSPERO: Don't be so mean! Let me see. (*He tries to take her by the arm.*)

VICTORIA: Leave me alone . . . Fresh! . . .

PROSPERO: Let me see or I'll take it away.

VICTORIA (*running away*): See—bread! Fresh bread!

MARIA (*from off stage*): Victoria! . . . Are you going to bring me that water?

VICTORIA (*leaving the bread on the bench*): I'm coming . . . Here, take it, if you want it . . . but remember I didn't give it to you. (*She goes to the well and lets down the bucket.*)

PROSPERO (*takes the bread, breaks it into two pieces which he puts into his pockets, and goes toward Victoria*): Wait . . . I'll help you.

VICTORIA: I don't need you.

PROSPERO (*mocking her authoritative tones*): "I don't need you . . . I don't need you." Get out of there! Who do you think you are? Disobedient young lady! (*He tries to take the rope away from her.*)

VICTORIA: Let me alone, I tell you. Let me alone. I don't need your help.

PROSPERO: All right. We'll both do it. Here we go, like this . . . Oop! That's heavy! You pull, too.

(*Victoria timidly backs away a little, holding an arm's length of rope, while Prospero reaches for the bucket.*)

PROSPERO (*after a pause*): Oh, the devil! The thing's empty.

VICTORIA: Oh, it isn't.

PROSPERO: Look!

(*Victoria bends over to look, and Prospero takes advantage of the moment to give her a resounding kiss.*)

VICTORIA: Oh! You . . . ! (*She hits him on the back with the end of the rope. The bucket falls back down the well.*)

PROSPERO (*delighted*): Ha! Ha! That hurt awful!

VICTORIA: Yes. Take that! See what I'm doing. (*She wipes her face with her sleeve.*)

PROSPERO: Hmm! Any day, you can wipe kisses off! (*Prospero takes the plowshare and goes off right.*)

In the final scene, Cantalicio, who has lost his arm in an accident, is about to leave his old home when his son returns, a successful man.

PROSPERO: Forgive me, Victoria. (*Taking her hands.*) How have you been?

CANTALICIO: Give her a hug! You both want to, and you aren't crippled, like me. (*They embrace. Enter Maria.*)

MARIA: Oh! You filthy—You impudent!—I'll teach you a thing or two! Bandit! What are you up to? (*She runs toward the frightened Victoria, who seeks protection beside Cantalicio. Prospero steps between them.*) I'm going to give you the thrashing of your life. Aren't you ashamed of yourself! But I'll fix you! Get inside there! Oh, you won't go, eh? (*Calling.*) Hey, Nicola! Nicola! Come here right away! There's a little matter to be attended to. Nicola! (*Angrily.*) Nicola! Come here! I caught Victoria at it again! (*Turning toward her.*) A daughter of mine! (*Recognizing Prospero.*) Heavens! And it turns out to be that creole Prospero! Nicola! Hurry up! (*Enter don Nicola.*)

NICOLA: What's wrong with you? Why are you neighing like a filly?

MARIA: Just imagine! I was coming to the patio and what do I see but this shameless girl with her arms around a man!

NICOLA: What? You saw Victoria?

MARIA: Just like the last time—

NICOLA: What does this mean? Damn it!

PROSPERO: It means that—even though this may not be the best time and I had no intention of doing it just this minute, it looks like I better ask you now for the hand of your daughter.

NICOLA: What, again? Who do you think you are? Tell me!

CANTALICIO (*aside*): This time they can't refuse to give her to him!

MARIA: I should say not! Not when a wedding is arranged between that contractor and her. To give her to that lazy creole now—

NICOLA: I told you to keep quiet! (*To Prospero.*) You, young man! First of all, I want to know what you're doing, coming to this house.

PROSPERO: I'm in charge of the threshing machine, sir.

MARIA: That's a lie!

NICOLA: I told you to shut up! (*To Prospero.*) All right; then, why aren't you over there running it?

(*Enter Horace.*)

HORACE: What's going on? Oh, hello, Prospero! How are things going? So you finally decided to come? You've found your old man, I see. We kidnapped him.

NICOLA: Ah, that's right, you were old friends, weren't you? But do you know what he was doing to Victoria? Eh?

MARIA: He had her in his arms. In his arms!

HORACE: Really? What was she doing?

MARIA: She was hugging him, too, the shameless girl! I caught them!

HORACE: So that's the way it is! (*To Victoria.*) Come here, you—sly girl! That's what's back of all your melancholy, is it? He's your sweetheart!

VICTORIA (*confused*): Yes!

HORACE: Then, Dad, there's nothing more to be said.

NICOLA: Eh! If you think the boy's worth while and if she likes him—It's all right with me, as long as he's a good worker.

PROSPERO: Thank you, Horace.

HORACE: So there you have Victoria. I suppose, Prospero, now you'll do our threshing free of charge. (*To Cantalicio.*) What about you, Cantalicio? Are you ready to call off your quarrel with the gringos?

CANTALICIO: With the gringos? Never in my cursed life! . . . With the gringa Victoria, fine! But that's all!

HORACE: Won't they make a fine couple! Daughter of pure gringo stock—son of pure creole stock! From them will come the strong race of tomorrow.

PROSPERO: It's in the making. Shake on it, old man.

CANTALICIO (*aside to Prospero*): In the making, nothing, you fool! It's made!

PROSPERO: Is that true, Dad? (*He runs toward Victoria.*) Beloved! Darling! (*Kisses her forehead. Everybody is surprised. At that moment, a long whistle is heard.*) The threshing machine is starting.

NICOLA (*pulling Prospero away*): All right, young man. Let's get to work. Let's get to work!

THE END

W.K.J.

DOWN THE GULLY

*Zoilo, the old creole, has lost his land, but the new
owner allows him to occupy it because of friendship with
his daughter, Prudencia. When Zoilo realizes the situation,
he moves down the gully with his wife Dolores, his daughter,
and his sister Rudecinda, into a run-down cabin. However
the women, with the crafty old Martiniana, a friend, try
to have at least the women move back to the more pleasant
farm house.*

*The hired man, Aniceto, discovers their plans and just
before the final scene has chased away Martiniana and her
buggy. Zoilo has a different idea.*

ZOILO (*to Aniceto*): Boy, go after that buggy that's leaving, and
bring it back.

(*Exit Aniceto after Martiniana. Zoilo paces up and down.
He stops at the barrel and drinks some water, with every
sign of satisfaction.*)

RUDECINDA: Have you ever seen such a bold, insolent person!
A down-right liar!

ZOILO (*sitting down*): Yes, that's so.

RUDECINDA (*regaining confidence*): By now you must be tired
of having us around.

DOLORES: Zoilo, Zoilo, forgive me!

ZOILO (*speaking simply*): I? You are the ones who ought to
forgive me. It's my fault that I didn't know how to treat
you as you deserved. I was always mean to you. I didn't
love you. I never treated you the way I should, during all
the years we lived together. I didn't teach you how to be
good, honorable, and industrious, and above all, a good
mother.

DOLORES: Zoilo, please!

ZOILO: And I treated you pretty bad, too, sister. I never gave you good advice. I persisted in making you unhappy. Afterward I squandered your share of the inheritance like some reckless fool. (*Pause.*) My poor daughters were victims of my bad example. I always got in the way of Prudencia's happiness. (*His voice chokes with emotion.*) As for Robustiana, that angel in heaven, I worried her to her death! (*With a sob, he hides his head in a fold of his poncho. Then he regains possession of himself.*) All right, get your things together to leave! The buggy'll be coming back in a minute.

DOLORES (*throwing her arms about his neck*): No, no, Zoilo! We aren't leaving. Forgive me! I understand it all now. We have been wicked women. Forgive—

ZOILO (*freeing himself with firmness*): Go away. Leave me. Go do what I told you.

DOLORES: In God's name, Zoilo! I beg you on my knees, forgive me. We promise we'll be different from now on.

ZOILO: Get up!

DOLORES: I swear I'll be a good wife. A good mother. A saint. We'll start again the happy life we used to have, because all the years we have left will be too few to love you and look after you. Say that you forgive me, I beg you! (*She clings to his legs.*)

ZOILO: Get out of here! Leave me alone. (*He shakes her off violently. Dolores remains on her knees, weeping.*) And you, sister, go on, get started. (*Rudecinda makes a negative gesture.*) Oh, so you don't want to go now? We'll see about that! (*He goes to the door of the ranch house, where he meets Prudencia.*) Oh, daughter, I missed you. Come, embrace your father.

PRUDENCIA: But what's happening?

ZOILO: Nothing. Don't be frightened. I want to make you all happy. I'm sending you to your man, and her to hers.

(*Exit Zoilo into the house.*)

PRUDENCIA: Holy Mother! What's going on? (*Upset.*) Mother, get up. (*Lifts her.*) Did he beat you? He's quite capable of that.

DOLORES: Poor, unfortunate daughter! (*She hugs her.*)

PRUDENCIA (*leading her to a bench*): What's all this about, for Heaven's sake? (*To Rudecinda.*) Tell me, was it Dad? (*Rudecinda does not answer.*) Oh, how terrible! (*Seeing Zoilo who reappears carrying a bundle of clothes.*) Daddy, Daddy, what's all this?

ZOILO: You're all going to your old home, that used to belong to old Zoilo. You got everything ready to leave, didn't you? Well, now I'm giving you permission to be happy. I won't stand in your way. Here are your clothes. Goodbye. I hope you'll be happy.

DOLORES: Zoilo, no!

ZOILO: Here comes your buggy. When I get back, I don't want to find any of you here. (*Goes slowly behind the ranch house. Enter Martiniana.*)

MARTINIANA: Didn't I tell you it was all the fault of that miserable Aniceto? But what's this? One on one side, one on the other? A bundle. I see Señor Whip had got in his dirty work. Tell me, women, did he beat you hard? Don't worry. A bleeding improves the quality of one's blood. What the deuce? You can't even go fishing without a fuss. Who'd have thought the old fool would wait till he was an old man before he beat his women. Tell me about it, somebody. Have you swallowed your tongues?

RUDECINDA (*getting up*): Shut up, Martiniana! (*Aniceto appears and watches the scene from a distance, with arms folded.*)

MARTINIANA: Well, thank goodness one of you came to! I was about to call Aniceto. So what about it? Are we going or are we staying?

RUDECINDA: We're going. Thrown out! That orphan Aniceto wrecked everything. Dolores! Hey, Dolores, stop sniveling. We've got to think about leaving. You heard what Zoilo said.

DOLORES: No, I'm staying. You go if you want to.

RUDECINDA: Why would you stay? Are you deaf? Prudencia, are you dressed? All right, then let's get going. (*To Dolores.*)

Come, get up. We can't have any fainting spells now. Martiniana, you carry the bundles.

MARTINIANA: At last you're doing the thing right. (*She picks up the bundle.*)

RUDECINDA: Get a move on, Dolores.

DOLORES: No, I want to see him, to talk to him first. I can't go this way.

RUDECINDA: He's in a fine mood for talking with you!

MARTINIANA: Do what we tell you. This is no time to listen to your conscience. They say, though it may be a poor comparison, that when an old woman repents, God is sad. Oh, while I remember it, would you be willing to give me or sell me this bed of Robustiana's? It would be nice for Nicasia because she has to sleep on a rawhide cot. If it would fit into the carriage, I'd load it myself, honey. It's the kind that lasts.

RUDECINDA: All right. Tomorrow we'll send for it. You can see what is happening to him, Dolores. What would he do about us?

MARTINIANA (*to Prudencia*): How about helping me carry these clothes, then? They're pretty heavy for an old woman. Just catch hold of this end. Forward march, as old Artigas used to say. (*Before leaving.*) Goodbye, miserable old ranch house. (*Aniceto follows them a few steps, then stops and watches thoughtfully as the women all leave. In a moment, Zoilo appears from behind the ranch house. He watches the scene and comes slowly forward till he reaches Aniceto.*)

ZOILO: My boy!

ANICETO (*surprised*): Eh?

ZOILO: Go part of the way with them, will you, then come back and get the little sheep ready to butcher. How about it? Please go with them.

ANICETO (*looking at him fixedly*): To butcher? All right, but —uh—will you lend me your knife? I lost mine.

ZOILO: What do you mean? Don't you have it right there?

ANICETO: The fact is—Well, you see—I'll tell you the truth. I'm afraid you might do something crazy.

ZOILO: What if I did? Wouldn't I have plenty of motive? Who's going to stop me?

ANICETO: Everybody. Me, for instance. Do you think that gang of good-for-nothings is worth the death of a good man?

ZOILO: I wouldn't kill myself for their sakes. It would be for my own.

ANICETO: No, boss. Calm yourself. What would you gain by getting reckless?

ZOILO (*rising*): That's the same thing as telling a relative at a wake: "Don't cry, friend. It can't be helped. One mustn't cry!" Damn it! What if you love that son, that relative? We're all good at consoling others and handing out advice. No one is good at taking orders. I'm not talking about you, my boy. People find a good, healthy, honest, industrious worker, and they rob him of everything he has, including his money saved up by the sweat of his brow, and the love of his family, his only consolation; they take away his honor, which is his reliquary. Damn it! They deprive him of all consideration and respect. They push him about, trample on him, beat him—even take away his name. And when that poor fellow, that old Zoilo, tired, worn-out, good-for-nothing, hopeless, crazy with shame and suffering—when once he decides to put an end to such a filthy life, everybody runs to stop him. "Don't kill yourself! Life is good!" Good for what?

ANICETO: For me, godfather.

ZOILO: I'm not talking about you, my boy. Well, then, all right. Suppose I didn't kill myself. I'm still alive. And now what do they do for me? Give me back everything I lost? My money, my family, my honor, my peace of mind? No, indeed! "We've done enough for you by not letting you die," they say. "Get along as best you can, old Zoilo!"

ANICETO: That's just the way it is.

ZOILO (*embracing him affectionately*): Well, my boy, round up the sheep, as I told you to. Go, leave me in peace. I won't do it. Go get the sheep.

ANICETO: That's more like it. Fine, fine!

ZOILO: It's a shame it isn't as easy to live as to die. Anyway, some day it has to happen.

ANICETO: Oh, what injustice!

ZOILO: Injustice? Old Zoilo knows all about that. Go on. Nothing is going to happen, I promise you. Here, take my knife. Round up the sheep. (*As Aniceto goes out, Zoilo watches him for a moment, then from the barrel he dips a jar of water and drinks greedily. He goes to the eaves and takes down the lasso which he hung there. He unhooks it. He tries it to test its flexibility, then he adjusts the loop with care. All the time he is whistling tunelessly. Placing himself under the ridgepole, he throws the rope over it, getting it tangled in the ovenbird's nest. In trying to work it past, he overturns the nest.*) That's the way God does things. The nest of a man is more easily upset than a bird's nest. (*He goes back to the task of fastening the rope securely. When he is sure it is firm, he returns to the center of the stage and drinks more water. Then he puts the loop around his neck and places a bench under the gallows.*)

CURTAIN.

W.K.J.

PEDRO E. PICO
1882–1945   Argentina

The hundred plays from the pen of Dr. Pico covered all phases of Argentine life to make him the outstanding Argentine dramatist of the early twentieth century. A master of dialogue, a painter of people and customs, from his first *La polka del espiante* ("The Spy Polka") (1901) to *Novelera*, ("Talebearer"), performed after his death, he challenged the playgoers to do something about the social problems of their country.

Pico was one of the few Latin-American dramatists able to make a living from his craft. Especially interested in the immigrant, he wrote *sainetes* (short dramatic sketches) describing his arrival, his crowding into the tenements, and even his attempt to find better quarters in the country. Naturalism, romanticism, even occasional melodrama came from his pen. Typical is the realistic but sentimental *Del mismo barro* (1918), the last third of which is here translated. Its lifelike conversation and vivid and varied characters make it among his best. It treats sympathetically some of the poor people on the fringe of Buenos Aires, who are scavengers of the city dump. Maco, driver of a dump truck, wants to take Chucha away from it, in which endeavor he is encouraged by "The Prof," a one-time schoolteacher in dire straits, but he is hindered by Dora, her mother, Black Cloud, an old colored woman, and Gold Tooth.

The scene is a garbage dump near Buenos Aires. In the corner amid the rubbish stands a small shack poorly built of packing boxes, tin cans, and pieces of canvas. The sky is heavy and dirty. It is growing dark.

COMMON CLAY

(*Maco leaves his truck that has just dumped its load, approaches Chucha stealthily, and surprises her with a kiss on the back of the neck.*)

CHUCHA (*indifferently*): Maco!

MACO: Did the Prof tell you? I've come to take you away.

CHUCHA: Some other time.

MACO: To the city.

CHUCHA: And what's in the city?

MACO: Another life. We'll find another world, a world of our own that will fit into our room. You'll see!

CHUCHA: What about my dog?

MACO: What about me?

CHUCHA (*animated*): I like the dog very much—more than anything or anyone. I found him one day among the refuse, skinny and sad and with a broken paw. I fixed him and ever since, I've had him around. That's why the Prof calls me Chucha. He says it means "Dog woman." Is that what it means?

MACO: Maybe. He knows a lot.

CHUCHA: Well, anyway, he always follows me. When that convict came after me, the dog went after him, small as he was, snarling and biting, till Black Cloud and Gold Tooth came.

MACO: You won't need the dog. I'll take care of you. I'll defend you. I'm not afraid of anything. I'm young. I'll bite if necessary, the same as your dog would, if he was older and stronger. Come with me!

(Black Cloud appears in the doorway of the shack, with a drink of mate in her hand.)

CLOUD: They won't let you have your dog, because he don't have no license, and the dog catcher will come looking for him.

MACO: What makes you butt in? *(He gets up.)*

CLOUD: Do you want a drink of *mate?*

MACO: Get out of here.

CLOUD *(to Chucha)*: Do you?

CHUCHA: No, thanks.

CLOUD: Bah! You're a fool. I'll bet that scoundrel has convinced you. Don't pay no attention to him, dearie; don't pay no attention to him. It's all a lie. It's like a song. Laugh at it, dearie. Laugh at it! The world! What a world! Society! I'm telling you in the city there are some people who wash their faces every day.

CHUCHA: Get out!

CLOUD: Don't you believe it?

MACO: It would be better, I suppose, to live in this filth!

CLOUD: You know the saying: "Them it don't kill, grows fat." Look at me, round as a barrel.

MACO: Let her make up her own mind.

CLOUD: Why are you ordering me?

MACO: Because I am.

CLOUD: O.K. I'll shut up, but you're a fool.

MACO: Soon as I start burning the stuff in this load, I'm leaving. Want me to wait for you?

CHUCHA: Yes, wait for me.

MACO: I'll go and fix up the truck. (*To Black Cloud.*) Good-by! You crazy woman! (*As he starts out, he bumps into Gold Tooth and the Prof.*) Here, get something to eat and drink. (*He gives the Negress some money and goes out.*)

CLOUD: Rascal!

(*The Prof comes forward and takes his regular place. Gold Tooth remains standing in the rear.*)

CLOUD (*coughing to attract attention of Chucha, who is deep in thought*): Ahem? Didn't I tell you? They've turned you against me. (*To Gold Tooth.*) It's a shame, don't you think?

GOLD TOOTH: What is?

CLOUD: Nothing. (*Gold Tooth shrugs his shoulders in indifference. Brief pause.*) So, you're leaving, are you?

CHUCHA: Yes.

CLOUD: Listen, dearie, maybe you'll tell me I ain't your mother and shouldn't ought to butt in, but what the devil! I've been around and I've seen things. How about you and me having a little talk?

CHUCHA: What for?

CLOUD: So you won't be a fool, and so you'll take another look at things. You ain't never been around clean people. It's enough to make you deny God. Come here.

CHUCHA: Here?

CLOUD: Here.

PROF: Nice work!

CLOUD: That's that. Why don't you go to the city, too, Prof?

PROF: I can't. What about you?

CLOUD: I don't want to. The smaller the world, the easier it is to know it. Maybe I can't say things like I mean, especially, but listen: here, you know everybody. That's something! We're all equal and all bums. All I want is enough to buy a little something to eat; the Prof don't bother no one if they lets him sleep; Gold Tooth don't hear nor bother nobody neither. Nobody bothers about anybody else. It's live and let live. I don't know if I've said this like I think it.

PROF: You're absolutely right.

CLOUD: But now, out there in the world, dearie, you're always meetin' up with new kinds of people. Foreigners, pure and simple. And since you don't know your way about, when you're off guard, they'll trip you up. Ain't nobody told you that? Ask your mother; ask the Prof and Gold Tooth. Ask any that goes around here gnawing bones.

GOLD TOOTH: I used to have money and a friend. Now, I ain't got nothing, not even my tooth.

PROF: You've already said that. (*A noise is heard. Some stones fall near Chucha.*)

CLOUD: What's going on?

GOLD TOOTH (*upstage*): Those kids!

VOICES (*off stage*): Make her dance! Dance, crazy woman! (*Shortly afterward, Dora enters excited, sweating, hair disheveled and her clothes disordered, followed by a gang of children who are teasing her and laughing at her. Dora's small children, Florcita and Mingo, are crying.*)

CHILDREN: Make her dance! Dance! (*When they see Black Cloud and Gold Tooth about to interfere, they retreat.*)

CLOUD (*to Gold Tooth*): Hand me a stick! Can't they see she is an old woman?

CHILDREN (*retreating slowly*): We wanted to see her dance.

CLOUD: I'll give them a dance. Let's see if they'll dance. (*The children flee. To Dora.*) Why didn't you stand up for yourself?

CHUCHA: She's always like this—dumb and senseless.

PROF: Poor woman. (*Dora sits down in silence and counts the buttons she has collected. Brief pause.*)

CHUCHA (*sits down beside her mother*): Tell me, mother— (*Dora looks at her without answering.*) Didn't you know? I'm going to the city. (*Incredulous look from Dora.*) Yes, I'm going. This isn't life, living in this dirt and filth, eating

scraps, sleeping on the ground. They say that it's worse in
the city. Well, maybe so, but I want to see it. I'm going.
You don't want me to go, do you? Tell me. You don't want
me to? Say it!

DORA (*muffled*): No.

CHUCHA: Why? (*Pause.*) Still you won't talk. Tell me, what
kind of life did you have in the city that makes your memory
so bitter? Why do you look at me so upset?

CLOUD: Your kid is aimin' to leave you. Say something to her,
old woman.

PROF: Speak to her!

CHUCHA: It's no use. I'll go without knowing, but I'll go, as
soon as Maco comes. (*She gets up.*)

DORA (*desperately clutching her by her dress*): With him?

CHUCHA: Yes.

DORA: There?

CHUCHA: There.

DORA: I don't want you to.

CHUCHA: Why don't you want me to?

DORA: They're bad! They're bad!

CHUCHA: Who's bad?

DORA: Men. All of them. (*Pulling at Chucha's dress.*) Don't
go, don't go!

CHUCHA: Tell me, then.

DORA (*pointing to the professor*): He knows!

PROF: Over there, on the other side of the ocean, she lived in
a real house, with two old people who loved her very much.

DORA: Yes.

PROF: They lived happily, but one day a very rich foreigner
knocked at the door. His hands were full of rings, a gold
chain and a broach, a diamond pin and lots of money.

DORA: Lots and lots of money!

PROF: He brought her here to sell her like an old rag. She belonged to everybody, everybody who wanted her. One year,
two years, five years, many years until her face was filled
with wrinkles like an old crumbling wall.

DORA: Yes, yes, yes.

PROF: Then she lived in the street, in the hospital, and in jail, and finally, when nobody wanted her, when she had sold her last rag and lost her last bit of shame, when the children pelted her like a dog and the men forgot her—those same men who had showered her with money while she was young and beautiful—then memories, the desire to forget, hunger, desperation, and hatred flung her here like a bit of garbage no one cared to pick up.

DORA: Yes, yes!

PROF: I saw her come.

CLOUD: Me, too, if you want to know.

PROF: If you want to know what? It's luck, and luck changes. Some save themselves from this. Some change completely, and you—Chucha, a part of the dump—may be the lucky one. Why not?

DORA: Don't go! Don't go!

(Chucha remains motionless, without looking at anyone. Upstage a fire begins. The cloud of smoke, slight at first, gradually gives a purple cast to the leaden sky. Various unsavory residents of the dump cross the stage. Some children enter, go left and take the road. A shrill whistle is heard. Seconds later, enter Maco.)

MACO: Chucha! *(He stops at sight of the others.)* Here I am! Ready?

DORA: Don't go!

CLOUD *(intervening)*: Rascal! You're a smart guy.

DORA: Don't go!

CHUCHA: Yes, I'm going. Let go of me, Mama. Let go! *(She frees herself.)*

MACO *(taking her in his arms)*: That's the girl. You're already beginning to be mine. Come! *(They go out together.)*

DORA: Chucha, dear Chucha! I'm your mother, your wretched mother. *(Bows her head and cries grievously. The astonished children try to see her face.)*

FLORCITA: Mama!

MINGO: Ma-a-a-ma!

PROF: It had to be. It was inevitable. It cost tears and pain and hardship, but it had to be. Life, that's life!

FLORCITA: Mama! Dear mama!

(*The brilliance of the fire lights the stage and makes even the garbage dump seem a thing of poetry.*)

W.K.J.

DARTHÉS and DAMEL
1889–   and 1890–   Argentina

Two Argentines, Juan Fernando Camilo Darthés, a retired businessman, and Dr. Carlos Santiago Damel, an ophthalmologist, began collaborating in plays while still university students, in 1911. Since then, under the signature "Darthés and Damel," they have written more than fifty delightful comedies, most of them hits on the Buenos Aires stage. The majority of them are set in the metropolis, and while their plots are often slight, their humor, brilliant dialogue, and fast movement bring popularity. One of them, *Los chicos crecen* ("The Youngsters Grow Up") (1937), won a national prize and has had more than four thousand performances in the whole Spanish-speaking world. *Amparo* (1934), also dealing with illegitimate children, had a thousand performances in two years, won a prize, and was filmed.

Their only play translated into English is *La hermana Josefina* ("Sister Josephine") (1939), about a quack doctor, adapted by María Luisa Hurtado Delgado for a University of Wisconsin performance in 1941, before she became famous as the actress Claudia Madero. Not till the end of the comedy is it learned that Josefina holds a medical degree from the capital. Because of prejudice against women doctors, she had moved to a small community where she played on the superstitions of the inhabitants to make them take her prescriptions. It ran originally for 114 nights and has been frequently revived. This is its opening scene.

THE QUACK DOCTOR

Act I.

Scene: The office of a quack doctor, a comfortable room with a window at the back and two doors on the side. The one at the right leads to a small hall, the other to the interior of the house. A big, worn table serves as a desk. Chairs of various styles and ages are scattered about the room. In a corner, a small column with a human skull, openly displayed. Over a small desk or table opposite, a crystal globe with gold fish, several books, a sand clock, several buzzers and switches for various colored lights. Prominently hung is a mummified lizard; in fact, anything that will add to the atmosphere of the place without crowding it too much.

As the curtain rises, Manuel is sitting at the table answering the phone. He is a middle-aged man of fifty, dressed like a peasant: shirt and trousers of coarse cotton cloth, sandals or alpargatas, a broad sash about his waist and a kerchief around his neck. The phone rings.

MANUEL: Hello. Yes . . . No, not today . . . I'm sorry, it's impossible. She can't see you till tomorrow. You'll be number thirty-two . . . Sorry, the other appointments are already taken . . . Yes, you can come for it. Goodbye. (*Hangs up, then gets up as if to go. Meditates and taking the receiver again, pushes a button.*) Pancho, take the next calls, will you? Yes, and don't disturb us until I tell you. Right! (*Hangs up. Sister Josephine enters, left. She is about thirty, attractive, intelligent, small, but energetic and expressive. She is smartly dressed.*)

JOSEPHINE (*taking her hat off and throwing it on the table*): Good morning, Manuel.

MANUEL: Good morning, Miss Jo. My, but you are up early this morning!

JOSEPHINE: Yes, I've just come from Tres Arroyos.

MANUEL: Did you wire the money?

JOSEPHINE: Yes. Four thousand pesos.

MANUEL: Four thousand in less than twenty days! I should say if we go on like this, we'll close the month with seven thousand.

JOSEPHINE: Well, don't you think it is about time? So many sacrifices. All we have to go through . . . Have you thought about it, Manuel?

MANUEL: It doesn't bother me any more.

JOSEPHINE (*pensively*): And after all, we are doing them good, aren't we?

MANUEL: Why, sure. Do you know that yesterday three more came from Buenos Aires? They are staying at the International Hotel.

JOSEPHINE (*sentimental*): It is going to be pretty hard to leave all this. (*Pauses. Changes tone of voice.*) There are almost fifty people waiting outside. Did you see anybody?

MANUEL: Who? Me? No. I spent all the time trying to hear what they were saying, but . . . when there are so many, it's a little difficult to know who is doing the talking.

JOSEPHINE: Let's see. Tune in, will you? (*Manuel goes to the desk and pushes a button. Immediately several voices are heard in confusion, then clearly a masculine conversation that is going on in the waiting room.*)

FIRST PATIENT: . . . and she was right about me. I took the second bath in the pond of the beavers Tuesday night when the moon was full, and all my pains disappeared.

SECOND PATIENT: Yes, I know, she is miraculous. Everybody talks about her. That's why I've come from so far away . . . You know where I live . . . Almost fifty miles from here . . . Just across the Valley of the Ghosts, in front of the late Oligario's house.

FIRST PATIENT: What's the matter with you?

SECOND PATIENT: Oh, it's not me . . . It's my wife.

FIRST PATIENT: Where is she? Did you leave her at the inn?

SECOND PATIENT: No, I didn't bring her.

FIRST PATIENT: How do you expect the sister to cure her then?

SECOND PATIENT: Well, I've brought one of her stockings, because the pain is in one of her legs, you know. She broke it, poor thing, three weeks ago . . . She walks with the tip of the foot looking right up to the sky. (*Josephine makes a sign to Manuel. He turns intercom. off.*)

JOSEPHINE (*standing up*): You can let them in, Manuel. (*Manuel opens the door. Several persons can be seen trying to get in, and voices are heard.*)

MANUEL (*using a commanding tone*): Wait! Don't push . . . You are all going to be seen, if you just have a little patience. Let's see . . . Number one and two can come in.

(*The two men whose voices have been heard through the intercom. enter. Manuel now closes the door.*)

JOSEPHINE (*addressing First Patient*): Did you bring the hens?

FIRST PATIENT: Yes, Sister, I left them in the kitchen, four of them.

JOSEPHINE (*her tone of voice has also changed*): Four? What do you expect me to do with four? I told you to bring eight, one for each painful joint, so as to cure the rheumatism. Are they white?

FIRST PATIENT (*humbly*): A little mixed.

JOSEPHINE: No good! I told you they had to be white, white and big. You know I have to open them, take out the entrails, then mix the liver with the ashes, willow leaves, and feathers from the wings, cutting it all in tiny pieces . . . then that mixture is applied to the painful spots, and in four or five days, the pain will disappear. But you ruin it, forgetting things . . . You can go now and don't come back without the eight hens. Don't forget! White and very big.

FIRST PATIENT: Well, if you think it's necessary, I'll bring them tomorrow.

JOSEPHINE (*taking some small folded papers from a drawer*):

Meanwhile you can give this, one each night. There are five. After that, come and see me again.

FIRST PATIENT (*as if to pay*): How much do I owe you?

JOSEPHINE: Forget it now. We shall talk about that when she is well again. (*As he is leaving.*) Tell me, for whom do you vote?

FIRST PATIENT: I don't know yet and I don't have to worry. They will tell me.

JOSEPHINE: I am the only one that "tells" around here. Do you understand? Before voting, come and see me. Ah, and bring me all your friends, too, even if they are not sick.

FIRST PATIENT: Yes, Sister.

MANUEL (*showing him to the door*): Say hello to Pelais when you see him, will you? And tell him that the cheeses he sent us were delicious, that we ate them and we don't have any more.

FIRST PATIENT: Yes, Don Manuel. (*Exit.*)

JOSEPHINE (*looking fixedly at Second Patient*): What about you?

SECOND PATIENT (*humbly*): I've walked more than fifty miles for your help.

JOSEPHINE: Where have I seen you before? (*Pause.*) (*Manuel goes to the desk and turns on a red light under the fishbowl. Josephine sits pensively at the desk, then looks at the gold fish.*)

MANUEL (*to Second Patient, who stands up rather afraid and surprised*): Shhh! Don't move. Let her concentrate. (*Moves to switches and darkens the room a little.*) Ayapurá! Mamboecope! . . . Help her, good spirits . . . Enter her body and soul . . . Illuminate her mind . . . Give light to her eyes so that she can see through the shadows of the soul. (*All this is said with a deep and penetrating voice and with queer gestures.*)

JOSEPHINE (*languidly*): Not so long ago . . . Yes, . . . Now I remember (*Closes her eyes.*) I've seen you helping your sick wife . . . Taking her by the arm . . . so that she would not fall . . . She was walking with the tip of her foot looking right up to the sky. Poor thing! You live very far away. Across the Valley of the Ghosts. (*Here the patient crosses himself quickly.*) In front of the late Oligario's house.

SECOND PATIENT: Yes, that's right. We live there.

JOSEPHINE (*not heeding him*): Show me the stocking you brought me.

SECOND PATIENT (*trembling with fear, hands her the stocking.*): Heavens! She's a witch! She knows everything.

MANUEL: Sure, she does. But be quiet and don't disturb her. (*Josephine has taken the stocking and put it on the crystal globe.*)

JOSEPHINE: The bones are badly joined. I wonder who did it. If you had brought her to me two weeks ago, perhaps . . . But now, I can do nothing.

SECOND PATIENT: Do you think nothing can be done?

MANUEL: Oh, yes, by not by her. This is a case for a knife. You had better go and see a surgeon.

SECOND PATIENT: How much do I owe you?

JOSEPHINE: Nothing. You can go. But tell me, who do you vote for?

SECOND PATIENT: At home we always vote with the government.

JOSEPHINE: It's all right, then. I'll call you when I need you.

(*The telephone rings. Manuel picks it up.*)

MANUEL: Yes, what is it, Pancho? . . . Who? . . . Doctor Zubiaga? . . . (*Josephine goes near the phone. To her.*) Dr. Zubiaga is here and wants to know whether you can see him?

JOSEPHINE: Let me talk to him. (*Taking the receiver.*) Pancho, that's all right. I'll talk to him. (*Excited, to Manuel.*) This is wonderful! Hello. Who's talking? Yes, doctor . . . I'm glad you called me. Are you sick? No? . . . What a pity! (*Laughs.*) Well . . . I just said it because here you know we specialize in doctoring. (*Laughs again.*) Did you say . . . Oh . . . I'll be delighted if you come . . . No, I won't make you wait . . . Impossible! You are my colleague . . . Patients? . . . Oh, yes, lots of them. All those that you don't cure. (*Laughs. She seems happy.*) But aren't you afraid somebody might see you? . . . Well, it might disgrace you. Imagine a real doctor visiting a quack doctor . . . Oh! I see you are not afraid . . . Good. Where are you? Oh, well . . . I'll have you shown in immediately. Goodbye. (*Hangs up.*)

MANUEL: Don't tell me you are going to see him.

JOSEPHINE: Why not?

MANUEL: You'd better be careful, Miss Jo. He'll get you into trouble.

JOSEPHINE: I just want to know what he wants. I'm dying of curiosity. I've got to go up and fix up a little. Show him in, Manuel, when he comes.

MANUEL (*protesting*): All right. All right, but don't tell me that I didn't warn you.

María Luisa Hurtado Delgado

SAMUEL EICHELBAUM
1894– Argentina

Eichelbaum, an Argentine of Russian and Jewish ancestry, is the great figure of the contemporary period. Beginning as a disciple of Ibsen in *La mala sed* ("Evil Thirst") (1925), for a time he filled his plays with tormented and disagreeable characters. Then in 1929 he directed his attention to psychological problems, like *Cuando tengas un hijo* ("When You Have a Child"), that takes high rank as a simple, realistic, but deeply emotional play.

Beginning in 1936, his dramas took a new direction, full of action, like *El gato y la selva* ("The Cat and the Jungle"). *El pájaro de barro* ("Bird of Clay") (1940) is a poetic, but realistic drama of an unmarried mother whose sculptor lover was interested only in the clay he molded. Universality is achieved in Eichelbaum's *Un tal Servando Gómez* ("A Certain Servando Gómez") (1942), but his most national, as well as his most universal play is *Un guapo de 900* ("A Twentieth Century Bully") (1940), whose final scene is here translated.

A couple of bullies of the 1900's are bodyguards of the politician Alejo Garay. One, Ecuménico, killed a rival politician who was making love to his patron's wife. When freed for lack of evidence as suspicion turned toward Don Alejo, Ecuménico, from a sense of honor and duty, confesses his crime to his wine-swigging mother.

A TWENTIETH CENTURY BULLY

ECUMÉNICO (*as if continuing a conversation, and with a smile that seems to define it*): The police are like midwives; like the old gossips of the neighborhood. They don't know anything more than what the blabber-mouths tell them. The police don't know anything. And the judges don't know half as much as the police know.

NATIVIDAD (*without paying any attention to what Ecuménico says*): I've been to Don Alejo's house, you know. I've just come from there.

ECUMÉNICO: Always their inquiries! Anyway they had to free me for lack of evidence. And lack of evidence is proof of innocence. Isn't that right, Mama?

NATIVIDAD: Yes, my son.

ECUMÉNICO: Look, Mama, you can't take a wretched man and bring him into line by throwing cold water in his face, but if you give him a little wine to drink . . . isn't that right, Mama?

NATIVIDAD: Uh huh!

ECUMÉNICO: Well, the kind of man I am, even wine wouldn't work. (*A long pause, after which he draws closer to Natividad, and despite what he is going to say to her, he accentuates his smile.*) Mama, I drove those others out because I was tempted to make a great blunder. . . . You're the only one I want to tell. (*He takes a chair and sits next to his mother, facing the audience, unlike her, who is showing her profile. After another pause, in a whisper.*) I killed him.

NATIVIDAD (*stupefied*): What did you say?

ECUMÉNICO: I had to cleanse Don Alejo.

NATIVIDAD: Cleanse him? Cleanse him from what?

ECUMÉNICO: The doctor. That miserable little quack who was helping himself to Don Alejo's wife.

NATIVIDAD: That's some story!

ECUMÉNICO: I saw it.

NATIVIDAD: You saw it?

ECUMÉNICO: The same as saw it. I saw all the filth.

NATIVIDAD: And what did you have to do with all this?

ECUMÉNICO: It was Don Alejo. It concerned Don Alejo. Was I, who knew all about it, going to let his name be dragged around in the dirt? Could I let a person of his stature, with heaven only knows how much courage, be messed up by a perverted adversary and a hollow woman? What do you think, Mama? The first thing I knew, a few party-members were whispering and telling tales while they twisted their mustaches. You know, Mama, that I quit Don Alejo. It turned my stomach to think that I was working with a . . . But I was his confidant and couldn't betray him. One day I walked in on the doctor and surprised him with that miserable woman. Then I made my move once and for all. I simply thought, Mama, that that was my proper course of action, and the same thing prompted me to move on that occasion that would have prompted me on any other; party procedure. I'm not a man to put up with that kind of cheating. (*A long silence. Ecuménico waits for a word of approval from his mother. Seeing that none is coming, he turns around to look for it in her eyes.*) Did I do wrong, Mama?

NATIVIDAD: I can't judge you, my son.

ECUMÉNICO: Yes, you can, Mama. You know that life for me is a fight. I have to kill or be killed.

NATIVIDAD: That's true.

ECUMÉNICO: Well then, Mama, why do you say that you can't judge me? I wanted to cleanse a man like Don Alejo, whom I've always fought for. Is that wrong? They were betraying him with the most sacred thing he had left: his wife, the woman he loved like an angel. I couldn't know about it and remain a good-for-nothing traitor. I killed so that he won't have to kill and shatter his heart knowing that his wife was deceiving him . . . with that blustering fool. Tell me, Mama, did I do wrong? Tell me straight.

NATIVIDAD: If I were a man I would have done the same thing.

ECUMÉNICO (*moved, he caresses the head of his mother, without looking at her*): Thank you, Mama. What luck, Mama, to have a mother like you! Because you understand me, Mama, like one man understands another man. Life must judge you accordingly. (*He hides his head in the lap of his mother and succumbs to his first shedding of tears. After a long pause, Ecuménico seems to recover from his strange emotion, composes himself, then straightens up, passes his hand over his face, then through his hair. Next he straightens the handkerchief that he wears knotted around his neck, brushes off his trousers, and goes to get himself some wine. When he sees that there is no more in the demijohn, he drinks the few drops that remain in the bottom of his glass. He approaches his mother and gives her a pat on the face like an expression of tenderness to a long-lost friend.*) Beautiful old sweetheart!

NATIVIDAD: You're a flatterer.

ECUMÉNICO: You look on life like a man. You're my mother, but I feel like you were my father, too.

NATIVIDAD: I'm not sure you're right. You know that I love your brother, Pancho, like he was a daughter, the daughter I haven't been able to have.

ECUMÉNICO (*after a new pause*): Now that you know everything that has happened, I don't want you to be in the dark about what's going to happen. Tomorrow . . . well not tomorrow because that's New Year's Day and I want us to spend it together, but the next day I'm going to present myself to the police for arrest. "Here I am. I have killed Doctor Ordónez. Do what you want to do."

NATIVIDAD (*frightened and surprised*): Are you crazy?

ECUMÉNICO: What do you mean, crazy, Mama? I know what I must do.

NATIVIDAD: What you're going to do is pure madness! Do you understand me?

ECUMÉNICO: I've got to do it.

NATIVIDAD: The law has punished so many innocent people, what can it matter to them that you go free?

ECUMÉNICO: See! Now you don't understand me.

NATIVIDAD: "I saw all the filth," you said. If that's so, you killed him because he was a scoundrel.

ECUMÉNICO: So? What did I have to do with the fact that he was a scoundrel? I'm not Don Alejo. If he had killed him, it would have been all right, but not me, Mama.

NATIVIDAD: You know, it's true. I really don't understand you. A little while ago you wanted me to judge you. I eased your conscience by telling you that if I were a man I would have punished, as you did, Doctor Ordónez' crime. And now you come out and say that you didn't have anything to do with the evil action of that rotten man. If you didn't have anything to do with it, why have you killed him? Explain that to me. Can you?

ECUMÉNICO: I don't know whether I'll be able to, because my head is pounding like a drum. I know that I had to punish that cheater who treacherously humiliated a great man like Don Alejo because he wasn't man enough to do it to his face. That woman is nothing to me, but when I found out that she was deceiving her husband, I stayed away from Don Alejo. I couldn't serve him now like I'd always done. It seemed to me that a man could not serve another who was fouled by a woman. Do you understand me, Mama? I looked at Don Alejo and kept seeing a monkey. And I don't know who, but somebody was always at my back saying, "Look! Don't you see that he's a cuckold?" To have continued with him, knowing what has happened to him, would have been betrayal. That dirty little doctor-bastard! . . . put me in the position of betraying Don Alejo. Me, betray him, Mama! You know that I'm not like dice that can fall on one side or the other. I fall where a man falls, even if some cutthroat is waiting for me around the corner. I had to give him what he deserved. I didn't intend to kill him. I'm telling you the truth. I wanted to give him a scare, that's all. But plans go wrong. He mistreated me. He tried to insult me. He called me a coward, just when I was trying to hold myself in check and not reach for my weapon. What was I going to do? (*Pause*) Well, I've got a death on my hands that I've got to pay for. (*He begins to walk around.*)

NATIVIDAD (*observes Ecuménico, and then draws near to him resolutely*): Look, Ecuménico, you know that I'm a woman tempered by all the fires. I have buried many children, your brothers and sisters. I have accompanied them to the cemetery and before they were buried I have looked at their dead faces, as you look at a picture. If I have ever begged God for anything, it hasn't been that He have pity on me, but rather on others. But now I'm not the way I used to be. I'm beginning to realize it. I am old, and ashamed to see myself grieved by your fate. I will not resign myself to see your freedom taken away. I don't want to die without you at my side, and I don't dare ask God for this for fear He'll punish me for the hardness and pride I have always had toward pain during my life. I prefer to beg from you the favor of remaining beside me, so that you may be the one who crosses my hands, when my eyes have closed forever. You have earned your liberty, Ecuménico. Promise me! No, don't turn your head away. Look me right in the eyes. If you have the courage to say no, don't turn away from me.

ECUMÉNICO: But I have *killed*, Mama! I don't want a freedom that burns my feet everywhere I walk.

NATIVIDAD: Those are trifles!

ECUMÉNICO: Trifles! You don't understand—it's useless. You don't understand. Don't you see that it belittles my life. In jail, even if it is forever, there is no man who is my equal, in courage, in loyalty, in honor. Behind the bars, even the skeleton of Ordónez would rise to give me its hand.

NATIVIDAD: But I would die without giving you mine. I would go from this world thinking that on the breast of some other woman you have confessed these things that keep you from me now, like from a flea-bitten cow. You won't do it—will you? (*Transition*) Look! Come here! (*She sits down and asks Ecuménico to do the same on the floor. He obeys her like a grownup and not like a child.*) You have a streak of hidden gray hair. It looks like a piece of fish net. Look! You've got a scar! And it's so big! When you were a very small child, your father, who had gone up to the roof to fix some big leaks, dropped a roof tile that fell and hit you on the head. The blood gushed out. I bandaged it with rags soaked in salt water and with great difficulty I managed to stop the wound from bleeding. Later when your father came down, I defied him to fight. When he didn't pay any attention to me and started to laugh, I slapped him across the face with the same roof tile that he had dropped on you. From that day on, he was afraid of me. (*Pause*) Do you hear me, Ecuménico?

ECUMÉNICO: Yes, Mama, I hear you, and you sound like another person.

NATIVIDAD: I seem to myself like another person. (*Continues examining his hair.*) And you seem like another person, too. Like a spirited horse, but tired. I look at your mane, and your neck, and your eyes, and your face, and it seems like the first time I've ever seen you. I need to see you standing up in order to recognize you, to look at your picture to know that you are my son. Piece by piece, you might belong to somebody else.

David A. Flory

ANTONIO ACEVEDO HERNÁNDEZ
1886–1962   Chile

Earliest of the outstanding modern Chilean dramatists
was Acevedo Hernández, whose first attempt, *En el
rancho*, was written in 1912 and published the following year. His serious plays of protest that gave him the
reputation of a Nihilist followed, interspersed with a
few dramatizations of folklore, and some anti-imperial-
istic outbursts. Never having studied playwriting, his
work is more forceful than technically excellent.

In 1933, Acevedo wrote *Chañarcillo*, consisting of
four episodes occurring about 1842 in the mines in
northern Chile. In the first one, miners gather in the
tavern. Among those who tease Anita, "La Risueña," is
tall, powerful Donoso, nicknamed "Cerro Alto." He
loses interest in the youngster at the entrance of Carmen, but she has eyes only for Juan, "El Chichara."
Jealous Cerro Alto challenges him and is badly
wounded. As he recuperates in his hut, La Risueña appears, to take care of him, in the second scene, here
translated.

This play was recently revised by Pedro de la Barra
and successfully performed by the University of Chile
Players.

Before he became too ill to write, Acevedo completed
El torrente (1952) and *Cuando la muerte habló*
("When Death Spoke") (1953).

CHANARCILLO

*The stage has become dark, and Scene 2 opens in the
lodgings or shop of Cerro Alto. The two characters in this
scene are Cerro Alto and Risueña. He is dressed but
stretched out on the bed, and she is at his side.*

CERRO: Risueña, you have a gentle hand, and my wounds no longer hurt. I've been feeling fine for a long time, but I didn't want to tell you because . . .

RISUEÑA: Because why?

CERRO: Because I didn't want you to leave. You are so kind and pleasant. Listen—next to my mother you are the only woman who has approached me like this . . . with gentleness . . . How could I put it? Look, we miners came from many places in search of adventure, and any type of work, we live from day to day, and die in the same manner. We take a woman without looking at her, as one would take a drink . . . and then we cast her aside the same way without knowing whether she is good or bad. Do you understand?

RISUEÑA: Good or bad . . . I . . . I wonder which I am?

CERRO: First, tell me, why are you taking care of me, hating me the way you do? Why have you stayed by my side until now?

RISUEÑA: Because you were hurt and alone . . . Because . . . I don't know why I took care of you, neither do I understand the pain I felt when they left you so badly wounded.

CERRO: It is because you are so good. You are a saint, woman. After all the harm I have done to you, still you have taken care of me like this. How would you have treated someone you really love? Look, I am thankful to Suave for having left me out of the plan because if he hadn't . . . I wouldn't have met you . . . we would never have met.

RISUEÑA: What a real guy Suave is! Why can't you be like him? You have the strength, they respect you, and if you weren't such a bully, such a dog, they would like you.

CERRO: I am a bad person, I am, Risueña. I used to have bad ideas about you. That night I wanted to have you . . . and afterward—out of pure fancy—to cast you aside in dead resentment. I wanted to break you into pieces. That night was no damn good to me. The devil had got into me. (*He pauses.*) Risueña, wonderful girl, forgive me!

RISUEÑA: Beg God's forgiveness, not mine. I have no reason to forgive you. Nobody has ever treated me in any other way.

They have all wanted me as a plaything, they desired my poor body, but none of them brought me love. I have been like the lost dogs. No one has bothered to understand that I am a woman with feelings . . . one who understands what it is to suffer, and also to love, and to want people to love me. I have been treated this way since I was a little girl. I have been made to cry a lot. Carmen and Suave have been the only ones in this world who have protected me. (*She pauses.*) Now that you are well, I'll leave. You'll return to your work, and I'll go back to my task of serving as a plaything for the miners . . . to end my life in an abandoned shaft or by the stab of a dagger. (*She wipes away a tear.*) Good-by. (*She leaves silently, but stops when he calls her.*)

CERRO: Risueña, don't leave me. I couldn't live without you. I've got you under my skin, in my blood. I'm very sorry for having offended you. You don't understand, do you? I think that when I'm with you, I won't be bad again. Do you understand? Stay with me, and try to forgive me, and love me. I don't promise you anything, I don't have to promise you anything. You know how life is. (*Risueña sobs.*) But listen! Are you crying? Did I hurt you by what I said?

RISUEÑA: Hurt me? No. It's because this is the first time anybody has wanted to be with me and protect me. It is the first time that a person has believed that he loves me.

CERRO: I feel that I love you now, and that I'll always love you.

RISUEÑA: Cerro, although you are lying, although you will throw me into the mine or abandon me in the desert, I'll have to live with you because I love you as nobody has ever loved you, because you'll no longer be a bully, but you will be mine. Because of me you have changed . . . The other you . . . The other you is back there fighting and killing. This one is my man. (*She embraces him.*)

CERRO: How lighthearted I feel. I could run, I could chase you until I caught you, I could go through the streets until I got tired. All through life I could carry you in my arms and kiss you. I didn't know that it was so good to be good. I never suspected that a woman was something else. It didn't occur to me that I could live and also be able to love.

(*They embrace, laughing like children.*)

RISUEÑA: We are going to tell them the news, especially Carmen, shall we?

CERRO: Of course! And afterward I must go to work, I think that now that I have you it will be difficult for me to go down into that dark, hateful mine, but we will not let the mine disrupt our thoughts.

RISUEÑA: If you really love me, you're going to see me everywhere. I'll be everywhere, calling to my man, my love.

CERRO: My little girl, my little woman, my love. Say, would you believe it? I feel like singing and crying, and I'm ashamed. It is sort of like a pain. Do something, my sweetheart, so that I won't cry, or at least so that I don't make a fool of myself.

RISUEÑA: Imagine that I am yours and that you carry me in your heart, that your heart is a mine shaft, and if you fill it with tears, then I'll surely drown. Take me with care, as you would take your mother, or as we will take our son, that our love will give us. Take me this way, with happiness and without any fears, and with the certainty that big as you are, I hold you completely in my tiny little heart that you say is the size of a little bird's.

CERRO: Risueña! (*They embrace again.*)

RISUEÑA: Do you know that now I could die of happiness?

CERRO: You still want to leave me! . . . But I swear that if you die I'll give you your first beating. (*They embrace.*)

Darol Davis and *Kathy Booher*

ARMANDO MOOCK
1894–1942   Chile

One of the two greatest Chilean dramatists of the early twentieth century and most widely performed of Latin-

American playwrights, Moock began his career with
Crisis económica (1914), that earned him twenty-eight
pesos in royalty. His genial comedies, numbering more
than four hundred, suggest the Álvarez Quintero brothers of Spain. He did not aspire to write deathless drama;
he was satisfied to let his audiences leave the theater in
a pleasant glow after meeting delightful people. From
at least sixty, he received royalties for an average of
two hundred performances apiece, and there were un-
numbered pirated showings. One one-act play, *Cuando
venga el amor* ("When Love Comes") (1920), with
simple plot but amusing dialogue, had more than 2,500
performances.

Moock also wrote plays of ideas, like *La serpiente*
(1920), especially after moving to Buenos Aires when
he thought Chileans failed to appreciate him. At one
time, he had twelve plays in production at the same
moment. His final works, the experimental *Del brazo
y por la calle* ("Arm in Arm in the Street") (1940)
with only two characters, and *Algo triste que llaman
amor* ("Something Sad Called Love") (1941) pro-
claimed by critics as his greatest play, marked a new
vein for him. But his most charming comedies are his
earlier ones: *Pueblecito* ("Small Town") (1918) popu-
larized by the actress Camila Quiroga, with over two
thousand performances in every Spanish-speaking country; *Mocosita* ("The Youngster") (1929) prize-winner
in Chile and Argentina; and *Rigoberto* (1935) a tragi-
comedy of the revolt of a weak man, henpecked by his
wife, his mother-in-law, and his daughter.

The opening scene of *Mocosita*, here translated,
shows Moock's skill at characterization, his ability at
exposition, and his humor in discussing small-town
problems. It also reveals the subservient position of
women thirty years ago, with Pituca as the symbol of
a new generation in her rebellion against Aunt Cruz's
counsel that it was woman's duty to suffer in silence
and let the boy she loved go away.

THE YOUNGSTER

Act I

In Chile there is a gray and drowsy little town. In this town stands a large old house with adobe walls, iron gratings at the windows, heavy carved doors, and a tiled roof. An old garden with ancient trees, laurel, orange, palm, and olive, surrounds the house. The dining room of the mansion is the setting of this play. It is also the meeting place of the family and friends.

Windows, both at the rear and the sides, as well as the rear door leading to the hall, are set in thick walls. The ceiling has uncovered beams. The arched door at the rear is divided, with both sections now open. A beautiful, hand-made grating over the rear window keeps out possible intruders. The room and what can be seen of the passageway are tiled. Beneath the sloping roof, upheld by pillars, the sky is visible.

Amid the foliage of the garden can be seen a well and an iron arch over it. The walls of the dining room are white-washed. There is a variety in the furniture. As time destroyed some of the chairs, they have been replaced by others from the parlor and by one big easy chair. Near the window is a table that serves as sewing stand, desk, and study table. On the walls hang calendars, colored pictures of farm machinery, and bulletins from the Department of Agriculture.

Care and order are everywhere apparent. It is a sunny spring morning. The canary is singing in its cage by the window, and roosters are crowing from the nearby chicken yard. A cat is purring in a patch of sunlight. The creaking of a windmill can be heard continuously.

Pituca, a tall, seventeen-year-old girl, is studying her lessons near the window. Her eyes are full of life and dreams. She is a picture of animation in her school apron. Her *braided hair falls to her prominent breasts. Suddenly the call of spring, evident inside the house as well as outside, makes her close her book and start singing at the top of her lungs a popular tango about love.*

From right enters Beatrice, an old women of sixty-five or seventy, with hair white more from worry than from years.

BEATRICE: Pituca, dear, don't sing so loud!

PITUCA: Why not? Isn't he awake yet?

BEATRICE: No. He went to bed very late last night. We had a talk. We had so much to say to each other. In spite of letters, ten years is a long time to be separated from a son.

PITUCA: Wish I could have seen him, Auntie Beatrice.

BEATRICE: You weren't up when he arrived, were you?

PITUCA: How could I be? Don't you know that Aunt Cruz— Aunt Cruz—Aunt Cruz! With the excuse that I ought to get to bed early to be ready for school, she wouldn't let me go to the station to meet him. "You can just as well see him tomorrow!"

BEATRICE: Poor Cruz! She isn't mean, but she's just the way my poor Juan Manuel was.

PITUCA: Not mean? Then why doesn't she like Juan? What has Juan done to her? Want me to tell you? Aunt Cruz, in spite of her praying, is going straight to——

BEATRICE: Pituca! Hush! Don't say that. Someone might hear you.

PITUCA: Let them! Let her! One of these days I'm going to tell her to her face. How angry she got when she heard that Juan was coming home! Last night she stayed around to be sure I went to bed, and kept telling me terrible things about him; all so I wouldn't like him.

BEATRICE: Cruz is like that because she loved his father, Juan Manuel, so much. He never forgave Juan for not wanting to stay on the farm with his brother, Pablo. She thought that because Juan disobeyed his father and went to the capital, he was going to hell.

PITUCA: How wrong she was! Now he's come back after ten

years a famous author, the pride of the town. You ought to read all the reviews that have been written about his novels.

BEATRICE: But since his stubborn father wouldn't forgive him, Cruz wouldn't, either. Besides, they say he writes things about the church that people ought not to say. I talked to him a lot about that last night and he said he wouldn't do it any more.

PITUCA: I want to talk to him, too, Auntie Beatrice. There are so many things I want to tell him and ask him. About Santiago and——

BEATRICE: Do you remember him? Why, you were hardly walking when he left.

PITUCA: I was seven. But has he changed much? Did he ask about me?

BEATRICE: He didn't have a chance.

PITUCA: Besides, why should he remember me?

(*They hear the voice of Cruz from the garden, rear. She enters.*)

VOICE OF CRUZ: Jesusa! Jesusa! Go and see why the black hen is cackling so much. See if she laid an egg.

PITUCA (*in a low voice*): Here comes Aunt Cruz. She gives me a pain.

BEATRICE: She's on a rampage. Lord help us!

CRUZ (*entering, removes a veil and approaches Beatrice*): I know why you're waiting for me.

BEATRICE: It's just because you're so late from church.

CRUZ: After mass, I stopped to talk to the priest about your son.

BEATRICE: Your nephew!

CRUZ: Nephew? God forgive me! (*To Pituca.*) Here, take these and put them on my bed, and then come back and listen to something you ought to hear. (*Exit Pituca, humming her tango.*) I told the priest that in spite of my protests, in spite of the fact that it hasn't been a year since the death of my brother who refused to forgive that reprobate Juan—I say in spite of my opposition and the expressed wish of his father that Juan never be allowed to set foot in this house again, he came back because you sent for him. (*Enter Pituca, singing.*) Will you stop that yelling, confound it!

BEATRICE: Let's not thrash that out again. He's my son and I wanted to see him.

CRUZ: He ought not to be your son. (*To Pituca.*) Keep quiet, I tell you. What are you making that noise for?

PITUCA: I'm singing because it's a perfect morning. Because the sun is out. Because it's spring, and because I'm happy.

CRUZ: Impudent girl! Well, I'd decided to leave this house, but since the priest told me to be patient and resigned and to redouble my prayers, I'll redouble them and I'm going to stay. But I'm warning you, Beatrice, to tell that man to be careful of what he says around her, and not to dare to talk to me.

BEATRICE: Don't exaggerate, Cruz! Juan is a good boy. He did what he did because he was obliged to, under the circumstances.

CRUZ: He disobeyed his father. He rebelled. He went through life speaking badly of God and scoffing at his representatives, and living a life of license. He's been associating with actors and actresses. Maybe you think I don't know anything about the kind of life he's led, and all his female—his—(*To Pituca.*) What are you doing, listening to all this?

PITUCA: You told me I ought to hear it, didn't you?

CRUZ: Well, it's not for your ears. Be off to school with you or you'll be late!

PITUCA (*gathering up her books*): Aunt Cruz! Aunt Cruz! Why do I call her Auntie? (*Exit Pituca toward her room.*)

CRUZ (*to Beatrice*): Yes, I know all about that, and so does the priest. And he's indignant.

BEATRICE: Please, Cruz, think of all Juan Manuel suffered and all he made me suffer with his stubbornness.

CRUZ: That's the last straw! To defend Juan, you want to stain the memory of your husband who was respected by everybody in town.

BEATRICE: But he suffered, Cruz. He listened to me crying and begging him to let Juan return. He'd tell me "No!" and slap his boot with his whip, but that was just to keep me from knowing how he felt. Later when he thought he was alone, I'd see him wiping his eyes. He loved Juan as much as I did, and he suffered, too, Cruz.

CRUZ: How many times did he say: "Tell Juan to come and ask pardon on his knees and I'll let him return." Why didn't Juan do it?

BEATRICE: Because he's proud and stubborn, just like his father. Because he thought he had done nothing wrong. He left because his father drove him out.

CRUZ: That's not the reason. Juan was wicked and perverse.

BEATRICE: Juan Manuel loved him, and in his heart he forgave him, and that's what you ought to do.

CRUZ: Me? Are you crazy? Do whatever you want to. You're in your own house. But you'll see that nothing good will come of this!

(*Exit Cruz. Pituca returns, followed by Celia, her twenty-three-year-old sister.*)

BEATRICE: Heavens, what a woman!

PITUCA: Did she go at last? Pay no attention to her, Aunt Beatrice. Let her rave. Don't you agree, Celia?

CELIA: Pituca's right, Mother Beatrice. Don't pay any attention to Cruz. She starts off like that but later, little by little, she'll come around and agree.

BEATRICE: That isn't the only thing that bothers me. Ever since it was announced that Juan was coming back, everybody seems to have changed in this house. Of course, I've felt so much happier, but——

PITUCA: Me, too! And everybody. Isn't that right, Celia?

CELIA (*slowly*): Yes, indeed!

BEATRICE: No, you're not happy, Celia.

CELIA: Me? Why not?

PITUCA: I hadn't noticed it.

BEATRICE: And Pablo hardly says a word. He tells me there's nothing wrong, but I can see that he's not happy about it.

CELIA: Well . . . You know he never got along very well with Juan.

BEATRICE: That was when they were small. They are so different, and their father helped encourage those differences. But now they are old enough to get along together. Yet it seems to me——

CELIA: I think you exaggerate. It's true that Pablo's been in a bad humor, but I think it is something about the crops.

BEATRICE: I hope that's it. Maybe because I'm so happy I sense it when others don't share my happiness.

PITUCA: I confess that I feel happy and I'm especially sorry I've got to go off to school without seeing Juan. Where did I leave my books? I don't know where my head is. Oh, I dropped them on my bed. (*Exit Pituca.*)

BEATRICE: Tell me, Celia, why didn't you go to the station to meet him? Why?

CELIA: Well, you know . . . It was so late when the train got here and . . . I . . . I didn't feel well, and . . .

BEATRICE: Don't lie to me!

CELIA: Mother Beatrice, I know it's silly, but before Juan left, he and Pablo were both in love with me, but you know Juan. . . . He . . . I don't know.

BEATRICE: So Pablo . . . ? I was afraid of that.

CELIA: But I assure you that Pablo's all wrong.

BEATRICE: You don't have to tell me, my dear. I know you and I know him.

(*Enter Pituca from her room, singing.*)

PITUCA: I'm going to be late. All the girls will ask me about Juan, and since I haven't met him, wait till you hear the lies I . . .

(*Exit Pituca.*)

W.K.J.

ISIDORA AGUIRRE
1919–   Chile

In the renascence of the Chilean theater, a number of
women are having a share. One is Isidora Aguirre, edu-
cated in Chile and in France. After several successful
one-act plays came *Las tres Pascualas* (1957) in which
she took a legend of south Chile of 1910 and rational-
ized it, to show how fantasy can grow out of fact.

She showed her versatility by the amusing *Dos y dos
son cinco* ("Two and Two Make Five") (1957) and
the grim *Población Esperanza* (1957). Then she provided the libretto for Chile's gay musical comedy *Pér-
gola de las flores* (1959), also developed from folklore.

In *Pascualas*, the mute Adela lives with her sister,
Elvira, and her fifteen-year-old daughter in the Cordillera in south Chile. Daniel, a scientist, pauses briefly
at their home, and before he realizes it, he has caused
all three to fall in love with him, so he escapes to Santiago.

Nené Aguirre's use of the colorful characters and
customs is seen in Act II when the servants and their
friends discuss a rural funeral, and in the epilogue
where the transformation of the truth into legend is
discussed. The final part of Act III, also included here,
deals with the death of the Three Pascualas.

THE THREE PASCUALAS

Act II, Scene 1

*Scene: A summer storm is approaching. In the patio,
Manuca is blowing the brazier to brew mate. Marcela, with
a shawl around her, is studying. Antonio, standing in the
shadows, is making a wreath of white wild flowers.*

MARCELA: "Butterflies are divided into the daytime variety and those that fly at night."

MANUCA: You're the night kind, and night is no time to be wandering about.

MARCELA: Who could sleep with that funeral music? (*She gestures toward where a typical funeral dirge is being played.*)

MANUCA (*as Antonio appears out of the darkness*): Are you still up, Antonio?

ANTONIO: I'm going over to say some prayers for the little angel. (*Indicates his wreath.*) So tiny to be drowned in the lake.

MANUCA: To say some prayers? You mean to tip the bottle. Folks used to have more respect for other people's sorrow!

(*Enter Gumercinda and Carmela, right, with a covered clay pot.*)

GUMERCINDA: Evenin', folks.

CARMELA: Good evening. How's everybody? What you all wrapped up for, Marcela?

GUMERCINDA: 'Fraid of catchin' p-neumony? God protect you!

MANUCA: Don't go looking around, Gume. We've got too much trouble round here already. Goin' to the funeral?

CARMEL: That's where we're headed.

GUMERCINDA: We stopped by to take you along.

MANUCA: I was there all afternoon. You go with Antonio.

GUMERCINDA: Here, grab ahold of this kettle, Carmela. (*To Manuca.*) We're taking some good nourishing soup to the mother for the wake. And a couple more things. (*They start out, left.*)

MANUCA: It was too bad, Gume, wasn't it? But God's will be done!

CARMELA: They shouldn't let the kid go down to the lake knowing how slippery the mud was.

GUMERCINDA: Come on, girl. Good night. You comin', Antonio?

MANUCA: Hush! Keep quiet and let's hear them sing. (*They listen to the monotonous music.*) I think I hear the voice

of Josefa, the baby's godmother. She has to lay her out, of
course.

MARCELA: When I went over there this afternoon, they had
the poor little girl seated on the chest, with paper wings.

MANUCA: That's the way she's supposed to be.

MARCELA: But did you see the expression on her face?

MANUCA: What do you expect? People's expression depends
on how they die. And that little baby died in the water, so
she'd have an expression like a fish. Listen to her godmother.
She'll be singing that song about:

> "May all your pains be, ended,
> You lily bud afar,
> For children that have perished
> Are strings in God's guitar."

(*They listen, wiping away their tears.*) Blessings on her!
And she puts such feeling into it. But it's wrong to mourn
the little angel. That only delays her entrance into heaven.

Act III

MARCELA: Everybody's evil! (*Throws herself at her mother's
feet, sobbing.*) Mama, Mama, take me to Santiago tonight!
Please, Mama, dear Mama! I won't bother you at all, but
please take me!

ELVIRA: You've got to stay here.

MARCELA: Why?

ELVIRA: On account of the house. And Adelaide. And your
father.

MARCELA: Why can't you look after them? I know you don't
go to Santiago for any business.

ELVIRA: Marcela!

MARCELA: It won't do you any good to go because you're
married.

ELVIRA: How dare you, you impudent girl? Don't forget you're
talking to your mother. (*Raises her hand.*) I'm going to—

MARCELA: Don't you touch me! (*They glare at each other.*

The bell rings.) If you don't take me to Santiago, I'm going to jump into the lake, the deepest part.

ELVIRA (*shocked*): Don't you dare go near the lake.

MARCELA: I certainly will. And I don't care what happens to me. If I die, you'll be happy, because I'm a nuisance. (*The bell rings again.*)

ELVIRA: I'll have you locked in your room. I'm going to talk to your father right now. (*Starts toward Alberto's room.*)

MARCELA: Go ahead. Talk to him! And I'll tell him that you hate me because you're jealous of me. And that you're sneaking off to Santiago after Daniel.

(*She runs out toward the field and passes the window on her way right. Elvira falls exhausted into a chair. Enter Manuca with the account book.*)

MANUCA: What's the matter, señora?

ELVIRA: Madness has got into everyone in this house. Daniel was right, Manuca. It's all the fault of that witchcraft. (*Manuca crosses herself.*) We were living peacefully, mother, sister, daughter. But now—everybody has gone mad.

MANUCA: Ain't you feeling well, Señora?

ELVIRA (*slowly*): Is it true the village is gossiping about us?

MANUCA: Bah. There's always wagging tongues.

ELVIRA: But why do they talk now about what's over long ago?

MANUCA: Where they see quarreling, Ma'am . . . People always notice the bad quicker than the good. Gossip travels fast. And since there are so many ways of telling a story—

ELVIRA: But, Manuca, I'm sure you don't go exaggerating. You know what really happened.

MANUCA: You're trembling, señora. You ought to look after yourself. You mustn't go tonight like this. I'm going to make you something to calm you. (*Elvira shakes her head.*)

ELVIRA: No, Manuca.

MANUCA: Even if it don't do you no good, it can't hurt you.

ELVIRA: Tell me when the workmen come from the garden. I must pay them before I go.

MANUCA: Señora Elvira, I wanted to ask you—Why don't you take the girl to Santiago? She's suffering.

ELVIRA: You tell Antonio to save the hardwood for the fireplace, the *tepu* they took out of the swamp yesterday.

MANUCA: She's upset, and something ought to be done. There in the capital she'll get over it.

ELVIRA (*more tense*): Tell him to look after the fence around the corral, and repair the holes.

MANUCA: You must try to understand her, Señora Elvira. After all, you three are suffering from the same thing.

ELVIRA: If he needs to, he can use the brambles.

MANUCA: If she gets desperate, there ain't no telling what she may do.

ELVIRA (*with her misery apparent in her voice*): Have them be careful about the poplars, when they grub out the brambles. Take them out with hoes and don't burn them out.

MANUCA: Yes, señora, but Marcela . . .

ELVIRA: Very well. Let them come along, both of them, if they'll leave me in peace. And don't say later that it was my fault. Go and tell them. What are you waiting for?

(*Manuca goes toward the stairs, weeping and laughing at the same time.*)

MANUCA: Marcela! Marcela, come here! Where are you hiding? (*She goes to the patio.*) Marcela, answer me!

(*Outside can be heard the dramatic peal of the alarm bell. They look at each other.*)

MANUCA: Who's ringing the alarm?

VOICES (*outside*): The lake! Help!

ELVIRA (*terrified*): The lake! Marcela! (*She starts out.*)

MANUCA: Señora! Wait! Adelita! Marcela!

ELVIRA: It's my fault! My fault! (*Both rush out, and pass the window. The scene blacks out. Incidental guitar music.*)

Epilogue

A return to the opening scene, that is, a night sometime later. In the background is the silhouette of the mountains. The lake is visible, dimly lighted.

MANUCA: I don't know why I'm lighting the brazier.

GUME: Only two months ago the house was full of life and noise, and now all three, silent in the bottom of the lake.

MANUCA: Did you arrange for candles for them, Antonio?

ANTONIO: Yes, for all three of them, on the north shore of the lake.

CARMELA: Under the oak. That's where they go.

MANUCA: I can still see my darling, that sly beggar. How a body worries about them from the day they're born, for fear they'll fall, for fear they'll catch cold. And how happy a body is when they are fat and healthy. And then afterward—

GUMERCINDA: We got to accept such things, Manuca. Especially us who don't have much longer to go on.

ANTONIO: That's true. Not much left for us.

MANUCA: It strikes when you least expect it. An accident—

CARMELA: Don't tell me it was an accident! They drowned because of love.

GUMERCINDA: Who knows why a body dies!

ANTONIO: Yea, all we know is, they die.

CARMELA: But that man put a spell on them. Everybody says so.

MANUCA: People will say anything.

GUMERCINDA: What's your opinion, Manuca?

MANUCA: The dumb one went to the lake because she was out of her mind. God forgive innocents who don't know what they're doing! And the girl died trying to save her. May the angels receive her in Paradise!

CARMELA: And the mother? I suppose you say she didn't mean to drown herself! Didn't we see her give up, right there in the middle of the lake?

MANUCA: She died trying to find her daughter, till her strength gave out. May the Holy Virgin receive her.

CARMELA: No use looking for explanations, Manuca. It was the stranger's spell.

MANUCA: That's ignorant talk.

ANTONIO: That's what I say. Talk of fools.

CARMELA: Don't try to tell me the three didn't die of love—
  unrequited love!

MANUCA: Who knows?

CARMELA: Everybody knows that those who die of love suffer
  the worst. How do you explain the wailing in the lake?

GUMERCINDA: Yea, that's true. Wailing and the ringing of
  bells.

MANUCA: It's nothing but the wind in the rushes.

CARMELA: Don't be so stubborn, Manuca. You know everybody is saying so. When the brook is noisy, there's always
  stones. And tell me, weren't all three of the women in love
  with him?

MANUCA: Yes, they were, all right.

CARMELA: Well, then?

MANUCA: Come up closer to the brazier, Antonio. You're dozing over there.

CARMELA: Are you finally convinced? Didn't all three of them
  die of love? (*The music of the original theme begins, the
  legend music, and gradually gets louder.*)

MANUCA: If everybody says so—(*Sighs.*) I guess it must be.

CARMELA: But now that the legend has started . . .

ANTONIO: That's true. It has started to spread! And nobody
  will be able to stop it.

The music grows louder as The Curtain Falls.

W.K.J.

JOSÉ JOAQUÍN GAMBOA
1878–1931   Mexico

Gamboa worked hard for a national Mexican theater.
With the Lozano García brothers, he sponsored a
theatrical revival in 1925, for which he wrote this farce,
Un cuento viejo ("An Old Yarn"), published complete. It represents, perhaps, a sort of moral holiday in
a career noted more for a sober attitude toward life.

He was well acquainted with European drama, as a result of a trip abroad while young. Then he returned to Mexico and, discarding his law career, became a literary man, starting first with a musical comedy, and then writing plays about social problems, marked by an unusual psychological analysis.

Mysticism and Symbolism came into his work toward the end, and his greatest play *El caballero, la muerte y el diablo* ("The Gentleman, Death, and the Devil") was performed just three weeks before his death.

AN OLD YARN

Characters

Doña Engracia, a widow
Clotilde, a younger widow
Don Periquito
Don Jacinto Luna
Pancho Arteaga
Pipirina
Rogelio, her sweetheart
A servant
The corpse of Aniceto Ortiz

Scene: Drawing room of Don Aniceto Ortiz who has been dead for some hours and is lying in state on a cot of planks. Candles stand on each side of it. The furniture is cheap, and gaudy pictures adorn the walls, several of bullfights. There is a portrait of the bullfighter Gaona under banderillas. Funeral wreathes with cloth flowers. The whole appearance is typical of a lower-class Mexican home.

As the curtain rises, doña Engracia, the widow, is uttering cries of grief which, if they had not been that, might have been mistaken for locomotive whistles.

ENGRACIA: Oh, Oh!
PERIQUITO: Calm yourself, Engracia. Don't take it so hard.

ENGRACIA: Oh, dear!

CLOTILDE: Don't grieve so! At least you had him quite a while. You see, my husband left me when he was still so young.

ENGRACIA: There's no one can fill this gap. No one. I'll never find another.

CLOTILDE: Neither will I.

ENGRACIA: You still have hope. You're still young. Oh, Oh!

JACINTO (*talking across the table with Pancho*): Heavens, how she takes on! Nobody in the neighborhood can get a wink of sleep. What a dreadful old woman!

PANCHO: After the life she led him, now he can rest.

ROGELIO (*trying to take Pipirina's hand*): Darling, you don't pay any attention to me.

PIPIRINA: Be quiet or they'll see us.

ROGELIO: But I love you.

PIPIRINA: Well, keep it to yourself.

ROGELIO: Aren't you going to the Resendi's dance tomorrow?

PIPIRINA: A wake is no place to talk about dancing.

ROGELIO: For heaven's sake! There's nothing we can do for that corpse! We came here to see each other. (*Glances roguishly at her.*)

PIPIRINA: We should have gone to the movies.

ROGELIO: But your mother thought—

PIPIRINA: My mother hasn't missed a wake since my father died.

ENGRACIA: Oh, dear! Oh, O-o-o-oh me!

PERIQUITO: Don't feel so bad about it, Engracita.

ENGRACIA: He was so good, so pious, so noble!

JACINTO (*to Pancho*): Is it any wonder there are cynics?

PANCHO: Well, you look sad, I must say!

JACINTO: Why should I? The War Office has promised me his job. Of course I stood next in line on the list. But I always did like him.

PANCHO: Now you'll like him more than ever.

JACINTO: Man, don't be flippant!

PERIQUITO (*to Engracia*): Tell me, what did your husband die of?

ENGRACIA: Of high blood pressure. He'd been ailing.

JACINTO: Ailing? Blood pressure! In a game of dominoes his opponent cheated him and he got so mad—

PANCHO: He had liver trouble.

JACINTO: Cirrhosis hepatica.

PANCHO: Hepa—what?

JACINTO: That means "liver."

ENGRACIA: After the bullfighter Gaona died, my Aniceto didn't raise his head. That man was his idol. And the tragedy of Esperanza Iris put the finishing touches. She was his idol.

PERIQUITO: He was a true Mexican. So patriotic!

ENGRACIA: He never let anyone run down Mexico. Once he almost killed an Englishman who didn't like chili sauce on turkey and said it showed that Mexicans didn't know good food and were uncivilized and weren't human. Just like that!

CLOTILDE: He was very quick-tempered, I'll agree, especially when anything disgusted him.

ENGRACIA: Yes, he was very Mexican. That's what I always say. Oh, O-o-oh!

JACINTO: Very Mexican! Every morning when he came into the War Office, he was tight.

ENGRACIA: But even in his drinking he was Mexican. He wouldn't touch anything but national drinks.

JACINTO: You mean like Berreteaga Rum.

PANCHO: Or Cuervo Brand.

JACINTO: Hush!

PANCHO: Sh! (*Each silences the other. Enter the servant.*)

SERVANT: Coffee is served.

JACINTO: Come on.

PANCHO: I didn't think they were planning to serve any refreshments here.

ENGRACIA: I'll stay here, close to him . . . close to him.

PERIQUITO: No, you must take something to keep up your strength.

CLOTILDE: That's right, Engracia, dear.

JACINTO: Just because he's gone to a better life, that's no reason you should fail to look after your own well-being.

ENGRACIA: Who needs me now?

CLOTILDE: Don't take it so hard. Come on. Let's get something to eat. (*Tries to lift her.*) You must eat, you know.

PERIQUITO: Well, somebody must start. We must realize that he isn't here to lead the way.

CLOTILDE: Don't speak of that, for goodness' sake!

PERIQUITO: He was always first to the table! But we must all die sometime.

CLOTILDE: You go first, Engracia.

ENGRACIA: Just for the sake of being with you. He was so good, so pious! Oh, me!

(*All exit solemnly but hungrily to the dining room. The stage remains empty for a moment, then cautiously through the door from the patio come Rogelio and Pipirina.*)

ROGELIO: Sh!

PIPIRINA: Hush!

ROGELIO: They didn't see us. . . . Pipirina. . . .

PIPIRINA: I don't believe so. The patio is dark.

ROGELIO: They're digging into the biscuits and the tamales.

PIPIRINA: To give them strength for the wake. And there were two bottles of Habanero rum. Imagine that!

ROGELIO: Are you going to kiss me?

PIPIRINA: Suppose the dead man sees us.

ROGELIO: Heavens, don't be superstitious!

PIPIRINA (*waiting for the kiss*): Well—

ROGELIO (*kissing her*): Darling Pipirina!

PIPIRINA: My Rogelio!

(*The dead man opens an eye.*)

ROGELIO: Another kiss!

PIPIRINA: Well,—Just one more.

ROGELIO: That's all. (*They kiss.*) Want another?

PIPIRINA: No, not now. Somebody might come.

ROGELIO: Nonsense! Everybody's busy. (*Pantomimes eating and drinking.*) That was a delicious kiss.

PIPIRINA: Well, maybe just one more.

(*They embrace for a long while. The dead man opens his eyes and sees them. They are seated close together on the sofa. Rogelio caresses her arms, her legs.*)

PIPIRINA: Listen, we aren't at the movies!

ROGELIO: No, we're in heaven. (*They caress.*) You're lovely!

PIPIRINA: Did you say you were learning to play the banjo?

ROGELIO: Um hum! How about another kiss?

PIPIRINA: This will be the last.

ROGELIO: The very last. Wonderful! (*Their kiss lasts still longer.*)

(*The dead man sits up and looks at them. They never see him.*)

PIPIRINA: Oh, when can we get married?

ROGELIO: Just as soon as I finish learning to play the banjo. I'm going to get in a jazz band—

PIPIRINA: Jazz?

ROGELIO: Yes, and I'll make lots of money.

PIPIRINA: And you'll love me a great deal?

ROGELIO: You bet!

PIPIRINA: As much as now?

ROGELIO: More, much more. Like this—

(*This petting is becoming too much for the dead man. He sits up, looks first with one eye, then with two, until he can't stand it any more. He gets out of the coffin, takes a couple of candles, and says to the audience:*)

DEAD MAN: I don't call this a wake. I'm going to move somewhere else, out to the patio.

(*With the glide of a ghost, he goes to the patio. The lovers are oblivious to anything on earth or beyond the grave.*)

CURTAIN

W.K.J.

FRANCISCO NAVARRO
1902–   Mexico

The diplomat and playwright Navarro has had an exciting career. After representing his country in four
New World posts, he spent two years in the Embassy
in Berlin, through eighty-five R.A.F. bombings, only
to be interned when his country declared war on the
Axis. *Alemania por dentro* ("Inside Germany"), his
book about his experiences, broke records with three
editions in five months.

As a dramatist, Navarro's beautifully written three-
act *La muerte en el bosque* ("Death in the Woods"),
about the suicide of Judas following his betrayal of
Jesus, was premiered in Madrid by Margarita Xirgú,
and later performed in Swedish while he was Ambassador in Stockholm. *La crepúscula* ("Twilight") was first
performed at the Schiller Theater, Berlin. His other
plays range from a fantasy in Mars in 2500 A.D. to a
naturalistic trilogy (1935) about Mexico: La *ciudad*,
El mar, and *La montaña*. The last half of *La ciudad* is
here translated. In the omitted beginning, patrons of
Altagracia's house of prostitution drink and talk.

THE CITY

*Scene: A house of prostitution in a suburb of Mexico's
capital. A cheap phonograph grinds out a tango. Some easy
chairs and old straight chairs back up against the wall. In
the center, a table with empty beer bottles. Isabel, Natalie,
and their two clients are playing poker, while Altagracia,
the madam, a woman about fifty, fat and crude-looking,
watches the scene, leaning on the tiny phonograph table.
The men are wearing grease-stained overalls and oilcloth
caps. Natalie, the younger of the girls, has a pale, weary-*

looking face, revealing traces of all sorts of vices through its
make-up. She has chestnut, almost tawny hair, and passion-
ate, brilliant, light-brown eyes. With a bored attitude she
puffs on a cigarette.

(*At the beginning Natalie gets bored and refuses to remain*
with Chueco unless he buys her something besides beer.
She calls him a cheap skate and gets knocked down. When
she defies him, he likes her spirit and buys her the cognac.
He orders the other clients to leave and Chueco and Natalie
are alone. Then follows the translated part.)

POLILLA: All right, old lady, we'll blow, and right now. So
long, you ungrateful people. So you don't want our company.
So we bore you. O.K. We're mules, and we're being driven
away. (*He puts his arm around Isabel and the couple stag-*
gers out the door.)

NATALIE: Why did you do that?

CHUECO: I wanted to be alone with you. I'm fed up with those
two drunks. I don't know whether I'm drunk, too, but I
want to see your eyes and nothing else. I can't forget the
way you looked while you were singing. You made me think
of love and marriage and——

NATALIE: Don't make me laugh!

CHUECO: Haven't you ever been in love or had an illusion that
for a minute or two took you out of the kind of life you
lead?

NATALIE: No, and I don't want one, either.

CHUECO: Look! I've got plenty of money. I just got paid down
at the railroad and I want to spend my pay envelope on you.

NATALIE: That's all right at night, but it's getting daylight. It's
almost five o'clock.

CHUECO: It must be the alcohol that's made me like this, half
sentimental, half—I don't know what. Maybe it's this time
of day. Don't you like this dawn hour a lot?

NATALIE: All hours are the same to me. It's the company that
matters.

CHUECO: When my train is rushing at full speed into the dawn and it's just beginning to get light, with the chill that dawn brings, I feel like somebody else. Many times at dawn I've dreamed about being with a woman like you.

NATALIE: You're easily satisfied!

CHUECO: Don't say that. I've almost—almost fallen in love with you.

NATALIE: Ha-ha-ha! Don't be foolish! No love affairs for me! They bring too many complications.

CHUECO: Not even my love?

NATALIE: Don't talk about such things. Love is a luxury that isn't made for women like me. Fall in love with a girl in your home town, a girl who'll give you children and all that goes with them. I'm in this life up to my neck and now there's no remedy. I just go on with it. What I don't like are the complications, jealousies, and boring things like that. How old are you?

CHUECO: Twenty-five.

NATALIE: Uh huh, I thought so.

CHUECO: Well, am I so young?

NATALIE: Yes, because I'm almost as old as you.

CHUECO: Don't you like me, then?

NATALIE: You're not bad, but that's not enough. I like to live in uncertainty. I like surprises, the unexpected. Love is monotonous. (*Change.*) Don't you like gambling? I prefer it to love. It's really got excitement.

CHUECO: I like gambling as much as I like you, and that's plenty.

NATALIE: That's what I'm crazy over. There was one night when I bet everything I had on one card and I ended in the street, but that didn't make any difference. The thrills that I got were priceless.

CHUECO: Since we both like gambling, I'll make you a proposition.

NATALIE: What?

CHUECO: Let's gamble our love on the cards. If I win, you'll come and live with me. If I lose, I'll never see you again.

NATALIE: Man, look! You want me to be frank with you. There's not the slightest thrill in that idea. It would be all the same to me to live with you or stay here. I need something more emotional, more brutal, more definite.

CHUECO: I'll put up all the money I brought here: 150 pesos.

NATALIE: No. Money is all right, but I've won it and I've lost it lots of times. But I've got an idea! Let's stake something that will really count, that will put our nerves on edge and chill us all over. What do you say?

CHUECO: Let's hear your idea.

NATALIE: But you've got to agree first.

CHUECO: That's all right by me. I say O.K. before you tell me.

NATALIE: You may be sorry.

CHUECO: You don't scare me. I'll go as far as you go. You aren't going to leave me behind.

NATALIE: Let's bet our lives.

CHUECO (*after a pause indicating surprise, which rapidly disappears*): You're drunk!

NATALIE: Maybe so, but I know what I'm saying. Do you agree? This will be really thrilling. Can you imagine the sensation of turning up each card. We'd live a thousand years in a moment.

CHUECO: Would you be willing to pay if you lost?

NATALIE: Sure.

CHUECO: O.K. It's O.K. by me.

NATALIE (*taking a pack of cards that is on the table*): If you win, then you kill me: if I win, I collect.

CHUECO: Do you really mean it?

NATALIE: You bet I do.

CHUECO (*after a pause*): Then let's get started. (*He takes a revolver from his hip pocket and lays it on the table.*) Aren't you scared?

NATALIE: Sure! That's why I think this is the most exciting game I ever played.

CHUECO: You have gambler's blood.

NATALIE: The first one who gets an ace wins. You shuffle.

CHUECO (*shuffling*): How I'm going to laugh when I see you whimpering with fear. If you lose, you better believe I'll kill you.

NATALIE: I tell you you don't know me yet. This thrill is worth dying for.

CHUECO: Cut!

NATALIE: Now I deal. (*She lays the cards slowly face up on the table, one in front of Chueco and the next in front of her.*) Ten! King! O deuce! Queen! Another king! (*Pause.*) Wait a minute. My hands are shaking.

CHUECO (*lighting a cigarette*): Want me to deal now?

NATALIE: No. It would change the luck and maybe I'd lose, and be killed.

CHUECO (*taking her hand*): Hadn't we better quit. Remember we're playing for keeps. But we can both quit now. Only from now on, we're not kidding.

NATALIE: Quit, nothing! This is priceless. The one who lives to tell about it will be a hero.

CHUECO (*after a pause*): O.K., go ahead and deal.

NATALIE: Queen! Three! Eight! Another ten! The ace! I win. (*Pause.*)

CHUECO: O.K. You win. There's the revolver. But give me a kiss first. I believe that I'm really in love with you.

NATALIE: Yes, yes. (*They kiss and embrace.*) And I love you much more than I ever did anybody before. You're the first man I've ever really admired, ever loved. (*She kisses him.*) But it takes this test to prove it. If I didn't kill you, I'd despise you.

CHUECO: You've got to go on and collect the bet. That's why I love you. You're no softy. Since I have to die some time anyway, it's better to end everything at the hands of a pretty woman like you than maybe to be flattened out some day between a couple of freight cars. Besides, I know that if you'd lost, you'd have died without a squeal. I don't want you to be better than me in any way. We're spittin' images of one another.

NATALIE: Good-by. You'll always be the only man I ever loved.
For the rest of my life I'll keep you in my heart and you'll
be my only lover.

CHUECO (*releasing himself from her arms and handing her the
revolver*): Here it is. Take it. (*Natalie aims and shoots.
Chueco falls, moves a little, and remains motionless.*)

ALTAGRACIA (*entering*): What's going on? What's happened!
Natalie! (*Natalie remains silent with her eyes fixed on the
dead man.*)

ALTAGRACIA (*grabbing her fiercely by the arm*): You killed him!
You killed him!

(*Enter Polilla, followed by Isabel. At sight of the corpse,
both are speechless.*)

NATALIE: We gambled our lives on a card and he lost. I was
collecting my bet.

W.K.J.

RODOLFO USIGLI
1905–   Mexico

One of the greatest of Latin-American dramatists is
the Mexican diplomat Usigli, who seems fated to create
controversy. His political satire *El gesticulador* was delayed in performance for three years because no one
dared handle it.

Usigli is an experimenter and has written on many
themes, like *Función de despedida* (1951) about an
actress' farewell tour, or the tragic *Niño y la niebla*
that had a run of 450 performances in 1950. With no
admirable character, it deals with the transfer of family
traits and hereditary insanity. *Juno es una muchacha*
(1952) about a feminine Jekyll and Hyde who is at
times a prostitute, had a similar long run. Usigli also
wrote an excellent history of Mexico's theater.

One of Usigli's best, however, is his "anti-historic"
Corona de sombra (1947), about the unfortunate Em-

peror Maximilian and Carlotta. Bernard Shaw gave it
high praise. Modern technique is used with a divided
stage and the use of flashbacks. The scene in which
Maximilian is executed is here translated.

CROWN OF SHADOWS

Act III, Scene 3

(*Maximilian's cell in the Capuchin Convent, in Queré-
taro. Maximilian appears seated before a desk; he finishes
writing. He rises and casts a glance beyond the small window of his cell and smiles mysteriously and sadly. Soon he
wistfully folds his letters. A guard opens the door of the cell
and lets Miramón enter.*)

MAXIMILIAN (*smiling*): Good morning, General Miramón.

MIRAMÓN: Good morning, Majesty.

MAXIMILIAN: It's certainly a beautiful dawn. Look at those red
clouds, trimmed with smoke, that give back the sunlight
little by little. I've never seen dawns or twilights like those
of the Mexican sky. Have you written to your wife and your
children?

MIRAMÓN: Yes, Sire, and Mejía is doing the same.

MAXIMILIAN: Poor Mejía, he has suffered so much on my account. At least, you can be sure that your letters will be
received. I don't know whether the Empress will ever be
able to read mine or not. The last news I had made me fear
for her sanity more than ever. (*He draws near to Miramón.*)
I must confess something to you. (*The guard opens the
door again. Mejía enters very dejectedly.*) You're just in
time, General Mejía. I want the two of you to hear this
letter. I don't know why, but I couldn't resist the temptation to write to my son.

MIRAMÓN AND MEJÍA: Sire! Sire!

MAXIMILIAN: No, to the son that I never had. (*He takes a*

sheet of paper from the table.) The fantasy of an amateur
poet. What difference does it make? All those who are going to die are granted one last wish. (*He unfolds the letter.*)
Do you want to smoke? (*He offers them his cigar box,
Mejía supplies a light, and the three men ritualistically light
their cigars.*) I'll miss the Mexican tobacco.

MEJÍA (*despairingly*): Sire!

MAXIMILIAN: Do you want me to read you my letter? It's very
brief: "My son, I am going to die for Mexico. To die is
seldom sweet; the man is absurd who fears death, instead
of fearing life, which is the fabricator of death. I have
traveled over all the seas and many times I thought it would
be perfect to submerge myself in any one of them, and
there find an end. But now I know that the sea resembles
life too much, and that her only mission is to carry men to
land, just as the mission of life is to carry man to death.
Now I know that man should always return to the land,
and I know that it is sweet to die for Mexico, because in a
land like Mexico no blood is sterile. I write to you only to
tell you this, and to tell you to think carefully about your
death, as I have tried to be careful about mine, so that your
death may be the very summit of your love, and the corona-
tion of your life."
That's all. The letter of a suicide!

MEJÍA: Majesty! (*There are tears in his voice.*)

MAXIMILIAN (*burning the letter and watching it being consumed*): Come, Mejía, Mejía, my friend! It's the last fancy
of my imagination. There's no need to grieve so.

MIRAMÓN: I never thought, Sire, that Your Majesty's love for
Mexico was so great.

MAXIMILIAN: Men little know each other in life, General
Miramón. We have carried our friendship to a rare extreme; for that reason we know each other better. Inci-
dentally, I must beg your pardon.

MIRAMÓN: My pardon, Sire?

MAXIMILIAN: I haven't kept you at my side all the time, as I
should have done.

MIRAMÓN: Then pardon me, Sire, for having opposed the abdication.

MAXIMILIAN: I can never thank you enough for that.

MEJÍA: It isn't just, Sire. It isn't just! You shouldn't die.

MAXIMILIAN: We all must die, General Mejía; one day is just like another. But see what a morning this is! See what a great privilege it is to die here!

MEJÍA: I don't care if I die, Majesty, I'm an Indian and I am a soldier, and I never took part in a battle without thinking that it would turn out as God wished. The only thing I ever asked Him was that I might not be killed in my sleep or treacherously. But you ought not to die. There are so many Indians here, so many traitors, so many bad people, but there are no others like you.

MIRAMÓN: The *republicanos* think that we're the traitors, General Mejía.

MEJÍA: I've thought of that. I've thought about it a thousand times! I know that it's not true.

MIRAMÓN: Perhaps we'll be a blemish on the pages of history, but the sincerity of our convictions will be proved by our doing what we are about to do.

MEJÍA: But not the Emperor! The Emperor *cannot* die.

MAXIMILIAN: Calm yourself, Thomas—permit me to call you that—and let me tell you what I see so clearly now. You told me one day of your dream of the pyramid, General Miramón, and that explains for me your whole attitude. You, Thomas, see in me, in my blood of ancient Europe, in my blond beard, in my white skin, something that you want for Mexico. I understand you. You don't want the native to disappear, but neither do you want him to be the only one in this land, because of a cosmic desire, because of an ambition that a land so large and beautiful as this may grow to contain one day all that the world possesses of goodness and of variety. When I think of the mad scramble that these three years of Empire have been, I feel lost before a terrible and shapeless riddle. Sometimes death is the only thing that gives things their real form.

MIRAMÓN: I have always admired you, Majesty, but never as much as now.

MAXIMILIAN: Call me Maximilian, my beloved Miguel. In the House of Austria there's an old funeral tradition. When an emperor dies, they knock three times at the door of the church. From inside, a cardinal asks who it is. They reply: "The Emperor our lord," and the cardinal answers: "I know him not." They knock again and the cardinal again asks who calls; they give the family names and titles of the deceased and the cardinal responds; "I know not who he is." A third time they knock from outside. A third time the cardinal asks. The voice from outside says, "A sinner, our brother," and gives the Christian name of the dead man. Then the door is opened to him. He who is going to die now is a sinner, your brother Maximilian.

MIRAMÓN: Maximilian, it tortures me to think what is going to become of Mexico. To kill you is a great political error, in addition to being a crime.

MAXIMILIAN: I am calm. It would have pleased me to live and govern in my way, and if we had been able to conquer Juárez, I wouldn't have had him shot. I would have saved him from the hate of Mexicans like Marquez and others, in order not to destroy the part of Mexico that he represents.

MEJÍA: Your valor leaves me speechless, Sire—Maximilian.

MAXIMILIAN: My valor? All my life I have been a weak man with strong ideas. The flame within me that burned and kept alive my spirit and my love and my desire for kindliness was my Carlotta. Now I am afraid.

MIRAMÓN: Afraid of what, Sire?

MAXIMILIAN: Afraid that my death will not have the value that I attribute to it in my consuming desire to dream. If my death should serve for nothing, it would be a terrifying destiny.

MEJÍA: No, Mexico loves you; but the rabble are performing dogs that dance to any tune that is played for them.

MAXIMILIAN: God grant it! A little love would suit me well. I am calm except on two points: I'm worried about what will happen to my Carlotta, and it pains me not to be able to understand what motivated López.

MIRAMÓN: That Tlaxcalan Indian!

MEJÍA: That Judas!

MAXIMILIAN: Don't say that word, Miguel, nor you the other word, Thomas. The Tlaxcalans helped Cortes achieve the first integration that Mexico needed. And to call him Judas is pure conceit. I am not Christ.

MEJÍA: They are crucifying you, Maximilian, crucifying you between those two traitors.

MAXIMILIAN: It would be too vain, Thomas, to think that our names will live so long and will resound in the world from century to century. No. Man sometimes dies like Christ, because man is made in the image of God. But one must be humble. (*Outside, a call to attention can be heard, and a roll of drums. The door is opened and the Captain enters.*)

CAPTAIN: Please follow me.

MAXIMILIAN: We are at your orders, Captain. May I put these letters in your hands? (*The Captain takes them in silence.*) Thank you. Go ahead, Miguel; go ahead, Thomas. I'll follow you. (*When Miramón is about to leave, Maximilian speaks again.*) Miguel . . . (*Miramón turns.*) Pride . . . that's it . . . yes, that's it . . . Miguel López betrayed us because of pride, because of vanity. God grant that this defect may grow no more in Mexico. (*He makes a friendly gesture. Miramón and Mejía go out. Maximilian remains a second. He looks around.*) Very soon, Carla! Very soon in the forest. (*He goes out. A silence. The light of the sun enters the cell, whose door has remained open.*)

THE VOICE OF CARLOTTA: And then?

THE VOICE OF MAXIMILIAN (*far away, but distinct*): Take the center, General Miramón. It belongs to you. Soldiers of Mexico! I die without malice toward you, who are going to fulfill your duties. I die with my conscience at ease, because it was not simple ambition for power that brought me here, nor does the shadow of a single deliberate crime weigh upon me. In my worst moments, I respected and made others respect the integrity of Mexico. Permit me to give you a memento. This ring for you, Captain. This watch, Sergeant; for you, valiant soldiers of Mexico, this money with the short-lived effigy of Maximilian upon it. (*Pause*) No. No, we will not have our eyes blindfolded. To die for Mexico is not to betray it. Permit me to hold my beard aside. Aim well at the chest, I beg you. Good-by, Miguel! Good-by, Thomas!

THE VOICE OF THE CAPTAIN: Attention! Ready! Aim! Fire!

(A *discharge of rifles*)
THE VOICE OF MAXIMILIAN: God!

At *the same time* . . .

(*Black out*)

David A. Flory

JOSÉ ANTONIO RAMOS
1885–1946   Cuba

The visit of an Italian actor to Cuba in 1906 got Dr. Ramos interested in playwriting and he produced several plays that were published in Barcelona. He was ambitious for a Cuban national theater, so he wrote and labored for it in the intervals of serving as consul for his country in the United States, Mexico, and Italy. He also studied Ibsen, as was evident in his prize-winning masterpiece, *Tembladera* (1916), called Cuba's closest approach to realism.

Inspired by a short verse of the martyr poet José Martí, about the divisions of a family during Cuba's attempts to secure independence, Ramos wrote *El Traidor* (1915). This translation of it was checked by Dr. Ramos. The play deals with Captain Juan García of the Cuban revolutionary army, whose son was fighting on the side of the Spaniards.

In the first half of the play, the melancholy captain

laments the treachery of his son, and is fighting the more fiercely to make up for it. But his soldiers are surprised and defeated on his old farm, and Captain García is mortally wounded. He tries to figure how to keep the Cuban flag from falling into Spanish hands. Finally digging a hole in the floor of his cabin, he buries it. The translation continues from here.

THE TRAITOR

GARCÍA: Their hands shall not sully the flag. Now I can die calmly, alone, all alone, but in my own cabin, on my own farm, kissing the soil of Cuba. (*His voice fails.*)

(*As he lies there, invisible in the gloom, the Spanish Lieutenant López and two Spanish soldiers enter cautiously, guns ready.*)

LIEUTENANT: Who goes there?

FIRST SPANISH SOLDIER: No one, Lieutenant. There were only those two.

LIEUTENANT: One's always stumbling over them, but now there are two rebels less. However, don't get over-confident, men. You remain here. The cabin will protect us in our attack on the village. When you hear shots, shoot anybody you see. And meantime, beware of traitors to Spain. You know we have Cubans in our ranks, and you can't trust those children of monkeys and buzzards. I'll look around.

THE TWO SPANISH SOLDIERS: Yes, Lieutenant. (*Exit Lieutenant López.*)

FIRST: There's something fishy about those Cubans.

SECOND: You're right. They don't usually go raiding without good reason.

FIRST (*stumbling over the body of the patriot Captain*): Confound it! Hey, look at this!

SECOND: What's up?

FIRST (*kneeling beside the Captain*): There's a man here.

SECOND: Is he dead?

FIRST: I guess so. (*Touches him.*) This is blood!

GARCÍA (*sitting up with great effort*): Finish me off! Here is where I want to die. Kill me!

FIRST: Well, if Lieutenant López finds you, you won't have to ask twice.

SECOND: Where is your company? (*Silence*)

FIRST: Won't you tell us?

GARCÍA: Kill me or let me die quietly. This is my land, my farm, my home. I want to die here.

SECOND: It's a trick. This isn't your house and you aren't alone. If you don't tell us, we'll use this machete on you.

GARCÍA (*summoning up strength to resent the insult*): Your mother is a liar, you Spanish scum! This *is* my house and my land. I left here two years ago and I came back tonight to revisit it. (*He tries to pull out his revolver.*) Even nearly dead, I'll let no man say I lie.

(*First Spaniard falls upon him and disarms him.*)

SECOND (*brandishing his machete*): Get out of my way and let me cut the guts out of that Cuban rebel!

FIRST (*protecting the Captain*): No!

SECOND: Get back.

FIRST: That's cowardly. You can't kill a man like that.

SECOND (*reluctantly sheathing his sword*): Bah! (*Pause*)

GARCÍA: Listen! (*To First Spaniard*) Yes, you! (*Holding out his hand*) This is the first time I've offered my hand to an enemy. I don't care whether I die five minutes early or late. I can't tell you more than that.

FIRST (*shaking his hand*): Don't thank me. He wouldn't have done it. We are Spanish soldiers, not murderers. If some of our men sometimes forget, the worse for them!

GARCÍA: Listen. I have a favor to ask which you can't very well refuse.

FIRST: What is it?

GARCÍA: A favor I beg you in the name of your father or your mother, or the children which you left behind you in Spain. I don't consider you a traitor because you fight on the side of your people.

FIRST: Well, what is your request?

GARCÍA: I want to be buried right here, in my own farm.

FIRST: But that——

GARCÍA: I—can't—talk—more. I'm dying.

FIRST: A soldier couldn't do what you ask.

SECOND: See here! Where are you wounded?

GARCÍA (*pointing to the spade*): Make—grave—right—here.

SECOND: Why, we're going to take you to town where you'll be cured, old fellow.

GARCÍA (*calling upon all his strength*): No! I want to die and be buried here. I beg as a Christian. It is a sacred request. I want you to bury me right here. I'm dying.

SECOND: What's your name?

GARCÍA: I won't tell you that. I'm nobody, nothing! My hope is to die and disappear without letting anybody know I'm buried here.

FIRST: Why?

SECOND: Yes, why? Tell me that. And if you don't speak up, we'll carry you to the village.

FIRST: Anyway, tell us your name, so we can at least know that.

GARCÍA (*as though to himself*): I don't want *him* ever to know where I'm buried.

SECOND: If this is where you live, we can easily find out who you are.

FIRST: Wait! (*To Captain*) Who're you talking about? Who don't you want to know? Tell me.

GARCÍA: I am father of a traitor. (*Silence*) That's what I am. That's the story.

FIRST: What traitor?

GARCÍA: That's the only name I use for him: Traitor. I gave him life. Now I curse him. Ask me nothing beyond that.

SECOND: Who is he? What's his name?

GARCÍA: Traitor. He has no other name.

SECOND: The man is stubborn.

GARCÍA: Come on. Finish me off. Stab me. Shoot me. My mind's anguish is worse than any kind of death.

SECOND: What'll we do?

FIRST (*starting to dig*): Do what he asks?

SECOND: But suppose he doesn't die?

FIRST: Look how weak he is.

SECOND: But after all, perhaps——

FIRST: What you promise to a dying man, you do.

SECOND: I didn't promise him anything.

FIRST: Because you have no sympathy; but just because I'm a Spaniard, I did.

SECOND: We might get into a lot of trouble.

FIRST: Look! What could be easier? The earth is soft, and before the Lieutenant gets back, it'll be all done.

SECOND (*picking up the spade*): In the ditch beside the road there are four of our men. They'd give us away.

FIRST: Forget them. This man was brave and honorable. I fight these Cubans but I don't hate them. After all, they're fighting to get freedom just as we fought the French.

SECOND: Better not let the Lieutenant hear you!

FIRST: That Spaniard might as well be a Russian. A murderer. That's what he is, a murderer!

SECOND (*approaching the Captain*): Wait! It looks to me as though he's dead.

FIRST (*taking off his hat*): May he rest in peace!

SECOND (*also removing hat*): He's been shot to pieces.

FIRST: I wonder if this grave will do.

SECOND (*lifting the body of the Captain*): Here, help me! If the vultures don't get him, everything will be all right. It would take an hour to make a grave of any depth.

FIRST: Let's leave him his machete. I'll throw his revolver away.

SECOND: Come on. There's no time to lose.

FIRST: His head's still showing.

SECOND: Then pile dirt over it. Probably no one will come around for several days.

FIRST: He said he just got here tonight.

SECOND: Then the rebels must be fairly near.

FIRST: The commander ought to know about that. Tomorrow or the next day, we're likely to have a battle with them.

SECOND: Listen! Footsteps! Don't you hear a man coming?

FIRST: Yes, hurry! We don't want to be found.

SECOND: If the moon comes out or dawn arrives while we're around here, we're done for.

FIRST: No chance of a moon. Look at those storm clouds.

SECOND: That black cloud looks as though it's coming right down to earth.

FIRST: There! Now he's fixed. Give me my gun.

SECOND: Let's scout around before we leave.

FIRST: Our conscience is clear. The poor fellow will rest in his own land. He has his last wish. (*Mournfully*) I wonder if we'll be that lucky.

(*Enter a Stranger who stops at sight of the soldiers.*)

SECOND (*raising his gun*): Halt! Who goes there?

FIRST (*imitating him*): Halt! (*The second takes aim.*)

STRANGER (*identifying himself in a quiet voice*): Camajuaní Company.

SECOND: It's about time you identified yourself. That's what you've got a tongue for.

FIRST (*to the other soldier*): Look! He's a Cuban.

SECOND: I don't understand what's going on around here. Remember the Lieutenant's warning. (*To Stranger*) Listen! What are you doing here? (*Silence*) Hey! Are you deaf or crazy? What are you doing here?

STRANGER: Nothing. Looking around.

SECOND: What is there to see? (*Louder*) I asked you what there is around here that you don't have where you live.

STRANGER: Nothing.

FIRST: Then why are you here?

STRANGER (*coming forward*): Who are you to order me around?

SECOND: You make us think there is something crooked going on, and when we see any suspicious· movements . . .

STRANGER (*as though to himself*): Suspicion, always suspicion, wherever I go.

FIRST: Who are you talking to?

STRANGER: Nobody. (*Angrily*) I have good reasons for coming here and that's why I came.

FIRST: And I have my reasons for saying it's likely to get you into trouble.

SECOND: It would take just a couple of shots. (*Seeing the Stranger's look of unconcern*) Come on, now! Tell us why you came here or I'll put a bullet through your head.

(*As the Stranger's hand moves toward his revolver, the First Soldier leaps on him and disarms him. The Second Soldier raises his gun.*)

STRANGER: Let me alone. I'm doing no harm.

FIRST: You're under arrest. You can do your explaining to the officials.

SECOND: Give me his gun. Now let's see. So you have your reasons. Well, you'd better not move.

STRANGER: Yes, my reasons. I belong on this farm. It was my home. I was born here. The thought of it and of my mother drew me here. But I have no call to explain to anybody. (*The soldiers release him and step away, with horror on their faces.*) Why do you look at me? What's there about me to make you stare like that?

FIRST: Look! I saw— Did you see—?

STRANGER: What was it?

FIRST (*backing farther away*): Nothing.

(*Still staring in horror and disgust at the traitor, both soldiers retreat slowly and in silence. Exeunt the soldiers.*)

STRANGER (*alone*): Why did they do that? What do they see in my face? (*He touches his face.*) Their look frightened me. (*Behind him the buried Captain slowly rears up.*) Why did they rush away from me? (*Shouting after them.*) Hey, why did you run away? Hey! (*The Captain, like a ghost, stands illuminated by a flash of lightning. The Stranger sees him.*)

No! It's not true! I don't believe in ghosts. (*Another flash.
The Stranger shrieks in terror. The Captain strikes him full
in the face.*)

GARCÍA: Traitor!
(*The traitor falls dead. A loud clap of thunder follows. The
wind howls terrifyingly. The Captain falls, and pulls toward
the grave the body of the traitor.*)

W.K.J.

JOSÉ MARÍA RIVAROLA MATTO
1917–   Paraguay

One of the increasing number of authors contributing
to Paraguay's theatrical renascence is a lawyer and
novelist, Rivarola Matto. *El fin de Chipi González*,
which he calls "A modern miracle play," was written
and performed in 1954. It combines fantasy with realism in its excellent picture of Paraguayan rural life. It
deals with a star football player whose destiny is fore-
seen by a devil. Doctor Rivarola later wrote the metaphysical *Coffin for a Money Lender*, and the two-act
religious *Sectarian*. None has been published.

Among the characters in the first scene of *The End
of Chipi González*, part of which is translated here, are:

> Saul, an angel
> Mom, a devil
> Luis Benítez, a rich citizen
> Chipi
> Pedro, his father
> Conché, his mother
> Lola, a girl looking for a husband

THE END OF CHIPI GONZÁLEZ

Act I. Scene 1. Morning

As the curtain rises, the stage is dark. A spotlight casts its light on the drops that represent the firmament. The ray of light focuses on a cloud. Saul slowly enters into its radius. Within the cloud are lights illuminating the actors from below, leaving the lower part of the stage in darkness. The spotlight is extinguished as the cloud illumination gets bright.

Saul is an angel, as beautiful and pure as the face of the actor and make-up permit. Blond hair falls over his shoulders. He wears a white robe caught at the waist by a white cord. He has no wings because that would involve theological argument, but on his head rests a golden halo, something allowed any aspirant to holiness. He has an air of pathetic boredom; to be immortal and bored are enough to encourage suicide.

SAUL: What horrible boredom! The only justification of eternity is the contemplation of God, to be in the divine presence. But when the Lord permits us to wander through the universe, even an angel feels oppressed by the monotony of these immense spaces where suns spin about and constellations of dead stars emerge and pass, shadowless, like black, coagulated masses of forgetfulness.

(Enter Mom. He stands behind Saul, smiling. He is one of the ordinary sort of devils that wander about by thousands. His hair is short for hygienic reasons and to keep cool. He wears two blunt horns coquetishly planted among his curls. He also wears a tunic, because he has discovered it is a comfortable garment. But it is gray, so as not to show dirt. In his country, water is scarce and laundry prices are high.)

SAUL: Sometimes I'm a bit envious of my brothers who in the Age of Genesis could descend to earth and love the fair daughters of man. It was an abasement, undoubtedly, but an angel could purify himself later, and so could better understand the worth of eternal glory.

MOM: You are ill, Saul! You need problems.

SAUL (*without surprise*): Oh, it's you, Mom? Cure my boredom with some ingenious temptation, won't you?

MOM: So that's the trouble? (*Sadly*) I'm sorry I can't help you. I'm only a bureaucrat in the Public Administration of Hell. I've even lost the last traces of my old wings. My time is spent making out lists. The same dull work for centuries! (*Sighs*) I'm not a devil any longer; I'm hardly a poor devil.

SAUL: Where I live, we have no bureaucracy.

MOM: I know. On account of the few souls you get, you've got room to let them wander wherever they want, through the valleys, villages, and flowery fields. An enchanting idyll! But we get so many souls that we have a terrific problem of organization.

SAUL: Well, why don't you cut down on your devices to tempt mortals?

MOM: Don't make me laugh! Centuries ago we gave up tempting mortals. All of us authentic devils live like slaves just writing regulations, finding places for the crowds, stopping the fights, trying to change the habits of the damned souls, to make them submissive and orderly, so they can all live together in Hell. (*He shrugs his shoulders.*) Nowadays, men tempt themselves and condemn themselves, but they have a savage pride. They are sure they can transform and master the whole of creation. That's what brings them in hordes to our region.

SAUL: Wouldn't you like to enjoy yourself watching them a little while at close range?

MOM (*shrugging his shoulders to indicate indifference*): All right, I haven't anything else to do. It's my vacation, you know.

SAUL: Well, God grant it relieves my boredom. I'll make an effort and enter into Time.

(*The light in the cloud is extinguished. The stage is illuminated. On the spectator's right is a small farm house with an open porch in the front, with coarse curtains at the side to keep out the rain. In the rear is the wall of the farm house, with a practical door. The backdrop allows one to go behind the house. It has a painted tree under which are scattered tools, wheels, tires, etc. To the left is evidence of vegetation with the horizon indicated, above which is suspended the cloud.*

From the beams of the porch hang tobacco leaves to dry, clusters of corn, and tools. A kettle and stove under the roof. Outside, a cot covered with leather hide under a mosquito netting framework. Several rustic benches and some home-made chairs of tree branches.)

LUIS (*loudly*): Good morning! Where's my old friend?

PEDRO (*from behind the house*): Is that you, Luis? Come in. Sit down. I'll be with you in a minute!

LUIS (*sitting*): What are you doing, Old Man?

(*Enter Pedro, right, from behind the house. He is about fifty, with white hair, but still vigorous. He is barefoot with his cotton trousers turned up, halfway to his knees. Wears a coarse straw hat with chin strap, and old-fashioned oval spectacles, with silver frames.*)

PEDRO: I was fixing the eaves. When I went looking for a file, I noticed that the wind last night had blown off some of the thatch.

LUIS: Any harm done?

PEDRO: No. (*Goes to the stove to get the horn cup in which yerba mate is brewed, and some water for the mate. Meanwhile*) The rain was certainly welcome. The plow sinks in this morning, and the earth has a good smell. The new moon came up full of water and it looks like we'll get more rain this month.

LUIS: Yes, I agree with you.

PEDRO: I'm plowing for cotton this year. They say it'll bring good money.

(Enter Conche right, with a bundle on her head. She is a woman of about forty, but looks older. Yet though shrunken, she is strong. Her eyes are red and her skin is stained by the smoke of the oven. Her long hair contains a couple of white pins, but hangs in two scanty pigtails. Her costume is a square-necked shirtwaist and faded skirt hanging to the middle of her shins. She is barefoot, and in the hand that she swings to balance the bundle is a worn machete.)

CONCHE: The manioc is growing fine. It's a pleasure to work the ground today.

PEDRO: What about Chipi? Didn't he come back with you?

CONCHE: He left early for the Kola farm. I haven't seen him since then.

PEDRO: That boy! *(He shakes his head.)* He's completely crazy about soccer football. On Mondays he can't work because he's got to boast about what happened in the game Sunday. And Tuesdays he starts practice again. And Wednesdays——

CONCHE: Heavens, Pedro! It's not as bad as that. Besides it's more better to play football than cards.

LUIS: Much better! But football has its bad points, too. My daughter Marta has a new dress that she won't wear because it has the colors of the "Presidente" team. She wants to sell it. She'll be wanting to wear football shoes to a dance one of these days.

PEDRO: The boy looks on his playing as work, and looks on work—*(hesitating)*—well, as work.

LUIS *(laughs, and then sighs)*: That's true, old man. Our youth, the hope of the country, thinks only of football, while we old folk—we couldn't see a goal post even with glasses.

CONCHE *(angrily)*: Shut up! You two used to go in for lots worse kinds of sport, and you still do! *(Confronting them.)* I know both of you, very well, I do! A fine pair of rascals! *(Pedro and Luis look at each other surprised and with a gesture of "The very idea!" But when Conche turns away, they can't hold back their satisfied snickers.)*

(Enter Chipi and Lola, left, holding hands. Chipi is a young man of twenty, tanned and strong. He wears a football jer-

sey, cotton trousers and sneakers. Lola is a blonde with green-
gold eyes, and light chestnut hair, tied back with a ribbon.
She has a slim, graceful body with the daring coquetry of
country girls who lack self-possession. A printed skirt and
tight white shirtwaist that accentuates her bust. She wears
hemp-soled shoes.)

CHIPI (*with straw hat in his hand*): Good morning, father.
(*He seeks a blessing.*)

LOLA: Good morning. (*Luis answers her. The others are listen-*
ing to the conversation between Chipi and his father.)

PEDRO (*nods at Lola, then raises his hand and repeats the bless-*
ing formula between his teeth): God bless you! (*Then with-*
out pause and with evident ill humor) Where were you all
morning?

CHIPI: I went looking for the ox that was missing when I got
up, on account of last night's storm.

PEDRO (*ironically*): I suppose the wind blew him far away.

CHIPI: Well, I went as far as the irrigation ditch and then in
the distance I saw some animals. I went to look, but he
wasn't among them. When I got back, I saw him beside the
road, near a haystack. I must have gone past without seeing
him.

(*The lights go out on the lower stage and there is illumina-*
tion again on the cloud. The action continues below in the
darkness till the people blend with the deep shadows and
disappear.)

MOM: Not much action in this spectacle, Saul.

SAUL: Don't worry! This is no backwater region. Things will
start moving.

MOM (*with bad humor*): I suppose so, because this fellow they
call Cipriano González, alias Chipi, is going to end up in
Hell.

SAUL (*astonished*): How can you know that Chipi will go to
Hell if you devils can't foresee the future? Don't you have
to let things develop till time for the punishment?

MOM: It's true we can't see into the future, but the vast number of lost souls, the lack of capacity of our plant, and the urgent need for expansion have forced us to inaugurate a system of technical studies to forecast the number of souls that we shall receive in any given period.

SAUL: And your technical studies can predict the destiny of each individual?

MOM: With remarkable accuracy. Our Statistical Institute of Probabilities is so scientifically organized that when a soul comes into the world, from an investigation of its genetic antecedents, with data on its education and information on its surroundings, we can put together everything into a final formula when it reaches puberty, and we can tell whether to heat up the furnace, or expect it to go elsewhere.

SAUL: Diabolical! Diabolical! I'd never have thought—! So Chipi González is damned?

MOM: He's on our list, and I can see from here the location of the furnace planned for him.

SAUL: What a pity! Poor damned Chipi González! Do you know, I've got a kindly feeling for him.

W.K.J.

RENÉ MARQUÉS
1919–   Puerto Rico

René Marqués, originally a short-story writer, came to the United States to study drama, and in 1950 wrote his *Sun and the Macdonalds*, about mixed blood in this country. More important was *La Carreta* ("The Cart") (1952) about three generations of a Puerto Rican family trying to break its bonds to the soil and immigrate to the United States. It won acclaim as Puerto Rico's greatest play.

Five plays later, *Purificación en la Calle del Cristo*, the success of the 1958 Festival of Puerto Rican Drama, established Marqués as one of the great dramatists of the hemisphere. It is a study of the decline of an old Spanish family in Puerto Rico, through inability to conform to changing conditions. Inés Bukhart de Sandoval ended the engagement of her sister Hortense by revealing the infidelity of her sweetheart. She feels the need now of making amends. She also has had to look after the other sister, lame Emilia. These three elderly characters tell the story by flashbacks to incidents forty and fifty years earlier.

The present scene occurs near the end of the final act. Hortense has died of cancer and they are planning to bury her.

THE HOUSE OF THE SETTING SUN

(Inés goes to the piano and leans on it. She notices the candelabra on the piano and replaces it on the table. Emilia makes a childlike gesture of protest. Inés takes the lamp back to its place on the piano. Another gesture of protest from Emilia. As she smooths the cover of the piano, she notices that some of the tassels are caught under the lid. She moves the flowers to free the tassels and sees the chest hidden in the piano by Emilia. She takes it out. Emilia jumps up. Inés opens the chest and takes out the copybook of poetry, comes downstage with it, and opens it.)

INÉS *(reading)*: "Only your hand can purify my heart." *(She sees Emilia looking at her frightened.)* Are these your poems, Emilia?

EMILIA *(stands in entreaty)*: Don't take them away from me, Inés!

INÉS *(approaching her slowly, and handing her the open notebook)*: I've never taken anything from you, Emilia. *(Puts the poems into her hands.)* Never! *(She turns away from Emilia.)* And I've never liked your poetry, either. Never! *(Emilia clasps the book to her breast and goes toward the piano.)* I remember all of them. There's something indescribable about them. Something—improper, Emilia.

EMILIA (*protesting*): My poetry is pure.

INÉS (*after a brief pause*): "Your limping foot paused on one word: *amor*."

EMILIA (*correcting her, offended*): "Your fawnlike foot," Inés.

INÉS: Yes, that's the one I mean. If you had written "Your limping foot," it would be something I could understand as yours. But "fawnlike foot," that's almost obscene, coming from you.

EMILIA (*still clutching her book and finally returning it to the piano*): It's no use discussing it with you. You never understood poetry.

INÉS: You're very wrong. I understand a lot about poetry. The poetry of the long silences, of hunger and misery, and pride. I understand the childish phrases and the words that wound. The poetry of old age and shadow, of the merciless sun and of disguised beggary. The poetry of Hortense's cancer, and the monstrous multiplication of cells in her beloved breast, and the silent pain that consumes. The horrible poetry of time, I understand that, too, Emilia. I had to know about them all so that you could preserve your poetry, Emilia, and Hortense could keep hers.

EMILIA (*amazed*): But Inés! You're speaking—you're speaking in poetry!

INÉS: Poor Emilia! You think that you alone can imprison poetry in your poor verses. But poetry escapes into the horrible life of each of our days. "Only your hand can purify my heart." Did it purify it, Emilia?

EMILIA (*confused*): I—No—I don't know.

INÉS (*passionately*): Does the consuming cancer purify, or the destructive fire? Does love or jealousy or hate purify? Or hell, or even death?

EMILIA (*terrified*): Inés, don't talk like that!

INÉS: Why not, Emilia? I've merely named death. And we've seen death face to face, haven't we? Mama Eugenia. The black nurse. Papa Bukhart, remember? (*The lights fade and a funeral march is heard.*) From the time that Mama Eu-

genia died, he abandoned this house with its fanlights like
the setting suns. And he went to the farm. He drove his
horses through the fields of sugar cane like a madman. And
that day— It was an afternoon in the month of October.
You and I were in this living room. A little later, Hortense
came down the stairs from her room. (*At this moment,
under a purple light, Hortense descends the stairs. She is
twenty-five. She is wearing a severe house dress of violet,
in the style of the turn of the century.*) Suddenly, we heard
frenzied knocks at the mahogany street door. (*Knocking
is heard at the street door downstairs, toward the left. Emilia
and Hortense jump at the sound. Inés, telling the story,
does not move.*) Then the horrible cry of Nurse. (*Hortense,
now at the foot of the stairs, runs to embrace Emilia. Both
look with apprehension toward the left. The normal light
is now gone. Only a bluish reflection illuminates the stage.
Footsteps can be heard in a rhythmic march on the steps
from the outside door to the hallway. The funeral march
sounds louder.*) There are steps on the stairs. They are coming nearer. Now they are in the hallway. Four colored field
hands carrying his body. They approach, moving rhythmi-
cally, with his body on a stretcher. They come into the
room. (*Hortense utters a scream.*)

HORTENSE: Papa Bukhart! (*Through the action of Emilia and
Hortense, the audience should be able to visualize exactly
what Inés is describing. She stands with her back to them,
still recounting the event.*)

INÉS: His body on the shoulders of four faithful black servants.
With his improvised shroud of dust and blood. Now they
are in the middle of the room. They set down the stretcher.
They raise the body. They place it in the old rocker where
he used to sit and dream, the dear, old, Vienna rocker.
(*Hortense and Emilia throw themselves at the foot of the
Vienna rocking chair and embrace it, sobbing.*)

HORTENSE: Papa Bukhart!

INÉS: Here were the three of us, sobbing, gathered as usual in the big room. The three portals with their double doors closed as usual onto the balcony. The three fanlights holding back the rays of the sun, with their colors of blue, yellow, red. And time divided in two. Behind was the world of safety and security. And the present was turning into a future full of disaster. As if death on that day was the sharp edge of a knife that puts a gash in time and lets escape from the wound a chaos of undreamed-of, enduring horrors. That's when I took up my cross. Nurturing your dreams, Emilia; your rancor and your pride, Hortense. (*She moves from downstage nearer to Hortense and Emilia. She raises Hortense and places her head against her own shoulder. She leads her to the stairs.*) Rest your head on the strong, broad shoulder of Inés, of the ugly Inés. How useless our struggle! Though we didn't sell our lands to the barbarians, at the end the barbarians got possession of them. (*She starts up the stairs, still guiding Hortense. The funeral march can still be heard.*) "Never sell your land, daughters." How badly you interpreted Papa Bukhart's warning! Land that is not used will always go to the barbarians, Hortense. You lived without knowing the outside world, the good and evil of the outside world. And without ever giving me a hint that would have relieved my horrible uncertainty. Only half revealing the secret. Because to have told all of it would have wounded your pride too much. Yes, you knew it. I loved your Ensign, too. You guessed at it when I revealed to you his treachery. How you loved to make me atone for my fault. The act of having destroyed your happiness. How we hated each other, loving each other so! How many years of atonement for Inés, the ugly Inés! Day after day, dragging my cross. (*They have reached the top of the stairs. Both pass out of sight. The voice of Inés can still be heard.*) With the dreams of my Emilia. With the weight of your pride.

(*With the fading of her voice comes a thundering knock on the outside door downstairs. The funeral march stops.*

The blue light disappears, and suddenly the normal light of day comes from beyond the doors, upstage. Emilia remains on the floor, her face almost buried in the cushion of the Vienna chair. The pounding with fists and the palm of the hand can still be heard from below. Emilia raises her head in fear. She looks in terror toward the left. She gets up.)

W.K.J.

A READING LIST

Readers who want to read other examples of Latin American literature scattered through various volumes may find things of interest in the following publications:

POETRY

Blackwell, Alice S., *Some Spanish American Poets* (University of Pennsylvania Press, 1937)

Blake, Agnes, *Pan American Poems* (Gorham, 1918)

Craig, G. Dundas, *The Modernist Trend in Spanish American Poetry* (University of California Press, 1934)

Darío, Rubén, *Eleven Poems of Rubén Darío* (Putnam, 1916)

Darío, Rubén, *Prosas Profanas and Other Poems*, translated by Chas. B. McMichael (Frank-Maurice, 1922)

Fitts, Dudley, *Anthology of Contemporary Latin American Poetry* (New Directions, 1942)

Grucci, Mallan, and Wickers, *Three Spanish American Poets* (Carrera Andrade, Pellicer, and Reyes) (Swallow and Crichlow, 1942)

Hills, Elijah C., *Odes of Bello, Olmeda, and Heredia* (Putnam, 1920)

Holmes, H. A. *Vicente Huidobro and Creationism* (Columbia University Press, 1934)

Translations from Hispanic Poets (Hispanic Society of America, 1938)

Underwood, Edna, *Anthology of Mexican Poets* (Mosher, 1932)

Walsh, Thomas, *Hispanic Anthology* (Hispanic Society of America, 1920)

PROSE

Brenner, Anita, *Tales from the Argentine* (Farrar and Rinehart, 1930)

Flores, Angel, and Poore, *Fiesta in November* (Houghton Mifflin, 1942)

Tales from the Italian and Spanish (Review of Reviews, 1920). The last part of vol. 8 is devoted to Latin America.

DRAMA

Bierstadt, E. H., *Three Plays of the Argentine* (Duffield, 1920)

Coester, Alfred, *Plays of the Southern Americas* (Stanford University Press, 1943)

Jones, Willis Knapp, *Short Plays of the Southern Americas* (Stanford University Press, 1944)

Sánchez, Florencio, *Representative Plays* translated by Willis K. Jones (Pan American Union, 1959)

Shay, Frank, and Loving, *Twenty-Five Short Plays, International* (Appleton, 1925)

———, *Fifty Contemporary One Act Plays* (Appleton, 1925)

GENERAL

The magazine *Inter-America*, vols. I–X, contains English translations of poems, essays, and stories from Latin American magazines. *The Pan American Union Bulletin* also contains occasional translations. *Poet Lore* has published a number of translations of Latin American plays and poetry.

INDEX

Authors and Major Works